HOW TO STUDY PICTURES

Windham Press is committed to bringing the lost cultural heritage of ages past into the 21st century through high-quality reproductions of original, classic printed works at affordable prices.

This book has been carefully crafted to utilize the original images of antique books rather than error-prone OCR text. This also preserves the work of the original typesetters of these classics, unknown craftsmen who laid out the text, often by hand, of each and every page you will read. Their subtle art involving judgment and interaction with the text is in many ways superior and more human than the mechanical methods utilized today, and gave each book a unique, hand-crafted feel in its text that connected the reader organically to the art of bindery and book-making.

We think these benefits are worth the occasional imperfection resulting from the age of these books at the time of scanning, and their vintage feel provides a connection to the past that goes beyond the mere words of the text.

As bibliophiles, we are always seeking perfection in our work, so please notify us of any errors in this book by emailing us at corrections@windhampress.com. Our team is motivated to correct errors quickly so future customers are better served. Our mission is to raise the bar of quality for reprinted works by a focus on detail and quality over mass production.

To peruse our catalog of carefully curated classic works, please visit our online store at www.windhampress.com.

HOW TO STUDY PICTURES

BY MEANS OF A SERIES OF COMPARISONS OF PAINTINGS AND PAINTERS FROM CIMABUE TO MONET, WITH HISTORICAL AND BIOGRAPHICAL SUMMARIES AND APPRECIATIONS OF THE PAINTERS' MOTIVES AND METHODS

BY

CHARLES H. CAFFIN

NEW YORK
THE CENTURY CO.
1921

Copyright, 1904, 1905, by
THE CENTURY CO.

Published October, 1905

TO
DOROTHY
AND
FREDA

CONTENTS

CHAPTER		PAGE
	Author's Note	xiii
I	Introduction	3
II	Cimabue—Giotto	8
III	Masaccio—Mantegna	20
IV	Fra Angelico—Jan van Eyck	37
V	Botticelli—Memling	52
VI	Perugino—Giovanni Bellini	68
VII	Raphael—Wolgemuth	85
VIII	Da Vinci—Dürer	109
IX	Titian—Holbein the Younger	125
X	Correggio—Michelangelo	142
XI	Veronese—Tintoretto	159
XII	Rubens—Velasquez	177
XIII	Van Dyck—Frans Hals	195
XIV	Rembrandt—Murillo	209
XV	Jacob van Ruisdael—Poussin	228
XVI	Hobbema—Claude Lorrain	242
XVII	Watteau—Hogarth	255

CONTENTS

CHAPTER		PAGE
XVIII	Reynolds—Gainsborough	272
XIX	Constable—Turner	287
XX	David—Delacroix	304
XXI	Rousseau—Corot	322
XXII	Breton—Millet	339
XXIII	Courbet—Boecklin	353
XXIV	Rossetti—Holman Hunt	371
XXV	Piloty—Fortuny	391
XXVI	Manet—Israels	404
XXVII	Puvis de Chavannes—Gérôme	423
XXVIII	Whistler—Sargent	441
XXIX	Monet—Hashimoto Gaho	457
	Concluding Note	479
	Bibliography	481
	Glossary of Terms	484
	Index	493

LIST OF ILLUSTRATIONS

		PAGE
MADONNA ENTHRONED	Cimabue	14
MADONNA ENTHRONED	Giotto	15
ST. PETER BAPTIZING	Masaccio	26
GONZAGA WELCOMING HIS SONS	Mantegna	27
THE ANNUNCIATION	Fra Angelico	42
VIRGIN AND DONOR	Jan van Eyck	43
MADONNA ENTHRONED	Alessandro Botticelli	58
VIRGIN ENTHRONED	Hans Memling	59
TRIPTYCH FROM THE PAVIA ALTAR-PIECE	Perugino	74

From a photograph by Emery Walker, London.

TRIPTYCH ALTAR-PIECE	Giovanni Bellini	75
MADONNA DEGLI ANSIDEI	Raphael Sanzio	90
DEATH OF THE VIRGIN	Michael Wolgemuth	91
VIRGIN OF THE ROCKS	Leonardo da Vinci	114
VISIT OF THE MAGI	Albrecht Dürer	115
MAN WITH THE GLOVE	Titian	134

From a photograph by Braun, Clément & Cie.

LIST OF ILLUSTRATIONS

		PAGE
PORTRAIT OF GEORG GYZE	*Holbein the Younger*	135
MYSTIC MARRIAGE OF ST. CATHERINE	*Correggio*	150
JEREMIAH	*Michelangelo*	151
THE GLORY OF VENICE	*Paolo Veronese*	166
From a photograph by Giraudon.		
THE MIRACLE OF ST. MARK	*Tintoretto*	167
DESCENT FROM THE CROSS	*Rubens*	186
From a photograph by Braun, Clément & Cie.		
LAS MEÑINAS (MAIDS OF HONOR)	*Velasquez*	187
From a photograph by Braun, Clément & Cie.		
MARIE LOUISE VON TASSIS	*Anthony van Dyck*	202
From a photograph by Franz Hanfstaengl.		
PORTRAIT OF A WOMAN	*Frans Hals*	203
From a photograph by Franz Hanfstaengl.		
SORTIE OF THE BANNING COCK COMPANY	*Rembrandt*	218
From a photograph by Franz Hanfstaengl.		
CHILDREN OF THE SHELL	*Murillo*	219
THE WATERFALL	*Jacob van Ruisdael*	234
SHEPHERDS IN ARCADY	*Nicolas Poussin*	235
THE AVENUE, MIDDELHARNIS, HOLLAND	*Meindert Hobbema*	246
THE LANDING OF CLEOPATRA AT TARSUS	*Claude Lorrain*	247
THE EMBARKATION FOR CYTHERA	*Antoine Watteau*	262
From a photograph by Braun, Clément & Cie.		
THE MARRIAGE CONTRACT	*William Hogarth*	263

LIST OF ILLUSTRATIONS

		PAGE
Mrs. Siddons as the Tragic Muse	*Sir Joshua Reynolds* .	278
From a photograph by Valentine & Son.		
Portrait of Mrs. Siddons . . .	*Thomas Gainsborough*	279
Valley Farm (Willy Lott's House)	*John Constable* . . .	294
Ulysses Deriding Polyphemus	*Joseph Mallord William Turner*	295
Oath of the Horatii	*Jacques Louis David* .	310
Dante and Virgil	*Eugène Delacroix* . .	311
Edge of the Forest of Fontainebleau	*Rousseau*	330
From a photograph by Braun, Clément & Cie.		
Dance of the Nymphs . . .	*Corot*	331
From a photograph by Braun, Clément & Cie.		
The Gleaner	*Jules Breton* . . .	346
The Gleaners	*Jean François Millet* .	347
Funeral at Ornans	*Courbet*	362
From a photograph by Braun, Clément & Cie.		
The Isle of the Dead . . .	*Boecklin*	363
From a photogravure by Bruckmann.		
The Blessed Damozel	*Dante Gabriel Rossetti*	378
From a photograph by Berlin Photo Co.		
Light of the World . . .	*Holman Hunt* . . .	379
Thusnelda at the Triumph of Germanicus	*Karl Theodor von Piloty*	394
From a photograph by Pach Bros.		
Spanish Marriage	*Mariano Fortuny* . .	395
From a photograph by Laurent & Cie.		

LIST OF ILLUSTRATIONS

		PAGE
GIRL WITH A PARROT . . . . . *Édouard Manet*	. .	414
THE OLD SCRIBE . . . . . . *Jozef Israels*	. . .	415
From the collection of Dr. Leslie D. Ward, by permission.		
INTER ARTES ET NATURAM . . . *Puvis de Chavannes*	.	430
From a photograph by Braun, Clément & Cie.		
POLLICE VERSO . . . . . . *Gérôme*	. . . .	431
By permission of Manzi, Joyant & Cie.		
PORTRAIT OF THE ARTIST'S MOTHER . . . . { *James A. McNeill Whistler* }	.	446
From a photograph by Braun, Clément & Cie.		
PORTRAIT OF THE MISSES HUNTER *John S. Sargent*	. .	447
By permission of Mr. Charles E. Hunter.		
OLD CHURCH AT VERNON . . . *Claude Monet*	. . .	466
SUNRISE ON THE HORAI . . . *Hashimoto Gaho*	. .	467

[xii]

AUTHOR'S NOTE

Some experience in lecturing has impressed upon me several points. In the first place, the majority of students have not the time to make an exhaustive study; while those who intend to do so ultimately, still need to begin with a simple summary that shall spread before them the salient features of the subject and afford a firm groundwork on which to build. Instead, therefore, of multiplying names, I have confined myself to fifty-six, which are pivotal ones by reason of what these artists accomplished or of their influence upon others. The selection must not be regarded as an attempt to pick out a list of the most famous names in painting; my real aim being to unfold the gradual progress of the art, to show how various motives have from time to time influenced artists, and how the scene of vital progress has shifted from country to country. I have tried to present a survey of the whole field of painting, not to write a history of artists or schools.

Again, while the student is buried in the history of one school, it is difficult for him to bear in mind what is being

AUTHOR'S NOTE

done by contemporary artists in other schools. Accordingly, as often as possible; I have treated side by side contemporary men of different nationalities, trying to show in each case something of the differences of environment and personality, and of motive and method. In this way also, I hope, the panoramic character of the story is increased.

Lastly, " by their works ye shall know them." An artist desires to be known and estimated by his works. Also it may be more useful to study pictures than lives of artists, because an appreciation of one picture leads to that of many. Therefore I have tried to combine with the historical aspects of the subject the matter which is usually treated separately in books of " How to study pictures."

I have adopted the parallel method: " Look on this picture and on this." Not, as a rule, to suggest that one is more admirable than another; but to stimulate interest and the faculty of observation, and to show how various are the motives which have prompted artists and the methods which they have adopted. In the sum total of comparisons I have tried to include as many as possible of the motives and methods which have from time to time prevailed, so that the student may gain a basis of appreciation from which to extend his observations with understanding and enjoyment.

For the object of study should be to put oneself in

AUTHOR'S NOTE

touch with each artist in turn, to enter into his point of view, to see as far as possible with his eyes, and to estimate his work, not for what it does not contain, but for what it does. In this way only can our appreciation of painting become catholic and intelligent. Then, we are no longer content to say " I know what I like," but " I know why I like "; and our likings are multiplied.

As we discover more and more of the diverse ways in which artists have put a portion of themselves, of their own lives, into their pictures, our appreciation becomes indefinitely enlarged, our sympathies continually broadened, our enjoyment perpetually increased. Thus may we enter into the life of the artist and reinforce our own lives.

CHARLES H. CAFFIN.

Mamaroneck, N. Y.

HOW TO STUDY PICTURES

HOW TO STUDY PICTURES

CHAPTER I

INTRODUCTION

"Having eyes, see ye not?"

THE world is full of beauty which many people hurry past or live in front of and do not see. There is also a world of beauty in pictures, but it escapes the notice of many, because, while they wish to see it, they do not know how.

The first necessity for the proper seeing of a picture is to try and see it through the eyes of the artist who painted it. This is not a usual method. Generally people look only through their own eyes, and like or dislike a picture according as it does or does not suit their particular fancy. These people will tell you: " Oh! I don't know anything about painting, but I know what I like "; which is their way of saying: " If I don't like it right off, I don't care to be bothered to like it at all."

Such an attitude of mind cuts one off from growth and development, for it is as much as to say: " I am very well satisfied with myself, and quite indifferent to the experiences and feelings of other men." Yet it is just this experience and feeling of another man which a picture gives us. If you consider a moment you will understand why. The world itself is a vast panorama, and from it the painter selects his subject: not to copy it exactly, since it would be impossible for him to do this, even if he tried. How could he represent, for example, each blade of grass, each leaf upon a tree? So what he does is to represent the subject as he sees it, as it appeals to his sympathy or interest; and if twelve artists painted the same landscape, the result would be twelve different pictures, differing according to the way in which each man had been impressed by the scene; in fact, according to his separate point of view or separate way of seeing it, influenced by his individual experience and feeling.

It is most important to realize the part which is played by these two qualities of experience and feeling. Experience, the fullness or the deficiency of it, must affect the work of every one of us, no matter what our occupation may be. And if the work is of a kind which appeals to the feelings of others, as in the case of the preacher, the writer, the actor, the painter, sculptor, architect or art-craftsman, the musician or the dancer, it must be affected equally by the individual's capacity of feeling and by his power of expressing what he feels.

Therefore, since none of us can include in ourselves the whole range of possible experience and feeling, it is through the experience and the feeling of others that we deepen and refine our own. It is this that we should look to pictures to accomplish, which, as you will acknowledge, is a very different thing from offhand like or dislike. For example, we may not be attracted at first, but we reason with ourselves: " No doubt this picture meant a good deal to the man who painted it; it embodies his experience of the world and his feeling toward the sub-

INTRODUCTION

ject. It represents, in fact, a revelation of the man himself; and, if it is true that 'the noblest study of mankind is man,' then possibly in the study of this man, as revealed in his work, there may be interest for me."

I am far from wishing you to suppose that all pictures will repay you for such intimate study. We may get inside the man to find that his experience of life is meager, his feeling commonplace and paltry. There are not a few men of this sort in the occupation of art, just as in every other walk of life, and their pictures, so far as we ourselves are concerned, will be disappointing. But among the pictures which have stood the test of time we shall always find that the fruits of the artist's experience and feeling are of a kind which makes lasting appeal to the needs of the human heart and mind, and that this fact is one of the causes of their being held in so high esteem. There is also another cause.

If only experience and feeling were necessary to make an artist, many of us would be better artists than a considerable number of those who follow the profession of art. But there is another necessity—the power of expressing the experience and feeling. This, by its derivation from the Greek, is the primary meaning of the word "art": the capacity to "fit" a form to an idea. The artist is the "fitter" who gives shape and construction to the tenuous fabric of his imagination; and this method of "fitting" is his technic.

So the making of a picture involves two processes: a taking in of the impression and a giving of it out by visible expression; a seeing of the subject with the visual and mental eye, and a communicating of what has been so seen to the visual and mental eyes of others; and both these processes are influenced by the experience and feeling of the artist and make their appeal to our own. And, I think, it should be clear from what we have been saying that the beauty of a picture depends much less upon its subject than upon the artist's conception and treatment of it. A grand subject will not of itself make a grand picture, while a very homely one, by the way in which it has been treated, may impress us profoundly.

The degree of beauty in a picture depends, in fact, upon the feeling for beauty in the artist and upon his power to express it. I have spoken of these two qualifications as if they influenced the picture separately; but, as a matter of fact, conception and technic are blended together in a picture, and as we pursue our study, we shall find ourselves embracing them simultaneously.

But at the outset we must proceed step by step, alternately studying the conception and the technic; and, in order that we may discover how variously, at successive times and in diverse countries, different men have conceived of life and have expressed their feeling and experience in pictures, I propose that we shall study them through a series of comparisons.

Our plan, therefore, will be:

"Look here, upon this picture, and on this";

not to decide offhand which we like the better, for in some cases perhaps we may not like either, since they were painted in times so remote from ours as to be outside our habit of understanding; but in order that we may get at the artist's way of seeing in each case, and

INTRODUCTION

reach some appreciation of his methods. In this way I hope that we may be able to piece together the story of modern painting; beginning with its rebirth in the thirteenth century, when it emerged from the darkness of the middle ages, and following it through its successive stages in different countries down to our own day.

It will very much increase the usefulness of this method if the student can obtain reproductions of other work by each artist, so as to test, by a particular study of them, the general principles that are being discussed.

CHAPTER II

GIOVANNI CIMABUE	GIOTTO DI BONDONE
1240 (?)–1302 (?)	*1266 (?)–1337*
Italian School of Florence	*Italian School of Florence*

FOR the first comparison I invite you to study the two examples of *The Madonna Enthroned*—one by Cimabue, the other by his pupil Giotto. Both are painted on wooden panels in distemper—that is to say, with colors that have been mixed with some gelatinous medium, such as the white and the yolk of an egg beaten up together; for it was not until the fifteenth century that the use of oil as a medium was adopted. The colors used in Giotto's panel are tints of blue and rose and white; in Cimabue's the blues and reds are deep and dusky; the background in each case being golden.

We notice at once a general similarity between these two pictures, not only in choice of subject, but in the manner of presentation: Madonna, the queen of heaven, upon a throne; her mantle drawn over her head; her right hand resting on the knee of the infant Saviour, who has two fingers of his right hand raised in the act of blessing; kneeling angels at the foot, and figures in tiers above them; all the heads being surrounded by the nimbus, or circular cloud of light, symbolic of their sacred character.

The reason of this general similarity is, that the choice of subject and the manner of its presentation were fixed by tradition; and long before this thirteenth century the tradition of Greek art had been lost, and in place of it was the Byzantine tradition, interpreted and enforced by the Christian church.

Briefly, the cause of the change was this. Greek art and Greek religion were indissolubly connected. The gods and goddesses were represented as human beings of a higher order; physical perfection was the ideal alike of religion and art. Therefore Christianity, in waging war upon heathenism, could not help attacking its art. Moreover, as the morals of the Empire became baser and baser, Christianity was driven more and more toward asceticism; meeting the ideal of physical perfection with the spiritual ideal of mortifying the flesh. So that pagan art, which itself had grown grosser as morals declined, became an object of exceeding hatred to the church. But some form of pictorial representation was needed to bring the truths of religion before the eyes of the faithful, and the church found what it required in the art of Byzantium.

This city was the gateway between the eastern and the western world, and the original Greek character of its art was speedily influenced by artists from the Orient. Now the ideals of the East and West are very different. Briefly, the longing of the East is for the Ultimate and Universal, while the West loves to dwell on the Particular, and to dwell upon the means rather than the end. While the Greek artist carved or painted some particular form, striving to give it perfection of shape in every part, so that through a series of means he might express his ideal of physical and spiritual perfection, the artist of the East reached his ideal through the abstract perfection of beautiful lines, of beautiful patterns of form and color. Thus, the one art is represented most characteristically by the sculpture on the Parthenon, the other by a decorated porcelain vase.

The arrival therefore, at Byzantium, of this art, so far removed from the Greek and Roman study of the human form, so beautifully decorative, was hailed by the church, both for the decorating of its sacred buildings and for the illuminating of the sacred manuscripts; and it was as decorators and illuminators that the Byzantine artists did their finest work. But, as the study of the nude figure had been abandoned, the ignorance of the artists regarding the real character of the human form increased; their types of figure became less and less like nature, and more and more according to a convention established by the church. Asceticism was preached, so the figure must be thin and gaunt, the gestures angular, the expression of the emaciated faces one of painful ecstasy. Moreover, there were certain dogmas to be enforced, and the church gradually dictated the manner of their representation; so that in time all that was required of or permitted to a painter was to go on producing certain conventional subjects in a purely conventional way. The divorce of art from nature was complete, and the independence of the artist lost in the domination of the church.

The story of the Italian Renaissance, which commenced at the end of the thirteenth century, relates how

CIMABUE—GIOTTO

the artist gradually emancipated himself and his art, giving new life to the latter by inoculating it with nature and with something of the classic spirit.

Now, therefore, we can understand why these two pictures of *The Madonna Enthroned* by Cimabue and Giotto are so similar in arrangement. They followed the tradition prescribed by the church. Yet the Florentines of Cimabue's day found his picture so superior to anything they had seen before, so much more splendid in color, if not much nearer to the true representation of life, that when it was completed they carried it in a joyous procession from the artist's home through the streets of Florence, and deposited it with ceremony in the Cappella de' Rucellai in the Church of Santa Maria Novella. The English artist Lord Leighton, in his picture commemorating the event, has represented Cimabue walking in front of the Madonna, with his pupil Giotto at his side; and in the procession appears Dante, who left this mention of the two:

> Cimabue thought
> To laud it over painting's field; and now
> The cry is Giotto's, and his name eclipsed.
> PURGATORIO, XI, 94. (*Cary.*)

The story is that Cimabue had chanced upon the boy as, like David of old, he watched his flock upon the mountain; and he found him drawing the form of one of the goats upon a rock with a sharp piece of slate. The master must have found some hint of genius in the work, for he straightway asked the boy if he would like to be his pupil; and, having received a glad assent and the father's permission, carried him off to Florence to his *bottegha*. This, the artist's studio of that period and for long after, was rather what we should call a workshop, in which the pupils ground and prepared the colors under the master's direction; and it was not until they had thoroughly mastered this branch of the work—a procedure which in Giotto's time was supposed to occupy about six years—that they were permitted to use the brushes. How often, as he worked in the gloom of the *bottegha,* must the shepherd boy have peeped wistfully at the master standing in the shady garden, before a great glory of crimson drapery and golden background, and wondered if he should ever himself acquire such marvelous skill.

He was destined to accomplish greater things, for his young mind had not been tutored to traditions, nor his young eyes constrained to admire the conventional. In the free air of the mountains the boy's spirit had wandered where it listed, and the eager eyes had learned to love and study nature. It was the love of form that had set him to try and picture a goat upon the surface of the rock; it was the actual appearance of objects that he sought to render when, in due time, he learned to use the brush.

If you turn again to a comparison of his Madonna with that of Cimabue, you will see what strides he had already made toward natural truth. Observe how the figure of the Virgin is made real to us, notwithstanding that it is covered, as in Cimabue's, with drapery; and while the Christ-child in each picture is represented in a similar garment, the form in Cimabue's does not

MADONNA ENTHRONED — CIMABUE
RUCELLAI CHAPEL, SANTA MARIA NOVELLA, FLORENCE

MADONNA ENTHRONED  GIOTTO

ACADEMY, FLORENCE

appear to be as strong and firm and life-like as in Giotto's. And if you examine the other figures in his picture you will find the same suggestion of substantial form that could be touched and grasped in the arms. Notice, further, how Giotto's feeling for truth has affected his arrangement of the forms. The throne actually occupies space of three dimensions—length, breadth, and thickness; so do all the figures, and they rest firmly upon the ground; the artist has called in the aid of perspective to enforce the reality of his group.

Now, how has he accomplished this appearance of reality? By the use of light and shade, and by making his lines functional—expressive, that is to say, of the structure and character of the object. Compare, for example, the figure of the infant Saviour in the two pictures. In Cimabue's the drapery is scored with lines which vaguely hint at folds and obscure the shape of the limbs beneath; but in Giotto's certain parts of the figure are made to project by the use of high lights, and others are correspondingly depressed by shade, while the lines of the drapery serve to indicate the shape of the form beneath.

This use of light and shade by Giotto, while it marks a distinct advance from the flat pattern-like painting of the Byzantine school, is still rudimentary; and, as if conscious of the fact, the artist has selected the most simple arrangements of drapery. Indeed, breadth and simplicity are characteristic of the whole picture. It was painted probably during the years of his apprenticeship to Cimabue, or, at any rate, under his influence, and shows much less freedom and assurance than the works of his maturity. These are to be found in frescoes upon the walls of the Upper and Lower Churches at Assisi; the Arena Chapel, Padua; the Bardi and Peruzzi Chapels, S. Croce; and the Chapel of the Bargello, Florence. Giotto was the first to introduce the faces of contemporaries into his pictures, and the *Paradise* on the walls of the Bargello contains the famous portrait of Dante in his early manhood. It had remained covered with whitewash for two hundred years, until once more brought to light in 1840. All these paintings were executed in fresco—that is to say, on the plaster before it was dry, with water-colors mixed in a glutinous medium, so that as the surface hardened the colors became incorporated in it. While the technical knowledge displayed in them is rudimentary, they are so simple and unaffected, so earnest and large in feeling, and tell the story with such dramatic effect, that they command the interest and enthusiasm of the modern student.

In his own day Giotto's fame as a painter was supreme; he had numerous followers, and these Giotteschi, as they were styled, perpetuated his methods for nearly a hundred years. But, like all the great men of the Florentine school, he was a master of more than one craft. "Forget that they were painters," writes Mr. Berenson, "they remain great sculptors; forget that they were sculptors, and still they remain architects, poets, and even men of science." The beautiful Campanile, which stands beside the Cathedral in Florence, and represents a perfect union of strength and elegance, was designed by Giotto and partly erected in his lifetime. Moreover,

CIMABUE—GIOTTO

the sculptured reliefs which decorate its lower part were all from his designs, though he lived to execute only two of them. Thus, architect, sculptor, painter, friend of Dante and of other great men of his day, Giotto was the worthy forerunner of that galaxy of brilliant men who thronged the later days of the Italian Renaissance.

CHAPTER III

TOMMASO MASACCIO
1401(?)–1428(?)
Italian School of Florence

ANDREA MANTEGNA
1431–1506
Italian School of Padua

SINCE the death of Giotto nearly a hundred years have elapsed, during which his followers in Florence and certain painters in Siena, notably the brothers Lorenzetti, have been continuing the effort to emancipate painting from the flat formalism of Byzantine art. But, although they have learned something more about expressing the roundness of form, have studied more closely the action of light upon objects and the expression and character of faces, and have begun to acquire some insight into the principles of foreshortening and perspective, they are inferior to Giotto in originality of feeling and grandeur of design. He had been a solitary genius.

However, at the beginning of the fifteenth century, there arose in Florence a new genius, who became to this century what Giotto had been to the fourteenth. At a bound he leaped above all competitors, set painting free from its shackles, and continued to be a stimulus to hosts of other painters, including Michelangelo and Raphael. This new genius was Masaccio; and he, after his short life of twenty-seven years, was followed by the Paduan

MASACCIO—MANTEGNA

Mantegna; this man, too, a genius, whose influence was wide-spread. By these two men painting was completely emancipated and set upon that sure and certain path along which it marched with gathering splendor toward the climax of the High Renaissance of the sixteenth century.

The great achievement of both these men, the original force from which all other improvements followed, was to realize for themselves and to impress upon others the independent dignity of painting as an art. Hitherto it had been regarded as the handmaid of religion, its highest function to set before the eyes of men the doctrines of the church. We have seen to what a condition it had thus been brought under Byzantine influences. Nor was Giotto able to do more than accept this secondary use of painting and then try to infuse more life into it. A century had to drag its length before Masaccio and Mantegna could say, in effect: "Before everything else we are painters; practisers of an art that, like sculpture, but much more than it, can make the external appearances of things visible to the eye. The invisible things of the spirit we will embody in our pictures if we can, but it is not with them that painting is first concerned. Its first duty is to develop that which belongs exclusively to itself. The teaching of doctrine, the telling of sacred stories and legends, we share with the men who use spoken or written words, and their power in this respect is fuller than ours; the suggestion of beautiful thoughts is quite as much, and more, within the power of the musician; but the representation of the external appearance of things, and especially of humanity, the crown of things, is the one point in which painting excels all other modes of expression. This is its special province; and our aim as painters must be, first and foremost, to represent the external appearances of things. This is at once our peculiar province and delight."

The joy of the painter in external things, we shall find, was shared at this time by thousands who were not painters. It was a symptom of the age. But, before discussing it, let us turn to the two pictures: Masaccio's *St. Peter Baptizing the Heathen* and Mantegna's *Gonzaga, Marquis of Mantua, Welcoming Home from Rome his Son, the Cardinal Francesco.* The former is religious in subject; but is it not clear that what chiefly occupied Masaccio's mind was to represent the incident as it may actually have occurred, with real men conducting themselves as they naturally might do under the circumstances? Observe especially the young man on the right with his arms crossed. In the first place, it is an enormous advance on Byzantinism that the artist, in this figure and the kneeling one, has represented the nude. Giotto had made a tentative step in this direction when, in his picture of the *Entombment,* he painted the figure of Christ nude as far as the waist. But here the baptism justified a nude representation of the whole of the figure, and Masaccio made full use of the opportunity. Note also in each case with what a regard for character as well as correctness of form; with an intent to make the nude a vehicle of expression. Compare the reverential composure of the young man who kneels with the trembling attitude of the other who stands on the bank shivering and nervously waiting his turn. Moreover, in each case, note the truth to nature represented in the pose: the shoulders, being drawn forward, are balanced by the bending of the knees and the drawing back of the body. For the present it will be sufficient to contrast with these nude figures the grand figure of St. Peter. The drapery is broadly and simply treated, as in Giotto's paintings, but with still greater ease and fluency of lines and masses that more thoroughly suggest the attitude and bulk of form of the figure. Lastly, observe the dignity of the saint's head, and the character and individuality portrayed in all the faces. It is humanity for its own sake, as separately represented in the individual, not the use of form for symbolical purposes, that interested Masaccio. With him painting became emancipated finally from Byzantinism.

When we turn to the Mantegna, it is probably again the character and individuality of the heads which first arrest our attention. They are portraits of the marquis, his sons, and courtiers: not beautiful, except perhaps in the case of the youth in the foreground. He is already a prothonotary of the holy see at Rome, one of the twelve ecclesiastical clerks who keep a record of the pontifical proceedings, and is destined to be a bishop. The gravity of life has weighed his young face with seriousness; in remarkable contrast to his elder brother, the Cardinal Francesco. The latter is soft and fleshly, as if fond of easy living; we are not surprised to learn that he is a lover of music, a connoisseur and collector of works of art, a man of refined and comfortable tastes. The faces of these two sons are curiously reflected in the stern, strong, but not untender head of the old father on the left, while the two little children have a strange infantile resemblance to the other members of the family. The remainder of the group consists of courtiers, men of pronounced character, shrewd and masterful. Throughout the whole there is a tendency toward stiff attitudes and liny draperies, at first sight not agreeable; but there is no mistaking the reality of these people; and we shall better appreciate the picture when we have discovered the influence that helped to form Mantegna's style.

It was through the lessons learned from sculpture that painting recovered its independent force. Both Masaccio and Mantegna displayed their genius by making these lessons so completely their own that they themselves became the models for succeeding painters. Being a Florentine, Masaccio must have been familiar from childhood with the bronze doors of the Baptistery by Andrea Pisano, the finest sculptural work of the fourteenth century in Italy; and, before he began the painting of *St. Peter,* Ghiberti had finished the first pair of his doors for the same Baptistery, and Donatello had executed, among other works, his statue of *St. George.* The last-named is remarkable for its naturalistic and at the same time elevated treatment of the human figure in the complete round, while Ghiberti's pictorial panels, which Michelangelo thought worthy of decorating the Gates of Paradise, no less naturalistic than the *St. George,* are richly elaborate compositions containing numerous figures—in some cases as many as a hundred—associated with architecture and landscape. The *St. George* is an example of the grandeur of form in the round; Ghiberti's work, of the illusion which can be

ST. PETER BAPTIZING   MASACCIO
BRANCACCI CHAPEL, CHURCH OF THE CARMINE, FLORENCE

GONZAGA WELCOMING HIS SONS — MANTEGNA
CAMERA DEGLI SPOSI, CASTELLO DI CORTE, MANTUA

produced by varying the elevation of the surfaces, so that, although nothing is in the round, everything has the appearance of being; and also by regulating the direction of lines and the gradations of planes, so that the scene depicted seems to extend back in a distant perspective.

This latter quality is conspicuous in Masaccio's as compared with earlier work. There is no longer a stretching of the figures across the picture in a flat band, almost on the same plane, with other figures placed above them, whose position in a further plane is only indicated by a diminution of their size; instead, a natural and concentrated grouping, in which the figures and landscape occupy in a natural way their several planes in the receding space. For this picture is no longer flat, but hollow and filled with air. Whatever Masaccio may have learned from the sculptors, this he gained from a direct study of nature. He proved himself a true painter by the skill with which he surrounded his figures with air and represented the varying effects of light upon the different objects. And these qualities, added to his knowledge of the human form and his strong, sincere treatment of it in composition and drawing, are the secrets of his greatness.

His chief works are the frescoes in the Brancacci Chapel of the Church of the Carmine in Florence, of which this *St. Peter* is one: a series finished later by Filippino. In 1428 he was summoned to Rome, and all further knowledge of "Careless Thomas" (for that is the meaning of his name) ceases. It was nearly fifty years before a worthy successor to him appeared in Florence, and meanwhile the story shifts to Padua and to Mantegna.

In 1305 Giotto had gone to that city and commenced the series of thirty-eight frescoes in the Chapel of the Arena, which are among his most famous works. But they bore no immediate fruit in Padua. More than a hundred years afterward, however, one Squarcione, a tailor and embroiderer, began to take an interest in art. Having considerable means, he proceeded to make a collection of pictures; and, traveling through Italy and, some say, Greece, made drawings and took casts of ancient marbles. Returned to Padua, he placed these on exhibition and opened a school of art. The most famous of his pupils was Andrea Mantegna, the son of a small farmer. The master had thought so highly of the boy that he adopted him as a son, thereby securing additional control over his labors. His shrewdness was justified, for at the age of twenty-one the young man was already executing important work on behalf of his master. The latter, in time, received a commission to decorate the chapel of the Ovetari family in the Church of the Eremitani; and here, quite close to the garden inclosing Giotto's chapel, Squarcione's pupils painted a series of frescoes, which became to the painters of North Italy what those by Masaccio in the Brancacci Chapel were to Florence.

At the commencement of this series, which was designed to represent incidents in the lives of St. Christopher and St. James, the master's best pupil was Niccolo Pizzolo, whose most promising career was cut short in a street brawl; but before the work's completion it was

MASACCIO—MANTEGNA

clear that the greatest of all was Mantegna. While the latter was still engaged upon this work, he made the acquaintance of the Venetian painter Jacopo Bellini, who, with his two sons, later to be so famous in the annals of Venetian painting, Gentile and Giovanni, was then sojourning in Padua. The acquaintance ripened into a close attachment, which was cemented by Mantegna's marriage to Jacopo's daughter.

His growing reputation caused him to be summoned to Verona, and while he was working in that city there came an invitation, frequently repeated, from Lodovico Gonzaga, Marquis of Mantua. For, by this time, the municipal authority of the free cities, which had flourished during the fourteenth century, had been usurped by powerful families.

The Communes, the Republics of Italy, after their period of self-assertion, of glory, of intense localized energy and furious internecine rivalry, began to get exhausted, to decay, to become weaker and weaker, by degrees to disappear altogether. And in their place there sprang up everywhere the great princely houses—the Medici of Florence, the Visconti and the Sforza at Milan, the Este at Ferrara, the Bentivogli at Bologna, the Montefeltri at Urbino, the Baglioni at Perugia, the Malatesta at Rimini and Cesena, and the Gonzaghi at Mantua.[1]

These despots intrenched themselves in castles to overawe the cities which they ruled, continually threatened by the outward attacks of one another, and by attempts at poisoning or assassination from enemies within. Yet they maintained magnificent courts, surrounding themselves with scholars, poets, and painters.

[1] Selwyn Brinton.

HOW TO STUDY PICTURES

In the strange and frightful isolation in which the Italian despot often lived, ever plotting himself to keep his insecure throne, ever watching against plots within the city and without, this brilliant society of dependants became his solace and his highest pleasure. Traverse that wonderful palace of the house of Este—intact, surrounded by its moat, dominating with its insolent pride the old city of Ferrara. Into the upper galleries and banquet-halls the sunlight pours. We seem to hear the musical laughter, the rustle of the rich old cinque-cento costumes; the walls are hung with paintings by Dosso Dossi or Titian—naked wrestlers, figures running, and the radiant deities of the old reawakened mythology. And below, beneath even the moat, lies the other side of the picture: the horrible dungeons, dark, noisome, shadowy, where the political conspirator, the inconvenient relative, the too outspoken citizen, the suspected wife, were thrust, and—soon forgotten.

Yet within some such courts this life must often have been very brilliant and wonderful. At Mantua the marquis had brought from Padua the great Greek and Latin scholar, Vittorino da Feltre, to be tutor to his children. A villa was allotted to the household, and a system of education commenced which deserved the admiration and fame it soon gained. Besides the rich and noble youths who thronged to Vittorino, no less than sixty poor scholars were fed, clothed, and taught at his own expense. Plain living and high thinking were there the rule; diet and physical exercises—wrestling, fencing, swimming, riding—were carefully considered; the highest classic authors, Virgil and Homer, Cicero and Demosthenes, were revered as the supremest masters of style.[1]

Into this refined society of scholars and courtiers was Mantegna summoned, and in the service of this marquis and of three of his successors he remained, with the

[1] Selwyn Brinton.

exception of two years spent in Rome, until the end of his life.

In the atmosphere of such a court he was completely at home, for here were focused into a brilliant epitome the great forces which, during this century, were leavening the whole of Italy and were also at work in Mantegna himself. These were, first of all, the moral qualities of self-assertion, belief in the dignity of man and in the grand possibilities of life, intense earnestness and eager seriousness; secondly, the mighty influence of the rediscovered Latin authors, and particularly of the Greek, the consequent admiration and worship of the antique, and the conviction that in it was to be found the key to unlock all the glorious possibilities of the modern life.

Mantegna, as we have seen, had been nourished upon antique sculpture; from his own standpoint as an artist, he was the equal of the classic scholars; they could learn from him, as he from them; he could share the effort of all to enlighten the present by the past. Therefore, if we turn again to this picture, still surviving on the wall of one of the rooms in the castle of Mantua, where all those people actually lived their proud, high-seeking, dignified, and, at times, terrible lives, we may be able perhaps to see it with truer eyes, and find it extraordinarily fascinating. We shall understand that it was with deliberation that Mantegna made the figures of the marquis and his sons particularly immobile, their draperies notably stiff. By thus emphasizing the resemblance of this portion of his picture to antique low-relief sculpture, he singled out these figures from the others for particular honor. That the whole group stretches across the composition with a general resemblance to an ancient bas-relief, is a tribute to the classic ideals which he and all those people worshiped. But that he was also a student of nature may be seen in the fine perspective of the landscape. A still finer example of perspective adorns the ceiling of this same room, which he decorated in such a way that one seems to be looking up at the sky through a circular opening, as we may see it actually through the eye of the Pantheon's dome. Around the circle is a balustrade, upon which stand a peacock and a basket of fruit; and leaning upon it are a girl with jeweled head-dress and a negress, who look down with laughing faces, while a band of winged boys play on the edge of the stone-work. Vasari relates what admiration this excited. Nothing so daring or so scientific had previously been accomplished in Italy.

The work, however, which seems to have pleased Mantegna himself best was his series of panels, painted on canvas, in all eighty feet long, representing the *Triumph of Cæsar*. Into this long procession he crowded the fruits of the study he most loved—as Vasari says:

the perfumes, the incense-bearers, the priests, the oxen crowned for sacrifice, the prisoners, the booty seized by the soldiers, the well-ordered squadrons, the elephants, the spoils of art, the victories, cities, and fortresses imitated on different cars, together with an infinitude of trophies, helmets, corselets, and arms of all kinds borne aloft on spears, with ornaments, vases, and rich vessels innumerable.

Of these paintings, marvelous exhibitions of knowledge, invention, and skill, Mantegna, who was most self-exacting and severe in the judgment of himself, said: "I really was not ashamed of having painted them." In 1628, two years before the sack of Mantua by the Austrians, they were sold to Charles I of England, and now are in Hampton Court Palace, irreparably damaged by "restoration." Fortunately they can still be studied in the magnificent series of wood-engravings made from them by Andrea Andreani at the close of the sixteenth century. Of portions also of the *Triumph* Mantegna himself made engravings upon copper.

For this profound student of the antique, of nature, and of the scientific principles of drawing and painting, found time, in the midst of his work with the brush and pencil, to execute many engravings, among the most famous of which are an *Entombment of Christ* and a *Judith with the Head of Holofernes*. The prints of his engravings, traveling broadcast through Europe as well as Italy, helped to teach others and to draw many students to Mantua to build up their own knowledge by study of the great master's paintings.

I wish it were possible to illustrate here the two engravings mentioned above, for they throw a strong light upon Mantegna's genius. They prove, on the one hand his extraordinary intensity of feeling, on the other his extraordinarily dispassionate self-control, and also his power over line to make it express emotion. In the *Entombment* the lifeless, expressionless body of the Saviour is surrounded with dramatic energy: the bearers straining on the burden, the mourners weeping or tossing their hands in anguish, the Virgin in collapse, St. John standing erect with clenched hands and open mouth, shrieking in utter horror that such a thing should be! It is the work of a man whose imagination has been filled with the terribleness of suffering. Yet, when he draws Judith, he represents her as a beautiful Vestal virgin, a visionary, like Joan of Arc, dreamily and daintily passing her hand over the head of the murdered general who would have enslaved her nation. No sight of blood, nothing of sensationalism; he himself betrays no feeling, looks at the matter quite objectively, sees only in the horror of the situation a chance for most exquisite beauty of expressional line.

Could you compare it with our present picture, it would help you to understand that the severity of the latter was deliberate. Yet, even without the comparison, a study of the accompanying illustration will reveal how the intentional severity of the upright lines of figures, tree, and column has been counteracted and assuaged by the curving line, like a loop of links, formed by the tender figures in the group, the young ecclesiastic and the little children; and, further, by the diagonal lines of the beautiful landscape.

The stern old Paduan expressed the intense energy of his age, tempered only occasionally with the softer sense of beauty.

CHAPTER IV

FRA ANGELICO	JAN VAN EYCK
1387–1455	*(?)–1440 (?)*
Italian School of Florence	*Flemish School of Bruges*

BEFORE proceeding along the path which Masaccio and Mantegna have struck out, we must pause to consider a painter who, although a contemporary of theirs, belongs more to the past. He was the last inheritor of the Giottesque tradition, and the last of the painters whose work is thoroughly religious.

I invite you to turn aside into a little quiet garden, as it were, secluded within cloister walls, where Fra Angelico, painter and monk, a brother of the black-and-white order of the Dominicans, devoted his life to religious paintings. Choosing, as an example of his work, *The Annunciation,* I have placed it in comparison with *The Virgin and Donor* by Jan van Eyck, who shares with his brother Hubert the honor of founding the Flemish School.

One reason for this comparison is that we are trying to gain a bird's-eye view of the story of painting; not allowing ourselves to become absorbed in any one spot to the exclusion of others, but scanning the whole field and noting the great movements as they spring up, now here, now there, sometimes related to one another, sometimes separate, but all of them features in the general progress of European civilization. Surely it is interesting to realize that at the commencement of this fifteenth century, when Italy was waking up to its second and greatest activity, the Flemish also were waking up to art, the first among the Northern nations. Again, I have selected this comparison, because it was religious subjects that chiefly occupied the Flemish painters, and Fra Angelico is the most remarkable example in Italian art of a religious painter of religious subjects. Moreover, he worked in a beautiful seclusion, and secluded also was the art of Flanders, a choice garden in the northern wilderness. It was an art, too, of minute perfection of finish, and such was Fra Angelico's.

There is in both these pictures a minute finish of detail which suggests—what is indeed the case—that each artist owed something to the miniature-painters who decorated with tiny scenes the pages of the manuscripts. But in Fra Angelico's there is a greater simplicity and, as the artists call it, a greater breadth of style; for this picture was executed when he was about fifty years old; by which time he had been painting for thirty years and had come, as we shall see, under many influences that did not reach the Flemish artist.

So let us begin by studying the latter's picture. It was painted for presentation to a church, and the portrait of the donor, the Canon Roslin, was introduced. This was a common practice in the Renaissance days. The picture was intended to serve the double purpose of being "to the glory of God and in memory of the donor." Clad in a dark robe brocaded with flower-forms of a bronze hue that catch the light, now richly, now delicately, like the body and wings of a May-bug, the canon is kneeling in an attitude of prayer, but gazes upon the Virgin with a piercing look of scrutiny. In this strong face we feel sure that the artist has painted an extraordinarily faithful portrait; and from the fact that the expression of the face does not correspond with the humble and devout gesture of the hands, we learn that although Van Eyck painted religious pictures, he was not a religious painter in the way that Fra Angelico was.

Note also the greater elaboration of Van Eyck's picture. After he had secured a dignified composition, in which the principal figures should count as large and handsome spots and the background be broken up by contrast into a more complicated fretwork of decoration, he then set himself to carry each separate part to the finest possible degree of accurate and perfect workmanship. Here appears the Flemish spirit, with its patient, tireless pursuit of minute beauty, such as produced a nation of craftsmen, skilled in illumination, in miniature-painting, in jewelry and the working of gold and silver, in embroidery and the making of tapestries and stained-glass windows. But Jan van Eyck and his elder brother Hubert, although they had this love of minute perfection, had also large ideas, and never allowed the little details to detract from the grand general significance of the whole work.

We may examine, for example, the figure of the Christ; it is painted with the precise daintiness of a miniature and is very baby-like, yet it has also remarkable character, an air of seriousness, as if it were conscious of being more than its little form would indicate. The Virgin's robe is crimson; her face is not beautiful, being of the heavy, wholesome, practical type of the women of the country; but she has a wealth of golden hair, painted with wonderful realism, and over it a little angel holds a golden crown of exquisite workmanship decorated with pearls. Or you may study with interest the patterning of the marble floor; the elegant arcade of arches and columns, with the glimpse of a leaded window on each side; or the little garden beyond, where lilies are growing in the borders, magpies strut on the paths, peacocks sun themselves upon the balustrades, and two little boys are looking out over the distant landscape. Here is a far-stretching scene in miniature: level country, characteristically Flemish, threaded by a river over which is a bridge connecting the town on the one bank with that on the other. People are passing over the bridge, or crossing the water in boats, or walking the streets, with an appearance of reality, although their stature is almost microscopic. Indeed, there is a great deal in the picture that it is impossible to discover in the black-and-white reproduction, which also gives little idea of the textures—that is to say, of the rendering of the different surfaces of marble, fabric, flesh, or metal and the rest, each according to its special quality—and none of the rich, full, firm coloring, brilliant as agate or precious stones.

This wonderful color is another reason of the fame of the Van Eycks. Artists came from Italy to study their pictures, to discover what they themselves must do in

THE ANNUNCIATION FRA ANGELICO
MONASTERY OF SAN MARCO, FLORENCE

VIRGIN AND DONOR   LOUVRE, PARIS   JAN VAN EYCK

order to paint so well, with such brilliance, such full and firm effect, as these two brothers. For the latter had found out the secret of working successfully with oil-colors. Before their day attempts had been made to mix colors in the medium of oil, but the oil was slow in drying, and the varnish added to remedy this had blackened the colors. The Van Eycks, however, had hit upon a transparent varnish which dried quickly and without injury to the tints. Though they guarded the secret jealously, it was discovered by the Italian Antonello da Messina, who was working in Bruges, and by him published to the world. The invention made possible the enormous development in the art of painting which ensued.

Little is known of the two brothers; even the dates of their birth being uncertain. Their most famous work, begun by Hubert and finished by Jan, is the altarpiece, *The Adoration of the Lamb*. Jan, as perhaps also Hubert, was for a time in the service of Philip the Good, Duke of Burgundy. He was entered in the household as " varlet and painter "; but acted at the same time as confidential friend, and for his services received an annual salary of one hundred livres (almost twenty-five dollars), two horses for his use, and a " varlet in livery " to attend on him. The greater part of his life was spent in Bruges.

In these two brothers the grand art of Flanders was born in a day. Like " the sudden flowering of the aloe, after sleeping through a century of suns," this art, rooted in the native soil, nurtured by the smaller arts of craftsmanship, reached its full ripeness, and expanded into blossom. Such further development as it experienced, we shall find, came from Italian influence; but the distinctly Flemish art, born out of local conditions in Flanders, was already full grown. The great French painter and critic, Fromentin, says of it: "Imagine a collection of the creations of the goldsmiths, executed in paint, in which one feels the handiwork of the enameler, the glass-worker, the graver, and the illuminator. Its sentiment is grave, for it is inspired by the sentiment of the monasteries; but it is under the patronage of princes, and its general character is resplendent."

And now let us turn back to Fra Angelico. Little is known of his early life except that he was born at Vicchio, in the broad fertile valley of the Mugello, not far from Florence, that his name was Guido, and that he passed his youth in Florence, probably in some *bottegha,* for at twenty he was recognized as a painter. But he had already come under the influence of the great preacher and scholar, Giovanni Dominici, who traveled up and down the length and breadth of Italy, exhorting all men to a holier life and founding the order of Dominican monks. At the door of their convent on the slopes of Fiesole, just above Florence, Guido and his brother Benedetto, an illuminator, sought admittance. They were welcomed by the monks, and, after a year's novitiate, admitted to the brotherhood, Guido taking the name by which he was known in after life, Fra Giovanni da Fiesole; for the title of " Angelico," the " Angel," or " Il Beato," " The Blessed," was conferred on him after his death.

Henceforth he became an example of two personalities in one man: he was all in all a painter, all in all a devout monk; his subjects were ever religious ones and represented in a deeply religious spirit, yet his devotion as a monk was no greater than his absorption as an artist. Consequently, though his life was secluded within the walls of the monastery, he kept in touch with the art movements of his time and continually developed as a painter. His early work shows that he had learned of the illuminators who inherited the Byzantine traditions, and had been affected by the simple religious feeling of Giotto's work. Then he began to learn of that brilliant band of sculptors and architects who were enriching Florence by their genius. Ghiberti was executing his pictures in bronze upon the doors of the Baptistery; Donatello, his famous statue of *St. George* and the dancing children around the organ-gallery in the Cathedral; and Luca della Robbia also was at work upon his frieze of children, singing, dancing, and playing upon instruments. Moreover, Masaccio had revealed the dignity of form in painting. Through these artists the beauty of the human form and of its life and movement was being manifested to the Florentines and to the other cities, whither their fame spread.

Among the rest, Angelico catches the enthusiasm and gives increasing reality of life and movement to his figures. Furthermore, from the convent garden he could see the marvelous dome, designed by Brunelleschi, steadily rising above the Cathedral. What wonder that his imagination was fired and that he became, like other cultivated men of the day, an earnest student of architecture! At length, in the summer of 1435, the brethren moved into Florence and took up their abode in the monastery of San Marco. The original house was being added to, at the expense of Duke Cosimo de' Medici, by his favorite architect, Michelozzo. Can you not imagine with what joy Angelico must have watched the work, moved alike by the devout pride of a brother in his order and by an artist's sympathy with beauty? For he was to decorate the refectory and the corridors and cells; and close indeed must have been the bond between the painter and the architect.

If you turn again to the *Annunciation* that he painted later on the wall of the upper corridor, you will see how large a part the architecture plays in the composition of the picture.

The arcaded loggia is clearly inspired by the one down-stairs in the courtyard, and the two Ionic columns are careful copies of those which Michelozzo had just completed. Moreover, the vaulted ceilings, the round arch and slender columns with an adaptation of the Corinthian capital, are all characteristic of the elegant dignity of the arcades which this architect and Brunelleschi were introducing into the interior courts of their buildings, while leaving the outside grave and often stern and massive, like a fortress.

And from this we may glean two points of interest: first, how the different kinds of artists of this period learned from one another, working together in a newly awakened enthusiasm for beauty; and, secondly, that Angelico himself, by contact with these outside influences, had broadened and strengthened his own style. He was now about fifty years old, and this picture, rep-

FRA ANGELICO—VAN EYCK

resenting his maturity, is far in advance of the earlier ones. They were apt to be crowded with figures and decorative details. This one is so open and spacious, freely letting in the quiet warmth of the twilight; and so simple in general plan and therefore decorative in a big way. Instead of a multiplicity of objects counteracting the effect of one another, a few leading features are enforced by repetition: the curved lines of the arches and ceilings, for example, and the upright ones of the columns and fence. And, in addition to the interlaced pattern formed by the contrast of these two sorts of lines, there is the massed contrast of the garden, interspersed as it is with little features, and of the broad, plain surfaces of the masonry, enlivened only by a few choicely selected details.

How this arrangement of beautiful simplicity, so elevated in its general design, so tender in its parts, accords with the character of the two figures and with the scene they are enacting! In the cool of the evening Mary has been surprised by God's messenger, Gabriel. He has but this moment alighted; his wings still glisten with the iridescence of the sky, and his body thrills yet with the rapidity of his flight, as he drops on one knee with bowed head and folded hands in adoration of her who is to be the mother of the Saviour. And at this apparition, flashing so suddenly across the quiet tenor of her days, Mary's face is troubled; but, as she harkens to the divine message, she too bows her head and folds her arms in adoration and in meek acceptance. " And Mary said, Behold the handmaid of the Lord; be it unto me according to thy word."

HOW TO STUDY PICTURES

Fitly corresponding to the sentiment of the occasion is the tender purity of the color-scheme. The angel's robe is pale rose-color edged with gold; Madonna's robe is a paler pink, and her mantle deep blue; while, beyond the whiteness of the architecture, the grass is starred with daisies, and above the fence peep clusters of roses backed by dark-green cypresses.

And fitly corresponding too is the habitation of the picture. You pass out of the traffic of the streets into the quiet retreat of Michelozzo's court, some afternoon, perhaps, when the sloping sun plays lovingly over a few of the arches and columns, while the rest are drowsing in various gradations of shadow. A door in the cloisters leads into the chapter-house, adorned with Fra Angelico's *Crucifixion;* a second opens into the refectory, where the brethren took their meals in presence of another of their brother's pictures; and when you have mounted the stairs you pass along the corridor, out of which open the little private cells, where the black-and-white-habited monks worked and slept and meditated: in one of them Fra Bartolommeo—after Angelico's time, but, like him, a painter—and in another Savonarola, a later prior of the order, who stirred Florence to the depths by his denunciations of sin, and was hanged by his enemies, his body being burned and its ashes thrown into the Arno. You pass along beside the cells, each with its little window and its sacred painting on the wall done by Angelico, until at the end of the corridor you come face to face with this *Annunciation*.

Stilled is the busy life of the place, the monks are gone, their habitation now a show-place trod by the steps

FRA ANGELICO—VAN EYCK

of visitors from all parts of the world. But the spirit of peace and piety still haunts the spot and finds its sweetest expression in this picture.

Compared with it, Van Eyck's *The Virgin and Donor* is mundane, of the world, worldly; it is the work of a great painter luxuriating in the opportunities which the sacred subject offered. Fra Angelico was no less ardent a painter, but his painting was saturated with the feeling also of devout religion. In the complete union of the artist and the devotee he stands alone in the history of painting. His gentle art and life represent, as I have said, a quiet back-water, secluded from the river of achievement that was gathering force and about to plunge on in full might through the fifteenth century.

CHAPTER V

ALESSANDRO BOTTICELLI
1446–1510
Italian School of Florence

HANS MEMLING
1425 (?)–1495 (?)
Flemish School of Bruges

WE have seen that the revival of painting began with the study of the appearances of objects and an attempt to represent them as real to the senses of sight and touch; that the painters learned from the sculptors, who themselves had learned from the remains of antique sculpture; and that the result was a closer truth to nature, in the representation both of the human form and of its movement. We have also seen how in Flanders Jan van Eyck developed a grand school of painting out of the national skill of craftsmanship in the minor arts of decoration,—goldsmith's work, stained glass, embroidery, tapestry, and the like,—and that to the truth of natural form he added also a true appearance of textures. Further, we have seen how in Fra Angelico appeared the most perfect flower of that old religious feeling which for centuries had been a light in the darkness of the world.

We have now to consider the effect produced upon painting by the revival of the study of Greek, which revealed to Italy of the fifteenth century a new light, in the joy of which the older light was dimmed. Botticelli typifies this new inspiration. I have coupled with him the Flemish painter Memling, in order to continue our study of the Flemish School, and also because both these artists, though they worked apart and under very different conditions, had one quality in common. A certain *naïveté* of mind appears in each, an unaffected simplicity, frank and artless, fresh and tender like the child-mind or the opening buds of spring flowers. In Memling's case it is tinctured with gentle sentiment; in that of Botticelli, with a wistful yearning toward the light of old Hellas which was just beginning to dawn on the world of his time.

If you visit the Campo Santo at Pisa, you will see some frescoes which were painted in the fourteenth century, perhaps by Orcagna, or, as others think, by the brothers Lorenzetti. Their subjects are, *The Triumph of Death, The Judgment,* and *Hell.* They are terrible in their tragic intensity. A party of ladies and knights are going a-hawking; but their horses start back, sniffing at three open coffins in which half-decayed corpses are lying. For one of those awful plagues which periodically devastated Europe is stalking through the land. In another part of the picture appears a throng of youths and maidens dancing in a rose-garden, whom Death is mowing down with a scythe; elsewhere wretched creatures, mutilated by torture, are imploring Death in vain to ease them of their anguish; good and evil spirits struggle for the souls of men; and apart from these grisly horrors are hermits, living their lives of abnegation with the birds and beasts among the rocks.

These frescoes depict with horrible directness the dark turmoil of soul and body in the middle ages; the cruelty of man to man; the ever-present dread specter of death; the judgment of God, inexorable, inevitable; the solitude of the monkish life, as the only refuge from a sinful and doomed world; lurid fire, and blackness hanging like a thick pall above it, and no escape except in the renunciation of the world and of the joy of living.

But a glimmer of light was trembling on the horizon. The possibility of beauty in the living of this life was beginning to swallow up the horror of death; the soul of man, so long pent up and imprisoned in savage darkness, had been suddenly liberated; for what is called " The New Learning " had unlocked the dungeons of thought.

The newness consisted in two things: first, that the learning concerned itself with new subjects; secondly, that the knowledge of Greek was recovered by the western world.

Dante's poems were the swan-song of the middle ages. Seventeen years before his death, Petrarch was born; nine years later Boccaccio; and the poetry of both and the stories of the latter are the evangel of the modern world. Instead of speculating on the mysteries that lie beyond the grave, their theme is the present life and living humanity.

Moreover, both of them were inflamed with a longing to know all that was to be known of the older classic authors of Italy, and of the Greek classics upon which the Roman were founded. They ransacked Italy for manuscripts, and procured from a certain Leontius Pilatus, a native of Greece, a rude translation of Homer into Latin; for with the Greek tongue itself they had no acquaintance.

The introduction of this into Italian culture dates from 1396, when Manuel Chrysoloras, a Byzantine scholar, was appointed professor of Greek at Florence. From him and from his pupils the knowledge of Greek literature spread rapidly over Italy, accompanied by an extraordinary enthusiasm for the antique: for Roman and Greek art, and for Greek thought and Greek ideals. Hence the artist's devotion to the beauty of the human form, the scholar's admiration of Plato's philosophy. Artists and scholars thronged the court of Duke Lorenzo de' Medici—Lorenzo the Magnificent, patron of arts and letters; and among the brilliant throng none was more highly honored than Sandro Botticelli.

He was the son of a citizen in comfortable circumstances, and had been " instructed in all such things as children are usually taught before they choose a calling." But he refused to give his attention to reading, writing, and accounts, continues Vasari, so that his father, despairing of his ever becoming a scholar, apprenticed him to the goldsmith Botticello: whence the name by which the world remembers him. In those days, as we have noted before, men were masters of more than one craft. Among Sandro's contemporaries, for instance, Pollajuolo was painter as well as goldsmith, and Verrocchio goldsmith, painter, and sculptor. Botticello's Sandro, a stubborn-featured youth with large, quietly searching eyes and a shock of yellow hair,—he has left a portrait of himself on the right-hand side of his picture of the *Adoration of the Magi*,—would also fain become a painter, and to that end was placed with the Carmelite monk Fra Lippo Lippi.

Read for yourself Browning's poem "Fra Lippo Lippi," and discover the friar's discontent at being obliged to represent religious subjects according to the conventions prescribed by his patron, the church. For he was a realist, as the artists of his day had become, satisfied with the joy and skill of painting, and with the actual study of the beauty and character of the human subject. Sandro made rapid progress, loved his master, and later on extended his love to his master's son, Filippino Lippi, and taught him to paint. But the master's realism scarcely touched him, for Sandro was a dreamer and a poet.

You will feel this, if you refer to the two pictures and compare his *Madonna Enthroned* with Memling's. The latter's is much more realistic. It is true that it does not, as a whole, represent a real scene, for the Virgin's throne with its embroidered hanging or dossal, the canopy or baldachin above it, and the richly decorated arch which frames it in, are not what you would expect to see set up in a landscape. These are the conventional features, repeated with variations in so many Madonna pictures intended for altarpieces. But how very real are the two peeps of landscape, drawn, we may feel sure, from nature: a great man's castle and a water-mill, two widely separated phases of life, suggesting, perhaps, that the Christ came to save rich and poor alike. This would be a touch of symbolism; another may appear in the introduction of the apple, intended to remind us of the circumstances of the fall of man, which the Saviour

MADONNA ENTHRONED **ALESSANDRO BOTTICELLI**
BERLIN GALLERY

VIRGIN ENTHRONED   **HANS MEMLING**

UFFIZI GALLERY, FLORENCE

came into the world to redress. But Memling was satisfied merely to suggest the symbolism; and then devoted himself to rendering with characteristic *naïveté* a little scene of realism. The angel on the left is simply an older child, playfully attracting the baby's attention with an apple; the Christ is simply a baby attracted by the colored, shining object; and the pretty scene is watched intently by the other angel. On the Madonna's face, however, is an abstracted expression, as if her thoughts were far away; and indeed they are, yet not in pursuit of any mystical dream, but following that quiet, happy pathway along which a young mother's thoughts will roam. She is, in fact, only a girl-mother whom the artist has surprised, while she sits, unconscious of everything around her, wrapped up in the inward peace and joy of motherhood.

So we find in Memling's picture, despite the religious conception of its arrangement, a preoccupation with the natural appearances of persons and things, a close study of the way in which facts present themselves to the eye. This is apparent equally in the landscape, in the carved and embroidered ornament, in the character of the figures, and in the little story which they are enacting. As I have said, the spirit of the picture is realistic.

But turn to Botticelli's. Here the spirit is allegorical. He was fond of allegorical subjects, especially of mythological ones treated in a vein of allegory. His *Birth of Venus* and *Allegory of Spring* are the most famous examples. In the present case the subject is religious, but we may doubt if the Bible version of the story was in the artist's mind. He was commissioned to paint a Madonna and Child with attendant angels, and, poet and dreamer that he was, took the familiar theme and made it the framework of an imagery of his own. This imagery, it may be fairly safe to believe, had less to do with the old Gospel story than with the later gospel of the New Learning. In the figure of the Child-Christ there is a grave dignity, an assertion of authority; and not improbably the artist meant it to be symbolic of the wonderful new birth of classic culture. The only gesture of infancy is in the left arm and in the hand groping for the mother's breast. And she has the same kind of face, bowed in timid meekness, very sad in expression, which Botticelli gave to his *Venus*. Mother of love, mother of God,—he blends the Christian and the pagan worship to represent the mother of the " Desire of all nations." The cult of the Virgin, partly at least, had grown out of the ancient cult of Venus; and Botticelli, working in an age that was looking back to the classic past and trying to adjust the present to it, felt in Madonna and in Venus the twin expressions of a single sentiment—worship of the highest beauty in the person of woman. But beauty of face, as some may think, he does not give to his queen of love; she is meek and timid, as I have said, oppressed with gentle sadness; too frail as yet for a world still full of violence and confusion; sadly conscious that she is not yet at home in her new habitation. And in the faces of the angels also, the young, fair creatures that stand around the throne, there is a similar expression of wistful and unsatisfied yearning. It was so that Botticelli's own spirit peered through the still lingering darkness of the medieval times toward that light from Hellas which was beginning to dawn, but of which he himself never expected to see the noonday. Hence the strain of sadness in all his pictures; they have the note of infinite but ineffectual desire. So, when we understand this, we forget the homeliness of many of his faces, and find in them a spiritual significance which, we learn to feel, is a very touching and beautiful expression of the artist's own mind, of his particular way of looking at the world of his own time.

He looked at it as a poet, moved alike by the love of beauty and by the beauty of love; and out of the world's realities he fashioned himself dreams, and these he pictured. So his pictures, as I have said, are not records of fact, treated with a very pleasing fancifulness and reverence, as in this Madonna of Memling's; but visions, the beauty of which is rather spiritual than material. He tried, as it were, to paint not only the flower, but also its fragrance; and it was the fragrance that to him seemed the more precious quality.

So now, perhaps, we can begin to understand the difference between his technic—that is to say, his manner of setting down in paint what he desired to express—and Memling's. The latter, serene and happy, had all a child's delight in the appearances of things, attracted by them as the infant in this picture is attracted by the apple, and offering them to us with the same winning grace and certainty that they will please as the angel in the picture exhibits. So it is the facts, obvious to the senses of touch and sight, that he presents, with a loving, tender care to make them as obvious to us as possible, elaborating even the smallest parts. You have examined the beautiful workmanship in the ornamentation of the arch and in the garlands suspended by the charming little baby forms; but have you observed the tiny figures in the landscape? The castle drawbridge is down, and a lady on horseback passes over it, following a gentleman who may be riding forth to hunt, since a greyhound courses along behind him. From the mill is issuing a man with a sack of flour on his shoulders, which he will set upon the back of the donkey that waits patiently before the door; while a little way along the road stands a dog, all alert and impatient to start. These incidents illustrate Memling's fondness for detail and elaboration of finish, and his delight in the representation of facts as facts: traits which were characteristic of this early Flemish School. But observe that these minutely finished distant details illustrate also the *naïveté* of Memling. From where he stood to paint the foreground group, the figures in the background would appear simply as little spots of color. He did not paint the facts as they appeared to his eye, but as in his mind he knew them to be—the child's way of drawing.

By comparison with Memling, Botticelli is a painter not of facts, but of ideas; and his pictures are not so much a representation of certain objects as a pattern of forms. Nor is his coloring rich and lifelike, as Memling's: it is subordinated to form, and often rather a tinting than actual color. In fact, he is interested in the abstract possibilities of his art rather than in the concrete. For example, his compositions, as has just been said, are a pattern of forms; his figures do not actually occupy well-defined places in a well-defined area of space; they do not attract us by their suggestion of bulk, but as shapes of form, suggesting rather a flat pattern of decoration. Accordingly the lines which inclose the figures are chosen with the primary intention of being decorative. You will appreciate this if you will turn to the two pictures and compare the draperies of the angels. Those of Memling are commonplace in their prosy realism, compared with the fluttering grace of Botticelli's. But there is more in this flutter of draperies than mere beauty of line: it expresses a lively and graceful movement. These angels have alighted like birds, their garments still buoyed up with air and agitated by their speed of flight; each body being animated with its individual grace of movement. Compared with the spontaneousness and freedom of these figures, those of Memling seem heavy, stock-still, and posed for effect.

Now, therefore, you are in a position to appreciate the force of the remark that Botticelli, "though one of the worst anatomists, was one of the greatest draughtsmen of the Renaissance." As an example of false anatomy you may notice the impossible way in which the Madonna's head is attached to the neck, and other instances of faulty articulation and of incorrect form of limbs may be found in Botticelli's pictures. Yet he is recognized as one of the greatest draftsmen, because he gave to "line" not only intrinsic beauty but significance; that is to say, in mathematical language, he resolved the movement of the figure into its factors, its simplest forms of expression, and then combined these various forms into a pattern which, by its rhythmical and harmonious lines, produces an effect upon our imagination, corresponding to the sentiments of grave and tender poetry that filled the artist himself.

This power of making every line count both in significance and beauty distinguishes the great master-draftsmen from the vast majority of artists who use line mainly as a necessary means of representing concrete objects. To distinguish it from the latter use we may call it the *abstract* use of line.

Yet, although unique, Botticelli's art was but a link in the gradual development of Italian painting; whereas Memling's, like the Van Eycks', represented a growth complete in itself. Little is known of Memling's life. It is surmised that he was a German by descent and born in Mayence; but the definite fact of his life is that he painted at Bruges, sharing with the Van Eycks, who had also worked in that city, the honor of being the leading artists of the so-called " School of Bruges." He carried on their method of painting, and added to it a quality of gentle sentiment. In his case, as in theirs, the Flemish art, founded upon local conditions and embodying purely local ideals, reached its fullest expression.

His contemporary, Rogier van der Weyden, who worked in Brussels and was the chief exponent of what is called the " School of Brabant," represented religious subjects with dramatic and emotional intensity; but his color was pale and thin, and his drawing angular and often extravagant in gesture. The sentiment of his pictures is Gothic: a term which sums up in a general way the religious feeling of the Northern races, more gloomy,

BOTTICELLI—MEMLING

intense, and painful than the Christianity of the South; producing the solemn, mysterious, intricate grandeur of the Gothic cathedral instead of the simpler, sunnier, and more elegant form of church built in the Romanesque style, which was a mingling of the Roman and the Byzantine methods of construction.

We shall have to say more about the Gothic feeling when we come to the consideration of the early German painting. Meanwhile the thing to note is that the Van Eycks and Memling, though living in an age that was influenced by this Gothic intensity, worked in an atmosphere of quiet and sunniness, cultivating, as it were, a little garden stocked with the simple flowers native to their country, and bringing it to perfection of development; so that this Flemish painting of the fifteenth century represents a little separate chapter in the history of art. At the beginning of the following century stands out the name of Quentin Massys (1460–1530), but his work has already ceased to be distinctively Flemish, and shows the influence of Italy. For as commercial relations increased between the two countries, the artists of Flanders lost their national characteristics and became imitators, at a very great distance, of the Italian masters. As we are treating in this little book only of the vital periods and phases of art, the art of Flanders will disappear from our horizon for nearly a hundred years, to reappear in colossal shape, in the person of Rubens, at the beginning of the seventeenth century.

Italy's yearning toward the antique, to which Botticelli gave expression, we shall find satisfied in the work of Giovanni Bellini and of Raphael.

CHAPTER VI

PIETRO VANNUCCI (called PERUGINO)
1446-1524
Italian School of Umbria

GIOVANNI BELLINI
1428 (?)-1516
Italian School of Venice

AT the end of the previous chapter we touched on the Gothic intensity which characterized the art of the North, in the midst of which the Flemish art of the fifteenth century, that culminated in the Van Eycks and Memling, was like an oasis of repose and rich pleasantness. For these artists escaped the rigorous influences around them, chiefly through their pure delight in the actual presentation of objects, which made them first and chiefly painters, and only in a secondary way interpreters of the Christian dogma and religious zeal.

You will remember that a similar painter-like love of presentation distinguished the contemporaries of Botticelli in Florence, and we spoke of them as realists, while Botticelli, as we noticed, was a poet and a dreamer. The two artists who now demand our attention, Perugino and Giovanni Bellini, were also contemporaries of Botticelli; and in them too the painter-like point of view was pronounced, but tempered with—perhaps we should rather say, subordinated to—a very high purpose of sentiment.

They were among the first artists in Italy to perfect

the use of the oil medium, the secret of which had been discovered from the Van Eycks and brought into Italy by Antonello da Messina. It permitted a fullness and richness of color and a fusing of all the colors into an atmosphere of golden warmth—qualities that corresponded with the sentiments that each of them desired to express.

Let us try to understand the sentiment which is exhibited in these pictures. Perugino's is different to Bellini's, and yet both have something in common. In each of these two triptychs you will feel the presence of a wonderful calm. It has been said of Perugino that he is the painter " of solitude; of the isolated soul, alone, unaffected by any other, unlinked in any work, or feeling, or suffering with any other soul—nay, even with any physical thing." You will realize the truth of this, I think, if you study the Pavia altarpiece. Not only in the expression of each face, but also in the gesture and carriage of the body, there is an absolute unconsciousness of surroundings, a complete absorption in some inward spiritual ecstasy. The archangel Michael, the Virgin, and the archangel Raphael, who holds the young Tobit by the hand, are beings without sin or sorrow or even joy; filled with the " peace that passeth understanding," that peace which comes of complete detachment from the world and of rapt communion with God. Nor is the type of the male figures masculine—it is said that Perugino's wife was the model for Raphael. Yet the pose of the Michael is not that of a woman; indeed, it would seem as if the artist's intention was to create a being who should be without thought or suggestion of sex; the embodiment, with as little bodily hindrance as possible, of a soul engaged in the beatitude of contemplation. His figures, then, do not represent Virgin, saints, and angels as such, but as personifications of intense soul-rapture. They are the souls and soul-saturated bodies which Perugino saw around him. For in the dying years of the fifteenth century Italy was torn with factions, a prey to sack and massacre at the hands of licentious bands of soldiers. Perugia itself, the little town on the hills of Umbria, where Perugino worked, was governed by treacherous and ferocious captains; its dark and precipitous streets were filled with broil and bloodshed, and its palaces with evil living. Yet it was one of the most pious cities in all Italy. Men and women sought refuge from the horrors of actual life in strange spiritual solitude, in life removed from all activities, steeped in devotion, passively contemplating a far-off ideal of purity and loveliness.

This was a very different thing from the active religious feeling of Fra Angelico: simple and childlike in its sunny faith; a product, as it were, of the open daylight; the lovable expression of a man who, as we have seen, entered humbly and intelligently into the activities around him. Yet Perugino's art, like Fra Angelico's, had its roots in the old Byzantine tradition of painting. You remember that the latter had departed farther and farther from any actual representation of the human form, until it became merely a symbol of religious ideas. Perugino, working under the influence of his time, restored body and substance to the figures, but still made them, as of old, primarily the symbols of an ideal. In him the Byzantine inspiration, so far as it was an expression of religion, reached its highest point of development.

It also reached a final development in Giovanni Bellini, though in another direction. This artist was the son of Jacopo Bellini, a Venetian painter, who, however, was settled in Padua during the time that Giovanni and his elder brother, Gentile, were in the period of studentship. Here, as we have seen, they came under the influence of Mantegna, who was also bound to them by the ties of relationship, since he married their sister. To his brother-in-law Bellini owed much of his knowledge of classical architecture and perspective, and his broad and sculptural treatment of draperies. Moreover, during these years Verrocchio was working on his equestrian statue of *Bartolommeo Colleoni*, " the most magnificent equestrian statue of all time ";[1] and Giovanni's father had been a pupil of Mantegna's master, Squarcione, with opportunities of studying the remains of antique sculpture that he had collected. So sculpture and the love of the antique played a large part in Giovanni's early impressions, and left their mark in the stately dignity of his later style. This developed slowly; indeed, during his long life of eighty-eight years he was continually developing; and the masterpiece, reproduced here, was executed when he was about sixty years old and Titian was one of his pupils.

The calm which pervades this picture is of a different kind from that which appears in Perugino's. Its suggestion is of stateliness, of the nobility of grand types of

[1] Dr. Bode

humanity. These figures have the ample quietude of strength in repose that belongs to those of Phidias upon the pediments of the Parthenon. Bellini, of course, knew nothing of these; but his study of such antique sculpture as had come within his observation, influenced by his own particular bent of mind, led him to a point of view very similar to that of the great Athenian. The latter's purpose had been to represent, not individuals, but types of humanity, ideally perfect, godlike beings, whose mental and physical powers were in complete poise. Hence his work is distinguished by grandeur of mass rather than by finish of detail. The successors of Phidias, on the other hand, showed an increasing tendency to individualize their figures by making them expressive of sentiment and emotion. A similar difference distinguishes Bellini from his successors in the Venetian School.

He is ranked as the greatest of the Venetian School of the fifteenth century—nay, more than that, as the greatest painter of the period—by no less an authority than Dürer, who, during his visit to Venice in 1494, wrote to a friend in a letter still preserved: "He is very old, but yet the best in painting." It must be remembered that at this date Titian was in his prime; so we may well ask upon what Dürer based his judgment. He knew his art theoretically and practically, so that he was able to appreciate the perfect mastery over the brush that was displayed alike by Titian and by Bellini; and, if he preferred the latter, it must have been because he himself was a very intellectual man and accordingly was in sympathy with the grave and elevated conceptions of

TRIPTYCH FROM THE PAVIA ALTAR-PIECE   PERUGINO
NATIONAL GALLERY, LONDON

TRIPTYCH ALTAR-PIECE GIOVANNI BELLINI
CHURCH OF THE FRARI, VENICE

Bellini rather than with the more sensuous and emotional art of Titian.

For this is the distinction between the two great Venetians. Bellini worked in a great calm, removed from passion. Swayed by intellectuality, serene and lofty and a little severe, he stands to the glowing, eager spirits that followed him as Phidias to Scopas and Praxiteles. In one respect, however, he shows the influence of his time. Observe the noble character in the heads of the four saints. He lived in an age when the portrayal of character was an important aim of art, and was himself a great portrait-painter—witness his noble portrait of Doge *Leonardo Loredano* in the National Gallery. During his long life he saw no fewer than eleven doges, and was state painter during the reigns of four.

To return to our picture. These bishops and monks have the bronzed, sunburned faces that may still be seen among the boatmen of Venice; the Virgin's complexion has the pure carnation tones of girls reared in a moist atmosphere; the cherubs, with their naked legs, recall the children that may still be seen fishing for crabs at sunset. In fact, the picture, as the French critic Taine remarked, " is full of local truth, and yet the apparition is one of a superior and august world. These personages do not move; their faces are in repose, and their eyes fixed like those of figures seen in a dream."

Here again is the symbol of an idea, as in the Byzantine paintings; but this time the symbol itself is founded on truth to actual local facts, and the idea is the elevation of these well-known facts into a lofty and ennobling type. It is not, as in Perugino's work, an escape from human nature into the abstract seclusion of the soul, but an assertion of the grandeur that may be inherent in humanity itself. Thus in Bellini's pictures the influence of the new learning of Greek culture and Platonic philosophy, toward which Botticelli groped tentatively, is seen in its highest and purest form.

And now let us try to discover something of the technical means by which Perugino and Bellini have expressed in these pictures their ideals. In one we have a notable example of Perugino's skill in combining figures with landscape; in the other, a hint of the dignity given to a composition by the introduction of architectural forms.

It was not until the seventeenth century that artists began to paint landscape for its own sake. By the Italians of the Renaissance it was treated as a background for figures; and while many artists—Perugino, for example, and the Venetians—made a close study of nature, they always kept inanimate nature subordinated to the human subject. The landscape in Perugino's triptych is a representation of Umbrian scenery, a beautiful vista of hills and river-threaded plain, stretching away to a low, distant horizon, with the delicate foliage of slender trees sprayed against the melting tenderness of the sky. To this beautiful effect of receding distance and of open sky, in the representation of which Perugino excelled, is largely due the impression that the picture produces. Just as the expression of the faces tells us that the thoughts of these beings are far away from the actual present, absorbed into infinite contemplation, so our gaze wanders on and on through the landscape, and finally loses itself in the luminous infinitude of the sky. The landscape, in fact, puts our own minds in tune with those of the persons in the picture. If it were not there; if, for example, the background were of gold, as in the old Byzantine pictures, I suspect that we should find these figures excessively sentimental; as, indeed, many of Perugino's pictures are, for it is only occasionally that he rises to the spirituality of this one. But, as it is, the sentiment of the figures is enlarged upon and interpreted by the setting, just as in a Greek play the emotions of the actors are explained by the chorus.

However, it is not only in interpreting such sentiment as Perugino seeks to express that this union of landscape and figures counts so much. One of the secrets of noble composition is the balancing of what artists call the full and empty spaces. A composition crowded with figures is apt to produce a sensation of stuffiness and fatigue; whereas the combination of a few figures with ample open spaces gives one a sense of exhilaration and repose. You may think there is a contradiction in the idea of being at the same time rested and exhilarated, unless you know the sensation of mountain-walking, when the zest of the upper air fills you with desire to exert yourself, and yet there is no fatigue in exertion; while the broad sweeps of the sky above you and of plain and valley below open lungs and imagination equally, and you feel full of peace and, simultaneously, of eagerness. And this illustration is not far-fetched, since it is a fact that a picture reaches our imagination through our ordinary experience of physical sensation. We know, for example, how soft and warm and caressing is the skin of a little child; and if, in the picture of a child, the flesh is painted in such a way as to suggest this lovely texture, it will stimulate our imagination with pleasure. And it is in the degree that an artist stimulates our imagination through our physical experiences, that he seizes and holds our interest.

I have spoken of the effect produced by a combination of full and empty spaces, but this may be nothing more than a fine pattern. When, however, besides giving us a pattern of flat ornament in two dimensions, the artist can make us realize the third dimension of nature, —distance,—he so much the more kindles our imagination. For how many of us, as children, have looked at that hill which bounded the horizon of our home and longed to know what lay beyond it? And, in after years, the sight of the ocean, or of peak ranged beyond peak in the mountains, or of a summer sky at night, or of many other distant prospects, allures our imagination to travel on and on and lose itself in space. Now the mere suggestion of distance in a picture, secured by accurate perspective, will not affect us in this way; the artist himself must have this sort of ranging imagination, and then he will not only make you feel the distance, but the existence of every successive plane of intervening space, inviting your own imagination to range. Perugino preeminently had this feeling and the gift of expressing it: a mastery of what has been called by Mr. Bernard Berenson the art of "space-composition." There are many other technical points in the pictures that we might dwell on; but as our purpose in this little book is to proceed step by step, one thing at a time, we will limit our consideration to this one point,—the more so as some of the others will be met with later in the work of Perugino's most illustrious pupil, Raphael.

So, too, in the case of Bellini we will consider only a single technical point—the value of architectural accessories in adding dignity to the composition. These three panels are inclosed in a gilt frame which itself is a very handsome example of Renaissance design and craftsmanship. You will observe that the character of the design is architectural, and that the pilasters, the cornice, and the arch repeat, and therefore enforce, the architectural features of the picture. The general effect of this architectural setting is a mingling of force and grave distinction and of richness.

If you carefully compare this triptych with Perugino's, you will get an insight into the different effects produced, according as the background is landscape or architecture. In the former the lines are irregular, softly undulating, and distance melts into further distance; in Bellini's picture, however, the lines are firm and exact, the background has structural weight and stability. In one case the imagination spreads and finally loses itself in conjecture; in the other it is contracted and concentrated. Perugino's conception is very wooing; Bellini's, more monumentally impressive.

Let us pause for a moment on this word "monumental," since it expresses a quality which will constantly confront us in our study of art. In one sense it is the antithesis of nature: it belongs to a structure reared by the hand of man. Instead of being the result of natural laws working invisibly and over great periods of time, it is the result of formal laws invented by man (sometimes, perhaps, through a hint from nature) and compressed into a well-defined compass. A structure must necessarily be smaller than nature, yet it may impress us with a greater sense of dignity and grandeur. Nature's grandeur, as seen, for example, among the peaks and cañons of the mountains, fills us with awe; we are in the presence of stupendous forces uncontrolled by visible laws. Whereas a great building, as St. Peter's, for example, is a triumph of law over disorder; everything has been planned, calculated, regulated; in the presence of it man is not crushed down into awed insignificance, but, realizing that all this grandeur around him is the work of man's hand and brain, he is lifted up into glorious enthusiasm, filled with pride in the grandeur of humanity and in the consciousness of having a share in it. A building which can impress us in this way we call monumental. It is worth while to look a little more closely and discover by what means this impression is produced.

Architecture is the most original of the fine arts, not being an imitation of nature, as painting and sculpture are, but an invention of man's own, founded first of all upon necessity, and then made to contribute to the aspirations that filled his soul. Yet its principles are based upon qualities which man learned to admire in nature: stability, for example, height, and breadth, and spaciousness. The prophet Habakkuk, wishing to bring home to man the awful power of God, says that in his presence "the everlasting mountains were scattered, the perpetual hills did bow." He knew that it was the stability, the permanence of the mountains and hills which impressed his hearers. Again, man in all ages has lifted his eyes from the earth to the height and immensity of the sky; he piled stone on stone to reach this majesty of height, and spanned his columns with arches, and then assembled his arches into the mimic wonder of a dome. Trees taught him the aspiring grandeur of vertical lines; the level horizon, the quiet dignity of the horizontal; distance and space, the beauty of long vistas and of spaciousness. After much experimenting he discovered the proportion of height and breadth and length that would best produce a harmonious whole, and then added ornament which should enrich without impairing the structural dignity and stability of the mass.

Learning from architecture, the sculptors—who, as you remember, in early times were quite frequently architects as well—applied these principles, and sometimes so successfully that their compositions are monumental. Upon these principles also the painter based his compositions; but, as the lines of nature and of the human figure are not formal and rigid, he recognized how much his picture would gain in force and stability if he actually introduced some architectural features. This was a common practice with the artists of the Renaissance, and is one of the causes of the noble dignity of their pictures.

Bellini, in this one, has not only introduced architecture, but has adapted the character of the figures to it. How large and simple in mass are those of the bishops and monks, in which again appears the quiet grandeur of upright lines! Even in the figures of the Virgin and

HOW TO STUDY PICTURES

Child there is a strongly sculptural suggestion: her pose is so firm and still, the cloak arranged in such simple and resolute folds. And the statuesque character of this figure in blue is enhanced by the open spaces around it of crimson and gold, which isolate it and increase its suggestion of everlasting stability and calm. Immobile and permanent as the everlasting hills, she sits there through the changes of time, guarded by men of the people ennobled into types of physical and mental grandeur, perpetual symbol of Bellini's intellectual elevation.

After filling the whole of the north of Italy with his influence and preparing the way for the giant colorists of the Venetian School, Giorgione, Titian, and Veronese, Bellini died of old age in his eighty-eighth year, and was buried, near his brother Gentile, in the Church of SS. Giovanni e Paulo. Outside, under the spacious vault of heaven, stands the *Bartolommeo Colleoni,* Verrocchio's monumental statue, which had been among the elevating influences of Bellini's life and art.

Verrocchio's influence must have been exerted also upon Perugino, if it is true, as Vasari asserts, that when he left Perugia to complete his education in Florence he was a fellow-pupil of Leonardo da Vinci in the sculptor's *bottegha.* If he gained from the master something of the calm of sculpture, he certainly gained nothing of its force. It is as the painter of sentiment that he excelled; though this beautiful quality is confined mainly to his earlier works. For with popularity he became avaricious, turning out repetitions of his favorite types until they became more and more affected in sentiment.

CHAPTER VII

RAPHAEL SANZIO
1483–1520
Italian School of Umbria,
Florence, and Rome

MICHAEL WOLGEMUTH
1434–1519
German School of
Nuremberg

BY the beginning of the sixteenth century the Renaissance in Italy had ripened into a golden harvest. Leonardo da Vinci, Michelangelo, and Titian were in their prime, and within the long lives of these older men blossomed Raphael's comparatively brief life of thirty-seven years.

My reason for introducing him into our story a little before his chronological place is that now I wish to bring into comparison with Italian art the contemporary art of Germany. It seemed necessary to couple Leonardo and Dürer; therefore I took advantage of the fact that although Leonardo was older than Raphael he survived him, in order to join the latter with Wolgemuth, who was Dürer's master. For it is in Dürer, and later in Hans Holbein the Younger, that German art in the sixteenth century reached so high a point. Yet we may well study Wolgemuth, the better to appreciate the greatness of Dürer and Holbein, and also because his work is characteristic of the general art of Germany before these two great masters.

How it differs from Raphael's! The difference is

wide and high as the Alps which separated the two civilizations of which these two painters were, respectively, a product. At this point, when Italy is approaching the zenith of her Renaissance, and that of Germany is about to dawn, it is well to glance back over the history of the two countries, which for over a thousand years had been acting and reacting upon each other.

Since the days of Julius Cæsar the German tribes had been in conflict with Rome, but upon the outskirts of the Empire. In the fifth century they began to crowd down upon Italy itself.

In 410 Alaric, at the head of his Visigoths, penetrated to the gates of Rome, took it, and subjected it to a six days' pillage. Then Italy was ravaged successively by Attila and his Huns, by Ostrogoths and Lombards, until the genius of Charlemagne welded all the conflicting elements of the western world into the Holy Roman Empire (800 A.D.). But after his death the unwieldy structure succumbed to its own bulk; his descendants strove among themselves for supremacy, and the power of the feudal nobles was established. There followed a century and a half of domestic war, in which unhappy Italy was desolated by nobles and by invasions of Huns and Saracens, and filled with corruption and barbarism. At last, in 962, Otho the Great of Germany, having revived in his person the title of Emperor of the Holy Roman Empire, set himself to curb the power of the nobles and of the church by encouraging the growth of the cities and giving them free municipal authority. The result was a long period of fighting between the Papacy and the Empire, out of which arose the factions of Guelphs and Ghibellines, who, under pretense of favoring, respectively, the church or emperor, committed every sort of atrocity. After two hundred years of social chaos, the destruction of Milan by the Emperor Frederick Barbarossa so enraged the Guelph cities of the north that they formed a league, defeated his army, and at the Peace of Constance (1183) secured their recognition as free cities, each with its council and chief magistrate, or *podestá*. But again the lull was only brief. The maritime cities fought with one another for the supremacy of the sea; while everywhere the lack of military spirit in the cities and their domestic jealousies made it possible for the leading family of the city, or for the captains of fortune, to usurp the power of the people and establish themselves as despots. We have already noted how the Gonzaga family so established itself at Mantua, and the Medici family at Florence, glossing over their tyranny by the patronage of art and letters. Italy, crushed, was again at the mercy of all comers: of the rival despots, of the foreign mercenaries that they hired, and of bands of condottieri who sold their savagery to the highest bidders. Finally even her commercial power was menaced and ruined. The capture of Constantinople by the Turks in 1453 cut off her trade with the Orient; in 1497 the Portuguese Vasco da Gama discovered the passage to India around the Cape of Good Hope; five years previously the Genoese Columbus had opened up the New World; and the subsequent discoveries and conquests of Cortez, Pizarro, and others diverted the stream of commerce, depriving Italy of her supremacy and giving it to the western nations.

HOW TO STUDY PICTURES

In the sixteenth century nothing remained to Italy but the glory of arts, of letters, and of science, which in this period of national and civic humiliation reached its highest point of splendor: a terrible example, once more, of the truth that the finest culture will not save a nation, unless it is allied to the hardier virtues of manly courage and morality.

We have seen in previous chapters how people sought refuge from the turmoil in religion; how others turned from the horrors of the present to the beauties of the past, unearthing the remains of classic sculpture, recovering the manuscripts of the Roman authors, and drinking deep of the "New Learning" through the study of Greek literature. It is because the work of Raphael, apart from its technical skill and charm, combines so admirably the religious and the pagan feeling,—the personal intensity and reverence of the one and the impersonal serenity and happiness of the other,—that he holds a place distinct from any other artist. But, before pursuing this subject, let us turn to the conditions in Germany which produced a Wolgemuth as the forerunner of the greater Dürer and Holbein.

As each successive wave of Gothic invasion into Italy retired back behind the Alps, it carried with it some infusion of the civilization that it had destroyed. From this mingling of ancient culture with the untutored simplicity of the North sprang the modern world, with Christianity for its nurse. Art was the faithful handmaid of religion; and, as the northern world progressed toward civilization, the two worked together as mistress and servant. Germany, which at first was the country

MADONNA DEGLI ANSIDEI   RAPHAEL SANZIO
NATIONAL GALLERY, LONDON

DEATH OF THE VIRGIN   MICHAEL WOLGEMUTH
MUSEUM OF FINE ARTS, BOSTON

now known as Bavaria, did not escape the rigors of war; it kept the Huns at bay and extended its rule to the shores of the Baltic. As the vast tracts of land were opened up, population increased, people began to congregate in towns and cultivate the arts of peace. A steady flow of commerce set in from south to north and back again; the main arteries of traffic being the Rhine and the Elbe, by which the products of eastern and southern countries were transported from Venice or Genoa to Bruges and Antwerp and the growing Hanse towns of the north. So, while the country at large was torn with strife, there grew up along the banks of the rivers or their connecting landways settlements of commercial people; towns, no longer centering round the castle of the local tyrant, but independent communities of peace-loving burghers, intent on their purses and ledgers rather than on swords and fighting. Midway in the path of commerce arose the famous cities of Nuremberg and Augsburg. Granted special favors by the emperors, they were free imperial cities, almost the only homes of liberty at that period; and they produced the two men who at that period rose to the highest rank in Germany as artists—Dürer and Holbein. Wolgemuth also was a native of Nuremberg.

This city was noted as early as the beginning of the fifteenth century for great mechanical activity and improvement in all kinds of machinery. She could boast the first German paper-mill and the celebrated printing-press of Antonius Koburger. In every branch of industry were men of skill and renown: watch- and clock-makers, metal-workers, and organ-builders, and particularly workers in gold. Nuremberg had the reputation of being the best-governed city in Europe; her merchants were nobles who extended their influence into every country, until it was said of her that her "hand is in every land." During the fifteenth century her progress in civilization was rapid; and the wealth of her citizens began to be spent more and more on things of beauty.

The German desire of the beautiful had first of all expended itself in the architecture of the cathedrals and churches. These differed from the ones of the South, first of all, as the vertical line differs from the horizontal; the aspiration of the eager, striving people of the North finding expression in soaring towers and spires, in high-pitched roofs supported upon lofty pillars.

This departure from the lower and more level lines of Southern architecture led to greater profusion and intricacy of the parts; to the multiplication and elaboration of details; to long-drawn-out naves and the addition of side aisles, producing in every direction vistas solemn and mysterious; to the enlargement of the window-spaces and the dividing of them by elegant traceries filled in with stained glass. These Gothic cathedrals differ from the Italian somewhat as the forests of Germany differ from the broadly sweeping plains and hills of Italy. And the German love of profusion and detail was exhibited also in the habit of decorating the exterior with sculpture and the interior with wrought metal-work and carved wood. Even to this day the dwellers in the Black Forest, like those who inhabit the forest regions of Norway and Sweden, spend the long days of winter in carving objects in wood. Wood-carving was one of the earliest of the arts in Germany; gradually it was supplemented by the sculpture in stone of floral or foliage designs, or of figures to decorate the cathedrals and churches—figures of saints, lean and angular, or of terrible and grotesque creatures. For the ancient religion from which Christianity had weaned the Northern tribes was that of Asgard, savage and cruel, believing in giants and dragons, and blending the fierceness of a wild beast with the imagination and ignorance of a child. So the Christianity of medieval Germany inherited what was terrible and grotesque. This is reflected in the sculpture, and thence passed into painting; for, at first, the latter was only a helpmate to the architecture and learned its first lessons from the sculptors. The early painters represented in their pictures what they were familiar with in wood and stone; so that not only are the figures dry and hard, but in the groups they are packed one behind another, heads above heads, without really occupying space, in imitation of the method adopted in the carved relief.

And this unpainterlike way of painting continued even to the middle of the fourteenth century, by which time, however, the painters began to take a more prominent position. For people who wished to show their respect to the church and at the same time to perpetuate their own memory found they could get a more pleasing effect, and probably at a less cost, in paint than in wood or stone. So there grew up a demand for votive pictures, to be set up over the altar or hung upon a pillar, and these represented sacred scenes, often with portraits of the donor and his family introduced.

The principal pictures of this character executed at Nuremberg in the last thirty years of the fifteenth century issued from the workshop of Wolgemuth. At first he was in partnership with Hans Pleydenwurff, and upon the latter's death married the widow and carried on the business in his sole name. For a business it really was; the workshop being rather like a factory than a studio. A number of assistants were maintained, and they were apportioned certain specific parts of the same picture; it being the duty of one to fill in the architectural features, of another to paint the hands and heads, of others to put in the ornamental portions or the various objects introduced, and so on. The work, indeed, was carried on like any other commercial enterprise.

We have seen something of the same kind of thing in Perugino's *bottegha:* assistants multiplying the master's types, and turning out a quantity of indifferent pictures, apparently for no higher purpose than to make money. Raphael, also, during his sojourn in Rome, when the demand upon his genius was taxed beyond his power of personally executing every commission, maintained his corps of assistants. But he never lost his high ideals as an artist; and, although a large portion of his famous decorations in the Vatican were actually painted by his pupils, the designs were his. Moreover, his genius for design was so extraordinary, inexhaustible in invention, always beautiful in plan, and the influence of his own elevated spirit so strong over his assistants, that even their work bears the impress of his creativeness.

RAPHAEL—WOLGEMUTH

The Madonna which illustrates this chapter is called "degli Ansidei," because it was painted for the Ansidei family, as an altarpiece to adorn the chapel dedicated to S. Nicholas of Bari in the church of S. Fiorenzo at Perugia. It is dated 1506, and belongs therefore to the end of the first of the three periods into which Raphael's life may be divided. For he worked successively in Perugia, Florence, and Rome, and is, in a measure, representative of the Umbrian, Florentine, and Roman schools.

The house in Urbino still stands where he was born in 1483. His father, Giovanni Santi (or Sanzio in the Italian form), was a painter of considerable merit; so Raphael's art education began in early childhood and was continued uninterruptedly through the remainder of his life, for to the very end he was learning, being possessed of an extraordinary capacity for absorbing and assimilating the ideas of others. He was only eight years old when his mother, Magia, died; but the father's second wife, Bernardina, cared for him as if he had been her own son; and her tenderness and his love for her may surely have helped to inspire the beautiful conception of motherhood which he portrayed in his Madonnas. In 1494 his father also died, leaving the boy, now eleven years old, to the care of an uncle, who, it is supposed, arranged for him to continue his studies under the painter Timoteo Vite, who was then living in Urbino. At about the age of sixteen he was sent to Perugia and entered in the renowned *bottegha* of Perugino.

This *Madonna degli Ansidei,* painted in his twenty-third year, is full of recollection of the master's influence. We may note the low-lying landscape with the vault of sky above it, and the union with these of solemn architecture; moreover, the " sweet Umbrian sentiment " in the expression of the faces; and that each figure seems alone with itself in spiritual contemplation. Even the rather awkward and affected attitude of S. John betrays the influence of Perugino.

But already the pupil has outstripped the master. The figure of S. Nicholas is nobler than anything that Perugino painted, and more full of character. With what truth it depicts the pose and bearing of an absorbed reader, while the character of the head gives a foretaste of those portraits by Raphael in later years, which, it has been said, have no superiors as faithful renderings of soul and body.

But in another respect he has already outstripped his master; namely, in the noble serenity of the composition. Perugino, as we have seen, in combining the figure and architecture and landscape, was a master of space composition, but never with so firm an instinct for grouping and arrangement that the masses shall be not only dignified in themselves, but perfectly balanced. For this is Raphael's supreme distinction. The Venetians surpassed him in color, the Florentines in drawing, but few, if any, have equaled him in his mastery over the filling of a space, whether it be inside a frame or on the larger surface of a wall.

Let us briefly consider this matter of composition, which is the artist's way of building up his effects. Much of our previous study has been occupied with the gradual approach of artists toward a more truthful representation of nature; so at this point we do well to remember that, although nature is the basis of art, art is not nature. The latter is a vast field from which the artist selects certain items, afterward arranging them in a certain way, so as to produce a certain impression on the spectator's mind through his eyes. Selection and arrangement, therefore, are the principles of composition.

Now the method of arrangement may either follow nature's, as in the case, for example, of a landscape; or it may be an artificial arrangement, based upon conventions, such as in this picture of Raphael's. But even in the case of the landscape the artist must select. He must decide, in the first place, how much to include in his canvas, and then how he will place it according to the size and shape of his picture, leaving out, very likely, some of the objects of the natural landscape, since their introduction would interfere with the balance and unity of his picture.

If you stand a little distance from the open window and look out, it is improbable that what you see of the landscape will have either of these qualities. Probably the view will appear what it really is—a fragment of the landscape, its details, more than likely, confused or crowded. Or, if you approach nearer to the window, the view will widen out, but still you will feel that your gaze is hindered by the window-frame. On the other hand, you look through a picture-frame, and you should be able to feel that what you see is a scene complete in itself, that it has unity. Again, if you examine some particular tree,—say, for example, an elm, especially when the leaves are off,—you may note how the limbs and branches, for all their diversities, seem to compose together to make a balanced whole. Its parts are so balanced, and their relation to the whole mass so perfectly adjusted, that you exclaim, " What a beautiful tree! " This principle of organic unity, which appears in all nature's tree and plant forms, the artist borrows to give unity and balance to the artificial arrangement on his canvas.

This arrangement, in the language of the studios, is made up of full and empty spaces. In a landscape, for example, the sky would be an empty space, though a sheet of water in the foreground, or even a stretch of meadow or distant hills, might be treated so. For it is in the way an object is treated that it becomes a full or an empty space; the full ones being those which are intended to assert themselves most. Thus, in Raphael's picture which we are studying they consist of the figures and the throne; the arch, which under some circumstances might be treated as a full space, here uniting with the sky and landscape to form the empty ones. And it is partly the equilibrium established between these and the full ones that makes the picture yield such a suggestion of wonderful composure. Another reason is the direction of the lines.

If you study them, you will find they present a contrast of vertical, horizontal, and curved lines; and will grow to discover that it is the predominance of the vertical direction—aided somewhat, it is true, by the dignity of the arch—which produces such an impression of elevated grandeur. Do not fail to notice what a share the repetition of line plays in this effect. It was by repetition that the predominance of the vertical lines was built up. But there are repetitions of horizontal lines also; for example, in those of the steps and the canopy, the cornice of the arch, and S. John's arm, as well as of the broken level line of the landscape. Moreover, there are repetitions of the curved lines, especially in the moldings of the arch. But these are repeated also in a subtler way; for example, in the nimbus of the Virgin, and in the arched dome of each of the heads.

Lastly, observe that the unity of the composition is made additionally sure by everything being adjusted to one point. The book on the Virgin's lap is the focus of the whole. The diagonal lines of the canopy, those of the cornice and of the steps, lead toward this spot; so do the direction of the Virgin's head and the downward glance of her eyes, the Child's gaze, the bishop's book, and S. John's right arm and its index-finger. While all these are radiating lines, they are inclosed—locked in, as it were—by the arch, the continuation of which into a circle is suggested by the direction of S. John's left arm.

All this is the reverse of natural arrangement, being the result of a most carefully calculated plan, based upon the knowledge that the actual directions of lines, their contrasts and their repetitions, exert upon the mind certain definite influences. You will observe that the basis of this design is geometric, as are nearly all the compositions of the old masters and of most modern painters; a continual shuffling and reshuffling of vertical, horizontal, and curved lines; a building of them up, so as to approximate to various geometric figures, such as the circle, the angle, the triangle, and the various forms of the quadrilateral, or any or all in combination. For some psychological reason, perhaps because these forms are rudimentary and elemental, they are instantly satisfactory to the eye, and when played upon by such a master of composition as Raphael produce the highest kind of esthetic enjoyment.[1]

By this time it should be apparent that the beauty of Raphael's picture does not depend primarily upon the expression of the faces, which is the first thing that many people look at, nor, indeed, upon any or all of the figures, but upon what artists call the "architectonics" of the composition; that is to say, upon the way in which the parts of the composition are built up into a unified structural design. This, apart from anything to do with the subject or with the actors in it, moves our emotion in that abstract, impersonal way that the sight of mountains, skies, and valleys, or the roar of the ocean or the tinkle of a brook, may do. "The play's the thing," said Hamlet; and so we may say of composition, that "composition is the thing." It is the framework, the anatomy, upon which the artist subsequently overlays his refinements and embellishments of color and expression.

If you will study the *Madonna degli Ansidei,* you will find that the tenderness of the Madonna's face, the

[1] The student would do well to study, in the light of what we have been considering, every illustration in this book, for the sole purpose of trying to discover in each case the part which composition plays in the impression of the whole picture.

rapture of S. John's, and the noble sweetness of S. Nicholas's are all of them echoes of the same qualities expressed in the whole composition; but that it is the actual direction of the lines, the shapes of the full and empty spaces, and their relation to one another, which make the chief impression, and that the expression of the faces is only a subsidiary detail, just as you are impressed by the total structure of some great building before you begin to apprehend its details.

Perhaps you will best understand the meaning and value of perfect composition by contrasting Raphael's picture with Wolgemuth's *Death of the Virgin*. In the latter there is no composition in the sense that we are using the word—that is to say, of an arrangement carefully planned to impress us by its abstract qualities. It presents only a crowd of figures more or less naturally disposed. Our attention is not engrossed by the whole, but scattered over the parts.

And this characteristic, we shall find, appears to a considerable degree in all German art. The German race has an instinctive appetite for detail. Its scholars and scientists are renowned for minute, patient, and thorough research; its artists, for accurate rendering of details. But this often leads to profuseness, in the intricacy and abundance of which the structural dignity of the whole is apt to be swallowed up. For you will find, as you continue your studies, that there is even more art in knowing what to leave out than in knowing what to put in; that simplification of the parts and unity of the whole are the characteristics of the greatest artists.

Among the various contrasts which are presented by

HOW TO STUDY PICTURES

the two pictures, one may be singled out. Wolgemuth has tried to represent the scene naturally, as it may have happened, and has introduced around the Virgin figures, studied from the actual men who walked the streets of Nuremberg in his day; while Raphael's persons are idealized types adapted from the real people to express the idea which was in his mind. It is the same with his arrangement of throne and arch and landscape. The scene is not a real one; it is made up of things selected in order to build up a structure of effect that would suggest to our mind the idea which was in his. Here is a sharp distinction in the way of seeing the facts of nature. One artist sees in them something to be rendered as accurately as possible; the other extracts from them a suggestion on which he may found some fabric of his own imagination. From the one we get an impression of reality which is apt to go no further than the mere recognition of the facts; from the other, a stimulus to our own imagination. One form of art chains us to earth, the other aids us to take flight as far as our capacity permits us.

What helped to form Raphael's ideal? First of all, the spirituality of Perugino's pictures. Then he visited Florence: at first only for a short time, but before he painted the *Madonna degli Ansidei*. During his second and longer visit he became intimate with the work of Leonardo da Vinci and Fra Bartolommeo. The influence of the former can be seen in the mysterious beauty of the face in the *Madonna Gran Duca;* that of the latter, in the supremely beautiful composition of *La Belle Jardinière;* while he gained also a freedom and greater naturalness in the drawing of his figures, and, through his friendship with the famous architect Bramante, a higher skill in the rendering of architectural forms and a deeper feeling for their grandeur. In fact, Raphael's capacity for being influenced by other artists was so remarkable that he has been called the " Prince of Plagiarists." But we must remember that the reproach which nowadays attaches to a man's making use of the motives of others cannot be extended to Raphael. The artists of the Renaissance freely borrowed from one another, and multiplied certain types of picture; the innumerable varieties, for example, of Madonna Enthroned having a family resemblance. Similarly in Japan, when an artist had mastered the rendering of a certain object, such as a bird's wing, other artists adopted his convention. Why should every one go back to the beginning and study for himself what had been already mastered? Much better to start with the accumulated capital of previous experience and knowledge, and, if the student has any originality of his own, draw from it a heightened dividend.

It was so with Raphael. To whatever he took from another he added something of himself; so that, though his borrowings were continuous and varied, he enriched the world with something personal and new. We have seen already how this present picture, while recalling Perugino, represents a distinct advance on that artist's capacity; and when he went to Rome, begged by Pope Julius II to decorate the *stanze,* or official chambers, of the Vatican, the composition of his first mural painting, the *Disputá,* is based upon a previous design of his master, yet surpasses in its completeness of decorative effect anything of Perugino's. In Rome, too, he had for models the ampler type of women which belongs to the south of Italy. Consequently his work becomes distinguished by still greater freedom and bigness of style. And, as he mixes with the world of great men who thronged the Eternal City, two other things are noticeable: his pictures become more human: the Madonnas embrace the infant Christ with the love of human motherhood; and, secondly, he is filled more and more with ardor for the antique.

He intersperses religious with classic subjects, and treats both in a classic spirit. It is as if Virgil had come to life again, but this time as a painter, whose aim was to link the later glories of the Renaissance with the early ones of Hellas; to make the legends of Hellas live again in the soul of the Renaissance; and to interpret the stories of the Hebrew Bible in Hellenic guise. The beautiful myths of Galatea, of Psyche and Venus, once more become realities visible to mortal eyes; Parnassus is again revealed; but now amid the constellation of Olympus appear the stars of Italian culture, Dante, Petrarch, and Boccaccio; and in silent companionship with them are the mighty ones of Athenian thought, Plato, Aristotle, Pythagoras, Socrates, and others, once more returned to earth and assembled beneath the arches of a noble building of the Renaissance. Through him the beauty of the antique world is recovered to the sight and soul of the modern.

But even more remarkable is what Raphael did with that other great volume of thought which had taken the place of the Hellenic. He not only started afresh the springs of Hellas, but that vast stream, derived from the Hebrews, which had flooded Christian Europe he conducted into Hellenic channels. He represented the Bible stories in Hellenic settings, retold them, as I have said, in the manner that a Virgil might.

When you remember that the New Learning was a revolt from the darkness and superstition of the middle ages; that in the beauty of pagan thought the beauty of the Christian was being neglected; and that, consequently, a clash between the two might have ensued in which one would have perished, you will understand the importance of what Raphael did. As a gardener will blend the pollen of two kinds of flowers and produce a third which unites the beauties of the two, so Raphael blended the Hellenic and the Christian in his religious pictures; and this new ideal so captivated the imagination of the world that for over three hundred years men pictured the religious story to their eyes and minds through the Hellenic atmosphere in which Raphael had placed it. It was not until painters had begun to value realism overmuch, to be more concerned with representing the appearance of things than the spirit enshrined in them, that they protested against the "incongruity" of clothing a Jewish fisherman in Hellenic draperies.

But Raphael himself and the people of his day felt no incongruity in this. They had become acquainted with the ideal beauty of antique sculpture, and of the serene elevation of Greek thought; crude ideas realistically represented were intolerable to them. Yet there was a beauty in this Christian thought at least as ele-

HOW TO STUDY PICTURES

vated and far more vital, because it touched the human heart of man in its relation both to this life and the future. How could it be made manifest?

We have noted already Raphael's method and its effect upon the world of his time, continuing to our own.

CHAPTER VIII

LEONARDO DA VINCI	ALBRECHT DÜRER
1452-1519	*1471-1528*
Italian School of Florence	*German School of Nuremberg*

HOW instantly these two masterpieces, Leonardo's *Virgin of the Rocks* and Dürer's *Adoration of the Magi,* seize our attention; yet how differently each claims our interest! In a general way, the difference consists in this, that the one is full of mystery, the other of clear statement. Leonardo has imagined a scene which appeals to our own imagination; Dürer has invented one that delights our understanding. The former's is a dream-picture, the latter's a wonderfully natural representation of an actual incident. In a word, while Dürer has tried to make everything plain to our eyes and understanding, Leonardo has used all his effort to make us forget the facts and realize the spirit that is embodied in them.

This contrast would alone make it worth while to compare the two pictures; but there are other reasons. These two men were contemporaries: Dürer, the greatest of German artists, most representative of the Teutonic mind; Leonardo, the most remarkable example of the intellect and imagination of the Italian Renaissance. It has been said of him that " he is the most thoughtful of all painters, unless it be Albrecht Dürer." So the fitness of comparing these two is evident.

Leonardo's early life was spent in Florence, his maturity in Milan, and the last three years of his life in France. Dürer, except for a visit of two years to Venice and of one year to the Netherlands, remained faithful to Nuremberg, the city of his birth.

Leonardo's teacher was Verrocchio—first a goldsmith, then a painter and sculptor: as a painter, representative of the very scientific school of draftsmanship; more famous as a sculptor, being the creator, as we remember, of the Colleoni statue at Venice. Dürer received his first lessons from his father, who was a master-goldsmith; his subsequent training, as an apprentice in the studio-workshop of Michael Wolgemuth.

Both Leonardo and Dürer were men of striking physical attractiveness, great charm of manner and conversation, and mental accomplishment, being well grounded in the sciences and mathematics of the day, while Leonardo was also a gifted musician. The skill of each in draftsmanship was extraordinary; shown in Leonardo's case by his numerous drawings as well as by his comparatively few paintings, while Dürer is even more celebrated for his engravings on wood and copper than for his paintings. With both, the skill of hand is at the service of most minute observation and analytical research into the character and structure of form. Dürer, however, had not the feeling for abstract beauty and ideal grace that Leonardo possessed; but instead, a profound earnestness, a closer interest in humanity, and a more dramatic invention.

DA VINCI—DÜRER

This sums up the vital difference between them; and it is worth while to consider, first, some of the causes of this difference, and, secondly, the effects of it as illustrated in their work, in respect both of choice of subjects and method of representing them.

No doubt it is true that genius is born, not made. But while it is a mistake to try and discover reasons for a man being a genius, it is proper and most interesting to note how his genius has taken on a certain shape and direction as a result of his environment.

Now, Dürer was born a German; Leonardo an Italian. A great deal of the difference between the ways in which the genius of these two men manifested itself may be summed up in this statement. The Italian race, under its sunny skies, has an ingrained love of beauty. The German, in a sterner climate—" How I shall freeze after this sun," wrote Dürer during his stay in Italy to a friend in Nuremberg—retains to this day the energy that carved its way through the vast forests of his country, and some of the gloomy romance that haunted their dark shadows. The German spirit is characterized by a " combination of the wild and rugged with the homely and tender, by meditative depth, enigmatic gloom, sincerity and energy, by iron diligence and discipline." Very remarkable qualities these, and to be found in Dürer's work, which is the reason that we describe him as being so representative of the Teutonic race.

But it was not only the difference of race that helped to mold the genius of these two men differently; each was a manifestation of the Renaissance of art and learning which was spreading over Europe: Leonardo of that form of it which appeared in Italy, and Dürer of that which was beginning to appear in Germany. Had Dürer been born in Italy and reared up under Italian influences, and Leonardo's life been associated with Germany, who shall say what a difference would have resulted to the work of each? For the aim and character of these two branches of the Renaissance were very dissimilar.

The Italian, as we have seen, began by seeking a return to truth of natural form; but was soon influenced by the classic remains, which abounded in Italy and were so eagerly searched for and studied, that a worship of the antique, the Roman and Greek, absorbed men's minds. Raphael, as we have noted, clothed the story of the Bible in classic garb; classic myths, classic thought and literature, filled the imagination of the artists and thinkers; religion and a revived paganism skipped hand in hand. I use the word "skipped," because of the joy which possessed the Italians of the fifteenth and early sixteenth centuries in the new realization of their racial love of beauty. Painter after painter before Leonardo's time had tried to give expression to it; he was the heir of their endeavors and the contemporary of a number of gifted men, who gathered at Florence and under the patronage of the Medici made it a reflection of what Athens had been under Pericles.

The different character of the German Renaissance we shall best appreciate by noting that it was a part of the great movement which produced Luther and the Reformation. It was first and foremost an intellectual and moral revival; in time to be the parent of that civil

VIRGIN OF THE ROCKS   LEONARDO DA VINCI
LOUVRE, PARIS

VISIT OF THE MAGI — ALBRECHT DÜRER
UFFIZI GALLERY, FLORENCE

and religious liberty which was to reshape a large portion of the world. And intimately identified with this movement was the printing-press.

Dürer was a great admirer of Luther; and in his own work is the equivalent of what was mighty in the Reformer. It is very serious and sincere; very human, and addressed to the hearts and understandings of the masses of the people. And he had a particular chance of reaching them, for Nuremberg under the enterprise of Koburger, a "prince of booksellers," as one of his contemporaries called him, had become a great center of printing and the chief distributer of books throughout Europe. Consequently the arts of engraving upon wood and copper, which may be called the pictorial branch of printing, were much encouraged. Of this opportunity Dürer took full advantage. He outdistanced all his predecessors in the art and brought it, at one bound, to such a pitch of perfection that his work was eagerly welcomed even in Italy, where pirated editions of his prints were published, and to-day he ranks first among wood-engravers and by the side of Rembrandt in engraving upon copper. Let us note the practical result of this upon his work as an artist.

Engraving as compared with painting is a popular art; many printings can be made from one plate or block and at comparatively slight cost, so that the artist's work reaches a great number of persons. It is easy to see how this might affect the character of his work: leading him to choose subjects with which the people were familiar; to treat them in a way that should secure their interest—that is to say, with simple directness and precision, and with dramatic earnestness that should appeal at once to the intelligence and the heart. That these qualities are characteristic of all Dürer's work, his paintings and engravings alike, may well have been due, in part at least, to his experience in the latter medium. But probably it would be more true to say that because these qualities were inherent in his personal character, they were reflected in his work and drew him particularly toward engraving.

It is quite possible, however, for pictures to be simple, precise, direct, and even dramatic, yet very commonplace. This Dürer's work never was; and that he contrived to make it so homely and natural and yet always dignified is because he was a genius, which is no more to be explained and accounted for in his case than in Shakspere's.

That he did not possess, as well, the gift of ideal beauty is due partly to the fact we have already noticed, —that the Renaissance in Germany was more a moral and intellectual than an artistic movement,—and partly to Northern conditions. For the feeling for ideal grace and beauty is fostered by the study of the human form; and this has been most flourishing in those Southern countries, such as Greece and Italy, where the climate favors a free, open-air life. In the Northern countries, clothes, being more necessary, assume a greater importance. They are a very important feature in this picture of Dürer's, and recall the elaborate costumes in those which we have examined by Van Eyck and Memling. Nuremberg, as we have remarked, was on one of the highways of travel between Italy and the cities of the

DA VINCI—DÜRER

North Sea, but, while commerce was passing freely in both directions, the influence upon painting came to Germany chiefly from Flanders. As there, so in Germany, painting was closely allied with the decorative crafts, and the painters delighted in the portrayal of fabrics, metal, and woodwork. In this *Adoration of the Magi* we can detect at once the same fondness for depicting stuffs, embroidery, and objects of curious and beautiful workmanship as in Van Eyck's *Virgin and Donor;* and in the originals there is apparent, not only a similar skill in minute and elaborate details, but also a corresponding use of strong, rich coloring. But, while it was from Flanders that Dürer derived his style in painting, he passed beyond his exemplars in the variety and scope of his skill and in mental and moral force.

In the first place, no one has excelled him in delineating textures. You may see in this picture with what truth the different surfaces of wood, stone, hair, fur, feather, metal-work, embroidery, and so on are represented. This skill in textures is even more wonderfully exhibited in the black and white lines of his engravings. But the point particularly to be noted is that his genius does not stop short with the skill; back of it is a great force of intellectual and moral intention. He has the artist's love of the appearance of things, but he uses every object, not merely for its own sake and for the pleasure of representing it, but that it may enhance and intensify the main motive of his subject. On this occasion it is to contrast the splendor of the visitors from the East with the lowliness of the Mother and Child, and with the meanness of their surroundings; to contrast the harshness of the ruins with the dignity of the Mother, the innocent sweetness of the Babe, and the profound reverence of the Wise Men. He makes the scene impress us so deeply: in the first place, because he realized it himself so deeply, tenderly, reverentially, and powerfully in his own mind; and, secondly, because he has given to each figure and to every object its own quality and degree of character. He felt, and could convey to others, the significance of form; by which term I am trying to express two things.

First there is in the character of objects—their color, shape, hardness or softness, dullness or brilliance—a capacity to arouse our enjoyment. They excite especially what has been called our "tactile" sense; that is to say, the pleasure we get from actually handling things, or from having them represented to us in so real a way that we can imagine what would be the pleasurable sensation of touching them. But there is another way in which objects may be significant. For example, the things in our houses mean more to us than they would if we saw them set on a shelf in a shop window. In the latter case we enjoy only their appearance; in the other they are a part of our lives. Just in the same manner objects may be arranged in a painting so as to interest us only by their appearance, or in such a way that they are an actual part of the life of the picture.

This is a distinction that it is worth while to grasp, and no one can better help us to do so than Dürer. We know at once that this *Adoration of the Magi* impresses us, and, when we study it, we discover that the secret of its impressiveness is the extraordinary significance which the artist has given to external appearances.

Here is the point at which the genius of Dürer and that of Leonardo, similar in many respects, branch out like a Y into separate directions. It is not with the external significance of objects, but with their inward and spiritual significance, that Leonardo was occupied. A glance at the *Virgin of the Rocks* [1] is sufficient to make us feel that the artist is not trying to impress us with external appearances. The outlines of his figures are not emphasized as in Dürer's picture; the cavern curiously formed of basaltic rock, and the little peep beyond of a rocky landscape and a winding stream, the group of figures in the foreground by the side of a pool of water —all are seen as through a veil of shadowy mist. They may be real enough, but far removed from the touch of man; less visible to eye-sight than to soul-sight. It was the passion of Leonardo's existence to peer into the mysteries and secrets of nature and life. He was at once an artist and a man of science; turning aside, for a time, from painting to build canals, to contrive engines of war, to make mechanical birds which flew and animals which walked; while the range of his speculations included a foresight of the possibilities of steam and of balloons, a discovery of the law of gravitation, and a rediscovery of the principles of the lever and of hydraulics. Mathematician, chemist, machinist, and physiologist, geologist, geographer, and astronomer, he was also a supreme ar-

[1] This illustration is reproduced from the picture in the Louvre. There is another example of the subject in the National Gallery, which is regarded by the majority of critics as a replica of the Louvre picture executed by another hand, probably under Leonardo's supervision.

tist. And always it was the truth, just beyond the common experience of man, hidden in the bosom of nature or dimly discerned in the mind of man, that he strove to reach. Partly he grasped it, partly it eluded him; much of his life was spent in restless striving after the unattainable; so to him life presented itself as a compromise between certainty and uncertainty, between fact and conjecture; between truth that is clearly seen and truth that is only felt. And in his pictures it was this mingling of certainty and elusiveness that he sought to express.

The means he employed were, first, extreme delicacy and precision in the study and representation of form, and then a veiling of all in a gossamer web of chiaroscuro. He did not invent the principles of light and shade in painting, but he was the first to make them a source of poetical and emotional effect. Others had used chiaroscuro to secure the modeling of form by the contrast of light upon the raised parts with shadow on those farther from the eye; but Leonardo was the first to notice that in nature this contrast is not a violent one, but made up of most delicate gradations, so that the light slides into the dark and the dark creeps into the light, and even the darkest part is not opaque, but loose and penetrable. In making this discovery he discovered also that the general tint of an object—the "local" color, as the artists call it—gradually changes in tone as the object recedes from the eye, owing to the increase in the amount of intervening atmosphere. By representing in paint these delicate gradations of light and shade he succeeded in obtaining a subtlety of modeling

DA VINCI—DÜRER

that has never been surpassed; while, at the same time, the successive layers or planes of tone reproduce in his pictures the effect of nature's atmosphere.

Nature's, observe; because other artists of his time introduced an atmosphere of their own, bathing the figures, very often, in a golden glow which they obtained by washing a glaze over the whole or parts of the picture; very beautiful, but quite arbitrary and conventional. Leonardo, however, like Masaccio, imitated the effects of real atmosphere, in which he anticipated, as we shall see, the nature study of Velasquez.

How subtle Leonardo's effects were may be noted in this picture; for example, in the modeling and foreshortening of the limbs of the two infants, so exquisitely soft as well as firm, and in the lovely mystery of the faces of the Virgin and Angel. The latter belong to the same type as his portrait of *Monna Lisa:* oval faces with broad, high foreheads; dreamy eyes beneath drooping lids; a smile very sweet and a little sad, with a suggestion of conscious superiority. For as he searched nature for her mysteries, so he scanned the face of woman to discover the inward beauty that was mirrored in the outward. He made woman the symbol of what beauty and the search for beauty meant to himself, adding that infinitesimal touch of scornfulness, in acknowledgment that, after all his strivings to know and capture beauty, its deepest secret eluded him. Much of his life was spent in the search after what eluded him; he loved more to reflect and study than to put his ideas into actual shape.

So, while he and Dürer were alike in moral and intellectual greatness, in their eager study of nature and in the elevation of their art, each had a different ideal which led them very far apart in the final character of their work. Dürer's is full of the meaning of appearances, Leonardo's of the mystery that lies behind them; the former is vigorous, direct, and powerfully arresting, the latter sensitive, strangely alluring, but baffling and elusive.

CHAPTER IX

TIZIANO VECELLI (TITIAN)   HANS HOLBEIN THE YOUNGER
1477-1576   *1497-1543*
Italian School of Venice   *German School of Augsburg*

IT is because of the difference between these two wonderful portraits—Titian's *Man with the Glove* and *Portrait of Georg Gyze* by Hans Holbein the Younger—that it is interesting to compare them. In doing so we shall contrast not only the difference in the personalities of these two artists, and the conditions under which they worked, but also the difference of their points of view and consequently of their methods. Let us begin by studying the second difference, to an understanding of which the pictures themselves will direct us.

If we should try to sum up in one word the impression produced by each, might we not say, "How *noble* the Titian is; the Holbein how *intimate*"? Both the originals are young men: Titian's unmistakably an aristocrat, but with no clue given as to who or what he was; Holbein's a German merchant resident in London, whose name is recorded in the address of the letter in his hand, and who is surrounded by the accompaniments of his daily occupation. Presently we shall find out something about the nature of his occupations; meanwhile we have surprised him in the privacy of his office, and are already interested in him as an actual man, who lived and worked over three hundred years ago, and very interested also in the objects that surround him. We note already that the flowers in the vase are just like the carnations of our own day, but that the character of his correspondence is very different. Evidently he is a prosperous man, but compare the fewness of his letters with the packet which one morning's mail would bring to a modern merchant. Each is fastened with a band of paper, held in place by a seal; he has just broken the band of the newly arrived letter; his own seal is among the objects that lie on the table. But I interrupt the fascinating examination of these details to ask whether we do not feel already that we are growing intimate with the man.

Can we feel the same toward the *Man with the Glove?* Certainly, when we have once possessed ourselves of the appearance of this man's face, we shall not forget it. But that is a very different thing from knowing the man as a man. There is something, indeed, in the grave, almost sad, expression of the face which forbids, rather than invites, intimacy. He, too, seems to have been surprised in his privacy; but he is occupied, not with his affairs, as Georg Gyze is, but with his thoughts. It is not the man in his every-day character with whom we have become acquainted; indeed, it is not with the man himself that we grow familiar, but with some mood of a man, or, rather, with some reflection in him of the artist's mood at the time he painted him.

For Titian found in the original of this portrait a suggestion to himself of something stately and aloof from common things; he made his picture interpret this mood of feeling; he may have been more interested in this than in preserving a likeness of the man; we may even doubt whether the man was actually like this. Certainly, this could not have been his every-day aspect, in which he appeared while going about whatever his occupation in life may have been; it is one abstracted from the usual, an altogether very choice aspect, in which what is noblest in his nature is revealed without the disturbance of any other condition.

It is, in fact, an idealized portrait, in which everything is made to contribute to the wonderful calm and dignity of the mood. The name of the original has not been handed down; there is no clue to who or what this man was—only this wonderful expression of feeling; and, as that itself is so abstract, exalted, idealized, baffling description, posterity has distinguished this picture from others by the vague title, *Man with the Glove*.

Here, then, is another distinction between these pictures of Titian's and Holbein's. The treatment of the former is idealistic, of the other realistic. Both these artists were students of nature, seeking their inspiration from the world of men and things that passed before their eyes. But Holbein painted the thing as it appealed to his eye, Titian as it appealed to his mind; Holbein found sufficient enjoyment in the truth of facts as they were, Titian in the suggestion that they gave him for creating visions of his own imagination; the one viewed the world objectively and was a realist, the other subjectively and idealized.

This, of course, is a distinction not confined to these

two artists. Indeed, all the comparison we have been making between their respective points of view is of general application. The distinction between the subjective, universal, and idealistic on the one hand, and the objective, particular, and realistic on the other, repeatedly confronts us in the study of art. In fact, every artist illustrates either one or other of these points of view, or, more usually, a combination of the two: hence, to appreciate the work of various men, it is necessary to grow to a clear understanding of these contrasts and of the innumerable degrees to which they may shade into each other. So large a subject cannot be exhausted by the comparison of any two pictures; yet from these by Titian and Holbein a considerable insight may be gained.

In what respect was Holbein a realist? In our study of art we should be very distrustful of words. We cannot do without them, but must remember that they have no value of themselves; that they are only valuable as far as they provide a shorthand expression of some idea. The idea, and not the word in which it is clothed, is the important thing; but unfortunately a word cannot have the completeness and finality of a mathematical formula. In arithmetic, for instance, $2 \times 2 = 4$ is universally true; but in the world of ideas there are so many "ifs and ans" that the exact statement is impossible. So beware of words, and, instead of being satisfied with phrases, try to think into and all around the thought that is behind the phrase.

What, then, is a realist? Naturally, one who represents things as they really are. But can anybody do that? If ten men the equals of Holbein in observation and skill of hand had sat down beside him to paint the portrait of Georg Gyze and his surroundings, would their pictures have been identical? Could even any two men, working independently, have painted the ink-pot alone so that the two representations would be identical? Have any two men exactly similar capacity of eyesight; and, if they have, will they also have exactly identical minds? The fact is, a man can draw an ink-stand only as its appearance physically affects his eye and makes a mental impression on his brain. In other words, objects, so far as we are concerned, have no independent reality; you cannot say, "This is what an apple really looks like," but only, "This is how it presents itself real to me." The personal equation intervenes; that is to say, the personal limitation of each individual.

So, in the strict sense of representing an object as it really is, no painter can be a realist; while, in the general sense of representing an object as it seems real to his eye and brain, every painter may be called a realist. Then how shall we discover the meaning of the word "realist" as used in painting? Let us look for an explanation in the two pictures.

Both painters represented what seemed real to them; but do we not observe that, while Titian was chiefly occupied with the impression produced upon his *mind*, it was the impression made upon the *eye* which gave greater delight to Holbein? No man who did not love the appearances of things would have painted them with so loving a patience. While to Titian the thing which appeared most real about this man, the thing most worth his while to paint, was the impression made upon his mind, so that what he painted is to a very large extent a reflection of himself, a mood of his own subjectivity, Holbein concentrated the whole of himself upon the objects before him. His attitude of mind was objective. His intention was simply to paint Georg Gyze as he was known to his contemporaries—a merchant at his office table, with all the things about him that other visitors to the room would observe and grow to associate with the personality of Gyze himself.

We may gather, therefore, that realism is an attitude of mind; one that makes the painter subordinate himself and his own personal feelings to the study of what is presented to his eye; which makes him rejoice in the appearances of things and discover in each its peculiar quality of beauty; which makes him content to paint life simply as it manifests itself to his eye, to be indeed a faithful mirror of the world outside himself.

It is not because Holbein was a realist that he is celebrated, but because of the kind of realist he was. You will find that realism often runs to commonplace; a man may see chiefly with his eye because he has little mind to see with; may take a delight in the obviousness of facts because he has no imagination; the material appeals to him more than the spiritual. But Holbein was a man of mind, who attracted the friendship of Erasmus, the greatest scholar of his age; and he brought this power of mind to the enforcing of his eye. The result is that the number and diversity of the objects in this portrait do not distract our attention from the man, but rather seem to increase our acquaintance with his character and

TITIAN—HOLBEIN THE YOUNGER

disposition. We recognize the order and refinement which surround him, and find a reflection of them in his face. On the other hand, when we examine the details, we find each in its way exquisitely rendered; for, as I have said, Holbein loved things of delicate and skilful workmanship, and left many designs for sword-scabbards, dagger-sheaths, goblets, and goldsmith's work.

Yet compared with the elaborated detail of Holbein's portrait, how large, simple, and grand is the composition of Titian's! The aim of the one artist was to *put in* everything that was possible *without injury to the total effect;* of the other to *leave out* everything but what was *essential.* Holbein's picture is a triumph of well-controlled elaboration; Titian's of simplification. I hope to show further that this distinction is characteristic of the personality of these two men; but, for the present, let us notice how completely each method suits the character of the subject: the man of affairs, calm and collected amid a quantity of detail, the man of contemplation, aloof from every distraction.

That Holbein painted all these details because he felt them to be really part of the personality of Gyze may be inferred from the fact that, though he loves to introduce little objects of choice workmanship, his treatment of the portrait of a scholar like Erasmus is very large and simple. Yet even then there is a minuteness of finish in the modeling of the flesh and in the painting of the hair and costume, which might easily be niggling and trivial, but that in Holbein's case it is only part of the singular penetration of his observation and extraordinary manual delicacy, brought to the rendering of something which he has studied with all the strength of his manhood.

Yet the breadth and simplification of Holbein are not like Titian's, being simply and sweetly dignified, where Titian's are majestically grand. Turn again to the *Man with the Glove*. Shut out with your fingers, first one of the hands, then the other, and then the sweep of shirt, and notice each time how the balance and dignity of the composition are thereby destroyed; for its magic consists in the exact placing of the lighter spots against the general darkness of the whole. By this time we realize that the fascination of this portrait is not only in the expression of the face and in the wonderful eyes, but also in the actual pattern of light and dark in the composition. Then, taking the face as the source and nucleus of the impression which the picture makes, we note how the slit of the open doublet echoes the piercing directness of the gaze; how the expression of the right hand repeats its acute concentration, while the left has an ease and elegance of gesture which correspond with the grand and gracious poise of the whole picture.

Grand and gracious poise! Not altogether an unapt characterization of Titian himself. At once a genius and a favorite of fortune, he moved through his long life of pomp and splendor serene and self-contained. He was of old family, born at Pieve in the mountain district of Cadore. By the time that he was eleven years old his father, Gregorio di Conte Vecelli, recognized that he was destined to be a painter and sent him to Venice, where he became the pupil, first of Gentile Bellini, and later of the latter's brother, Giovanni. Then he worked

MAN WITH THE GLOVE   TITIAN
                        LOUVRE, PARIS

PORTRAIT OF GEORG GYZE   **HOLBEIN THE YOUNGER**

BERLIN GALLERY

with the great artist Giorgione. From the first, indeed, he enjoyed every privilege that an artist of his time could desire. The Doge and Council of Venice recognized his ability; the Dukes of Ferrara and Mantua followed suit; and, as the years went on, kings, popes, and emperors were his friends and patrons. In his home at Biri, a suburb of Venice, from which in one direction the snow-clad Alps are visible and in the other the soft luxuriance of the Venetian Lagoon, he maintained a princely household, associating with the greatest and most accomplished men of Venice, working on until he had reached within a year of a century of life. Even then it was no ordinary ailment, but the visitation of the plague, that carried him off; and such was the honor in which he was held, that the law against the burial of the plague-stricken in a church was overruled in his case and he was laid in the tomb which he had prepared for himself in the great Church of the Frari.

No artist's life was so completely and sustainedly superb; and such, too, is the character of his work. He was great in portraiture, in landscape, in the painting of religious and mythological subjects. In any *one* of these departments others have rivaled him, but his glory is that he attained to an eminence in all; he was an artist of universal gifts,—an all-embracing genius, equable, serene, majestic.

The genius of Holbein also blossomed early. His native city of Augsburg was then at the zenith of its greatness; on the highroad between Italy and the North, the richest commercial city in Germany, the frequent halting-place of the Emperor Maximilian. His father,

HOW TO STUDY PICTURES

Hans Holbein the Elder, was himself a painter of merit, and took the son into his studio. A book of sketches made during this period by the young Hans, preserved in the Berlin Museum, shows that he was already a better draftsman than his father. In 1515, when he was eighteen years old, he moved to Basel, the center of learning, whose boast was that every house in it contained at least one learned man. Here he won the friendship and patronage of the great printer Froben and the burgomaster Jacob Meyer. For the former's books he designed woodcuts; for the latter he painted a portrait, and, later, the famous *Meyer Madonna*. In this the Virgin is represented as standing, and the Meyer family kneeling: the father and his two sons on the right, and opposite to them his deceased first wife and his then living second wife and only daughter. In 1520, the year of Luther's excommunication, he was admitted to citizenship at Basel and to membership in the painters' guild: sufficient testimony, as he was only twenty-three, to his unusual ability.

In that same year Erasmus returned to Basel, and accepted the post of editor and publisher's reader to his friend Froben. Erasmus spoke no modern language except his native Dutch, and Holbein seems to have been ignorant of Latin, yet a friendship sprang up between the two, and the artist designed the woodcuts for the scholar's satirical book, "The Praise of Folly," and painted his portrait. About this time he made the famous series of designs of the *Dance of Death;* the drawings of which were so minute and full of detail that when Hans Lützelberger, their engraver, died in 1527, it was ten years before another wood-engraver could be found sufficiently skilled to render the action and expression of the tiny figures.

But book illustration was poorly paid and the times were lean ones for the painter, since the spread of the Reformation had cut off the demand for church pictures. Holbein found himself in need of money, and accordingly, by the advice of Erasmus, set out for London with a letter of introduction from the scholar to Sir Thomas More, the King's Chancellor.

"Master Haunce," as the English called him, arrived in England toward the close of 1526. The London of that day presented some crude contrasts. Side by side with buildings of Gothic architecture had arisen later ones of Renaissance design, but the average houses were still of wood and mud, huddled together in very narrow streets, the rooms small and the flooring of the lowest story merely the beaten earth. The houses of the upper class lined the bank of the Thames, and it was in one of these, situated in what was then the village of Chelsea, that Sir Thomas More lived. Here Holbein was welcomed, and made his home during this first visit to England. He painted portraits of many of the leading men of the day, and executed drawings for a picture of the family of his patron, which, however, was never painted; for, two years later, in consequence of an outbreak of the plague, he returned to Basel.

But Basel was no longer what it had been: Froben was dead; Erasmus, Meyer, and others of the cultivated class had abandoned the city, which was in the clutches of the Reformers, who showed their zeal for religion by a crusade against art. Consequently, in 1531, Holbein returned to England. But here, too, had been changes; More was in disgrace, so that Holbein, cut off from court patronage, attached himself to the merchants of the Steelyard.

These were the London representatives of the Hanseatic League, a combination of commercial cities, at the head of which were Lübeck and Hamburg. It had been formed as early as the thirteenth century, for mutual protection against piracy and to promote the general interests of trade, and had established factories, or branches, in various places, as far removed as London and Novgorod. These, under special privileges derived from the respective governments, gradually absorbed the main business of the import and export trade. Georg Gyze was a member of the London factory, a merchant of the Steelyard, and in his portrait the steelyard or scale for the weighing of money, the symbol also of the merchant guild, hangs from the shelf behind his head.

By 1537 Holbein had come to the notice of Henry VIII, and was established as court painter, a position which he held until his death. This seems to have occurred during another visitation of the plague in 1543; for at this date knowledge of the great artist ceases. When he died or where he was buried is not known.

What a contrast between his life and Titian's! One the favorite, the other the sport, of fortune. For though the greatness of both was recognized by their contemporaries, Titian lived a life of sumptuous ease in the beautiful surroundings of Venice, while Holbein, often straitened for money, never wealthy, experienced the rigor of existence; more or less a victim to the religious convulsions of the time, forced by need and circumstances to become an alien in a strange land, dying unnoticed and unhonored. The world to Titian was a pageant, to Holbein a scene of toil and pilgrimage.

Titian viewed the splendor of the world in a big, healthful, ample way; and represented it with the glowing brush of a supreme colorist. On the other hand, Holbein is eminent in German art because he finally emancipated it from Gothic thraldom. He was the foremost artist of the German Renaissance, beside whom Dürer seems to belong to the middle ages. Yet the latter's art must be joined with his to produce a complete representation of the genius of the race. In both are manifested the decorative feeling, the eager curiosity, the love of elaborate detail that distinguish German art. But, while Holbein reflected the conscientiously earnest, matter-of-fact spirit, Dürer reflected also the romantic temperament that underlies it. After these two, if we except Lucas Cranach, no painter in German art demands the student's attention until the nineteenth century.

CHAPTER X

ANTONIO ALLEGRI (called CORREGGIO)
1494 (?)–1534
Italian School of Parma

MICHELANGELO BUONARROTI
1474–1564
Italian School of Florence

IT would be impossible to imagine a greater contrast than the one presented by these two pictures—Correggio's *Mystic Marriage of Saint Catherine* and the *Jeremiah* by Michelangelo. And the difference is all the more worth studying because these artists are the most typical representatives of two very different phases of that wonderful outburst of energy which we call the Renaissance.

We have seen how two currents of striving united in Raphael's work; how he satisfied the old religious yearning as well as the newly aroused passion for the antique; how he reclothed the Bible story in classic guise. We have seen, too, that in Leonardo da Vinci were revealed the subtlety of his time, its eagerness for perfection, the dawn of the spirit of scientific inquiry, which, reawakened by the study of Aristotle and Plato, was searching into the mystery of the universe and man's relation to it; and that in this peering forward Leonardo anticipated some of the facts of science rediscovered and established by later philosophers and scientists.

We can now study in Correggio that element in the

[142]

CORREGGIO—MICHELANGELO

Renaissance conveniently called " pagan "; which, for the present, may be briefly summarized as a tendency to look back further than the beginning of the Christian religion, further, even, than the classic times, to that dream of a golden age, of perfect peace and happiness and innocence, when men and women lived a natural life, and shared the woods and streams, the mountains and the fields, with satyrs, nymphs, and fauns. Correggio has been called the " Faun of the Renaissance."

But in those splendid yet terrible days of the Renaissance peace was continually disturbed by wars and civil strife; innocence crept to shelter from the wickedness which shamelessly prevailed; and happiness went hand in hand with anguish. Italy of that day was like a huge caldron into which all the human passions, good and evil, had been flung, while underneath it was the fire of an impetuous race, that after long smoldering had now leaped up with volcanic force. The seething tumult of these contending passions is reflected in the work of Michelangelo.

While Correggio represents the exquisite fancifulness of that period, Michelangelo is an embodiment of its soul.

Compare again these two pictures. Correggio has here taken for his subject one of the beautiful legends of the church. Catherine was a lady of Alexandria who, living about 300 A.D., dared to be a Christian, and eventually died for her faith by the torment of the wheel, which latter appears as an emblem in many of her pictures. She had a vision in which it was made known to her that she should consider herself the bride of Christ;

and the theme of this mystic marriage was a favorite one in the turbid times of the Renaissance, when women sought the cloister as a refuge from the wickedness and tyranny of the world.

But how has Correggio treated this subject? Does he make you feel the sacrifice of Catherine; or suggest to you anything of the religious fervor and devotion with which the vision must have inspired herself? In the background are little figures, scarcely to be seen in the illustration, which, if you search into them, tell of suffering; but they do not really count in the impression which the picture makes upon us. What we get from it as a whole is a lovely, dreamy suggestion, as of very sweet people engaged in some graceful pleasantry. The mother is absorbed in love of her child, wrapped up in the consciousness, common to young mothers, that her child is more than ordinarily precious. The baby itself is a little, roguish love, a brother of the little Cupids and *putti* that abound in Correggio's pictures, eying with the watchful playfulness of a kitten the hand of Catherine. The latter plays her part in the ceremony with little more feeling than that of any other child-worshiper; while the St. Sebastian, with his bunched locks reminding us of ivy and vine leaves, has the look of the youthful Dionysos, the arrow recalling the thyrsus which the young god used to carry.

There is not a trace of religious feeling in the picture, or of mystic ecstasy—only the gentle, happy peace of innocence. There may be violence out in the world, but far away; no echo of it disturbs the serenity of this little group, wrapped around in warm, melting, golden atmosphere. Elsewhere may be hearts that throb with passion, consciences sorely eager to do right or stricken with the memory of sin; but not in this group. These beings are no more troubled with conscience than the lambs and fawns; their hearts reflect only the lovableness of their sunny existence, as the placid pool reflects the sunlight. They are the creatures of a poet's golden dream.

Compare with them the *Jeremiah*. Here, instead of delicate gracefulness, are colossal strength, ponderous mass, profound impressiveness; back and legs that have carried the burden, hands that have labored, head bowed in vast depth of thought. And what of the thought?

More than two thousand years had passed since Jeremiah hurled his denunciations against the follies and iniquity of Judah, and in his Lamentations uttered a prophetic dirge over Jerusalem, hastening to become the prey of foreign enemies. And to the mind of Michelangelo, as he painted this figure of *Jeremiah*, sometime between 1508 and 1512,—that is to say, between his thirty-fourth and thirty-eighth years,—there was present a similar spectacle of his own beloved Italy reeling to ruin under the weight of her sins and the rivalries of foreign armies, and perhaps also a prophetic vision of how it would end. As Jeremiah lived to see the fall of Jerusalem, so Michelangelo lived to see the sacred city of Rome sacked in 1527 by the German soldiery under the French renegade Constable Bourbon.

It is the profundity of Michelangelo's own thoughts that fills this figure of *Jeremiah*. Like the Hebrew prophet's life, his own was a protest against the world. Jeremiah fled to Egypt; Michelangelo into the deepest recess of his own soul. In this figure of *Jeremiah* he has typified himself.

Whether consciously or unconsciously, who shall say? Always the artist puts into his work a portion of himself, and of this feeling in himself that he is striving to express he is of course conscious. But this feeling is the sediment left in him from many experiences, some—the most of them, probably—forgotten; so, as he labors to express it in his painting or statue, he very likely is not conscious of its personal application to himself, being absorbed by the work before him. And still more likely is this unconsciousness in the case of great artists; for in them there is more than memory and experience, more even than knowledge and imagination: something inexplicable to us, not to be understood by themselves; what we vaguely call soul, and the ancients, more vaguely still, but with nearer approach to truth, called " afflatus " —divine inspiration.

The French philosopher Taine wrote: " There are four men in the world of art and literature so exalted above all others as to seem to belong to another race— namely, Dante, Shakspeare, Beethoven, and Michelangelo."

They are of the race of the Titans, the giant progeny of heaven and earth. The old race warred with heaven, but was finally subdued and sent down to Tartarus. Three, at least, of these modern Titans, Dante, Beethoven, and Michelangelo, were at continual war in their souls with conditions that environed them, and found hell on earth. Not that the world treated Michelangelo worse than many others: but, as Taine says, " suffering must be measured by inward emotion, and not by outward circumstances; and, if ever a spirit existed which was capable of transports of enthusiasm and passionate indignation, it was his." Such a man as Michelangelo could not escape from the tempest of the world by wrapping himself up in dreams of a " golden age," as Correggio did.

Once more compare the two pictures, to observe the difference of their technic. One reason of difference is that Correggio's is painted in oil on canvas, Michelangelo's in fresco on the plaster of the ceiling. The meaning of the word " fresco " is " fresh," and the peculiarity of the method consisted in painting on the plaster while it was still damp, so that the colors, which were mixed with water, in the process of drying became incorporated with the plaster. The wall or ceiling to be so decorated was coated with the rough-cast plaster and allowed to dry thoroughly; after which a thin layer of smooth finish was spread over as large a portion of the surface as the artist could finish in one day. Meanwhile he had prepared his drawing, and, laying this against the surface, went over the lines of it with a blunt instrument, so that, when the drawing or cartoon was removed, the outline of the figures appeared, incised in the damp plaster. Then he applied the color, working rapidly, with a full assurance of the effect which he wished to produce, since correction, or working over what had already been painted, was not easy.

On the contrary, with oil paints the artist can work at his leisure, allowing his canvas time to dry, working over it again and again, and finally toning it all together by

HOW TO STUDY PICTURES

brushing over it thin layers of transparent colors, called glazes. It was by the use of these latter that Correggio obtained the warm, melting atmosphere in which his figures are bathed, and which is one of the distinguishing characteristics of his style. We can realize at once how this method was suited to the dreamy luxuriance of his imagination; while, on the contrary, more in harmony with the genius of Michelangelo was the immediate, smiting method of the fresco. For in the strict sense of the word he was not a painter; that is to say, he was not skilled in, and probably was impatient of, the slower, tenderer way in which a painter reaches his results. He was not a colorist, nor skilled in the rendering of light and atmosphere; but a great draftsman, a great sculptor, and a profound thinker. He labored with his subject in his brain, and then expressed it immediately with pencil or charcoal, or more gradually by blows of the mallet upon the chisel. But in either case it was the thought, straight out from himself in all the heat of kindled imagination, that he set upon the paper, or struck out with forceful action of the tool.

He used to say that he had sucked the desire to be a sculptor from his foster-mother, the wife of a stone-cutter; and in his later life, when sore oppressed, he would retreat to the marble-quarries of Carrara under color of searching for material. To him each block of marble, rugged, hard, and jagged, held a secret, needing only the genius of his chisel to liberate it; and in the same way his own soul was imprisoned in a personality eternally at odds with the world, that to the seven popes whom he successively served during his long life of eighty-nine years seemed very hard and unyielding.

MYSTIC MARRIAGE OF ST. CATHERINE — CORREGGIO
LOUVRE, PARIS

JEREMIAH   **MICHELANGELO**

SISTINE CHAPEL, ROME

CORREGGIO—MICHELANGELO

It is the feeling of the sculptor that we recognize in this painting of *Jeremiah;* the feeling for solidity and weight of mass, for stability of pose; a preference for simple lines and bold surfaces, arranged in a few planes. To appreciate this distinction, compare Correggio's picture: its intricacy of lines, the distance of its receding planes, but more particularly the character of its composition, consisting of so many varieties of lighted and shadowed parts, and the absence of suggestion that the figures are firmly planted. While Correggio has relied upon beautiful drawing, upon exquisite expression of hands and faces, and on color, light, and shade, and his golden atmosphere that envelops the whole, Michelangelo relied solely upon form—the form of the figure and of the draperies. This is to admit that, judged from the standpoint of painting, he was not a great painter. He himself told Pope Julius II, when the latter requested him to paint this ceiling of the Sistine Chapel at Rome, that he was not a painter, but a sculptor; yet, after he had shut himself up for four years, and the scaffold was removed, a result had been achieved which is without parallel in the world.

Very wonderful is the profusion of invention spread over this vast area of ten thousand square feet. The fact that there are three hundred and forty-three principal figures, many of colossal size, besides a great number of subsidiary ones introduced for decorative effect, and that the creator of this vast scheme was only thirty-four when he began his work—all this is wonderful, prodigious, but not so wonderful as the variety of expression in the figures.

HOW TO STUDY PICTURES

If there is one point more than another in which Michelangelo displayed his genius it is in this, that he discovered the capability of the human form to express mental emotions. While the ancient Greeks sought, in their rendering of the human form, an ideal of physical perfection, and the later Greeks, as in the group of Laocoon and his sons attacked by serpents, sought to express the tortures of physical suffering, Michelangelo was the first to make the human form express a variety of mental emotions. In his hands it became an instrument, upon which he played, like a musician on his organ, extracting themes and harmonies of infinite variety. And just as it is within the power of music to call up sensations, which we feel deeply and yet cannot exactly put into words, which elude us and merge themselves in the abstract and the universal, so Michelangelo's figures carry our imagination far beyond the personal meaning of the names attached to them. We know, for example, who Jeremiah was, and what he did; but this figure, buried in thought, of what is he thinking? To each one of us, thoughtfully considering the picture, it has a separate meaning.

On the other hand, we could come very near to a mutual understanding of the emotions aroused by Correggio's picture; although he too, as we have seen, was intent upon representing, not the concrete fact of a marriage, but the abstract ideas of peace, happiness, and innocence. Therefore, the difference between the ways in which these two pictures affect us is not one of kind, but of degree. Both detach our thoughts from the concrete and carry our imagination away into the world of abstract emotions; but while Correggio's appeals to us like a pastoral theme by Haydn, Michelangelo's is to be compared to the grandeur and soul-searching impressiveness of Beethoven.

Michelangelo, therefore, compels us to enlarge our conception of what is beautiful. To the Greeks it was physical perfection; to Correggio physical loveliness joined to loveliness of sentiment; but Michelangelo, except in a few instances, such as his painting of *Adam* on the Sistine vault, and his sculptures of the *Pietà* and of the figure of the *Thinker* over the tomb of Lorenzo de' Medici, cared little for physical beauty. As far as we know, he reached the age of sixty-four years without ever being attracted by the love of woman; then he met the beautiful Vittoria Colonna, widow of the Marquis of Pescara. They were mutually drawn together by the bond of intellectual and spiritual sympathy; their communion was of soul with soul; and Michelangelo, now moved by love to be a poet, expressed his soul in sonnets, as beforetime he had done in sculpture and painting.

The beauty, therefore, of his sculpture and paintings consists finally in the elevation of soul which they embody and the power they have to elevate our own souls. Their beauty is elemental; for example, the picture we are studying is not so much a representation of Jeremiah, as a typal expression of a great soul in labor with heavy thoughts. Accordingly, in Michelangelo's figures, lines of grace are for the most part replaced by lines of power—the power of vast repose or of tremendous energy, even of torment, either suppressed or desperate. Though a master of anatomy and of the laws of composition, he dared to disregard both if it were necessary to express his conception: to exaggerate the muscles of his figures, and even put them in positions which the human body could not assume. In his latest painting, that of the *Last Judgment* on the end wall of the Sistine, he poured out his soul like a torrent. What were laws in comparison with the pain within himself which must out? Well might the Italians of his day speak of the *terribilità* of his style: that it was, terrible!

In a brief study of so great a man it is possible to allude to only one more feature of the picture—namely, its architectural details. These, real as they look, are painted on the level surface of the vault. It is characteristic of Michelangelo that, having this vast space to decorate, he should begin by subdividing it into architectural spaces, since he was architect as well as sculptor, painter, and poet. For a time the building of St. Peter's was intrusted to his care, and in the last years of his life he prepared plans for it and made a model of its wonderful dome. There was much dispute as to whether the groundplan of the building should be of the design of a Greek or of a Roman cross. Bramante had urged the former and Michelangelo adhered to it, intending the dome to be its crowning feature. Unfortunately, in the beginning of the seventeenth century the nave was lengthened, and this change from the Greek to the Roman cross has interfered with the view of the dome from nearby and otherwise diminished its effect.

Michelangelo died in Rome, February 18, 1564, after dictating this brief will: " I commit my soul to God, my body to the earth, and my property to my nearest relations." His remains were conveyed to Florence, and given a public funeral in the Church of Santa Croce.

Compared with this long and arduous life, Correggio's seems simple indeed. Little is known of it, which would argue that he was of a retiring disposition. He was born in the little town of Correggio, twenty-four miles from Parma. In the latter city he was educated, but in his seventeenth year an outbreak of the plague drove his family to Mantua, where the young painter had an opportunity of studying the pictures of Mantegna and the collection of works of art accumulated originally by the Gonzaga family and later by Isabella d'Este. In 1514 he was back at Parma, where his talents met with ample recognition; and for some years the story of his life is the record of his work, culminating in that wonderful creation of light and shade, *The Adoration of the Shepherds*, now in the Dresden Gallery, and the masterpiece of the Parma Gallery, *Madonna and Child with St. Jerome and the Magdalene*.

It was not, however, a record of undisturbed quiet, for the decoration which he made for the dome of the cathedral was severely criticized. Choosing the subject of the *Resurrection,* he projected upon the ceiling a great number of ascending figures, which, viewed from below, necessarily involved a multitude of legs, giving rise to the *bon mot* that the painting resembled a "fry of frogs." It may have been the trouble which now ensued with the chapter of the cathedral, or depression caused by the death of his young wife, but at the age of thirty-six, indifferent to fame and fortune, he retired to

HOW TO STUDY PICTURES

the comparative obscurity of his native place, where for four years he devoted himself to the painting of mythological subjects: scenes of fabled beings removed from the real world and set in a golden arcady of dreams. All that is known regarding his death is the date, March 5, 1534.

CHAPTER XI

PAOLO CALIARI (called
VERONESE)
1528-1588
Italian School of Venice

JACOPO ROBUSTI (called
TINTORETTO)
1518-1594
Italian School of Venice

THE art of Venice, it has been said, " was late in its appearance, the last to come, the last to die, of all the great Italian schools." It reached its culmination in Titian, whom we have already considered, and in Paul Veronese and Tintoretto, his contemporaries. Most characteristically, perhaps, in the last two.

For the grandeur of Venetian art does not consist in its representation of the motives which exercised the other schools of Italian art. It was not saturated with the religious motive, or with the classical; nor intent on realistic representation. It combined something of each, but only as a means to its purpose of making art contributory to the joy and pageantry of life. While the searching spirit of the Renaissance was reflected in Da Vinci, its soul in Michelangelo, and the Christian faith and classical lore united in Raphael, the motive of the Venetians was the pride of life: pride particularly in the communal life of Venice, in her institutions, in her unsurpassed beauty, in her royal magnificence as the Queen City of the East and West.

HOW TO STUDY PICTURES

Eleven hundred years before the birth of Paul Veronese, A.D. 421, a handful of Roman Christians, driven out of Aquileia by the Lombards, had taken refuge upon Torcello, one of the sandy islands amid the lagoons. In time they spread to other islands, Malamocco and Rivalto, from which they repelled an attack made by Pepin, the son of Charlemagne, thus throwing off the yoke of the Eastern emperors. Rivalto was then selected as the seat of government; Venice was founded, and in A.D. 819 the doge took up his residence on the spot still occupied by the Ducal Palace. Nine years later a Venetian fleet brought from Alexandria the body of St. Mark; he was adopted as the city's patron saint; his emblem, the lion, became the symbol of the Venetian government; and a church was erected in his honor, where now stands the great cathedral, adjoining the palace of the doges.

Henceforth these two structures became the embodiment of the city's spiritual and temporal life; the assertions of her proud independence and superb ambitions; the visible expressions of her strongly personal religion and intense patriotism. From the first she set her face to the sea, and by her geographical position became the entrance-port through which the wealth of the East poured into Europe. So, when she planned her great church of St. Mark's in the eleventh century, it was to Byzantium that she turned for craftsmen and artificers, and the edifice, which rose through this and the following centuries, was Oriental both in style and in the lavishness of its decoration. It came to be like a colossal casket, the outside and inside of which was being embellished continually with more precious and sumptuous display. Some architects will tell you it is a monstrosity, because it lacks the dignity of form, the harmony between the whole and its parts, that are essential to a great composition.

It is not, however, on the score of form that it challenges the admiration of the world, but as an example, the most superb in Europe, of applied decoration. Its exterior is incrusted with carven work, brilliant with gold, sumptuous with columns of most precious marbles: with costly marbles, also, its interior is veneered; its vaultings covered with glass mosaics, its windows filled with colored glass—the glass-work fabricated on the island of Murano, originally by Byzantine artists. The interior is a miracle of color, seen under every conceivable variety of lights and shadows; by turns gorgeous, tender, stupendous, or mysteriously lustrous, impregnated everywhere with an atmosphere of infinite subtlety. Not form, as I have said, but color, light and shade, and atmosphere; and these are the qualities that prevail in Venetian painting. They are a heritage from the Byzantine influence, reinspired continually by the waters and skies of Venice; and they were the only adequate means of representing pictorially the variegated opulence of Venetian life.

Let us glance for a moment at the growth of the power of Venice. In the thirteenth century,—namely, 1204,—under her Doge Dandolo, she took Constantinople and planted her colonies on the shores of the peninsula of Greece and on the adjacent islands. During the fourteenth century she waged war with her naval rival, Genoa, conquered her, and extended her own power over the neighboring cities of Vicenza, Verona, and Padua, until the whole district of Venezia was under her sway, while her colonies extended along the shores of the Adriatic and Mediterranean as far as Trebizond, on the northeast coast of Asia Minor. By the commencement of the fifteenth century her glory was in its zenith. The French ambassador, De Commynes, writing to his sovereign, describes Venice as the " most triumphant city I have ever seen, and one which does most honor to ambassadors and strangers; which is most wisely governed, and in which the service of God is most solemnly performed."

But the wave, having reached its summit, was already beginning to decline. In 1453 the conquest of Constantinople by the Turks began the undermining of the commerce of Venice with the Levant; and, following the voyage of Vasco da Gama round the Cape of Good Hope, the trade with India gradually passed into the hands of the Portuguese. Then, in 1508, the Pope, the German Emperor, and the King of France conspired against Venice in the League of Cambrai; and although she " remained herself untouched upon the waters of the Lagunes, she lost her possessions on the mainland "; while through the years which followed, almost single-handed, she held the Turks at bay. Yet it was in the long-drawn-out decline of her power that her art reached its supreme height. With Titian, whose long life bridged the fifteenth and sixteenth centuries, it is still magnificently poised; with Tintoretto and Paul Veronese, both of whom belonged entirely to the latter century, it is an art of display and some exaggeration.

VERONESE—TINTORETTO

Peculiarly characteristic of Venetian art was the pageant picture representing some great religious or state function redounding to the glory of Venice. The most beautiful city in the world, her own external life was a continual pageant, but on frequent occasions her canals and piazza were the scenes of officially regulated ceremonials. The arrival and departure of ambassadors were events of particular magnificence; the church's processions, such as those of Corpus Christi, were conducted with a splendor that was only surpassed in the great state pageant wherein Venice was annually wedded to the Adriatic.

The Doge's Palace, embodiment of her power as a state, under the rule of its doge and Council of Ten, was five times damaged by fire, and after each catastrophe repaired with greater magnificence. In the fire of 1576 the paintings by Bellini, Alvise Vivarini, and Carpaccio which had adorned the interior were consumed; and those which now decorate its walls and ceilings are the work of the later artists, notably of Titian, Tintoretto, and Veronese. With very few exceptions, the subjects of the pictures set forth the glory and power of Venice, which find their highest expression in the Hall of the Great Council, that body of one hundred nobles, nominally the government, but actually superseded by the inner Council of Ten. The walls are covered with large mural paintings, representing triumphal incidents of war and diplomacy. Around the frieze are portraits by Tintoretto of seventy-six doges, a black tablet with the inscription *Hic est locus Marini Falethri decapitati pro criminibus* hanging where should be the portrait of Doge Marino Faliero, a traitor to the terrible Council of Ten.

HOW TO STUDY PICTURES

The splendor of the whole culminates in the center of the eastern ceiling, in the *Glory of Venice* by Paul Veronese.

The illustration of it here reproduced should be held above the head, in order that the angle of vision may correspond with that at which the original is viewed. Then it becomes apparent with what wonderful skill the architecture and the figures have been made to conform to the conditions of seeing the picture. High up against the magnificent architectural setting, of that imposing kind with which the architect Palladio was delighting his contemporaries, between pillars of Oriental design, such as adorn the *Beautiful Gate of the Temple* in Raphael's cartoon of Peter and John curing the lame man, Venezia sits enthroned. She is robed in ermine and blue silk, gold embroidered, and above her fair-haired head a winged figure, poised in air, suspends a crown, while another, higher up upon a cloud, blows through a trumpet. Grouped at the foot of the throne, and resting upon clouds, are five female figures, symbolizing, from the right, Justice, Agriculture, Peace, Commerce, and Victory, and beside the last sits the male figure of a soldier, holding a branch of laurel. From a balcony beneath them men and women in beautiful attire look up with faces of radiant happiness and devotion, while down below, two horsemen appear among a crowd of persons.

"This picture," writes the artist E. H. Blashfield, " is so rich and so silvery in its color "—the latter appearing in the architectural parts—" that it may be called magnificent in its technic as in its motive. As a subject, it is exactly what Veronese loved best to treat, and among

THE GLORY OF VENICE　　　　　　PAOLO VERONESE
HALL OF THE GREAT COUNCIL, DUCAL PALACE, VENICE

THE MIRACLE OF ST. MARK   ACADEMY, VENICE   TINTORETTO

his works only *The Marriage at Cana* and *The Family of Darius* can rival it. . . . No picture shows a more masterly arrangement: a style at once so sumptuous yet elevated, figures whose somewhat exuberant loveliness is saved from vulgarity by an air of pride and energy, magnificent material treated with such ease and sincerity."

We should particularly remark the last words, "ease and sincerity." As to the ease of Veronese, I quote from various sources: " His facility of execution has never been equaled." " Every one of his canvases, replete with life and movement, is a feast for the eye." "Veronese was supreme in representing, without huddling or confusion, numerous figures in a luminous and diffused atmosphere, while in richness of draperies and transparency of shadows he surpassed all other Venetians or Italians." " He is of all painters, without a single exception, the one whose work shows most unity."

As to his sincerity, it arose from the fact that he was simply what he was—a painter. He does not appeal to our intelligence, as Titian, or to our sense of dramatic poetry, as Tintoretto. His is the Kingdom of the World, the pride of strong and beautiful bodies, the splendor of external appearances; and he gave himself to it with the single purpose of representing what appealed to the eye. " Joyous, free, proud, full of health and vigor, Veronese is the very incarnation of the Italian Renaissance, that happy time when under smiling and propitious skies painters produced works of art with as little effort as trees put forth their blossoms and bear their fruit."

HOW TO STUDY PICTURES

"These being the prominent features of his style, it remains to be said that what is really great in Veronese is the sobriety of his imagination and the solidity of his workmanship. Amid so much that is distracting, he never loses command over his subject, nor does he degenerate into fulsome rhetoric." In the exuberance of his fancy and the facility of his brush, moreover in the skill with which he " places crowds of figures in an atmospheric envelope, bathing them, so to speak, in light," he resembles Rubens. "But he does not, like Rubens, strike us as gross, sensual, fleshly; he remains proud, powerful, and frigidly materialistic. He raises neither repulsion nor desire, but displays with the calm strength of art the empire of the mundane spirit." Equally in this quality of sober restraint he differs from Tintoretto. "Where Tintoretto is dramatic, Veronese is scenic."

This distinction is well worth analyzing. It may seem for a moment as if the two ideas were identical; but "scenic" has to do with the things apparent to the eye, "dramatic" with the unseen workings of the mind, as expressed in word or gesture. A pageant is scenic; but the attempt to reproduce the thought, which moves each individual to separate expression of his feelings, would bring it into the category of dramatic. The distinction is made clear by a comparison of the *Glory of Venice* with Tintoretto's *Miracle of St. Mark*. We feel a desire to know the story represented in the latter. This in itself is to admit a difference. Veronese being, as I have said, simply what he was — a painter — needs no commentary. The purport of his picture is at once self-evident. You will be told by some that this self-evidentness is the proper scope of painting; that "art for art's sake" should be the sole object of the painter; that the representation of anything else but what is apparent to the eye is going outside the province of the art; and that the preference which so many people have for a picture which makes an appeal not only to the eye, but to the intellect or the poetic and dramatic sense, is a proof of vulgar taste which confuses painting with illustration. The best answer to this is that not alone laymen, but artists also in all periods,—artists of such personality that they cannot be ignored,—have tried to reinforce the grandeur of mere appearances with something that shall appeal to the mind and soul of men.

Tintoretto was one of them; not by overt intention, but because the poetic and dramatic fervor was in him and it had to find utterance. The points of main importance are the value of the story that he represents and his manner of representing it. Now, to the Venetians, any incident connected with their patron saint was of extreme interest, recognized at once and enjoyed. The one pictured here has reference to the legend, that a Christian slave of a pagan nobleman had persisted in worshiping at the shrine of St. Mark; whereupon his master haled him before the judge, who condemned him to be tortured. But as the executioner raised his hammer, St. Mark himself descended from heaven and the weapon was shattered. We see the saint, hovering above the crowd; the executioner in his turban, turning to the judge to show the broken hammer; the judge leaning forward in his seat, and the various individuals in the crowd pressing round with different expressions of amazement. Following a custom of the time, Tintoretto has introduced the portrait of himself three times: in the bearded man who leans forward between the columns on the left, in the figure immediately to the right of the executioner, and again in the face that appears beneath the judge on the extreme right of the picture. No Venetian of Tintoretto's time could be unresponsive to such a theme, so realized; any more than an American of to-day could fail to be impressed, were there an artist capable of representing some incident in the life of Washington in such a way as to involve all that the idea of Washington presents to the American imagination.

Now as to the manner of presentment: Tintoretto, when a youth, wrote upon the wall of his studio as an ideal to be reached: " The drawing of Michelangelo, the coloring of Titian." His father being a dyer of silk (*tintore*), the lad at first assisted in the work, hence his nickname, " Il Tintoretto," " The Little Dyer." However, as he showed an aptitude for drawing and painting, the father obtained permission for him to work in Titian's studio; but for some reason his stay with the great master lasted only a few days. For the rest, he was his own teacher, studying and copying the works of Titian in the churches and palaces; and, having obtained casts of Michelangelo's figures upon the Medicean tombs, drawing them from every possible point of view. It is said that he also made little figures in clay, and suspended them by a string from the rafters in his studio, that he might learn how to represent them in mid-air, and as they appeared when viewed from underneath.

It was very difficult even in Venice for a young untried painter to obtain recognition; but at last an opportunity occurred. In the Church of Santa Maria del Orto there were two bare spaces nearly fifty feet high and twenty broad; he offered to paint them for nothing but the price of the materials; and, the offer being accepted, produced *The Last Judgment* and *The Golden Calf*. He was now about twenty-eight years old. So great was the impression produced by these works that he was shortly after invited to paint four pictures for the Scuola di San Rocco, one of which was the picture we are studying. There were many of these schools in Venice, and they vied with one another in securing the services of painters to decorate their walls. The brothers of the Confraternity of San Rocco gave Tintoretto a commission for two pictures in their church, and then invited him to enter a competition with Veronese and others for the decoration of the ceiling in the hall of their school. When the day arrived, the other painters presented their sketches, but Tintoretto, being asked for his, removed a screen from the ceiling and showed it already painted. "We asked for sketches," they said. "That is the way," he replied, "I make my sketches." They still demurred, so he made them a present of the picture, and by the rules of their order they could not refuse a gift. In the end they promised him the painting of all the pictures they required, and during his lifetime he covered their walls with sixty large compositions. After the fire of 1577 in the Ducal Palace he shared with Veronese the larger part of the new decorations.

Among his pictures there is the *Marriage of Bacchus and Ariadne,* described by John Addington Symonds as "that perfect lyric of the sensuous fancy"; with which the same writer couples his *Martyrdom of St. Agnes,* "that lamb-like maiden with her snow-white lamb among the soldiers and priests of Rome," as an illustration " that it is not only in the region of the vast, the tempestuous, and the tragic, that Tintoretto finds himself at home; but that he has proved beyond all question that the fiery genius of Titanic artists can pierce and irradiate the placid and the tender secrets of the soul, with more consummate mastery than falls to the lot of those who make tranquillity their special province."

Yet it is his phenomenal energy and the impetuous force of his work that are particularly characteristic of Tintoretto and earned for him the sobriquet among his contemporaries, " Il Furioso." He painted so many pictures, and on so vast a scale, that some show the effects of over-haste and extravagance, which caused Annibale Carracci to say that, " while Tintoretto was the equal of Titian, he was often inferior to Tintoretto."

But the *Miracle of St. Mark* is one of his grandest pictures; admirable alike in the dramatic movement of the figures, the beauty of the coloring, and the emotional use that has been made of light and shadow. If we compare it with Veronese's we shall discover the difference between the dramatic and the scenic. The figures in the latter have a sumptuous repose, finely adjusted to the general strain of triumph that resounds from the whole picture; but in Tintoretto's the wonderfully foreshortened body of St. Mark plunges through the air with the impetuosity of an eagle. "There is not a figure in the picture that does not act, and act all over; not a fold of drapery nor a tone of flesh that does not add to the universal dash and brilliancy." The coloring of the costumes includes saffron, blue, gold, and deep crimson; the sky is of greenish hue passing to a golden haze over the horizon; while the body of the slave is a center of luminousness. For the chief characteristic of the picture is Tintoretto's use of light and shade.

He uses it with dramatic and emotional effect; " with him," as has been said, " it is the first and most powerful of dramatic accessories; he makes light an actor in his vast compositions." We shall see how Rubens, fresh from Italy, used light and shadow in this emotional way in his *Descent from the Cross;* but usually, like Veronese, he enveloped his figures in clear full light; while Tintoretto makes his emerge into light from darkness. Some of his pictures, whether from effects of time or the manner of their painting, are to-day black and coarse-looking; but in the best and well-preserved ones, as in our present example, the shadows themselves are luminous with color.

While his life was a tranquil one, spent for the most part in his studio, his mind teemed with ideas; his conceptions came to him in lightning bursts of inspiration, the whole scene vividly clear; rapidly and without hesitation transferred to the canvas. Hence some of his work is exaggerated in force and confused in composition. Such, at least in its present condition, is the vast canvas of *Paradise* in the Ducal Palace, the largest oil-painting in the world, measuring thirty by seventy-four feet, upon which he painted during the last six years of his life. He lies buried in Santa Maria del Orto, the church in which his first important work was done forty-eight years before. Veronese, the younger man, had been dead six years.

With these men died the last of the giants of the Italian Renaissance. That mighty movement had run its course, and was succeeded by decline. The vital force of painting now reappeared in other lands.

CHAPTER XII

PETER PAUL RUBENS
1577-1640
Flemish School

DIEGO RODRIGUEZ DE SILVA VELASQUEZ
1599-1660
Spanish School

THE student of art, when he reaches the period of the seventeenth century, turns a sharp corner. He has been traveling for three centuries in Italy, with brief visits at long intervals to Flanders and Germany, the second of his trips to the latter including a visit to England. But, as he turns the corner of the seventeenth century, Italy is left behind, Spain attracts his attention to the west, while far to the north Holland and, a second time, Flanders beckon him.

For in Italy the last of the great artists passed away with Tintoretto. The country itself had become the prey of despots who were in the hire of foreign rulers; and the loss of political liberty was accompanied by lower social standards, by intellectual and artistic decline. There were still clever painters, but they were little men, without originality, content to reproduce the manner of their great predecessors; copying chiefly their weaknesses; trying by extravagances to disguise the absence of originality in themselves.

At this period, to find something vital in art,—something, that is to say, that grows and ripens because of the independent force of life within itself,—we must turn to Spain and to the North. Immediately three of the greatest names in art rise to our notice: Rembrandt, Rubens, and Velasquez. It is with the last two that we are concerned at present.

The pictures selected as a basis for the study of these two giants are *The Descent from the Cross* by Rubens and *The Maids of Honor* (*Las Meñinas* in the Spanish) by Velasquez. The former was painted when Rubens was thirty-five. He had completed his education by a sojourn of eight years in Italy, where, in the service of the Duke of Mantua, he had had special opportunities of study, being employed during part of the time in making copies of masterpieces for his patron.

He was now returned to Antwerp, and one of the first works in which he declared himself to be a master was *The Descent from the Cross*. It shows him to be under the Italian influence, and not yet the original artist that he became. *The Maids of Honor,* on the contrary, was painted by Velasquez only four years before he died, and represents the finest flower of his maturity.

Possibly our first impression of the Rubens picture will be, "How beautiful!"—of the Velasquez, "How curious!" In the one case the figures almost fill the canvas and are grouped so as to decorate it with an imposing mass of light and shade and a beautiful arrangement of lines; whereas in the other the figures are all at the bottom of the canvas, and do not present a similarly beautiful pattern of lines and masses. The one looks like a magnificent picture; the other seems to be rather a real scene, as indeed it was.

RUBENS—VELASQUEZ

The story of *Las Meñinas* is that Velasquez was painting a portrait of the king and queen, who sat where the spectator is as he looks at the picture, and their little daughter, the infanta Margarita, came in with her maids of honor, her dog, and her dwarfs, accompanied by her duenna and a courtier. The little princess asks for a drink of water; the maids of honor hand it to her with the elaborate etiquette prescribed by the formalities of the most rigidly ceremonious court in Europe. The scene presented so charming a picture, that the king desired Velasquez to paint it. The artist has included himself in the group at work upon a large canvas, on which it is supposed he was painting the portraits of the king and queen when the interruption occurred. Their reflection appears in the mirror at the end of the room, and the chamberlain, Don José Nieto, stands outside the door, drawing a curtain. The scene is indeed represented with such extraordinary realism that the French critic Gautier writes, " So complete is the illusion that, standing in front of *Las Meñinas,* one is tempted to ask, ' Where is the picture? ' "

It is the mature work of a painter whose motto was, "Verdad no pintura" ("Truth, not painting"). By comparison, the principle which Rubens followed is "Painting and truth." Let us see how the two ideas are illustrated in the respective pictures.

The Descent from the Cross arouses one's feeling of awe and pity to an extraordinary degree. This is partly due to the actual moment in the great tragedy of the Redemption which the artist has seized. The terrible anguish of the Crucifixion is past; to it has succeeded the pathetic nothingness of death; the poor, limp body is being tenderly cared for by the faithful few who have come, under the cover of night, to render the last office to the Dead. Joseph of Arimathæa is superintending the lowering of the precious burden; young John, the beloved disciple, supports its weight; Peter has mounted the ladder with characteristic eagerness, but the memory of his denial is with him, and, fixed in contemplation of the divine face, he lends no hand; and the three Marys are there, the one stretching out her arms with a mother's yearning for embrace, the Magdalene grasping the foot that she had once bathed with her tears. Each attendant figure, though so different in its individual expression of feeling, joins with the others to complete a unity of deepest reverential tenderness. Then in contrast to these strong forms, so full of life and feeling, is the relaxed, nerveless body of the Dead. I wonder if ever the pitiful helplessness of death, or the reverent awe that the living feel in the presence of their beloved dead, has been more beautifully expressed.

Let us try to discover by what actual resources of the painter's art Rubens has achieved this result. We have mentioned the contrast between the bodies of the Dead and the living figures. It is an illustration of the painter's power to stimulate what has been called the "tactile imagination"; that is to say, to suggest the physical sense of touch and the feelings in the mind aroused by it. A lesser artist might have conceived this way of presenting the scene and drawn all the figures in the same positions, making, in fact, the same appeal to our eye, and yet not affected us in the same way, because he would make no appeal to that other sense of *touch,* which really in most people is the more easily roused. For people more readily appreciate hard and soft, rough and smooth, stiff and limp, hot and cold, than the colors and shapes and grouping of objects. It is this sense of touch which Rubens had so wonderful a skill in suggesting. Look, for example, at the modeling of the shoulders and head of Peter. What strength and bulk and sudden tightening of the muscles, as he turns and holds himself still! The line of the shoulders and the direction of the eyes point us to the Saviour's head. It has dropped of its own weight, as the hand of the man above let go of it. The left arm is still grasped by the other man—at the elbow, observe, so that his hand not only helps to sustain the weight of the body, but keeps the forearm stiff. We feel that, when he lets go, it too will fall lifelessly. Compare also the huddled, actionless position of the Saviour's form with the strong body of John, braced so firmly by the legs. So, one by one, we might examine the figures, feeling in our imagination the physical firmness and muscular movement that each would present to the touch, coming back again and again to the feeling, How limp and flaccid is the dead body!

This last feeling might produce in us either disgust or pity. Rubens has insured the latter, partly by depicting in the living figures a reverence and tenderness in which we instantly participate; also, by the persuasive beauty of the composition.

Let us study the latter, first in its arrangement of line, secondly in its arrangement of light and shade, though the two are really blended. Every figure in the composition has either the beauty of grace or that of character; and the most beautiful is the Saviour's, which has the elongated, pliant grace of the stem and tendrils of a vine. And the drooping flower upon it is the head, to which all the principal lines of the composition lead. Start where you will and follow along the direction of the figures, your eye finally centers upon the Saviour's head. It is the focus-point. And note that on the edges of the group the lines begin by being firm and strong in character, gradually increasing in suppleness and grace as they draw near the sacred figure, until finally all the dignity and sweetness of the picture come to an intensity in the Head. Lest the central figure should be lacking in impressiveness as a mass, its effect has been broadened by the winding-sheet, against the opaque white of which its own whiteness of flesh is limpid and ashy in tone. Apart from the flesh-tints, the other hues in the picture are black, almost black-green, and dull red. Thus by its color as well as by the lines the figure of the Saviour is made the prominent spot in the composition. Moreover, placed as it is upon the most brilliantly lighted part of the picture, its own tenderer lighting is made more emphatic.

The figure is being lowered, as it were, down a cataract of light which leaps up in a wave at the bottom, and scatters flakes of foam around it. These alight on the faces, hands, and sometimes on an arm or foot, in every case just those parts of the composition which are important in the expression of gesture or sentiment.

In this distribution of light, as well as in the arrangement of the lines, there has been a careful building up of effect, everything calculated to arouse the emotion and make at once a magnificent spectacle and a profound impression. Painted as an altarpiece to be viewed from a distance, it is an example of the "grand style," belonging to that "high-bred" family of pictures represented most nobly in Italian art. Compared with it, *The Maids of Honor* may appear to have little grandeur.

While the Rubens presents a beautiful pattern of decoration, the Velasquez seems barren, more than half the canvas being given up to empty space. The figures in the former have a grand flow of line, those in the latter seem stiff and awkwardly grouped. The Rubens excites our emotion, the Velasquez our curiosity.

Before studying closely *The Maids of Honor,* we must recall the fact that in 1628 Rubens visited the court of Spain for nine months; that Velasquez watched him paint and came under the fascination of his personality; that he saw Rubens's admiration for the great Italian pictures which hung in the king's gallery; that by the advice of Rubens he shortly afterward visited Italy, and studied in Venice, Milan, and Rome. In fact, Velasquez was well acquainted with the grandeur of Italian painting; and in the middle period of his life, between 1645 and 1648, had an opportunity to execute a grand example of decorative painting. The king commissioned him to decorate the walls of the new summer palace, Buen Retiro, whereupon Velasquez painted the famous *Surrender of Breda.* It represents Justin of Nassau handing the keys of the city to his conqueror, Spinola, the last of the great Spanish generals. It is a noble decoration and at the same time one of the finest historical paintings in the world, contradicting the assertion made by some painters that the two ideas are incompatible.

Some years before it was painted Rubens had completed a series of historical decorations, which are now in the Louvre, to celebrate events in the life of Marie de Médicis, queen of Henri IV of France, and mother of Louis XIII. Here again is shown the difference between Rubens and Velasquez; for these pictures by Rubens present a blaze of color, a profusion of sumptuousness, a pageant of imagination in which gods and goddesses and allegorical figures mingle with the actual personages. Velasquez, on the contrary, while keeping in mind the decorative necessities of the canvas, kept himself also to the simple and very touching circumstances of the incident. Even in the enthusiasm of painting a great decoration, he preserved his regard for "truth."

So it was not because of ignorance of what other great painters had done, or of what he himself could do to rival them on their own ground,—for *The Surrender of Breda* could hang without loss of dignity beside a Titian,—that he turned his back upon all traditions of the Italian grand style, and in the years of his maturity produced *The Maids of Honor,* a new kind of picture. It was new because it was the product of a new kind of artist's eyesight; of a new conception of realism.

We have seen in Holbein's *Portrait of Georg Gyze* an example of that kind of realism which is solely occupied in giving a faithful representation of the figure and

DESCENT FROM THE CROSS 　　　　　　　　**RUBENS**
ANTWERP CATHEDRAL

LAS MEÑINAS (MAIDS OF HONOR) VELASQUEZ
PRADO GALLERY, MADRID

its surrounding objects. But if you compare that portrait with Velasquez's picture, you will feel, I think, that the attention is scattered over Holbein's picture, while in the case of Velasquez's the eye immediately takes it in as a whole. The little princess is the center of the scene, the light being concentrated on her, as it is around the principal figure in Rubens's picture; but, though our attention is centered on the child, it revolves all round her and immediately embraces the scene as a whole. The realism of this picture is a realism of unity. Moreover, it gives us a single vivid impression of the scene, such as the king received; so we may call it also a realism of impression.

To illustrate what is meant by realism of impression let us contrast an example of the extreme opposite: *1807 —Friedland,* by Meissonier, in the Metropolitan Museum, New York. It is not necessary to have seen it to appreciate the difference; enough to know that it represents a regiment of cavalry galloping past Napoleon, saluting him as they charge the enemy; and that the armor and weapons and accoutrements of all these men are painted with the finish and exactness of a miniature. No eye in the world could have seen the bridles and bits and spurs and buttons, and the thousand other sharply defined details, as those soldiers galloped by. While each detail represents realism, their sum total is, from the point of view of the painter or of the spectator, false. The reason is that Meissonier has painted, not what he could see, but what his mind informed him must be there.[1] And what is the result? The picture does not

[1] See the chapter on Memling, page 64.

affect us as a whole; but people study over it, moving their eyes, as if from word to word or from line to line on the page of a book; and then, because every item looks so real, they exclaim, "How wonderful!"

Velasquez's picture, on the other hand, makes an instant and complete impression, because he has included in it only as much of detail as the eye could embrace at one glance; more, however, than a less gifted and an untrained vision could encompass. But it was Velasquez's distinction that he had a marvelous power of receiving a full impression and of vividly retaining it in his mind until he had rendered it vivid upon the canvas.

If we turn back again to a comparison of *The Descent from the Cross* and *The Maids of Honor,* do we not realize a much more instantaneous and vivid impression in the Velasquez? The Rubens, also, is a noble example of unity, but it is a unity of effect produced chiefly by the balance of the dark and light parts; yet the method adopted is arbitrary, as compared with the Velasquez. To state it briefly: Rubens has put the light where he needed it for his composition; Velasquez has taken it as he found it. Streaming through the window, it permeates the whole room, not striking the figures simply on one side and leaving the other dark, but enveloping them and penetrating to the remotest corners of the ceiling. Even in the reproductions, you can see how much more real the light is in the Velasquez; how it is bright on the parts of the figures that lie in its direct path; less bright in the half-lights, where it strikes the figure less directly; reflected back, as for example from the dress of the little princess on to that of the maid on her left; how it steals round everything and penetrates everywhere. For Velasquez recognized that light is elastic and illuminates the air. Also he noticed that the light was whiter on objects near the eye, grayer and grayer on objects farther and farther back, owing to the intervening planes of atmosphere hanging between like veils.

Hence he was the first to discover a new kind of perspective. Men long ago had learned to make the lines vanish from the eye; to make the figures diminish in size and shape as they recede from the front; and to explain the distance by contrasts of light and shade. But he perfected what had been anticipated by Leonardo—the perspective of light. By the most delicate and accurate rendering of the quantity of light reflected from each and every part of the room and the figures and objects in it, and by recognizing the veils of atmosphere, he gave to the figures the reality of form and to the room its hollowness and distance.

Painters distinguish between the color of an object and its color as acted upon by light. Thus, in the case of a white dress, they would say that white was its "local color." But it is not white like a sheet of paper; it varies in degrees of whiteness according to the quantity of light reflected from its various parts. And these varying quantities of light reflected from the various planes of the objects, they call "values." Velasquez excelled in the rendering of "values."

This attention to values, or the truthful rendering of light, involved other truths: for example, that the outlines of objects are not, except in special cases, sharply defined,—the light plays round their edges and thereby softens and melts them; and the objects themselves do not appear as if they were cut out in paper and pasted on the canvas, but are masses of more or less illuminated color, merged in the surrounding atmosphere. Consequently, Velasquez gave to the contour-lines of his figures an elusiveness; sometimes they are strong and assertive, at other times they melt into the atmosphere. And as light shows itself to our eyes by being reflected from the infinite molecules of the air, so Velasquez's rendering of light introduced an appearance of real atmosphere into his pictures. You have only to compare this one of his with Rubens's to be sure this is so.

Having thus briefly (and therefore inadequately, I am afraid; for it is a large and difficult subject) glanced at the things that Velasquez tried for, we are in a better position to understand how his realism was a realism of impression. Firstly, he saw his subject at a single glance, eye and hand instantaneously coöperating; and he confined his impression to what a less keen eye, assisted by him, could also take in as a single impression. Secondly, by his marvelous penetration into the action of light, and his skill in rendering it, he set upon the canvas the scene as he had received the impression of it, with such subtle fidelity that our own observation is stimulated, and we receive the impression vividly.

By this time the picture should no longer appear to be empty; nor the figures crowded at the bottom. We should feel that the background and ceiling are connected, by that vertical strip of light up the edge of the canvas, with the figures in the foreground, so as to make a unified composition of balanced masses of light and less light. In the wonderful truth to life of the figures —the exquisite daintiness of the little princess, the affectionate reverence of the maids, the grotesqueness of the dwarfs, and the courtly sensitiveness of the artist's figure —we should have entered into the intimate human feeling of the whole group and ceased to be troubled by the curious style of the costumes.

These costumes, more than likely, and the fact that Velasquez lived in the palace painting courtly scenes and portraits, had much to do with his striking out a new style. How could he introduce such hooped skirts into a picture in the grand manner of Italian painting? His great genius was therefore compelled to find another outlet, and did so in directions which were new and permanent additions to the art of painting.

Rubens, on the other hand, not less original, took from the Italian style what could be of use to him, and then built upon it a style of his own. It is distinguished by a wonderful mastery of the human form and an amazing wealth of splendidly lighted color. He was a man of as much intellectual poise as Velasquez, and, like the latter, was accustomed to court life. But while Velasquez, bound to the most punctilious, ascetic, and superstitious court in Europe, was driven in upon himself, and became more and more acutely sensitive,— Rubens, traveling from court to court with pomp as a trusted envoy, had the exuberance of his nature more and more developed. As an artist, he had the wonderful faculty of being habitually in a white heat of imagination, while perfectly cool and calculating in the control of his hand. Hence the enormous output of his brush. It might be said that he was as prolific in the representation of the joy and exuberance of life as Michelangelo was in the representation of the life of the emotions.

Velasquez, for nearly two centuries, was forgotten outside of Spain. Italian art continued to be the model to imitate; and even when a return to the truth of nature was made at the beginning of the nineteenth century, sixty years passed before this great example of "Truth, not painting" was "discovered." Then a few painters visited the museum of the Prado at Madrid, which contains most of his pictures; others followed, and the world became gradually conscious that in these pictures of Velasquez, especially in the wonderful series of portraits of the king and members of the court, which he made during forty years of royal intimacy, there was revealed a great and solitary genius. Since then he has exercised, as we shall see, such an influence upon modern painting that he has been called "the First of the Moderns."

CHAPTER XIII

ANTONY VAN DYCK *FRANS HALS*
1599–1641 *1584 (?)–1666*
Flemish School *Dutch School*

THE commencement of the seventeenth century witnessed the birth of a new nation and of a new art—the Dutch. When the emperor Charles V abdicated in 1555, he allotted Austria and Germany to Ferdinand I, Spain and the Netherlands to his son Philip II. The rule of Spain was in one way beneficial to the Netherlands, or Low Countries (Holland and Belgium), since it opened to them the trade with the New World and the West Indies. Antwerp rose to greatness. "No city except Paris," says Mr. Motley, "surpassed it in population or in commercial splendor. The city itself was the most beautiful in Europe. Placed upon a plain along the bank of the Scheldt, shaped like a bent bow with the river for its string, it inclosed within its walls some of the most splendid edifices in Christendom. The world-renowned Church of Nôtre Dame, the stately Exchange, where five thousand merchants daily congregated—prototype of all similar establishments throughout the world—the capacious mole and port—were all establishments which it would have been difficult to rival in any other part of the globe."

Such it was before the "Spanish Fury." In 1567 the Duke of Alva arrived with ten thousand veterans for the purpose of stamping out the Reformed faith; established his "Council of Blood"; beheaded the Counts of Egmont and Horn after a mock trial; and commenced a reign of terror and bloodshed. In the six years of his governorship he boasted that he had put to death eighteen thousand persons besides those killed in battle; for the people had risen under William the Silent, and the war for independence was begun. In 1579, by an agreement at Utrecht, the seven northern provinces united for mutual defense; the southern holding back, because they adhered to the Roman Catholic form of faith. Antwerp, however, though not in the League of United Provinces, became a focus-point of the struggle, and in 1585 capitulated to the Duke of Parma.

Thirty-one years later the English ambassador paid a visit to the place, and wrote home to a friend:

> This great city is a great desert, for in ye whole time we spent there I could never sett my eyes in the whole length of the streete uppon 40 persons at once; I never mett coach nor saw man on horseback; none of our own companie (though both were workie dayes) saw one pennieworth of ware either in shops or in streetes bought or solde. Two walking pedlars and one ballad-seller will carry as much on their backs at once, as was in that royall exchange either above or below,—and the whole countrey of Brabant was suitable to this towne; faire and miserable.

When Philip II died in 1598, Spain was exhausted almost to prostration, and his successor was glad to conclude an armistice of twelve years with the United

Provinces. But at its conclusion war was resumed, and it was not until 1648 that by the peace of Westphalia the independence of the northern provinces of Holland was finally assured.

Meanwhile, during those seventy years of conflict in which a new nation was in the forming, a new art had been born. While the northern provinces were fighting for their liberties, a number of painters came to manhood, whose work was of such originality as to constitute a new school of painting—the Dutch School; "the last," as Fromentin says, "of the great schools, perhaps the most original, certainly the most local."

It was original because it was local. Across the Scheldt in Antwerp, Rubens was in the prime of his powers (among his retinue of pupils was Van Dyck); but, though his fame must have crossed to the Dutch, his influence did not. That people, stubborn against foreign domination, was stubbornly fashioning a kind of art of its own. Its artists were independent of Rubens, of the great Italian traditions, of everything but what concerned themselves. By their religious views they were separated from the chance of painting altarpieces or mythological subjects, and by their revolt they were cut off from viceregal patronage, such as the Flemish enjoyed. A nation of burghers, busy with war and commerce, they developed, out of their own lives, their love of country, and pride in themselves, a new art.

In one word, the Dutch art was an art of portraiture. It began with the painting of portraits of persons, and then proceeded to the painting of landscapes and of the outdoor and indoor occupations of the people, and to the painting of still-life,—all with such simple intention to represent the things as they appeared, and with such fidelity to the truth, that the whole range of subjects may be classed as portraiture. It was not "grand art," but it was intimate and sincere.

The first of the great men, chronologically, was Frans Hals, whose *Portrait of a Woman* we are comparing with Van Dyck's *Marie Louise von Tassis.* There is a story related by Houbraken, which may or may not be true, that Van Dyck passing through Haarlem, where Hals lived,[1] desired to see the painter; but, though he called several times, he could not find him at home. So he sent a messenger to seek him out and tell him that a stranger wished to see him; and, on Hals putting in an appearance, asked him to paint his portrait, adding, however, that he had only two hours to spare for the sitting. Hals finished the portrait in that time; whereupon his sitter, observing that it seemed an easy matter to paint a portrait, requested that he be allowed to try and paint the artist. Hals soon recognized that "his visitor was well skilled in the materials he was using; great, however, was his surprise when he beheld the performance; he immediately embraced the stranger, at the same time crying out, 'You are Van Dyck; no person but he could do as you have now done.'"

Assuming the story to be true, how interesting it would be if the two portraits existed, that one might see what Frans Hals, accustomed to the heavier type of the

---

[1] He was born in Antwerp, whither his family moved for a time in consequence of the war. They seem to have returned to Haarlem about 1607.

VAN DYCK—HALS

Dutch burghers, made of the delicately refined features of Van Dyck, and how the latter, who always gave an air of aristocratic elegance to his portraits, acquitted himself with the bluff, jovial Hals, who was as much at home in a tavern as in a studio! For no two men could be more different, both in point of view and method, though they were alike in one particular, that each was a most facile and skilful painter.

Let us turn to the two portraits, which are very characteristic examples of these two masters. First of all, examine the hands. You have recognized, no doubt, that hands are very expressive of character. In good portraits there is always a correspondence of feeling and character between the hands and the head. Hals was a master in this respect. There is also an absolute unanimity between the expression of the hand and that of the face in the Van Dyck, even to the curl of the forefinger, which echoes with extraordinary subtlety the curious slanting glance of the eyes.

But when we learn that this artist kept servants in his employment whose hands he used as models for the hands of his sitters, we begin to wonder where this idealizing of nature stopped, and whether the face and carriage of the figure also may not have come in for a share of it. As we know, too, that it was his habit to make a rapid study of his sitters in black and white chalk upon gray paper, and to hand it to his assistants for them to paint the figure in its clothes, which were sent to the studio for that purpose, after which he retouched their work and painted in the head and hands, we feel a suspicion that Van Dyck was as much interested in illustrating his own ideas of elegance and refinement as in reproducing the actual characteristics of his sitters.

We shall hardly feel this in the *Portrait of a Woman* by Hals. Of the fact that the woman looked in the flesh just as he has represented her on the canvas, we are as sure, as if we had looked over his shoulder and watched her grow to shape beneath his brush. He has put in nothing but what he saw, left out nothing that could complete the veracity of the record.

We turn back to the Van Dyck, and have ceased to wonder if Marie Louise were really like this. Her portrait is an exquisitely beautiful picture—let it go at that; and then again we turn to the Hals, and again we have forgotten that it is a portrait. It is a real woman that we face, one of stout and wholesome stock, whose husband may have had a hand in the shaping of the new republic, who may have been the mother of sons who fought in the long struggle for freedom. Those hands! —one loves them; strong hands, coarsened by their share in the work of life, now folded so unaffectedly in the calm and peace of living, which right good doing has won. When you look at them, and, still more, when you read their fuller story in that high, broad forehead, with the strong, big skull beneath it, as indicative of steadiness of purpose as the wide-apart eyes; in that resolute nose, with its lift of energy in the nostril; and in the firm, kindly, wise mouth, you realize how it was that Holland, having by its energy and patience set a barrier to the ocean, could keep at bay the power of Spain; and achieve for itself, after long waiting, liberty of life and thought.

MARIE LOUISE VON TASSIS   ANTHONY VAN DYCK
LIECHTENSTEIN GALLERY, VIENNA

PORTRAIT OF A WOMAN   FRANS HALS
NATIONAL GALLERY, LONDON

VAN DYCK—HALS

This portrait, while self-sufficient as a record of a woman who actually lived, is more than that: it is a type of the race to which she belonged. It is a type, too, of the whole school of Dutch painting; so straightforward, intimate, and sincere. Moreover, such a marvel of painting!

The Dutchmen of the seventeenth century, having abandoned the large field of decorative composition, settled down in the small space of their canvases to a perfection of craftsmanship that has never been surpassed in modern art. From the standpoint of pure painting, they formed a school of great painters; differing among themselves in motives and manner, but alike in being consummate masters of the brush.

Hals set his figures in clear light, so that the modeling is not accomplished by shadows, but by the degree of light which each surface of the flesh or costume reflected. In this respect he worked like Velasquez, but in a broader way. He distributed the lights and painted in the colors in great masses, each mass containing its exact quantity of light; and so great was his skill in the rendering of values that he could make a flat tone give the suggestion of modeling. Thus in the almost uninterrupted flat white tone of this woman's ruff we do not miss the absence of many lines to indicate the folds of muslin.

Compare the treatment of the ruff in Van Dyck's portrait; indeed, the explicit way in which the whole of the elaborate costume is rendered. Nothing is left to the imagination. Everything is told with rhetorical elaboration. The contrast of the Hals portrait offers an instructive example of what painters mean by the word "breadth," and a lesson also in the effect of breadth on our imagination; for we get from the broad simplicity of this portrait a strong invigoration, whereas from Van Dyck's a pleasant intoxication. Yet, while we miss the breadth in the Van Dyck, do not let us overlook the freedom with which it is painted, so that there is nothing small or niggling in all these details; they are drawn together, like the drops of water of a fountain, into one splendid burst of elegance.

In the latter, however, the character of the woman is considerably smothered. Perhaps it was the case that she had little character, that she was simply a fine lady of fashion; or it may be that that aspect of her was the one which chiefly interested the artist. He seems to have been particularly impressed with her eyes, which indicate at least a trait of character; and in a very subtle way he has made the attitude of the figure and the gesture of the hands and head correspond to it. So in a limited way the picture is representative of a type.

Hals, on the other hand, did not fix upon any particular trait or feature: he broadly surveyed all the externals of his sitter, and represented them as a whole; and with such clear seeing that, although he never penetrates into the mind of his subject,—as we shall find Rembrandt did,—he does get at the heart of it, and, in his straightforward characterization of what he sees, suggests that character lies beneath it.

In this respect his work is very like the man himself. He must have had fine qualities of mind; else how could he have seen things so simply and completely, and rendered them with such force and expression, inventing for the purpose a method of his own, which, as we have seen, was distinguished by placing his subject in the clear light and by working largely in flat tones? To get at the essential facts of a subject, and to set them down rapidly and precisely, so that all may understand them and be impressed by them, represent great mental power, and place Hals in the front rank of painters. Yet, as a man, he allowed himself to appear to the world an idle fellow, over-given to jollification, and so shiftless that in his old age he was dependent upon the city government for support. That he received it, however, and that his creditors were lenient with him, seem to show that his contemporaries recognized a greatness behind his intemperance and improvidence; and, when in his eighty-second year he died, he was buried beneath the choir of the Church of St. Bavon in Haarlem.

In great contrast to Hals's mode of living was Van Dyck's. He was early accustomed to Rubens's sumptuous establishment; and, when he visited Italy with letters of introduction from his master, lived in the palaces of his patrons, himself adopting such an elegant ostentation that he was spoken of as "the Cavalier Painter." After his return to Antwerp his patrons belonged to the rich and noble class, and his own style of living was modeled on theirs; so that, when at length in 1632 he received the appointment of court painter to Charles I of England, he maintained an almost princely establishment, and his house at Blackfriars was the resort of fashion. The last two years of his life were spent in traveling on the Continent with his young wife, the daughter of Lord Gowry, Lord Ruthven's son. His health, however, had been broken by excess of work, and he returned to London to die. He was buried in St. Paul's Cathedral.

He painted, in his younger days, many altarpieces, "full of a touching religious feeling and enthusiasm"; but his fame rests mainly upon his portraits. In these he invented a style of elegance and refinement which became a model for the artists of the seventeenth and eighteenth centuries, corresponding, as it did, to the genteel luxuriousness of the court life of the period.

On the other hand, during the latter century Hals was thought little of, even in Holland, whose artists forsook the traditions of their own school and went astray after other gods—to wit, those of the Italian "grand style." It was not until well on in the nineteenth century that artists, returning to the truth of nature, discovered that Hals had been one of the greatest seers of the truth and one of its most virile interpreters. To-day he is honored for these qualities, and also for the fact that, out of all the Dutch pictures of the seventeenth century now so much admired, his are the most characteristic of the Dutch race and of the art which it produced.

CHAPTER XIV

REMBRANDT VAN RIJN BARTOLOMÉ ESTÉBAN MURILLO
1606-1669 1618-1682
Dutch School Spanish School of Andalusia

AS remarkable as the sudden uprising of a native art in Holland is the fact that it almost immediately reached its maturity, and, in the person of Rembrandt, produced one of the foremost artists of the world. He is one of the few great original men who stand alone. You cannot trace his genius to the influence of his time or to the work of other men who preceded him; nor, although he had followers, could any of them do what he did. He shines out in solitary bigness.

So it is not so much for comparison as for convenience in continuing our method of study, that I couple his name with Murillo's. Yet, having done so, we may find that they have something in common; a common center round which Murillo makes a small circle, Rembrandt an infinitely larger one. Each was a realist as well as an idealist; both painted light, and both translated religious themes into the dialect of the common people.

In his *Children of the Shell,* Murillo chose for subject the infancy of the Christ and St. John; the latter represented with a staff-like cross in token of his future career as preacher and pilgrim, while the application of the legend upon the scroll, " Ecce Agnus Dei," to the little Saviour is further illustrated by the introduction of a lamb. These symbols were prescribed by the church's tradition; Murillo put them in partly because his patrons demanded them, and partly because he himself was a devout Christian; but in other respects he is influenced by a man's love of little children and an artist's desire to create a beautiful picture. He takes for his type the warm-skinned, supple, brown-eyed children that played half-naked in the bright sunshine of Seville; their beauty of limb and grace of movement being characteristic of their free, open-air life. This part of the picture is real enough; a bit of nature translated into paint. But the act in which they are engaged, and the way in which it is represented, suggest an idealization of the facts; and this ideal feeling is increased by the soft vaporous light in which the little bodies are bathed; a kind of light " that never was on sea or land," a product of the artist's imagination.

The people of Murillo's own day loved his work because they could enter into it and understand it, for it portrayed in its virgins, children, and saints the type of figures with which they were familiar, with the sweet gentleness of sentiment that reflected the dispositions of this Southern race. For by that time the darkness of the Inquisition had cleared away; the Jesuits were winning the devotion of the people by beautifying the churches; monks and nuns had abandoned the rigor of self-inflicted torture, and were seeking by lives of kindliness and by holy contemplation to have visions of the divine love. Pictures were demanded that should represent this happier change. Elizabeth, the saintly Queen of Hungary, engaged in doing acts of mercy to the sick and poor; St. Anthony of Padua, the holy Franciscan monk, blessed with an ecstatic vision of the Child-Christ in the midst of a choir of infant angels; the Holy Family, poor peasant folk, but radiant with heavenly light and love—these, and the like, Murillo painted, and in such a way that the people of his day could recognize the counterparts of themselves, men and women and children, familiar to their daily experience, and yet lifted up above them in a light far lovelier than that of their own beautiful sunshine—a spiritual light. So they loved his work; and for the same reason—that it is of earth and yet above it, humanly natural and yet spiritually ideal—it has continued to be loved.

Rembrandt's picture, on the other hand, *The Sortie of the Banning Cock Company*, did not satisfy the men for whom it was painted. It is one of the kind known as a "corporation picture": an aggregation of portraits. Sometimes it was the council of one of the trade guilds; sometimes the governing body or the surgical force of a hospital; very often one of the numerous militia companies, that wished to be commemorated. Franz Hals painted many of these pictures; so also did another popular Dutch painter, Bartholomeus van der Helst. Both these artists gave great satisfaction to their patrons; for they took care that each member, who had paid his quota toward the expense of the picture, should have his portrait clearly delineated. It was, after all, a correct concession to a quite reasonable vanity. Besides, the whole tendency of Dutch art, as we have seen, was toward direct and intimate portraiture, and the racial tendency of the Dutch mind toward straightforwardness and clarity and precision in all things. The people, on the one hand fighting against the encroachments of the ocean and the invasion of the Spaniard, and on the other extending their trade over the world, were living very real lives, and their artists as a body were realists.

Rembrandt had proved himself a realist when he painted, in his twenty-sixth year, *The Anatomy Lesson,* in which the famous Dr. Tulp is represented conducting a lecture in dissection before a class of surgeons. It was a work of marvelous realism, and immediately secured for the young painter a number of commissions from those who wished to have their portraits painted, and caused his studio to be sought by students eager to learn from him. It made him famous.

Ten years later he was asked to paint this picture of Captain Banning Cock's company of musketeers. With the assurance of genius, he dared to depart from the usual way of representing such a subject. Instead of grouping the company in their guild-house, he represents them issuing from it, as if the occasion were a shooting-match. The captain, dressed in black with a red scarf, is giving directions to his lieutenant, whose costume is yellow with a white scarf around his waist; the drummer is sounding the call, which arouses the barking of a dog; the ensign shakes loose the big flag; a sergeant stretches out his arm as he gives an order; picket-men are hurrying out, a musketeer is loading his gun, a boy running beside him with the powder-horn;

and in the midst of the group, "as if," says Mr. John La Farge, "to give a look of chance and suddenness to the scene, is the figure of a little girl, strangely enough with a dead fowl strung from her waist." She appears to be engaged in some form of play with a boy, who has a leaf-crowned helmet on his head and is turning his back so that it is his leg which is chiefly visible.

Rembrandt, in fact, chose an instant of sudden and general animation, and by his genius made it thrill with the appearance of actual life. The picture, as originally painted, was larger than at present; but when it was removed to the Amsterdam town hall it did not fit the space on the wall and was cut down in size, a slice being taken off the right side and the bottom. This barbarous treatment has particularly interfered with the relation of the two front figures to the rest of the group, giving them too much an appearance of stepping out of the picture, whereas in its original size we may be sure the balance of the composition was complete.

To draw its various parts into one supreme impression Rembrandt abandoned the custom of setting all the figures in a clear, even light, and welded the whole together in an elaborate pattern of light and shade. This had become darkened by dirt and smoke, so that the picture was taken by French writers of the eighteenth century for a night scene, and styled *Patrouille de Nuit,* and Sir Joshua Reynolds followed their error by calling it *The Night Watch.* Subsequent cleaning, however, has proved that, notwithstanding some darkening of the color as the result of time, the picture represents a daylight scene. The company streams out of the dark doorway into bright sunlight, which plays upon it with innumerable accidental effects.

In such action of light, with its glints of surprise and manifold variations, there is joy to the artist, especially to one whose mind was so alive to what is momentary and unusual as Rembrandt's; a mystery, also, and abundance of mental and artistic suggestion, in the varying depths of shadow. Moreover, it may have seemed to him the most effectual way of securing the unity and momentariness of the impression. If every part had been shown with equal distinctness, it would have been impossible for the spectator to receive from it the instantaneous shock of wonder and surprise that he now experiences. His attention, instead of being immediately focused, would have been scattered over a hundred details. As it is, he sees the picture as a whole, and, before he begins to consider the parts, receives a single, profound impression.

This original treatment, so entirely at variance with traditions of corporation pictures, cost Rembrandt the patronage of the civic guards, and his commissions fell off from that time forward.

That Rembrandt was wrong to paint this particular picture in this way is also the opinion of the great French critic and artist, Eugène Fromentin, because the occasion was not a suitable one for putting into practice this peculiar method of lighting. Fromentin's argument, briefly summarized, is as follows:

Rembrandt was compact of two natures: one, the realist; the other, the idealist. At times he was impressed with the facts of things—the main, essential facts of a landscape or of a human personality; and, whether he is painting with the brush or drawing on copper with the etching-needle, the result is a wonderful synthesis or summary of the truth of actual appearance. At other times it is the truth beneath the surface, the invisible truth, that fascinates him; and in his attempts to express this he discovered for himself a new treatment of light. It was something different from the chiaroscuro, or arrangement of light and shade, which other artists used for the threefold purpose of giving substance to form, of producing an effect of aërial perspective, and of making the picture brilliant and impressive in pattern. He, too, used this method of chiaroscuro, but he carried it much farther than any other artist before or since, so that it is called, after his name, the Rembrandtesque treatment. He immersed everything in a bath of shadow, plunging into it even the light itself; he surrounded centers of light with waves of darkness. The darkness itself in his pictures is transparent; you can peer into it and discover half-concealed forms; everything provokes curiosity; there is mystery; and it acts upon the mind, so that the real and the imaginary become mingled. It is at once reality and a dream.

Rembrandt discovered for himself this power of making chiaroscuro a source of emotional feeling; but he went even farther. Light exists independent of the objects it shines upon, and he tried to paint only with the help of light, to draw only with light, to make the light itself express ideas and emotions. To succeed it was necessary to make great sacrifices; to relinquish much that was dear to his other self, the realist: the strong drawing and firm modeling, the magnificent certainty of effect. These are qualities that might be looked for in a picture of citizen-soldiers, such as *The Sortie of the Banning Cock Company,* but are absent from it. It was required of him by the circumstances that he should paint a reality; what he produced was a vision of light glimmering like phosphorescence on darkness.

This picture was Rembrandt's first big effort to embody his new conception of the possibilities of painting, and his whole after life was a struggle to reconcile the two sides of his nature, culminating in 1661, eight years before his death, in that triumph of mingled realism and idealism, *The Syndics of the Cloth-workers' Guild.* And in many single portraits are revealed the wonderful resources of this treatment of light and shade for the purpose of expression. The heads are enveloped in darkness, out of which emerge the features, the eyes especially arresting the attention. Through the depth and poignancy of their gaze one seems to look into the very soul of the subject. This faculty of profound suggestion, the power of a man who sees into the heart of things and makes others partake of his imagination, appears also in his etchings.

Rembrandt is recognized as the Prince of Etchers, by reason both of the range and quality of his prints, which include landscapes, portraits, Biblical subjects, and studies of beggars and of other picturesque specimens of poverty. Sometimes they are executed with extraordinary economy of means, a few lines in opposition to the spaces of paper giving the impression of a

SORTIE OF THE BANNING COCK COMPANY   RIJKS MUSEUM, AMSTERDAM   REMBRANDT

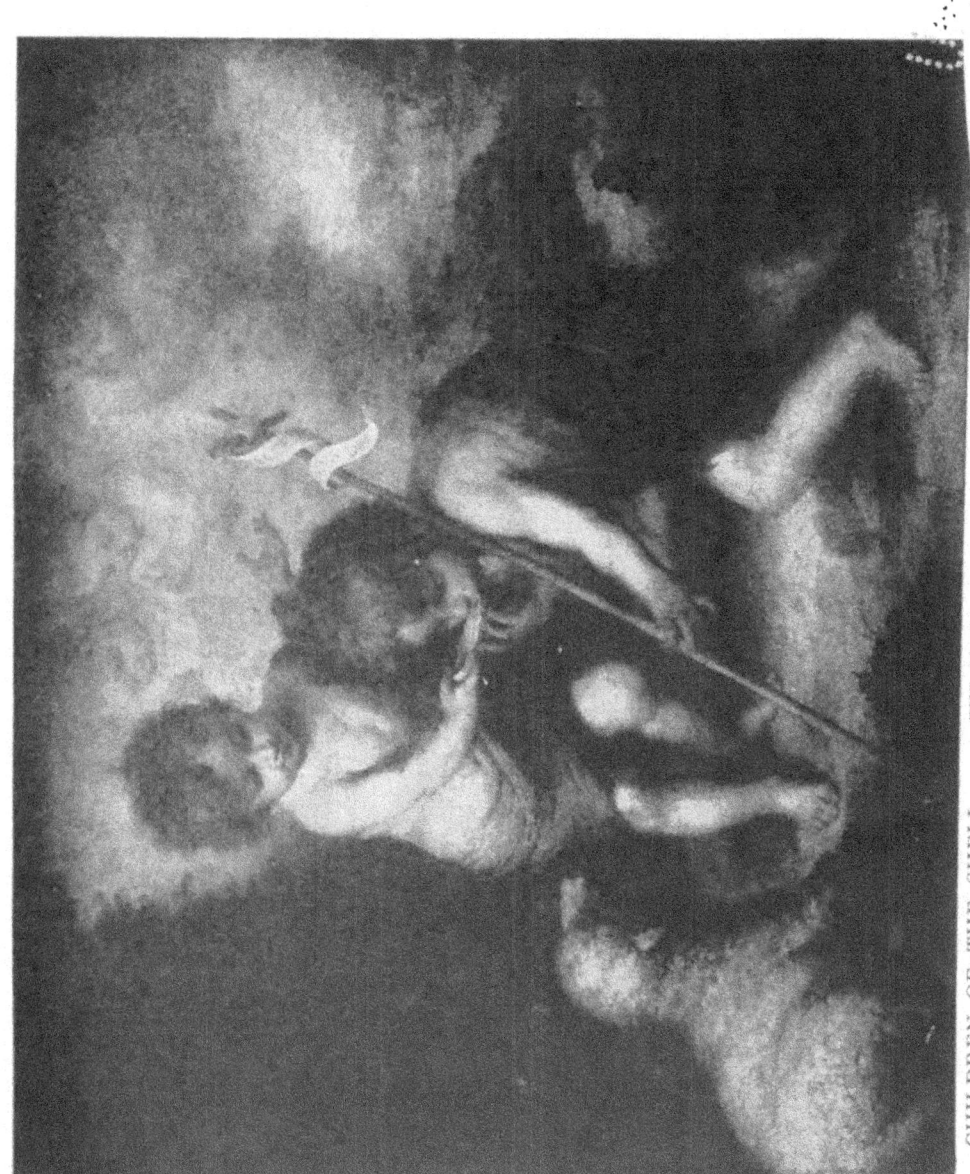

CHILDREN OF THE SHELL   THE PRADO, MADRID
MURILLO

far-reaching landscape flooded with sunshine; sometimes they are worked up into richness of texture, or again are elaborate creations of light and shade.

Etching being an art which demands certainty of brain and hand and yet admits of so much illusion, we may understand why throughout his life Rembrandt, realist and idealist, was so fond of it. The method is briefly this. A polished copper plate is covered with a film of melted wax, which is then blackened with smoke by holding it over a lamp or candle. The artist with a needle, or any correspondingly sharp-pointed instrument, draws his design in the wax; thus baring the copper where the lines appear. He then plunges his plate into a bath of nitric acid, which bites into the parts exposed, the surfaces still covered with the wax resisting the eating in of the acid. When the plate has been bitten and the wax removed, a roller, covered with printing-ink, is passed over it, that the ink may settle into the channels. The surface is then cleaned, and dampened paper is laid over it and pressed down in a printing-press, so that the paper sucks up the ink from the hollows of the lines. This actual process of printing is the same as is used in the case of steel-engravings; but in the latter the lines have been dug out by a sharp instrument in the hard metal; whereas in the case of etching the hand moves freely and easily through the soft wax; and, further, instead of the groove in the metal being sharp and hard from the tool, it is soft and furred by the insinuating tooth of the acid. An etching, therefore, is richer in its blacks, with a more generous contrast of light and shade, and at the same time, if the artist chooses to make it so, more delicate. It is, of all the methods of art, the one which responds most immediately to the volition of the artist; it is preëminently the artist's art. That Rembrandt should have practised it throughout his life, and have attained in it a proficiency which no other artist has surpassed, is of itself sufficient to place him in the foremost rank of art. The artist who has most nearly approached him in scope and excellence as an etcher is Whistler.

We started with a comparison of Murillo and Rembrandt, and have discovered, if I have told the story right, that the smaller thing, which Murillo attempted, he did to the satisfaction of his contemporaries and of posterity; whereas Rembrandt, striving for something infinitely greater, had his successes and his failures, was misunderstood by the people of his day, and during the century which followed, when the influence of Italian painting, spreading over Europe, had penetrated even into Holland, was neglected. The story of their work corresponds with the story of their lives.

Murillo's proceeded smoothly and pleasantly. He was born in Seville, the birthplace also of Velasquez. At the age of eleven he was apprenticed to an uncle who was a painter, and his gentle nature and diligence soon made him a favorite with his master and his fellow-students. He managed to live by painting little pictures of sacred subjects on linen; offering them for sale at the *feria,* or weekly market. It was the custom to bring paints and brushes to the fair, so that patrons could have the pictures altered to suit their taste; and, as he sat among the stalls, he had plenty of opportunity of studying and sketching the city urchins and beggar boys that lay or frolicked in the sunshine. He afterward painted many of these, and they are among his best work, so true to life and vigorously executed. In this way two years passed.

Then there returned to Seville a fellow-student of Murillo's, who had exchanged painting for soldiering and been with the army in Flanders. But the sight of the works of Rubens and Van Dyck had revived his love of painting, and he had visited London to study under the latter artist. He was now back in Seville with some copies of Van Dyck's work, and with so many stories of what he had seen, that Murillo was stirred with the ambition to go to Rome. He trudged on foot to Madrid, and called on his fellow-townsman, Velasquez, to secure letters of introduction. The great artist received him kindly, and, being struck with his earnestness, invited him to stay in his own house. Velasquez was called away in attendance on the king, and during his absence Murillo made copies of paintings in the royal galleries by Ribera, Van Dyck, and Velasquez himself. The latter, on his return, was so pleased with the progress the young man had made, that he advised him to go to Rome; but by this time Murillo had no desire to leave his country. He stayed in Madrid for further study, and then returned to Seville after three years' absence.

One of the mendicant brothers of the little Franciscan monastery had collected a sum of money, which the friars determined to expend upon some paintings for their cloister. The amount was too small to attract the well-known artists of the city, so with much compunction they gave the commission to the young, untried Murillo. It was the opportunity he wanted; and he made such good use of it that his reputation was at once established. Henceforth his time was fully occupied in decorating churches and in painting for private individuals; he was admitted into the best society, made a rich marriage, became the head of the School of Seville, and all the time was beloved of the people.

A fall from a painter's scaffold cut short his activity. Incapacitated from work, he lingered for two years, spending much of his time in prayer in the church of Santa Cruz, beneath Campana's painting of *The Descent from the Cross;* and beneath this, by his request, he was buried.

The date of Rembrandt's birth is doubtful, being variously assigned to 1606, 1607, and 1608. His father, Harmen van Rijn (Harmen of the Rhine), owned a mill on the banks of the Rhine at Leyden. When quite young the boy was sent to the Latin school in order that, as Orless, the best authority upon his early life, puts it, " he might in the fullness of time be able to serve his native city and the Republic with his knowledge." However, his inclination toward drawing was so marked that his father placed him with Jacob van Swanenburch. Three years later he went to Amsterdam to study under Lastman, who had spent many years in Rome. But with him Rembrandt stayed only six months, and then returned to Leyden, " resolved," as Orless says, " to study and practise painting alone in his own fashion." He stayed at home six years, working much from the members of his family, and frequently etching his own head, with various kinds of facial expression.

In 1630 he moved to Amsterdam, which henceforth was to be the scene of his life. The city at that time had recovered from the shock of war and was rapidly growing in commercial prosperity and liberally encouraging the fine arts. For a time all went well with Rembrandt. *The Anatomy Lesson,* painted in 1632, had made him famous; commissions poured in and students flocked to his studio. Two years later he married a young lady of property, Saskia van Uylenborch, to whom he was deeply attached, and whose portrait he painted or etched eighteen times, besides using her as a model in various pictures. He was able now to indulge his taste for beautiful things; was a generous buyer of other artists' work, and filled his handsome house in the Breedstraat with treasures. Ten years of domestic happiness and magnificent production followed his marriage, and then, in 1642, the clouds gathered.

In that year he was involved in disputes, as we have seen, over *The Sortie of the Banning Cock Company;* but, worse than that, his beloved Saskia died, leaving an infant son, Titus. In the emptiness of his home and heart, the great artist buried himself with ever deeper purpose and grander energy in his work. It is characteristic of this sad time that his portraits of himself cease for six years. Then appears an etching, in which he no longer represents himself in splendid clothes, with fierce mustache and flowing hair; but as a simple citizen. His hair and mustache are trimmed; a large hat covers his head, his tunic is unadorned; he is seated at a window, drawing, but lifts his head and gazes full at the spectator with his piercing eyes. During this time he owed much to the sympathy of the burgomaster Jan Six, a scholar and connoisseur; and now the burgomaster's mansion, the celebrated Six Gallery at Amsterdam, owes much of its fame to the examples which it contains by Rembrandt.

In 1656 he was overtaken by financial troubles, due to legal disputes with the trustees of his wife's will, to his liberality toward his family in Leyden, and to his own love of buying works of art and his lack of business ability. He was declared a bankrupt, his house was sold, and his treasures were dispersed at auction; and, by the time that his creditors were satisfied, there was nothing left for him. But his devotion to his art was unabated; the years which followed were distinguished by a series of noble paintings and etchings, among them *The Syndics*. It is good to know that he had friends, and that his last years, though contracted in means, were comfortable. In the last portrait of himself, painted a year before his death, he has depicted his face wrinkled by time and care, but laughing heartily. It sums up the triumph of the man and the artist over evil fortune.

After his death he was soon forgotten. Through the eighteenth century Dutch painters, like those of other countries, turned to Italy for inspiration; Rembrandt's homely naturalism, representing, for example, the Bible scenes, peopled with rude peasants instead of fine men and graceful women in classic robes, was scorned as vulgar; his marvels of light, condemned for the " slovenly conduct of his pencil "; his portraits, that search into the souls of his subjects, despised for their "laborious, ignorant diligence." He was neglected, while Murillo continued to be abundantly admired.

Now, however, when painting has shaken itself free from conventional traditions and once more turned to nature, Murillo is esteemed less highly, and Rembrandt has been restored to his place among the giants.

CHAPTER XV

JACOB VAN RUISDAEL
1625 (?)–1682
Dutch School

NICOLAS POUSSIN
1593–1665
Classical School of France

AT this point of our survey of the field of painting France swings into the line of vision. There had been other French painters before Poussin, but the latter was the greatest up to his time, and has had so important an influence upon subsequent French art, that in our selection of prominent names he comes first.

When we compare his *Et Ego in Arcadia* with Ruisdael's *Waterfall*, we are conscious at once of a vast difference of feeling, both in the attitude of each painter's mind toward nature and in the impression produced upon our own. We experience before Ruisdael's a sense of strenuousness and sadness, very different to the serenity and idyllic sweetness of Poussin's. We are face to face, in the one case with the realities of life, in the other with the pleasant dream of a world that only exists in the imagination. Yet Poussin composed the surroundings of his figures from real landscape—that of Italy; probably, however, not from one scene, but with a selection from many; while Ruisdael's landscape, which has such an air of stern reality, was actually borrowed—in its general character, at any rate—from the work of another painter, Allart van Everdingen.

It will occur to you, perhaps, as strange that a Dutch painter of the seventeenth century should have borrowed from any one instead of studying straight from nature; just as it may have struck you that the scenery of the *Waterfall* is not suggestive of Holland.

The fact is that Ruisdael, during his first and, as many consider, his best period, painted pictures thoroughly Dutch in character, studies of the landscape round his native city of Haarlem, showing a marked fondness for massed clouds and warm sunshine. But they met with little encouragement from his own countrymen, and he moved to Amsterdam. In the latter city was established Allart van Everdingen, who had begun as a painter of the sea, taking trips on the Baltic for the better study of his subject. But on one occasion the vessel had been driven by storm on to the coast of Norway; and, while he waited for a chance of getting home, he made a number of sketches of the country, with its rocky shore and pines and waterfalls. Returned to Holland, he used this material for pictures, which, partly because of their unusualness, were very popular. Ruisdael, then, finding his own work neglected, determined to give the public what they seemed to want, and out of his own head invented landscapes similar in character to Everdingen's. Their very wildness and sternness may have attracted him, fitting in with the sadness and gloom that were gathering over his own spirit; for this picture and all the productions of his later life are imprinted with melancholy. And well they might be; for he was evidently of so little account in his own day, that the date of his birth is doubtful, and scarcely more is recorded of his life than that, after working unsuccessfully in Haarlem, he moved to Amsterdam, and thence returned to his native city in poverty, to die in an almshouse.

In respect of sadness he is akin to Rembrandt, who also lived in the company of sorrow; and these two artists strike the only note of intense feeling in the Dutch art of the seventeenth century, which, as a whole, is distinguished by its equable and contented attitude toward life. Yet in the intensity of Rembrandt there is no bitterness; and even in this landscape of Ruisdael's we may discover a strain of tenderness. For, contrasted with the inhospitable wildness of the coast and the restless tumult of water are the quiet composure of the little spire nestling amid the trees, and the gentle evidences of quiet life in the string of cattle passing down to drink. But the noblest feature of the scene is the fine sky with its masses of cloud. The mountainous land and waterfall may have been invented or borrowed; but this at least has been studied by Ruisdael from the nature of his own land. And the skies of Holland are proverbially grand, partly because the prevailing course of clouds is from the west, so that huge volumes of vapor come continually rolling in from the North Sea, and partly because the land, being uniformly level, affords least obstruction to the vast appearance of the sky and to the gathering and passage of the clouds. None of the Dutchmen of the seventeenth century had been so impressed with the vastness and buoyant force and freedom of the sky as Ruisdael; in which respect he anticipated the achievements of modern Dutch artists, who have found in the skies of Holland an inexhaustible theme.

I think it is capable of demonstration that every landscape-painter of powerful imagination and serious poetic feeling has reveled in the representation of the sky. It is as if his spirit leaps from the definiteness and circumscribed limits of the earth into the limitless, unexplorable vastness of the air. The ground is local, tethering him by the foot to what man can examine and know; the sky, however, at some point ceases to be merely an envelope to the earth and mingles with that ether in which the whole universe swims. May we not believe that Ruisdael, compelled to fashion an unreal, or, at least, an alien land, to tempt his customers, satisfied both his love of country and the sincerity of his study of nature by the ardor with which he threw himself into the representations of the skies? Nor is there anything unduly sentimental in such a belief, for the artist is also human, and has his pride in himself and his preferences, and does best what best he loves.

And now let us turn again to the picture by Poussin. " I too have been in Arcadia "; in that sweet spot, undisturbed by nature's violence or the tumult and clang of human life. It exists nowhere, and yet everywhere is to be found. It was Poussin's fortune to discover it.

He was born of a noble but poor family in Normandy, that hardy country from which William went forth to conquer England, and, some eight hundred years later, Millet, to conquer, after a long-drawn-out conflict, the appreciation of his own countrymen. Poussin learned painting in the local town of Les Andelys, and then proceeded to Paris, where he spent much of his time in drawing from casts and in copying prints after Raphael and the latter's pupil, Giulio Romano. By the time that he was able to visit Rome, he was in his thirtieth year, a man of matured mind, nourished upon the antique and upon the suave, balanced style of Raphael; with a standard, therefore, fixed, and a mind capable of doing its own thinking.

It was well for him that it was so, since the Italy of his time was in its decadence. The last of the great masters had died with Tintoretto. They had been succeeded by many clever painters, but by none of commanding genius. On the one hand were Guido Reni and Carlo Dolci, saturated with sentimentality; on the other, Salvator Rosa, following Caravaggio in depicting what was impetuously powerful, and yet again Tiepolo, a brilliant and vivacious decorator. Poussin, amid this uncertain flux of energy, attached himself to Domenichino, a painter of much strength but poor as a colorist. Meanwhile he pursued his study of sculptured low-reliefs, practising modeling as well as drawing.

The effect of this is apparent in the grouping and drawing of the figures in this picture, for they are arranged as in a low-relief: the woman slightly in advance of the two stooping figures, while the fourth figure is only slightly behind these. The three planes in which the figures stand are flattened as far as possible into one; and the figures are relieved by the contrasts of light and shade, instead of being detached in their separate en-

THE WATERFALL   NATIONAL GALLERY, LONDON   JACOB VAN RUISDAEL

SHEPHERDS IN ARCADY   LOUVRE, PARIS   NICOLAS POUSSIN

velopes of atmosphere. The method, in fact, is a sculptor's rather than a painter's.

This is the first point to notice; and the second is the influence of Raphael. The latter can be traced in the serene composure of the whole composition, obtained by the perfect balance of the full and empty spaces, and by the harmonious grace of the lines that oppose and repeat one another with studied calculation, as well as by the grace of gesture and suave refinement of expression that characterize the figures. Both these influences combined to make the rendering of the subject an ideal one; and, except in the superior tact of taste displayed by Poussin, do not distinguish his pictures radically from those of the many other followers of Raphael and the antique. But here steps in a third influence, that of the Italian landscape; and, by combining the latter with the other two, Poussin originated something new, and became a model for other painters, establishing a principle of perfection that has served as a standard for French painting down to the present day.

Before his time the landscape was subordinated to the figures; even Titian, whose landscapes are so beautiful, felt them primarily as backgrounds. But in this picture of Poussin's it would be hard to decide whether the landscape accompanies the figures or the figures the landscape. In fact, both ingredients are of equal importance.

The love of landscape is particularly characteristic of northern nations, and it would seem that Poussin had it, but not in the way in which the Dutchmen felt it. They loved the landscape for its own sake; Poussin, for the way it could be made to contribute to the feeling of his figures. The latter were mostly classical in feeling; and thus he became the father of the so-called " classical " or " heroic " landscape. We can understand how it happened.

The visitor to Italy is apt to find that the Italian landscape makes a unique appeal. In every direction it seems to suggest pictures, presenting itself to the eye in ready-made compositions; moreover, it is continually a pictorial setting to the towns and villas, and, in the neighborhood of Rome especially, to the antique ruins. Many of us must have felt this; and, also, that there is a curious relation between the pictures in the Italian galleries and the landscape outside; that the latter, in fact, with its inexhaustible suggestion of stately compositions, must have had a great influence upon the imagination of Italian artists in the direction of helping to suggest the " grand style " of Italian painting.

To this Italy, then, of pictorial landscape came Poussin, already full of the spirit of Raphael and of classic sculpture, and with a fresh eye that recognized a kinship of feeling between the landscape and the style of figure-work which he had learned to admire. He had discovered a country in which the classical figures and those of Raphael could move and have their being. If we turn to the picture we shall feel, I think, how completely the persons belong to the scene in which we find them: they are naturally at home in it; they are part of it; it is Arcady, and they are Arcadians.

Strolling along in the pleasant sunshine, the woman and the three shepherds have chanced upon a tomb.

There are traces of an inscription on it; and the father, stooping to rub away the lichen and moss, reveals the words, "Et Ego in Arcadia." I too, a nameless one, crumbling forgotten within these stones, I too have lived and loved in this region of innocent delight, where man is in perfect accord with his surroundings; rising and lying down with the sun, and nourished upon the bosom of mother earth; mind and body healthy, since conduct and desire are in conformity with nature. It is the country of youth, eternally young in an old world, wherein the children sport and happy lovers stray, and even the aged may linger if they have kept some freshness in their souls. Correggio and Raphael had lived there; and it is the latter, maybe, who calls from the tomb to welcome Poussin to the charmed spot.

We have thus examined the character and feeling of Poussin's work, and found that it was not originally inspired by nature, but founded on a direct study of the antique and upon Raphael's interpretation of the same; and that, when it did receive an inspiration direct from nature, the latter was not used naturally, but to harmonize with the ideal conception of the figures. Let us now inquire how it was that his work became the source of what is called the "classic" and "academic" in French art.

We must remember that the French race has a strong infusion of Latin blood, and that it had been brought under the influence of the legal and social system of the Romans. At the break-up of the empire Italy was overrun with foreigners, and the character of its people became changed, the continuity of its institutions and traditions broken. These, however, survived in France; and the French, much more even than the Italians, are the inheritors of those qualities and ideals which made up the greatness of the Roman people.

Briefly, they comprised a fondness for system and a capacity for organization; a tendency to skilful adaptation rather than to originality; less regard for ideas than for fundamental principles, and especially for those of construction, for what is technically called the "architectonics." The Romans were great builders, and reduced the art of construction to a system, so that the major part of it could be carried out by unskilled labor. With this intention, they laid special stress upon form, logical relationship between the parts and the whole, and the dignity of the mass.

Let us see how the inheritance of these qualities by the French affected the history of their painting. In Poussin's time the throne of France was occupied by Louis XIV, whom the court painter Lebrun was flatteringly depicting in his paintings and tapestries as a Roman conqueror. Full of the Roman spirit, he played the *rôle* of an organizer. To perpetuate the purity of the French language, he established the Institute of France, composed of forty members. To this day the selection of these "Immortals" is determined less by their contribution to thought than by the perfection of their style,—by their mastery, in fact, of the architectonics of their craft. With the same zeal for system and organization, Louis founded an academy of painting and sculpture and an academy in Rome for the instruction of French artists. These, being official institutions, needed a system of principles. This was discovered in the art of Poussin.

In it was exemplified a diligent regard for the architectonics; a careful building up of parts so as to produce a balanced and harmonious whole; a preference for ideal or abstract perfection of line and form and spacing over the representation of character or sentiment; an avoidance of what is original in favor of a tactful reproduction of ancient models; and, in general, the preëminence of style over subject-matter. Poussin's color was a weak point; but that mattered little, for color—both the skill in it and the appreciation of it—is an affair of individual temperament, whereas line and form and composition are fundamental. It was on the side where painting touches sculpture and architecture, not in its special province of color, light, and atmosphere, that a standard of excellence could be established.

Granted the usefulness of establishing a standard, no better one could have been devised. For, although, as we shall discover, the existence of a fixed official standard will tend toward dry formalism, and almost every painter that achieves greatness will do so by breaking away from the rigidity of the academic style, yet the advantage of the system will continue. Its maintenance will be justified by the very high general average of skill that it insures.

It is Poussin's title to a place in history that he was the father of this classic or academic system, which has made the École des Beaux Arts in Paris the greatest training-school of art in the modern world.

CHAPTER XVI

MEINDERT HOBBEMA   CLAUDE GELLÉE *(called LORRAIN)*
1638 (?)–1709   *1600–1682*
Dutch School   *Classical School of France*

THE village of Middelharnis is one of the places that lay claim to be the birthplace of Hobbema, the town of Koeverden and the cities of Haarlem and Amsterdam being the others. This picture, *The Avenue,* gives us a clear idea of the approach to it, as it appeared in 1689, when Hobbema is supposed to have painted it. It is a bit of portraiture of nature, whereas Claude's picture—you might guess it from the title, *Landing of Cleopatra at Tarsus*—illustrates the use of nature to build up a classic composition; the borrowing from many sources, and the arrangement of the details to produce a scene which the artist's imagination has conceived to be ideally beautiful.

We ought to be able to enjoy the one and the other, but we do not feel toward both in the same way. It is very probable that we shall begin by preferring the Claude. If so, it is largely because the lines and masses of its composition are more seductive. The hulls, masts, and spars of the shipping on one side balance the lines of the architecture on the other, and between them is a gently dipping curve of faint forms, which separate the luminous quiet of the open sky from the glittering movement of the water and the busy animation of the figures. Besides the actual beauty of balance between the full and empty spaces of the composition, we get the added enjoyment of contrast between a sense of activity and a still deeper one of permanence and repose. Everything has been nicely calculated to stir our imagination pleasurably. We find ourselves thinking that if there is no spot on earth like this, it is a pity; that there ought to be one, and that the artist has made it possible. In fact, he has created it; and thereby we are the happier.

We are little concerned with Cleopatra, and scarcely care to distinguish which of the figures is Mark Antony's. The feeling is that a shore which was once a ragged ending of the land, where the sea began, has been made a stately approach of terraces, leading up to noble buildings; that in these, as in the shipping, man's creative power is apparent; that the scene is an improvement upon nature.

Now we turn to the Hobbema. It is a composition of vertical lines contrasted with horizontal; a much harsher arrangement of spaces—of nature unadorned, we might almost say; or, at any rate, taken as the artist found it. We are disposed to feel, perhaps, that he was lacking in imagination, and that his work, as compared with the ideal beauty of Claude's, is homely and uninteresting; that, to use an expression of the eighteenth century, when writers and artists prided themselves on having a " pretty fancy," it is " pedestrian "; that it does n't soar, but walks afoot like the common people.

Certainly Hobbema was not inventive, like Claude; he did not devise or try to construct an ideal Holland out of his imagination. But imagination may display itself also by its sympathy with, and insight into, things as they are; and it was this kind of imagination that Hobbema possessed. He loved the country-side, studied it as a lover, and has depicted it with such intimacy of truth, that the road to Middelharnis seems as real to us to-day as it did over two hundred years ago to the artist. We see the poplars, with their lopped stems, lifting their bushy tops against that wide, high sky which floats over a flat country; full of billowy clouds, as the sky near the North Sea is apt to be. Deep ditches skirt the road, which drain and collect the water for purposes of irrigation, and later on will join some deeper, wider canal, for purposes of navigation. We get a glimpse on the right of patient perfection of gardening, where a man is pruning his grafted fruit-trees; farther on, a group of substantial farm-buildings. On the opposite side of the road stretches a long, flat meadow, or " polder," up to the little village which nestles so snugly around its tall church tower; the latter fulfilling also the purpose of a beacon, lit by night, to guide the wayfarer on sea and land: a scene of tireless industry, comfortable prosperity, and smiling peace, snatched alike from the encroachments of the ocean and from the devastation of a foreign foe, by a people as rugged and aspiring as those poplars, as buoyant in their self-reliance as the clouds. Pride and love of country breathe through the whole scene; and we may be dead to some very wholesome instincts if we ourselves do not feel drawn, on the one hand, toward its sweet and intimate simplicity, and, on the other, toward the fearless matter-of-factness of its composition.

THE AVENUE, MIDDELHARNIS, HOLLAND   MEINDERT HOBBEMA

NATIONAL GALLERY, LONDON

THE LANDING OF CLEOPATRA AT TARSUS   CLAUDE LORRAIN
LOUVRE, PARIS

HOBBEMA—CLAUDE LORRAIN

Indeed, if we have entered into the spirit of it, we may find that this picture, as well as Claude's, has its ideal beauty: if by this term we understand that kind of beauty which is distinguished by the idea revealed in it. In other words, it is not only imaginary subjects which may be ideal: there may also be an idealization of facts. Their outward appearance may be so rendered as to make us feel also their underlying significance, the soul, as it were, within them. In this way a portrait may be idealized. I am not thinking for the moment of the kind of idealization indulged in by Van Dyck, who gave to all his sitters, men and women, an elegant refinement corresponding to the idea of elegance and refinement in himself. That is more like the kind of idealization in Claude's picture. But let us take the case of a portrait of your own mother. One painter may paint it so that anybody, comparing it with the original, will say it is a good likeness; whereas another may have the imagination to penetrate beneath the exterior of the woman and reproduce something of what you know of her as a mother. He gets at the soul of the face.

Similarly the portrait of a landscape may reproduce the sentiment which attracts one to the country-side; the love of the painter for it, the attachment of those who live in it, what it is to them as part of their lives. Such a landscape is in a measure ideal. The modern French have coined a phrase for it—*paysage intime;* for which I can find no better translation than "the well-known, well-loved country-side." They coined it to describe the kind of landscape that was painted by Rousseau, Dupré, Corot, and some other French artists who made their headquarters at the little village of Barbizon on the borders of the forest of Fontainebleau; and these men, as we shall see, were followers of Hobbema and the other Dutch artists who had lived two hundred years before.

Very little is known of Hobbema's life. He appears to have been born at Amsterdam in 1638, but, as we have seen, other towns claim to be his birthplace. It is probable that he was the pupil of his uncle, Jacob van Ruisdael, and certain that he lived in Amsterdam. He died poor; his last lodging being in the Roosegraft, the street in which Rembrandt, also poor, had died forty years before. His works were little appreciated in Holland until nearly a hundred years after his death, and most of them found their way to England.

Claude, on the contrary, enjoyed in his lifetime a European reputation. Yet his early life was modest enough. He was born of poor parents in the little village of Chamagne, near the right bank of the Moselle, in what is now the department of Vosges, but in 1600 was the duchy of Lorraine. His real name was Claude Gellée, but from his native country he received the name of Claude le Lorrain, or, more shortly, Claude Lorrain. It is supposed that as a child he was apprenticed to a pastry-cook, and, when the years of his apprenticeship were completed, set off with a party of pastry-cooks to Rome. The Lorrainers were famous in this capacity, and the young Claude had no difficulty in finding employment. He was engaged by a landscape-painter, Agostino Tassi, as cook and general housekeeper, with the privilege of cleaning his master's brushes. He gained from him, however, instruction in painting, and seems to have become his assistant. When he was twenty-five years old he revisited France and stayed two years, returning then to Italy, where the rest of his life was spent. On the journey back he fell in with Charles Errard, who was one of the original twelve members of the French Academy and was later employed in establishing the famous French school at Rome, and in 1666 was appointed its first director.

For many years Claude worked on diligently in a modest way, until, about his fortieth year, he attracted the attention of Cardinal Bentivoglio, who not only gave him commissions, but introduced him to the Pope, Urban VIII. The latter, intent on maintaining the temporal power of the church, was continually erecting fortifications, in which he did not spare the most precious monuments of antiquity. Hence arose a joke which played upon his name—he was a member of the famous Florentine family of the Barberini—"Quod non fecerunt barbari, fecerunt Barberini." But he was an excellent scholar and fond of pictures, and became very much attached to Claude. The rest of the artist's life is one of fame. The three popes who succeeded Urban were his patrons, as were the noblest families of Italy, while commissions came to him from his native land, from the Netherlands, Germany, Spain, and even far-off England.

Besides his paintings he left forty-four etchings. He also executed two hundred sketches in pen or pencil, washed in with brown or India ink, the high lights being brought out with touches of white. On the backs of them the artist noted the date on which the sketch was developed into a picture, and for whom the latter was intended. The story is that his popularity produced many imitators, and that he adopted this means to establish his proprietorship of the subject in each case. But the more probable theory regards these sketches as a record which the artist made in a general way of his work. He collected them into a volume, which, known as the *Liber Veritatis,* has been for more than a hundred years in the possession of the Dukes of Westminster. It was in rivalry of this book that the English painter, Turner, as we shall find, produced his book of drawings, which he called *Liber Studiorum.*

Claude, like that other French artist, Nicolas Poussin, who was seven years his senior, belonged to Italy rather than to France. Both introduced something new into the field of subject. Like Poussin, also, Claude conceived the idea of giving ideal or heroic beauty to the landscape, that it might correspond to the heroic incidents in which his figures were engaged. But he went a step further in the direction of pure landscape; making his figures of comparatively little importance, and concentrating his effort upon the ideal or heroic character of the landscape, into which also he incorporated the beauty of architecture. He was a close student of nature, sketched and painted in the open air, and, like his Dutch contemporary Cuyp, filled his skies with the appearance of real sunshine. But the use that he made of nature was unnatural.

Instead of being satisfied to paint it as it is, for its own sake, as Hobbema was, he felt, like Poussin, that the province of art was to improve upon it. So Poussin, more particularly through his figures, and Claude, through landscape, were the founders in French art of what is called the classic or academic motive, which would reject everything that is "common" or "vulgar," and paint only types as near as possible to perfection. In order to secure this in the case of a figure subject, it will be necessary to paint the head from one model, the body from another, the hands from another, and so on; or, at any rate, to copy any single model only in the parts which seem beautiful, while the others must be brought to perfection by the painter's skill. So, in the case of a landscape, the painter selects a morsel from this place, and others elsewhere, and puts together out of his head a composition that shall present an ideally beautiful arrangement of lines and masses. This exactly suited the taste of the times, in which Racine was writing classical tragedies and Le Nôtre was laying out the gardens of Versailles with combinations of grottoes, fountains, architecture, and landscape. The result was that Claude's pictures had an extraordinary popularity, which extended on into the eighteenth century and far into the following one. He was regarded as the greatest of landscape-painters.

When, however, Frenchmen, following the example of Constable in England, began to turn to nature directly, they, as he, discovered what Hobbema had done, and made his work the foundation of their own efforts; carrying, however, the truth to nature for its own sake even farther than he did. For, although Hobbema depicted the natural forms of trees and the appearances of the sky and of light, he did not reproduce the varied coloring of nature, confining his palette mostly to grays and browns and a certain sharp green. Nor had he the skill to paint real atmosphere or to make the trees move in it. Even in his pictures, close to nature as they are, there is visible a conventional method of representation; that is to say, a habit of painting according to a plan which he had discovered for himself rather than with a continually fresh eye for the various manifestations of nature. It was reserved for the painters of the nineteenth century to be the truer nature-students of the *paysage intime*.

CHAPTER XVII

JEAN ANTOINE WATTEAU　　WILLIAM HOGARTH
1684–1721　　　　　　　　　*1697–1764*
Eighteenth-Century School of France　*Early English School*

WATTEAU has been called the first French painter; Hogarth was certainly the first English one. The previous painters in England had been foreigners, such as Holbein, Rubens, Van Dyck, Lely, Kneller, visiting the country for a longer or shorter stay. Those preceding Watteau, while French by birth, were altogether foreign in their art. We have seen how the greatest of them, Nicolas Poussin and Claude, lived in Italy and based their respective styles on the study of classic and Italian art and landscape. On the other hand, Lebrun, a pupil of Vouet who had studied in Italy, occupied the position of painter in ordinary at the court of Louis XIV, elaborating vast compositions and designs dictated by the monarch's vanity and intended to extol his fame, representing him as a classic hero and always in the act of conquest. Despite the size of his canvases, Lebrun was not a great painter, and there was nothing distinctively French or original about his work. On the contrary, both these qualities appeared in Watteau, hence the assertion that he is the first of French painters. And this notwithstanding the fact that he was really of Flemish birth, a native of Valenciennes, which had recently, however, become a part of the French dominions.

In his case, as in Hogarth's, a new kind of art sprang into existence, full-grown almost from its birth; both eminently characteristic of their times; the one distinctly French, the other as unmistakably English. Also, it is extremely interesting to note that each artist was, in a greater or less degree, influenced by the sister art of the drama.

Let us try to get an understanding of these two men by first examining the examples of their work. *The Embarkation for Cythera*—the island near which Venus was fabled to have risen from the sea, especially dedicated to her worship—was painted by Watteau upon his admission to full membership in the French Academy when he was thirty-three years old. It caused a great sensation, being entirely different from the official classic standard maintained by the Academy,—"a rainbow-hued vision of beauty and grace, such as had not been seen since the golden days of the Venetian Renaissance,"—yet strangely in touch with the French spirit of its own day. For the Grand Monarch had been dead two years, succeeded by his great-grandson Louis XV, a child now seven years old; and under the regency of Philip, Duke of Orleans, the dreary formality of the old court had been replaced by the gaiety of the new. True, the country was plunged in misery, and the shadow of the terrible Revolution which was to burst in the next reign was already drawing near. But at court the people frisked and frolicked, like lambs unmindful of the butcher; pleasure and love-making were their occupations, and Watteau's picture represents the graceful side of all this, detached from its wickedness and inhumanity.

Look at the picture—the trees, the water, and the sky all seem real; so, too, the ladies and gentlemen in their rainbow-tinted silks and satins. Yet the scene is also unreal; part of a world in which there is no ugliness, no hunger, no need of work or self-denial; a dream of the poets of old Greece reclothed in the semblance of the eighteenth century. Nor is it only the presence of the cupids that touches this strain of unreality; wreathed, as they are, in joyous circles in mid-air, clinging about the masts of the vessel, or winging their flight through the shrubbery as they summon the human votaries of pleasure. For the gilded vessel is ready to set sail to the isle of happiness, lying somewhere in that dreamy distance; lovers are already aboard, and the rest are being urged to follow. A statue of Venus adorns the woodland spot; yet it is but a symbol of the joy that awaits these pleasure-seekers in the island of dreams— when they reach it.

For it is the beauty of what is not yet attained, of the unattainable, expressed in this picture, that is one of the sources of its poetic unreality; and another is the exquisite pattern of its composition—the spacing of the foreground and the trees against the sky; the rhythmic curving line of moving figures; the delicate varieties of light and shade; and in the original the brilliant harmony of color. All is too absolutely attuned to what is only beautiful to be real; and yet, to repeat what has been said above, its poetry is based on realism. For "Watteau has this note of a great artist, that as a foundation for his poetry, his dream, his idealism, he lays a constant and minute study of nature."

When Watteau was a lad in Valenciennes he was continually filling his mind with the appearances of things and practising his hand in drawing; especially absorbed on the occasion of the fairs, when the market-place was gay with booths, and mountebanks and actors vied with one another in their antics and gestures. He reached an extraordinary facility in representing figures in action. To this he added from his studies in the Louvre a perfection of coloring derived from Rubens, Titian, and Veronese.

During those days of the Regency the light French comedies were again in favor, and the Italian comedies, which had been banished from the old monarch's court, had been invited back. Once more in the salons and gardens of the Luxembourg sported Gilles (the Italian equivalent of Pierrot), Columbine, Harlequin, Pantaloon, the doctor of Bologna on his donkey, and Polichinello,—characters evolved by Italian wit out of their prototypes as played by the Roman mimes. Sometimes the players acted in dumb-show, at other times from written plays, and often with words improvised by themselves, but always with their Italian skill of expression by gesture and facial play, in which they have been rivaled only by French actors and by the Chinese and Japanese. Watteau on some occasions derived his subjects directly from the Italian comedy, as in his famous picture of *Gilles* in the Louvre; but in all his work the indirect influence is plainly visible.

His figures move through the scene as if they were

enacting a comedy: in the case of our present picture, a very elaborate spectacle, but of lightest touch; no emotion, only the daintiest play of fancy; yet in its artistic aspect most serious and accomplished. For Watteau was no trifler; an earnest and indefatigable worker; serious even to sadness, a man of frail physique; nervous, irritable, not fond of company; a looker-on at life, not a sharer in its joys, except in the joy of his own art; and when he painted this vision of loveliness he was already dying of consumption. Note also with regard to his figures that, on the one hand, except in the case of the *Gilles,* they are small. Therefore we are not concerned with them individually and intimately, but only in relation to the whole scene, in which they play like puppets, creatures of exquisite grace, of easy movement, detached from us, inside the proscenium opening of the gilt frame. On the other hand, note the actual relation of those figures, in point of size, to the landscape. The latter is not subordinated to them, as in the Italian paintings, nor are they mere spots of accent in the surroundings, as in Claude's pictures and in the Dutch landscapes; but the two elements are so adjusted to each other, that, to use a theatrical expression, the *mise-en-scène* is perfectly balanced. It was this balance, coupled with the dramatic vivacity of the figures, which made Watteau's pictures a new thing in art.

Its newness is linked to that of Hogarth's by the influence that the drama exerted over both; otherwise there is no similarity between the two men in motive, though in their craftsmanship they were alike in being both accomplished painters. But while Watteau, as we have said, was a sad, retired man, who found inspiration for his landscape studies in the beautiful gardens of the Luxembourg palace, which he peopled with the creatures of his own imagination, though having all a realist's feeling for, and knowledge of, nature and the human figure; Hogarth, a jovial little man, fond of his London and thoroughly acquainted with its aspects and the life of its people, laid his scenes in the streets, the drawing-rooms, churches, attics, madhouses—always in some scene thronged with the rich, the poor, the actual people living in his day. He neither extenuated, "nor set down aught in malice." But, added to this painter's joy of representing what he saw (and with what minuteness of detail you can see from this picture, remembering, as you study its extreme finish, that Hogarth began life as apprentice to an engraver, and that in after life he engraved a large proportion of his pictures)—added, I say, to this purely pictorial motive is that of telling a story, and one, too, which has a moral.

First of all let us read the story of this picture; or, rather, this Act I of a very serious comedy of six tableaux, entitled *Marriage à la Mode*. The scene is the drawing-room of Viscount Squanderfield (note the allegorical significance of the name); on the left his lordship is seated, pointing with complacent pride to his family tree, which has its roots in William the Conqueror. But his rent-roll has been squandered, the gouty foot suggesting whither some of it has gone; and to restore his fortunes he is about to marry his heir to the daughter of a rich alderman. The latter is seated awkwardly at the table, holding the marriage contract,

THE EMBARKATION FOR CYTHERA ANTOINE WATTEAU
LOUVRE, PARIS

THE MARRIAGE CONTRACT — WILLIAM HOGARTH
NATIONAL GALLERY, LONDON

duly sealed, signed, and delivered; the price paid for it being shown by the pile of money on the table and the bunch of canceled mortgages which the lawyer is presenting to the nobleman, who, as you observe, refuses to soil his elegant fingers with them. Over on the left is his weakling son, helping himself at this critical turn of his affairs to a pinch of snuff, while he gazes admiringly at his own figure in a mirror. The lady is equally indifferent: she has strung the ring on to her handkerchief and is toying with it, while she listens to the compliments being paid to her by Counselor Silvertongue. Through the open window another lawyer is comparing his lordship's new house that is in course of building with the plan in his hand. A marriage so begun could only end in misery; and the successive stages of it are represented in the following five pictures of this famous series, which was issued in engraved form in 1745.

Of this masterpiece of Hogarth's, considered as the gradual unfolding, tableau by tableau, of a dramatic story, Austin Dobson writes: "There is no defect of invention, no superfluity of detail, no purposeless stroke in the whole tale. From first to last, it progresses steadily to its catastrophe by a forward march of skilfully linked and fully developed incidents, set in an atmosphere that makes it as vivid as nature itself, decorated with surprising fidelity, and enlivened by all the resources of the keenest humor." This is very high praise; but, observe, there is not a word in it which would be inapplicable if it were a play or a novel and not a series of pictures, that Mr. Dobson were criticizing. As Hogarth was not a dramatist or novelist, but a painter, we need some further indorsement. Let Gautier, the French critic, speak: "Throughout the *Marriage à la Mode* series Hogarth perfectly merits the name of a great painter." Compare with this an extract from the writings of the American critic, Mr. John C. Van Dyke: "There can be no doubt that Hogarth's instincts were those of a painter. His feeling for color, air, values, his handling of the brush, his sense of delicacy and refinement in the placing of tones, all mark him as an artist whose medium of expression was necessarily pigment. The fact that his audience applauded him for his satires rather than for his painting does not invalidate the excellence of his art." And many other judgments to the same effect could be quoted.

So it is because Hogarth was distinguished by these qualities, which are among the hall-marks of painting, that he is reckoned a great painter; and because he was the first of Englishmen to be thus distinguished, and the subjects of his pictures are character studies of life in England, that he is considered the first of the English painters. For similar reasons, Watteau is called the first of the French painters.

The difference between the art of these two contemporaries, each representative of his race and period, is most interesting. The Gallic genius, influenced by intellectuality, seeks in each branch of art its separate special perfection; while the Anglo-Saxon, like the German, mixes sentiment with his abstract love of beauty: a sentiment either of emotions or imagination, of morality or religion. The Frenchman does not, as a rule, confuse his mediums of expression: that is to say, what can best be said in words, he leaves to literature; and, when through painting or sculpture he makes an appeal to the eye, it is to the eye, as far as possible, exclusively, that he is wont to appeal. There are many exceptions to this in French painting, the very popular Greuze being one; but, as a rule, the racial genius of the French is displayed in bringing to the highest point of perfection the special capabilities of the medium, whether in words, or paint, or what not. On the other hand, the Anglo-Saxon and the German, moved by sentiment, are apt to use their art to get at the sentiment of their fellow-men; quite as intent upon what they wish to say as upon their mode of saying it; sometimes more so. They will borrow, therefore, from other arts, as Hogarth did from those of the satirist and dramatist, and, we may add, of the preacher and the moralist.

To this ruling difference between the genius of these races there are numberless exceptions, yet the essential difference remains and must be grasped by all who would appreciate fairly the merits of both. Nor need we try to discover which is the better motive. To the French, their own undoubtedly, because it is fashioned out of their own characteristics. A heritage from Poussin, it has resulted in a very high average of accomplishment; so that no writers are more clever in writing than the French; no painters so generally skilled in painting; no sculptors, as a body, so expert in their particular craft.

On the contrary, while individual painters of the German and Anglo-Saxon races have regarded themselves primarily as painters and reached a high degree of accomplishment in their technic, there has been a tendency to think the subject of the picture of more importance than the way in which it is painted, and the latter has suffered in consequence. Hogarth, as we have seen, was not one of these; yet the admiration given to the story-telling and moral aspects of his work has done much to lead other painters to overlook the proper scope of painting, its true possibilities and limitations.

He himself was a perfectly typical product of his time, reflecting at least four very vital influences: Puritan morality; the power and independence of the middle classes; the love of the drama, and the rise of English prose.

The first two are closely interwoven. At the commencement of the eighteenth century there was this great difference between the conditions of England and France, that while in the latter the opposite extremes of the aristocracy and the proletariat stood wide apart, in England there was a powerful and independent middle class. It had its origin in the fifteenth century, when the mutual destruction of the nobles in the Wars of the Roses "gave honest men," as the saying was, "a chance to come by their own." It grew in numbers and in wealth, eagerly identifying itself with freedom of thought and speech, until by the seventeenth century it had developed that Puritan conscience which made a stand at once for morality and for religious and civil liberty. It was temporarily triumphant and then superseded in the matter of government by the Restoration, when lower moral standards and indifference to religion came to be in vogue. But the Puritan conscience survived, as it still does to-day; and in Hogarth's time made itself felt in a variety of ways. In a religious guise it reappeared in the preaching of John Wesley, and the rise of the Methodists; in literature, in the satirical writing of Swift, Addison, Steele, and Pope.

But the great event of literature during the latter part of the eighteenth century was the development and growth of English prose, particularly, in connection with our present study, of the modern novel. There sprang up a group of story-tellers: De Foe, Richardson, Goldsmith, Fielding, Sterne, and Smollett. Literature, seriously, humorously, or satirically, was interested in human life. The Puritan conscience, the sturdy middle-class common sense, the novelist's keen observation of life, tinged sometimes with bitterness, but always with humor—these are the influences to be detected in Hogarth's work.

Its affinity to the drama is no less evident. The figures are grouped in a scene rather than composed with the empty spaces of the background. They are strung across the scene, almost in the same plane, and are illuminated as if from footlights, the light of which does not explore the background. To appreciate this artificial form of grouping and lighting, the picture should be compared with Velasquez's *Las Meñinas*. In a moment we perceive that one is natural, and the other stagy.

In his portrait of himself, in the National Gallery in London, Hogarth has introduced a palette, on which is drawn a curved line. This is what he called the line of beauty and of grace. One may possibly trace his use of it in this picture: in the gesture of the right arm and hand of the heir; in the curve of the lady's pocket-handkerchief; more subtly through the line of her head and the hands of the Counselor Silvertongue; with a certain broken humility in the head and left arm of the lawyer who hands the mortgages, and with a pompous stiffness in the head and left arm of his lordship.

In his early efforts at painting, Hogarth produced miniature "Conversation Pieces"; that is to say, little subjects of figures grouped in the act of conversation: a style of picture which, as he said, had novelty. It was akin to the genre pictures, those subjects of real life which had occupied the Dutch of the seventeenth century. But there was this difference. The Dutch artists, depicting scenes of real life in the home, or streets, or taverns, were concerned almost entirely with the pictorial aspect of the subject; they did not include, as a rule, any study of character, much less any story-telling or dramatic motive. They looked at the outside, not the inside, of life. Hogarth was the first of the painters to do the latter. In his objective realism he is related to Dutch seventeenth-century art; but, under the influence of English literature of the eighteenth century, he went further and originated a new motive in painting. While Italian art in the eighteenth century was variously reproducing a faint recollection of its past, Holland itself aping the Italian, and Watteau shrinking from the present in a golden vision of dreams, Hogarth attacked the real. He is the father of modern realism in painting.

The great difference, then, between him and Watteau is that his pictures represent a study of character which

WATTEAU—HOGARTH

analyzes the causes and results of human actions, while the French artist floats upon the beautiful surface of things. The one is terrible, seeing the world so clearly as it was; the other, altogether lovable in his disregard of what is gross and horrible, in his imagined perfection of beauty. But, in relation to the respective conditions of their countries at the time, Watteau's art was as a tangle of flowers, covering pleasantly a bottomless pit of destruction; Hogarth's, a rude awakening to a wholesomer condition; the one, a sad and sick man's craving after ideal beauty; the other, a healthy recognition of what was wrong.

CHAPTER XVIII

SIR JOSHUA REYNOLDS
1723–1792
Early English School

THOMAS GAINSBOROUGH
1727–1788
Early English School

IN the same year, 1784, that Sir Joshua Reynolds's picture, *Mrs. Siddons as the Tragic Muse,* was exhibited at the Royal Academy, the famous actress sat for her portrait to his rival, Gainsborough. Sarah Siddons was then in her twenty-ninth year, in the prime of her beauty, and in the first flush of that popularity which was to make her the queen of the English stage for thirty years. She was the eldest daughter of a country actor, Roger Kemble, three of her brothers, John Philip, Stephen, and Charles, and one sister, Elizabeth, being also distinguished on the stage; while Charles's daughter, Fanny Kemble, carried on the theatrical traditions of the family until 1893. As a girl, Sarah acted in her father's companies; at eighteen married an actor named Siddons; and made her first appearance at Drury Lane Theatre in 1775, when she played Portia with Garrick. But on this occasion she failed to make a good impression, and retired in disappointment to the provinces, where she worked hard for seven years. Upon her reappearance in London in 1782, as Isabella in "The Fatal Marriage," her success was instantaneous. She became identified with parts of tragic pathos and queenly dignity, her favorite ones being Lady Macbeth, Queen Constance, Queen Katharine, Jane Shore, Isabella, Ophelia, Imogen, Portia, and Desdemona. Her power seems to have consisted not so much in the delivery of the words as in her "presence, mien, attitude, expression of voice and countenance, and in her intense concentration of feeling, which lifted and dilated her form, transporting her audience as well as herself." Her last appearance on the stage was in 1818. Thenceforth until her death, in 1831, she lived in retirement, as honored as a woman as she had been as an actress.

We can compare the two aspects of her personality in these pictures. Sir Joshua's exhibits her in an attitude of rapt contemplation, as if gazing into the world of the imagination and listening for the voice of inspiration; dressed in a costume which at the end of the eighteenth century passed for heroic. In Gainsborough's picture she appears as she may have done when Fanny Burney met her, in 1782, while paying an afternoon call at a friend's house. Mrs. Siddons had just become famous. She was on everybody's tongue, and Miss Burney makes this entry in her diary: "We found Mrs. Siddons, the actress, there. She is a woman of excellent character, and therefore I am very glad she is thus patronized. She behaved with great propriety; very calm, modest, quiet, and unaffected. She has a fine countenance, and her eyes look both intelligent and soft. She has, however, a steadiness in her manner and deportment by no means engaging. Mrs. Thrale, who was there, said: 'Why, this is a leaden goddess we are all worshipping! however, we shall soon gild it.'"

HOW TO STUDY PICTURES

Her hair is frizzled and powdered after the fashion of the time, and surmounted by a large black, feathered hat; she wears a blue-and-gray-striped silk dress, with a buff shawl hanging from her arm, and holds a brown muff. The curtain at her back is red. On this arrangement of colors hangs a tale.

Sir Joshua, in the eighth of the discourses which, as president of the Royal Academy, he delivered to the students in 1778, laid down the principle that the chief masses of light in a picture should always be of warm, mellow color, and that the blue, gray, or green colors should be kept almost entirely out of these masses, and "be used only to support and set off these warm colors; and for this purpose a small proportion of cold colors will be sufficient. Let this conduct be reversed," he added; "let the light be cold and the surrounding colors warm, as we often see in the work of the Roman and Florentine painters, and it will be out of the power of art, even in the hands of Rubens or Titian, to make a picture splendid and harmonious."

It is said that Gainsborough took up the challenge and produced the *Mrs. Siddons* portrait; though others assert that it was in another famous portrait, *The Blue Boy,* that he did this. Whether or not it is true that he deliberately painted these pictures to refute his rival's theory, matters very little beside the fact that they do refute it. For one of the chief charms of Gainsborough's work is the delicacy of his color-harmonies, in which he was entirely original. But this story brings out very sharply the difference between these two artists: Reynolds regulating his art and life on safe and arbitrary principles; Gainsborough, an original student of nature, influenced by a dreamy, poetic temperament; the one, also, a man of the world; the other, simply an artist.

Sir Joshua was born at Plympton, four miles from Plymouth, in Devonshire, in 1723. His father, rector of the grammar-school, early trained him in classical studies, intending his son to be an apothecary; but he displayed such an inclination for drawing, diligently copying the prints which fell in his way, that the father yielded and sent him to London as a pupil of Hudson, then popular but now held in little esteem. After two years he returned to Devonshire and established himself as a portrait-painter in Plymouth, where he was taken up by Commodore Keppel, who, being appointed to the Mediterranean station, invited the young painter to accompany him on his ship, the *Centurion*. Thus he was able to visit Rome, spending two years there in very close study, especially of the works of Raphael and Michelangelo. It was while painting in the corridors of the Vatican that he contracted a cold, which brought on the deafness which afflicted him during the rest of his life. Leaving Rome, he visited Parma, where he fell under Correggio's influence; then Florence and Venice, in the latter city studying the works of the great colorists. On his way home he stopped in Paris, making acquaintance with the work of Rubens. Arrived in London, he settled in St. Martin's Lane, and painted a portrait of his patron, Commodore (by that time Lord) Keppel, which laid the foundation of his fortunes. Later he established himself in Leicester Square, where his house, No. 47, may still be seen opposite the site of Hogarth's.

HOW TO STUDY PICTURES

Van Dyck had been dead a hundred years. Though his memory was a great tradition in England, no Englishman had succeeded to his fame, and yet portraiture was the trend of painting that chiefly interested the English. Reynolds, coming back from his travels with well-considered rules which he would follow if it were possible for him to paint historical or ideal subjects, immediately adapted himself to circumstances and applied these rules to portrait-painting. Every portrait should be a picture as well as a rendering of the features of the original. He had learned how Michelangelo made the attitude and gestures of his figures so full of expression; what triumphs of light and shade were produced by Correggio; the dignity and sumptuousness of Venetian coloring; the decorative splendor of Rubens's pictures; the exquisite sentiment of Raphael's women and children, and the dignity that this artist gave to his heads of men. He had learned all this and much more, and set himself to combine as much of these different qualities in his portraits as he could. "No one," said James Northcote, a pupil of Reynolds, who wrote his life, " ever appropriated the ideas of others to his own purpose with more skill than Sir Joshua. The opinion he has given of Raphael may with equal justice be applied to himself: 'His materials were generally borrowed, but the noble structure was his own.'"

For example, in the *Mrs. Siddons* the pose of the figure, especially in the carriage of the head and left arm and hand, recalls Michelangelo's painting of *Isaiah* on the ceiling of the Sistine Chapel; while in the latter's *Jeremiah* may be seen the suggestion for the attendant

MRS. SIDDONS AS THE TRAGIC MUSE — SIR JOSHUA REYNOLDS

GROSVENOR HOUSE, LONDON

PORTRAIT OF MRS. SIDDONS — THOMAS GAINSBOROUGH
NATIONAL GALLERY, LONDON

figures, *Crime* and *Remorse,* in the Reynolds picture. If you compare the *Siddons* and the *Isaiah,* you will be conscious at once of particular similarities and yet of general difference. Each figure is represented as being under the influence of inspiration, as if listening to a voice. The latter in the case of the *Isaiah* is near, in that of the *Siddons* afar off; the prophet is *taking it into* himself to write it in the book; the actress, with her right arm extended, looks as if she may spring from her seat and impetuously *give out* of herself what she feels. Then note the different treatment of the draperies: in the *Isaiah* it is sculptural, the drapery is felt as part of the figure; in the *Siddons* it is arranged so as to make you forget the figure in the amplitude and superbness of its garniture, just as the actual personality of a great actress is enlarged and made magnificent by the atmosphere of emotion which surrounds it. It was so that Reynolds, intimate friend of the great actor Garrick and of the brilliant orator Burke, tried to represent the mighty impressiveness, the emotional grandeur, and intellectual splendor of the nobly spoken word. Throughout all Reynolds's work there is a strong inclination toward the dramatic representation: even the children — and none ever painted sweeter ones than he — unconsciously play some little part. Moreover, Reynolds lived in the grand world, and painted all the great and the fashionable people of his time; and sought to apply to portraiture the principles of the "grand style" of painting.

Look back to Gainsborough's *Mrs. Siddons*, and see how free from anything dramatic or "grand" it is; how simple and straightforward; true and sure in the drawing, so that one can enjoy the suggestion of vigorous, alert body and soft, firm flesh. It gives enjoyment to our tactile sense, which is much less excited by the Reynolds picture. On the other hand, quite as noticeable is the delicacy of the picture: its delicate refinement of expression and the delicate rendering of the face and hair; while we have already alluded to the choice and original beauty of the scheme of color-harmony. Altogether there is a rare quality of distinction in this picture which we shall not find in the Reynolds, for all its grandeur. It is also a much finer kind of distinction than appears in Van Dyck's pictures; and I think we may discover why.

This quality of distinction in a picture is not so much a reproduction of something in the subject as of something in the artist; else we might expect to find it as evident in Reynolds's picture as in Gainsborough's. No, you may find this quality also in a painted landscape; it is an expression of the mind and imagination of the artist, even as the touch of a musician is an interpretation not only of the music, but of the way in which the music affects him—an expression of himself, in fact.

Now Van Dyck, as we have seen, was very fond of the grand world and fashionable life, and, having great personal refinement, gave an air of exceptional refinement to his portraits; but it is very largely a refinement of beautiful clothes and elegant manners. We can hardly imagine Van Dyck condescending to paint a picture of a *Girl and Pigs,* as Gainsborough did; and he certainly did not paint landscapes,—whereas Gainsborough, while painting portraits for a living, painted landscapes for his own pleasure, and lived at Hampstead during the summer, that he might be constantly in fellowship with nature.

It was this love of nature and of simple things, and the faculty of seeing beauty in them, that gave such a choice distinction to his work, because it was the expression of his own simple, lovable personality. He had beauty in himself, and all his life it fed on simple delights—the joy of nature, of domestic happiness, of music, and of his own art.

He was born in the little town of Sudbury, on the river Stour, in the beautiful county of Suffolk, not far from East Bergholt, the birthplace, some fifty years later, of the great landscape-painter Constable. As a boy, he loved to ramble in the country, sketching; and showed so much inclination for it, and so little for any other kind of study, that when he was fifteen he was sent to London and placed under the care of a silversmith, who procured him admission to the St. Martin's Lane Academy. Here he worked for three years under the painter Frank Hayman, who was distinguished by being addicted more to wine and pugilism than to art. Gainsborough's eighteenth year was an eventful one. First, he hired three rooms in Hatton Gardens and set up as a painter on his own account; then, meeting with little encouragement, returned to Sudbury; there fell a victim to the charms of a young lady of seventeen, Miss Margaret Burr, who had an annuity of one thousand dollars; married her, and established himself in the country town of Ipswich. After this eventful year, he worked on for fifteen years happily and quietly, continually studying in the open air and executing such small commissions for portraits as came to him, until he had succeeded in discovering for himself a manner of painting suited to his needs, and had developed an extraordinary facility.

In 1760, by the advice of a friend and patron named Thicknesse, he moved to Bath, at that time the most fashionable city outside of London. Its hot medicinal waters had been famous in Roman times, and still the gay world congregated there to drink them and to dance and talk scandal in the Pump-room, where Beau Nash reigned as an autocrat among the wits and macaronis.[1]

Gainsborough's success was immediate, but with increasing wealth there was no alteration in his simple method of living. He worked four or five hours a day, and devoted the rest of his time to the society of his wife and a few friends who were musical. For music now became a passion of his life, so that it was said he painted for business and played for pleasure, constantly mastering some fresh instrument.

So passed fourteen years, when, in 1774, Gainsborough moved to London, was commissioned by George III to paint a portrait of himself and the queen, and became the rival of Reynolds. He died in 1788, having contracted a chill while attending the trial of Warren Hastings, and was buried by his own request in Kew churchyard. On his death-bed he sent for Reynolds. There had been misunderstanding and estrangement between the two. It was now forgotten. Reynolds caught his last dying words, "We are all going to heaven, and

[1] Slang word for the fashionable dandies of the day.

Van Dyck is of the party"; acted as one of the pallbearers at his funeral; and subsequently pronounced a eulogy. In it he said: "If ever this nation should produce genius enough to acquire to us the honorable distinction of an English school, the name of Gainsborough will be transmitted to posterity in the history of the art, among the very first of that rising name."

Reynolds himself only survived Gainsborough four years. He was buried with much pomp in St. Paul's Cathedral, near to the grave of its architect, Sir Christopher Wren.

The contrast between these two artists is almost the difference between art and artlessness. Reynolds was learned in what other painters had done, and had reduced his own art to a system; he was a man of the world, and represented his subjects with a well-bred consciousness of good manners. Gainsborough found out almost everything for himself; never lost the simple, natural way of looking at things and people, and painted, not according to rule, but at the dictates of what he felt. Reynolds planned out his effects; Gainsborough painted on the spur of the impression which the subject aroused. Reynolds's art was based on safe general principles; Gainsborough's was the fresh and spontaneous expression of his temperament,—depending, that is to say, on feeling rather than on calculation. His temperament, or habit of mind, was dreamy and poetic, gentle and retiring, including a small range of experience. Reynolds, on the other hand, was a man of large experience and of business capacity; intimate with Samuel Johnson, Oliver Goldsmith, and other celebrities of the day;

HOW TO STUDY PICTURES

a man of knowledge and clever conversational power, whose pictures by their variety prove his versatility. Consequently, when the Royal Academy was established in 1768, he was elected president by acclamation, and was knighted by George III, an honor that has ever since been bestowed on the holder of this office.

These two men were at the head of the group of portrait-painters who, in the latter part of the eighteenth century and early years of the succeeding one, added luster to the new growth of art in England. Foremost among the other names in the group are Romney, at times quite as able as Reynolds or Gainsborough; Sir Henry Raeburn, a Scotchman; John Hoppner; and Sir Thomas Lawrence.

CHAPTER XIX

JOHN CONSTABLE *JOSEPH MALLORD WILLIAM TURNER*
1776-1837 1775-1851
English School *English School*

WHAT a contrast these pictures present of splendid audacity and serene simplicity! The one an amazing vision of the imagination; the other, a loving record of something intimately familiar. Turner's was painted in 1829; one of the finest works of this master, who is a solitary figure in landscape art, unapproached by others, although, as we shall see, he combined several motives that others had been or would be seeking after. Constable's picture appeared six years later, an excellent example of the painter who may be regarded as the father of modern landscape.

The Valley Farm, known also as *Willy Lott's House,* is on the little river Stour in the county of Suffolk, England, near the mill at East Bergholt where Constable was born; for he, like Rembrandt, was a miller's son. It is a characteristic bit of English scenery, not grand or romantic; just a tiny bit of a little country, the conspicuous features of which are its verdure and rich cultivation; so homelike that those who love it, as Constable did, get to have a companionship with every detail, learning to know the line of its hills, the winding of its streams, and the position and character of every tree and object in the familiar scene. It was along the banks of this little river that he strayed in boyhood; and to it that he came back, after a stay in London where he studied at the schools of the Royal Academy, and copied the pictures in the galleries, especially those of Hobbema and Ruisdael. But he soon tired of looking at nature through the eyes of other men. "There is room enough," he wrote to a friend, "for a nature-painter. Painting is with me but another name for feeling; and I associate my careless boyhood with all that lies upon the banks of the Stour; those scenes made me a painter and I am thankful." This is the kind of spirit which, we have seen, actuated the Dutch landscape-painters of the seventeenth century; and, indeed, their love of nature was reincarnated in Constable. For in the lapse of time their contribution to art had been forgotten; the Dutchmen themselves had followed after strange gods, and, like the painters of France and England, had forsaken the direct study of nature for an attempt to reproduce the grandeur of the classic landscape. Reynolds, who drew his inspiration from Italy, had set its stamp upon English portraiture; and Claude, the Italian-Frenchman, was the landscape-painter most admired.

If we compare this picture of Constable's with the *Landing of Cleopatra at Tarsus* by Claude (page 247), we shall note how wide apart they are. Beside the formal stateliness of the latter, wherein everything, carefully selected from various sources, has been arranged so as to produce a noble effect, *The Valley Farm* seems huddled and formless, homely. For Constable rejected the rules of composition then in vogue, to build up an artificial stateliness, painting the scene as he saw it, with a native instinct for balance of the full and empty spaces. Again, if we compare it with Hobbema's *The Avenue, Middelharnis* (page 246), we shall note that, while both are simple records of the natural country-side, there is a difference. We can detect a movement of the foliage of the trees in Constable's which is not in Hobbema's picture; we perceive more than the actual forms of the trees, they are alive, trembling in the air. Further, we may observe more suggestion of atmosphere in the later than in the earlier picture; the sky is less a background than a canopy, the air of which pervades the whole scene. Once more, there is a marked difference between the feeling of these two pictures; that is to say, we may note a difference in the attitude of mind with which Hobbema and Constable, respectively, approached their subject. We have no doubt that each was in love with his subject, and painted it because he was; but Hobbema did not think it necessary to say so in his picture. He viewed his subject objectively, as something outside himself; whereas Constable, with whom "painting was another name for feeling," has put his love into the picture, has made the scene interpret his own mood. His picture is subjective.

He was not satisfied with a copying of nature. It was to him so real and personal a companion, that, in the first place, he tried to make it live in his pictures; that the clouds might move and overhang the spot, that its atmosphere might penetrate every part of the scene, and that trees and water, and the very plants by the roadside might move and have their being in it; and secondly, he put his own personal affection into his representation. Then, too, in the matter of color, which cannot be gathered from the reproduction, he dared to paint nature green, as he saw it, and the skies blue, with the sunshine either yellow or glaring white. This scandalized the people of his day. "Where are you going to place your brown tree?" said a patron of his, speaking of an unfinished picture. For the older men, even Gainsborough to some extent, transposed the hues of nature into browns and grays and gold, producing a very charming harmony of tone, but one that was arbitrary; not true to nature's facts, but adopted as a pictorial convention.

It is, then, because of this closer fidelity to the hues of nature, and to the effects of movement, of atmosphere and of light, which are the manifestations of its life and moods, and because he interpreted nature according to his own mood,—was, in fact, the first of the temperamental landscape-painters,—that Constable is called the father of modern landscape. For these are the qualities that particularly have occupied the artists of the nineteenth century, and have caused the most original and vital branch of painting at the present time to be that of landscape.

On the threshold of this new movement stood Turner, alone among his fellow landscape-painters, the most imaginative of them all, who was less concerned with the truth of nature than with her splendors and magic. No one has equaled him in suggesting the mystery of nature in its sublime forms. One turns to the *Ulysses Deriding Polyphemus*, not to be drawn toward it and made to feel at home, as in the case of the Constable, but to be lifted up and filled with wonder of its strangeness and mysterious grandeur.

The incident depicted in it is from Homer's Odyssey. The hero, Ulysses, in his voyage from Troy to his home in Ithaca, stopped at the isle of the Cyclops, and with his followers approached the cave of Polyphemus. The monster devoured six of the crew; but the hero plied him with wine, brought from his vessel, and, while he slept, put out his single eye by gouging it with a red-hot stake. The mariners then escaped to their ship, while Polyphemus in his pain and impotent rage flung rocks in the direction of their voices. We see his huge form writhing on the top of the cliff; the sailors scrambling up the masts to loosen the sails; the red oars flashing upon the water; a bevy of sea-nymphs around the prow drawing the ship to safety through the green water; the latter, gilded with the reflections of the rising sun, that paints with gold and crimson the little clouds, floating in the vaporous sky, wherein are rifts which reveal further depths of blue.

But really the incident was of very little account to Turner, except as it furnished him with a peg upon which to hang the splendors of his own imagination; far enough away from our actual experience to permit him a perfect liberty of treatment. Fourteen years earlier he had painted *Dido building Carthage,* in which he emulated the liberties that Claude had taken with nature. It lacked the purity of coloring of the latter's work, yet its composition revealed Claude's mannered elevation of style, and served to show that, if he were so minded, Turner could compete with the landscape-artist then held in highest repute. But his mind was set upon further things; having proved that he could rival Claude, he would now be Turner—himself. At this time he paid the first of three visits to Italy, and the picture we are studying, painted after his return, reveals a heightened sense of color, and the magnificence of his imagination, probably, at its highest point.

A man may shut himself up in his house and lead a very solitary life, as Turner did, and yet unconsciously be a part of the influences of his time. And those early years of the nineteenth century were a period of reaction against the eighteenth century reign of prose, its cold calculation and small and elegant precision. The spirit of Romanticism was in the air. It is not usual, however, to regard Turner as a Romantic painter, yet his work combines qualities which reappear more distinctly in other men. We shall consider the Romantic movement in painting in another chapter; meanwhile here are two definitions of it, that will include Turner, as having, at least, romantic tendencies. Walter Pater says, " It is the addition of strangeness to beauty that constitutes the romantic character in art "; again, Dr. F. H. Hedge, " The romantic feeling has its origin in wonder and mystery. It is the sense of something hidden, of imperfect revelation."

The mystery of this picture, its spaces of light and darkness, that the eye explores but cannot fathom, we are conscious of at once. Moreover, when we think about it, we are sure that, if our eye could pierce the shadows and closely discern the formation of the rocks, definitely learn the structure of the ship and the appear-

VALLEY FARM (WILLY LOTT'S HOUSE)   JOHN CONSTABLE
NATIONAL GALLERY, LONDON

ULYSSES DERIDING POLYPHEMUS   JOSEPH MALLORD WILLIAM TURNER

NATIONAL GALLERY, LONDON

ance of its sailors, peer into the distance and discover exactly how each mass of cliff succeeds another—if, in a word, our eye could grasp everything and convey the facts distinctly to our understanding, we should not enjoy the picture as we do. It is the sense of something hidden, of imperfect revelation, that is one of the sources of its enjoyment.

And then the strangeness of the picture,—that arch of rock, an actual aspect of nature, though an unusual one; the huge, roughly hewn figure of Polyphemus; a sky, full of surprises to people who seldom see the daily pageantry of sunrise,—but it is less in detail than in general character that the picture is strange. The artist has taken a theme of old times, when the world was young and things loomed very big to its unformed imagination. For to the ancient child-mind the world seemed very big, and its empty, unexplored spaces, peopled with shapes and fancies that were vague and large. Whether it was the myths of old Greece, or those of the Norse mountains, or German forests—the earliest ones are concerned with personages vast in size, only half formed in shape, vague and elementary; and it is the suggestion of this vastness and shapelessness, of the early beginning of things, this great strangeness, in a word, that helps to make the present picture so impressive.

Once more compare it with Constable's. One is part of a vast new world; the other, a little spot that for ages the hand and heart of man have shaped.

Whether Turner felt toward nature the wonder which his pictures inspire in us, may be doubted. His life was a strange contradiction to the splendor and imagination of his work. Like many other great landscape-artists he was city-bred. The son of a barber in London, he early showed a talent for drawing, and the father hung the child's productions on the wall of his shop and sold them to his customers. By degrees the boy obtained employment in coloring architectural designs, and at fourteen was entered as a pupil in the schools of the Royal Academy. The following year he exhibited his first picture. He worked with indefatigable energy, and during vacations went on walking tours, sketching continually and painting in water-colors; so that, by the time he was twenty-four and admitted as an associate to the Academy, he had exhibited pictures which ranged over twenty-six counties of England and Wales. During this early period his most conspicuous success was made in water-color, in which medium he developed an extraordinary facility and skill. He would brook no rivalry. Girtin was at that time the most admired artist in water-color; he set to work to surpass him. Having done so, he practically abandoned this medium for oil-colors, and then threw down, as we have already noted, a gauntlet to the popular admiration for Claude. That artist had published a "Liber Veritatis." Turner would outrival him with a "Liber Studiorum," though the drawings, engraved under the artist's supervision, were not studies but finished water-color pictures. In fact, this collection of seventy-one out of the hundred plates originally planned, while a monument to Turner's genius, is also the assertion of a rivalry that, in itself unworthy, was conducted in a spirit scarcely fair. For Claude's "Liber Veritatis" is simply a sketch-book, and the sketches were engraved after their author's death, indeed, not until Turner's day. But the latter's finished productions were issued under his own eye.

Turner's rule of conduct, in fact, was "aut Cæsar aut nullus." Having established his supremacy over rivals, at least to his own satisfaction, he set himself to conquer a universe of his own. During a period of twelve years, beginning with this picture of Ulysses and ending with that of a tug-boat towing to a wrecker's yard a ship of the line, *The Fighting Téméraire,* and *The Burial of Wilkie at Sea,* he did his greatest work. For then his imagination was at its ripest and richest; displayed particularly in the majesty of moving depths of water, in skies of vast grandeur, and in the splendor of his color-schemes; moreover, the workmanship of his pictures was solid, and he still based his imagination on the facts of nature. But, as time went on, the need of continual experimenting — which every genius feels — seemed to take undue possession of him, so that the study of nature became constantly less and the independent invention more and more. It was no longer the forms of nature that interested him, but her impalpable qualities of light and atmosphere, and perhaps even more the intoxication of the actual skill in using paint, until one may suspect that he was more enamoured of the magic of his brush and paints than of the qualities of nature which he was supposed to be representing. So daring, almost to the point of recklessness, were his experiments, that his later pictures have deteriorated, until their original appearance can only be guessed. On the other hand, in his fondness for atmospheric effects, and particularly in his efforts to raise the key of light in his pictures, he was anticipating, as we shall see, some of the most interesting developments of nineteenth-century painting.

And during all these years, while as an artist he was absorbed in the pageants, the mystery, and the subtlety of light and atmosphere, his life as a man was morose and mean; his house in Queen Anne Street dirty and neglected; and, finally, it was in a still more squalid haunt in a wretched part of London, which he frequented by his own choice, that he was found dead. When his will was opened, the curious contradiction that he was fond of hoarding money and yet refused to sell the majority of his pictures, was explained. He had left his works to the National Gallery, his money as a fund for the relief of poor artists. A strange mingling of greatness and sordidness, of boorish manners and kindly humanness!

Constable, on the other hand, led a happy, simple life in the village of which he wrote in one of his letters, published by his friend, the painter Leslie, " I love every stile and stump and lane." It was an out-of-door life, for he painted, as he expressed it, " under the sun "; observing the big clouds as they rolled inland from the North Sea, with their attendant effects of light and shadow. For it is these shadow effects of the northern countries that have made them the home of the natural landscape. In sunny Italy, where the air is for the most part bright and clear, the landscape makes an appeal of lines and masses; the artist finds in it suggestion for composition, hence the stately pictures by Nicolas Poussin and Claude, who lived in Italy, and of the English Wilson, who visited Italy and saw nature through the Italian influence.

But in a country where the sunshine is comparatively rare, Constable learned to appreciate the value of it; the ample comfort of its occasional breadth, the subtle charm of its brief gleams, piercing the rain-cloud and sparkling upon the grass and leafage. The sky, not spread with an undisturbed ceiling of light, but built high with clouds, that shift continually and change their aspects, taught him to observe the varying luminosity of the atmosphere; not to take light for granted, or to represent it by some uniform recipe for glow, but to study the infinite variety of its manifestations—with what degrees of strength or faintness it saturates the air, and how it colors the objects upon the ground.

Constable became, in fact, the first of the modern school of open-air painting. Some of his pictures were exhibited at the Paris Salon during the years 1822 to 1827, and the interest that his work aroused and the impression produced by it are to be reckoned, as Delacroix himself affirmed, a powerful influence in the creation of the French school of *paysage intime*. The Englishmen, however, of that date, paid Constable little honor. It is true he was made an associate of the Royal Academy in 1819, after which he moved from Suffolk and established himself in what was then the village of Hampstead on the northern outskirts of London; but it was not until he had been honored with a gold medal by the French that the Academy admitted him to full membership. Nor did this increase the public's appreciation; he died at Hampstead in very meager circumstances, but with the happy expectation that some day his pictures would be understood and valued. The expectation has been fully realized.

Such tardy recognition has been the lot of many painters great enough to create something new. Turner would not have been so highly esteemed in his own generation, but that Ruskin, the most admired writer upon art in his time, was his enthusiastic advocate, extolling him, indeed, with an extravagant enthusiasm that has been followed by a reaction. Ruskin claimed for him every virtue of a painter; and the later discovery, that he was not so great as his advocate claimed, has somewhat obscured how great he was.

Moreover, the world has now become so persuaded of the beauty of the natural style of landscape-painting, that it is distrustful of the imaginative. In its praise of Constable it pooh-poohs Turner.

This is a foolish and ignorant attitude of mind. The proper one for the genuine student is to recognize that in art, as in any other department of life, a man should be judged, not by standards of measurement, but by what he himself is. Now to a man who loves nature Constable must appeal; but where is the man whose love of nature, being simple and real, has not, once or twice or oftener, felt taken out of himself, so that the facts of sky and earth seemed little to him beside the wonderful exaltation of spirit that the same suggest? It may be on some mountain, or in the presence of a sunset, or beside a little brook, anywhere, at any time, but some time or other to the lover of nature will come a moment in which the facts of the landscape are swept into forgetfulness, and all he is conscious of is a sense of his soul being strengthened, purified, exalted. It is so that Turner's best pictures may affect him.

As we approach the development of modern art, we become more and more involved in the question of nature-study. But let us realize that nature is practically the same to-day, yesterday, and forever; it is our own attitude toward it which is variable. Nature is a mirror in which the artist and ourselves are reflected. Therefore, it would be just as foolish to affirm that a mirror should reflect only such and such objects, as to limit our appreciation to particular kinds of artistic motive. The proper attitude of mind is one of being actively ready to receive impressions of all kinds.

CHAPTER XX

JACQUES LOUIS DAVID
1748-1825
Classical School of France

FERDINAND VICTOR EUGÈNE DELACROIX
1799-1863
Romantic School of France

EACH of these pictures—David's *Oath of the Horatii* and Delacroix's *Dante and Virgil*—represents a breaking away from what had gone before. David's was a protest against the art of Watteau and his successors, Van Loo, Boucher, and Fragonard; Delacroix's, in turn, a protest against the art of David. The one was an attempt to revive the purity of Classic style by going even further back than Poussin, namely to the ancient Roman sculpture itself; the other, to express the fervor of modern life through the medium of romance. David's picture is cold, calculated, and self-conscious; Delacroix's impassioned, less formal in arrangement, the characters being absorbed in their various emotions.

Compare the two pictures, first of all, from the standpoint of their subjects, in each case a dramatic one: David's drawn from the early days of the Roman Republic, Delacroix's from Dante's "Inferno." And, first, the David. Jealous of the growing power of the young city, the neighboring tribe of Curiatii has invested it; Rome's very existence is imperiled. There are three brothers in the ranks of the enemy who, like Goliath in the Bible story, march up and down in front of their comrades, challenging any three Romans to fight with them. Let a combat of three against three decide the issue. Now within the walls is one Horatius, who has three stout sons. He will give them up, sacrifice them if need be, as champions of the Republic. They are eager for the honor, notwithstanding that their own sister is betrothed to one of the three Curiatii. But between their loyalty to country and to sister they have no hesitation. They will fight for country; and to this highest of all purposes the father with prayer and blessings devotes them.

But observe the three brothers in the picture. Their attitudes are almost identical, like those of well-drilled supers on the stage. Let us admit that this device expresses the unanimity of their feeling; they are moved as one man, with a single patriotism, and, as we may judge from the hand of one encircling another's waist, by a single bond of brotherly affection. Yet still there is more than a suspicion of staginess in their pose. Perhaps David had seen Corneille's tragedy of the Horatii, written one hundred and forty-five years before; at any rate, its representation became very popular in Paris after the appearance of this picture, influenced by which the great actor, Talma, played the part, no longer in a periwig and court-clothes, but in the Roman costume. Again observe the secondary group of women. Do we feel convinced that the elder daughter betrays real grief, or her sister genuine sympathy, or that the mother's act of enfolding the little children in her arms is more than a bit of maternal conventionalism? In a word, are we really stirred by all this representation of pathos and heroism?

Now let us study, from the point of view of subject, the *Dante and Virgil*. The incident depicted may be read in Dante's "Inferno," Canto III, though the details are not closely followed in the picture. The poet of Florence, escorted by him of Mantua, has reached the shores of Acheron, that lake encircling the city of Dis (Pluto), against which leap up the fiery waves of Phlegethon. Upon the shore linger the souls of those who lived in life without praise or blame, moaning to be taken across the water, even if it be to hell. But Charon drives them back with cruel words and blows of his oar, as he takes the shade of Virgil and the living man into his crazy boat. To its gunwale cling the unhappy shades, one convulsively gripping it with his teeth; another has lost hold and sinks into the water, in which two more flounder, clutching each other as the living will when drowning. Above these writhing forms stands Dante, aghast with horror, leaning toward the Mantuan, who alone is calm, serenely fixed amid the tumult, eternally poised and youthful.

In this picture Delacroix has attempted to seize and convey by an immediate representation all the anguish and the tumult that the poet's song renders by separate stages. It was the work of a youth of twenty-three, already a master. David, a veteran of seventy-four years, when he saw it, exclaimed, "Where does it come from? I do not recognize the style."

For it does not depend upon line as David's picture,

DAVID—DELACROIX

but upon colored masses. It is true that the figures in the water are arranged so as to produce a certain wild rhythm of movement, like agitated waves; but none of the figures are inclosed in hard lines, the contours having neither the assertion nor the precision of David's. To repeat, it is an arrangement of colored masses: of dark greenish-blue sea, the pallid ivories of flesh tints, Virgil's drabbish-green robe, and Dante's drab one; his crimson *becchetto,* and the echo of its color in the fainter distant glow of fire,—a turbid harmony of color, wherein the nude bodies appear as a *motif* of pain and the crimson is a crash of wrath. It is the work of a man who feels in color, as a musician does in sounds, and who plays upon the chromatics of color, somewhat as the musician upon the chromatics of sound. It is the work, not of one who uses color merely to increase the reality of appearances, as the majority of painters do, but of one of that smaller band, headed by the Venetians and Rubens, who make the color itself a source of emotional appeal. Delacroix was a colorist; and David, drilled in the Academic school which says line and form are the chief essentials, seeing the picture, asked, " Where does it come from?"

It came, in the first place, out of the imagination of a colorist, who conceives his pictures in color; sees them, I mean, in his mind's eye, as a composition of color, before he begins to resolve the whole into its parts, and work out the separate details of form. Indirectly it came out of the heart of the Romantic movement which had spread over Europe. Delacroix was inspired by the influence of Goethe, Scott, Byron, Victor Hugo, and the other poets and writers who had broken away from the coldly intellectual viewpoint of the eighteenth century, and its study of manners, to explore the passions of the human soul, and the variegated colorful life of the emotions.

David was a part, Delacroix a product, of the French Revolution, which opened a new chapter in the history of the world and also in that of painting. It had begun in protest against an extravagant and wanton court and an impotent monarch; had passed through a period of madness and horror, and culminated in an extraordinary outburst of national enthusiasm and individual energy. France, as a nation, was reborn, and—which had more influence upon the world at large—out of this Revolution, and the American one which preceded it, was born anew the idea of individualism. David represented the protest, and had no small share in promoting it; Delacroix, the fervor of personal feelings, let loose by individualism.

It was in 1784, in Rome, after he had completed his studies at the French Academy, that David produced the picture of *Brutus* and this *Oath of the Horatii*. In them he went back to the original Roman models upon which the Classic style of Poussin, then the model of the Academic school, had been founded. Here are the semicircular arches and the vaulting, which were the most characteristic developments of Roman architecture, and columns such as the artist may have copied from the Baths of Marcellus. And against this background the figures are set as if carved in low relief, like those on the column of Trajan, of which David was so fond. By

OATH OF THE HORATII LOUVRE, PARIS JACQUES LOUIS DAVID

DANTE AND VIRGIL   LOUVRE, PARIS   EUGÈNE DELACROIX

DAVID—DELACROIX

comparison with Italian painting and with that of France during the seventeenth and eighteenth centuries, this picture of the Horatii was severely simple. Then, too, what a simple severity of lofty patriotism it represented!

Its success in France was immediate. The people, tired of the voluptuous insipidities of Boucher and the others, welcomed its severity; while the principles of freedom and love of country that it inculcated gave at once a definite voice to the floating theories of the time. Republicanism, the old Roman brand of it, simple, unselfish, frugal, began to be considered the panacea for all the ills from which the French branch of the Latin race was suffering. David proved to be the strong man, fitted to the hour, and his influence, first asserted in this picture, played a big part in the subsequent Revolution. When the latter commenced he was forty years old. He was elected a deputy in the Convention, and appointed Minister of Fine Arts. In this capacity he was a despotic dictator; imposing his Roman taste even upon the costumes of the deputies and ministers, and from these upon the people, and organizing public fêtes in the manner of Republican Rome. "He applied art to the heroism of the day, gave it the martial attitude of patriotism, and inspired it with the spirit of Robespierre, Saint Just, Marat, and Danton. Robespierre is said to have spoken from the tribune slowly, rhythmically, artistically. Under the same starched methodical precision David concentrated the volcanic force of his appeal to patriotism." In the first consciousness of individualism, everybody was strutting and posturing self-consciously, like actors upon a stage. The times were artificial and theatrical.

And how greatly this man was penetrated by the spirit of his age is illustrated in his manner of presenting to the Convention his portrait of Marat. The people asked for their murdered man back again, longing to look once more on the features of their truest friend. "They cried to me: 'David, take up your brush, avenge Marat, so that the enemy may blanch when they perceive the distorted countenance of the man who became the victim of his love for freedom.' I heard the voice of the people, and obeyed."[1]

His portraits, however, are free from this sort of rhodomontade, intensely direct and real. "In them, he is neither rhetorical nor cold, but full of fire and the freshness of youth. Before any face to be modeled, he forgot the Greeks and Romans, saw life alone, was rejuvenated in the youthgiving fount of nature, and painted—almost alone of the painters of his generation—the truth.

"David was one of the first of the men of the Revolution to come beneath the spell of the Little Corporal. One day while he was working at his studio at the Louvre, a pupil rushed in breathlessly: 'General Buonaparte is outside the door.' Napoleon entered in a dark-blue coat 'that made his lean yellow face look leaner and yellower than ever.' David dismissed his pupils, and drew in a sitting of barely two hours the stern head of the Corsican. Thus he passed into the service of Napoleon."[1]

He was appointed Imperial Court Painter, and

[1] Richard Muther: History of Modern Painting.

executed that colossal picture which has handed down to posterity a true presentation of the ceremonial pageant that took place in Notre Dame on December 2, 1804. The moment selected is that in which Napoleon, already crowned, is placing the crown upon the head of the empress. The *Coronation* was the great work of his imperial, as the *Marat* had been of his revolutionary period. He had been so intimately identified with both that, after Napoleon's final fall in 1815 and the succession of Louis XVIII, he was banished and sought refuge in Brussels, where he died in 1825. He left behind a legacy of so-called "classicalism," carrying on that of Poussin, which under various modifications has been preserved by the official Academy, as the basis of instruction in and the proper aim of painting. These academic principles, however, no longer confine the student to an imitation of Roman subjects and models. But, even as David permitted himself to be a naturalist in his portraits and in other subjects, such as the *Death of Marat* and the *Coronation,* so the Academy encourages still the study of nature, but within certain limitations.

It lays especial stress upon what it calls the ideal line, and ideal beauty of form and composition. Nature must be corrected to conform with the ideal representations handed down to us from Greek and Roman sculpture, and the paintings upon Greek vases. As Delacroix, mocking at these principles, said: "In order to present an ideal head of a negro, our teachers make him resemble as far as possible the profile of Antinous, and then say, 'We have done our utmost; if, nevertheless, we fail to make the negro beautiful, then we ought not to introduce into our pictures such a freak of nature, the squat nose and thick lips, which are so unendurable to the eyes.'"

This extreme view, which would exclude any subject that is not capable of being idealized, is no longer maintained by the Academy. Yet it still insists upon the prime importance of the line; and, as a result, the figures in academic pictures are usually in graceful poses and inclosed by sharp outlines. A comparison of the *Horatii* with Delacroix's *Dante and Virgil* will show the distinction very clearly. But, as a matter of fact, in nature the forms of objects are not sharply outlined. Even when a dark tree cuts against a light sky, the atmosphere that intervenes between it and our eyes tends to blur its edges. Now these effects of light and atmosphere depend not so much upon the way the picture is drawn as upon the way it is painted, and this again is connected with problems of color.

Accordingly, the Academician, precise about form, disregards problems of light and atmosphere and color; while the colorist, who cares most for these qualities, and sees nature as an arrangement of colored forms in harmonious relation, very often disregards the beauty of form, and, because of what he aims at, cannot make the lines of his objects so precise and ideally perfect. On the other hand, it is the little irregularities and indistinctness of line that give character to forms and suggest that they have the capacity of movement and are alive. The academic figure, notwithstanding its beauty, is by comparison inert and rigid. You may realize this point by a reference to these two pictures we are studying. The figures of the men in the *Horatii* have come to gestures and positions of energy, and hold them as if cast in bronze. The women have been placed in pretty attitudes of amiable sentiment, and remain as if modeled in wax. But in the *Dante and Virgil* there are life and movement: terrific action, put forth and sustained in the figures of Charon and of the two men who grip the gunwale; action of another kind in the Dante, as he gazes with horror and balances himself in the rolling boat; even the latter moves, and the shades, although exhausted to impotence, are moving.

This picture of Delacroix's has been called "in a pictorial sense the first characteristic picture of the century." That is to say, while the art of David and his followers was virtually a translation of sculpture into painting, Delacroix's once more asserted the independence of painting, and its possession of certain qualities and possibilities which no other art possesses in the same degree. For, in the place of the tinted forms of the Academicians, Delacroix had introduced the wonder of color, used for purposes of expression by such masters as the Venetians and Rubens.

Delacroix, in fact, was one of the greatest colorists of the nineteenth century, using the word in the sense of one who thinks and feels and expresses himself by means of color. He nurtured himself upon the works of the colorists in the Louvre, especially upon Rubens. Every morning before his work began, it is said, he drew an arm, a hand, or a piece of drapery after Rubens. It was from Rubens also, and Titian, that Watteau, the great poet-painter of the eighteenth century, had drawn inspiration. And Delacroix, like him, was proud, self-reliant, delicate from his youth up, and for many years sick in soul and body. But, whereas Watteau drew from the licentiousness of the Regent's court the food for his dreams of poetry, Delacroix into his closed studio admitted the mighty impulses which had been let loose by the Revolution.

Liberty had given larger bounds to individualism, and the first of the arts to reflect this was literature. The measured prose, conventionally correct verse, and somewhat pedantic rhetoric of the eighteenth century had been succeeded by an outburst of the imaginative faculty. The movement began in Germany with Goethe; in England with Wordsworth and Scott, Coleridge, Byron, Shelley, and Keats; and in France with Victor Hugo. During a visit to London, in 1825, Delacroix saw the opera of Goethe's "Faust" performed in English, while he had already discovered Shakspeare, Byron, and Scott to be his favorites. His own romantic nature flamed up by contact with theirs; he was possessed with their souls and became the first of the Romantic painters. He took many of his subjects from the poets of his preference, not to translate into literal illustrations, but to make them express in his own language of painting the most agitated emotions of the human heart.

But the representation of agitated emotions necessitated the introduction of a good deal that was horrible to those who swore by the ideal line and perfect balance of composition. "How can ugliness," they cried, "be beautiful?" Victor Hugo produced his play of "Hernani" in 1829; and around him and Delacroix was waged the battle between the Classicists and the Romanticists. Poussin's phrase was repeated by the Classicists—"Painting is nothing more than drawing." "Had God intended to place color at the same height as form," wrote Charles Blanc, "he would not have failed to clothe his masterpiece man with all the hues of the humming-bird." And this "critic" called Delacroix "the tattooed savage who paints with a drunken broom."

To these and similar denunciations, continued for many years, Delacroix himself in one of his writings has contributed a reply. It pleads for a wider conception of the idea of beauty. Winckelmann, the great German archæologist of the eighteenth century, had asserted, "The sole means for art to become, aye, if possible, inimitably great, is the imitation of the ancients." "The marble manner only requires a little animating." "The highest beauty is that which is proper neither to this nor to that person"—that is to say, *not individual.* This was practically the doctrine of the Classicists. To it Lessing, another German, replied that truth to nature was the first condition of beauty; and Goethe expanded it by saying that everything natural was true as far as it was beautiful. The English Keats chimed in, "Truth is beauty, beauty is truth." Delacroix's words are: "This famous thing, the Beautiful, must be—every one says so—the final aim of art. But if it be the only aim, what are we to make of men like Rubens, Rembrandt, and, in general, all the artistic natures of the North, who preferred other qualities belonging to their art? . . . There is no recipe by which one can attain to what is ideally beautiful. Style depends absolutely and solely upon the free and original expression of each master's peculiar qualities"—*upon individuality,* in fact.

There are, among others, some important considerations in these views of the Romanticists, which may be put in the following familiar way. It is quite possible for an exceedingly pretty girl to be very stupid; there is also such a thing as the beauty of character; we enjoy the beauty of the slimness of the silver birch, and the rugged stanchness of an oak; there is a charm about a Gloucester fisherman as well as an *Apollo Belvedere.* On the whole, we do well to be interested in people for what they are rather than for what they might be; individual character is always worth studying; when it is exhibited under the stress of powerful emotion, it is conspicuously so. The artist himself may be a man of marked individuality of character; it is better for the world that he should express himself freely, instead of within the tight groove of some conventional method.

The Classicists were intrenched in the official fortress of the Academy, and for long years resisted the attempts of Delacroix to obtain entrance. Indeed, it was not until twenty-two years after his death, when a great collection of his works was exhibited, that France realized how grand an artist it had lost. Before he died, other men with other motives, as we shall see, rose up to challenge the official standard of excellence; for the history of painting in the nineteenth century, centering in Paris, has been one of continually new assertions of individualism. Our sympathies, quite possibly, will be with the rebels, but that should not blind us to the value of the academic principles of painting.

DAVID—DELACROIX

If there is to be an official and permanent standard, the Classic is the best for the purpose. The standard to be serviceable must be one that can be reduced to a reasonable certainty. In painting, composition and line are the elements which can most readily be formulated; and, when founded upon the canons of antique art, are established upon a basis that the continuing judgment of the world has approved. Given this central body, there is the perpetual inducement for independent spirits to fly off at a tangent from it, which is productive of vitality. The classical ideal provides at once firm groundwork for the average student and a starting-point for independent genius. Permanence and progress are alike insured.

CHAPTER XXI

THÉODORE ROUSSEAU	*JEAN BAPTISTE CAMILLE COROT*
1812–1867	*1796–1875*
Fontainebleau-Barbizon	*Fontainebleau-Barbizon*
School of France	*School of France*

THREE miles from the landscape-forest which adjoins the Palace of Fontainebleau lies the little village of Barbizon. After 1832 it became the headquarters of a group of painters whose school and studio were the forest. They were the second protest of the nineteenth century against the formalism of academical teaching, and, though the artists varied individually, they were all united in their first-hand study of nature, so that they are distinguished as the Fontainebleau-Barbizon School.

Once before there had been a Fontainebleau School, the term being applied to that group of Italian artists —among them Leonardo da Vinci, Andrea del Sarto, and Cellini—whom Francis I invited to decorate his palace. With these men the subject had been the human figure, used with the artificial intention that decoration permits; whereas the group that appeared three hundred years later was concerned with nature, represented naturally. It comprised Rousseau, the acknowledged leader, Jules Dupré, Corot, Diaz, and Daubigny; the sheep and cattle painters, Troyon, Van Marcke, and Jacque; and

ROUSSEAU—COROT

Millet, the painter of the peasant. This new group was related to the Dutch School of landscape-painters of the seventeenth century, through the English Constable.

The latter, learning of the Dutchmen, had revived the natural study of landscape and carried it further than they, introducing into his pictures the greens of nature, truer effects of air and light, and the suggestion of movement in the foliage. During the years from 1822 to 1827 Constable's pictures had been appearing at the Salon, and had been awarded a gold medal. Delacroix, the colorist, was attracted by them; and other painters, tired of the frigid unreality of the classic school, welcomed these nature-studies, and through them were induced to study also the works of the old Dutch landscapists in the Louvre. Among the many, thus influenced, was Rousseau, who had worked in the studio of the classicist Lethière, but, dissatisfied with the latter's grandiloquent canvases, had taken to wandering about the plain of Montmartre with his paint-box, and in 1826 had produced his first little picture.

But another influence played its part in shaping the future of the new school. Romanticism was in the air; Delacroix and others were making their pictures the medium of emotional expression. Accordingly, by the time that the Barbizon men had found themselves, their art was distinguished not only by truth to nature but also by poetic feeling. Of the two whom we are considering, we may say that Rousseau was the epic poet of the group; Corot, the lyric.

Of this lyric quality in Corot's work we may be conscious if we turn to *Dance of the Nymphs*. It yields a suggestion of music and of songfulness; exactly how, it may be hard to explain; but, perhaps, the reason is that there was constant music in the heart of the man who painted it. He sang as he worked, played the violin at intervals, and regularly attended the opera. Comparing himself with Rousseau, he once said, "Rousseau is an eagle. As for me, I am only a lark, putting forth some little songs in my gray clouds."

On the other hand, the epic quality in Rousseau's picture may not be so immediately recognizable; we shall better appreciate it when we have examined the motives of his work more closely. Comparing the example here reproduced with the one by Corot, we note this great difference, that Rousseau's shows a solidity of form and a power of clear decision in the lines inclosing the forms, whereas Corot's masses are by comparison dreamy and unsubstantial, the outlines blurred. Rousseau insists upon the form of objects and the character of their forms, while Corot escapes as far as possible from the actual things and renders the effect which they produce upon the senses. He sought to represent the essences of things; the fragrance, as it were, rather than the flower.

Both these men were city-bred. So, indeed, have been most of the great landscape-painters; a fact which may seem strange, until we remember how apt we all are to long for that which is farthest away from our actual life. Corot's parents were court dressmakers in the days of the first Napoleon, in comfortable circumstances, so that their son never wanted for money. Rousseau's father was a tailor, living up four flights of stairs; and

ROUSSEAU—COROT

Rousseau himself was well on in manhood before he ceased to know the bite of poverty. Corot received the usual classic training and then went to Italy; but it was not until he had paid three visits to that country, and had reached the age of forty-six, that he came under the influence of Rousseau and the course of his art was changed. Even then some ten years elapsed before he perfected that style upon which his fame chiefly rests. Rousseau, on the other hand, found his true bent early.

The critic, Burger-Thoré, writing in 1844, asks a question of Rousseau. "Do you remember," he says, "the years when we sat on the window-ledges of our attics in the Rue de Taitbout and let our feet dangle at the edge of the roof, looking out over the chaos of houses and chimneys, which you, with a twinkle in your eye, would compare to mountains, trees, and outlines of the earth? You were not able to go to the Alps, into the cheerful country, and so you created picturesque landscapes for yourself out of those horrible skeletons of walls. Do you still recall the little tree in Rothschild's garden which we caught sight of between two roofs? It was the one green thing that we could see; every fresh shoot of the little poplar wakened our interest in spring, and in autumn we counted the falling leaves." "From this mood," as Muther says, " sprang modern landscape-painting, with its delicate reserve of subject, and its vigorously heightened love of nature."

Notwithstanding this nature-love in his heart, the young Rousseau at first devoted himself to mathematics, aiming to become a student at the Polytechnic Institution. The fact is interesting as showing that he combined the instincts of an artist and a scientist, a point we shall return to later. Meanwhile, as we have seen, he entered Lethière's studio, and watched him paint such subjects as *The Death of Brutus* and *The Death of Virginia*. But there was nothing in them to satisfy the youth's love of nature, and he began his wanderings with his paint-box in the country round Paris. The year 1833 found him for the first time in the forest of Fontainebleau, and the following year, at the age of twenty-two, he painted his first masterpiece, *Côtés de Grandville*. It was accepted at the Salon, and awarded a medal of the third class.

No further concession, however, could be allowed to a young man so dangerously independent from the academical standpoint, and for thirteen years, indeed until after the Revolution of 1848 and the fall of the " Bourgeois King," Louis Philippe, his pictures were excluded from the official exhibitions. Even then, officialdom, although it could not ignore this leader of a new movement, slighted him by singling out his followers, Dupré, Diaz, Troyon, for the Legion of Honor in preference to himself. It is true they were older men, but what Diaz thought of the slight to Rousseau may be gathered from the words in which he responded to the courtesies tendered him at the official banquet. Rising on his wooden leg, he gave the toast, " Here's to our master who has been forgotten." In the following year, 1852, Rousseau himself was admitted to the Legion. At the Universal Exposition of 1855, the world discovered how great an artist he was; but by this time other shadows were beginning to creep over his life.

ROUSSEAU—COROT

He had married a poor, unfortunate creature, a mere child of the forest, the only feminine being he had found time to love during his toilsome life. After a few years of marriage she was seized with madness; and, while he tended her, Rousseau himself became the victim of an affection of the brain, which darkened his last years. The end came in 1867, the year of another Universal Exposition. He had served as one of the heads of departments on the jury, and in the natural routine should have been awarded the higher rank of officer in the Legion of Honor; instead of which it was given to a man twelve years his junior, Gérôme. It was the climax to the tragedy of his life, and he survived it only a few weeks. In the churchyard of Chailly, near Barbizon, his body rests beneath a stone erected by Millet— a simple cross upon an unhewn block of sandstone, which bears a brass tablet with the inscription, "Théodore Rousseau, Peintre."

What a contrast the happy peace of Corot's life presents! His father had apprenticed him to a linen-draper, but after eight years consented to his becoming a painter. "You will have a yearly allowance of twelve hundred francs," he said, "and if you can live on that you may do as you please." Twenty-three years later, when the son was elected to the Legion of Honor, this allowance was doubled, "for," as the father remarked, "Camille seems to have some talent after all."

We have already alluded to his beginnings as a painter, how he went through the usual course of study of the figure and attempts at classical landscapes after the manner of Poussin. When he paid his first visit to Italy, he was so attracted by the moving life on the streets of Rome and Naples that he longed to transfer it to his sketch-book. But the figures would not remain still long enough to be treated methodically, as he had learned to draw; so he set himself to try and obtain with a few strokes the general effect of the moving picture, and with such success that after a time he could rapidly suggest the appearance of even so intricate a scene as a ballet. This skill was to stand him in good stead, when he should seek to represent the tremble of foliage in the morning or evening air. It taught him also, by degrees, the value of generalization; of not representing details so much as of discovering the salient qualities of objects, and of uniting them into a whole that will suggest rather than definitely describe.

But all this time the inspiration of his work was Italy and the Italian landscape; it was not until he had returned from his third visit thither, and was forty-six, that the landscape of France began to appeal to his imagination. He became acquainted at last with Rousseau, and with the aim of the Barbizon artists to represent nature as surrounded by air and light, and he set to work to learn the method of painting these qualities, reaching finally a style that is peculiar to himself.

It is so closely a result of his personal attitude toward nature, particularly toward the dawn and evening, which were his favorite moments, that a letter to Jules Dupré, in which he describes his sensations at these moments, gives one an understanding of his style.

One gets up early, at three in the morning, before the sun; one goes and sits at the foot of a tree; one watches and waits.

EDGE OF THE FOREST OF FONTAINEBLEAU   LOUVRE, PARIS   ROUSSEAU

DANCE OF THE NYMPHS   LOUVRE, PARIS   COROT

ROUSSEAU—COROT

One sees nothing much at first. Nature resembles a whitish canvas on which are sketched scarcely the profiles of some masses; everything is perfumed, and shines in the fresh breath of dawn. Bing! The sun grows bright, but has not yet torn asunder the veil behind which lie concealed the meadows, the dale, and hills of the horizon. The vapors of night still creep, like silvery flakes, over the numbed-green vegetation. Bing! Bing!—a first ray of sunlight—a second ray of sunlight—the little flowers seem to wake up joyously. They all have their drop of dew which trembles—the chilly leaves are stirred with the breath of morning—in the foliage the birds sing unseen—all the flowers seem to be saying their prayers. Loves on butterfly wings frolic over the meadow and make the tall plants wave—one sees nothing—yet everything is there—the landscape is entirely behind the veil of mist, which mounts, mounts, sucked up by the sun; and, as it rises, reveals the river, plated with silver, the meadows, trees, cottages, the receding distance—one distinguishes at last everything that one had divined at first.

How spontaneous a commentary upon his pictures of early morning—nature in masses, fresh and fragrant, the "numbed-green" of the vegetation, the shiver of leaves, and the twinkling of flowers, the river plated with silver, and the sky suffused with misty light!

In the same letter he describes the evening:

Nature drowses—the fresh air, however, sighs among the leaves—the dew decks the velvety grass with pearls. The nymphs fly—hide themselves—and desire to be seen. Bing!—a star in the sky which pricks its image on the pool. Charming star, whose brilliance is increased by the quivering of the water, thou watchest me—thou smilest to me with half-closed eye! Bing!—a second star appears in the water, a second eye opens. Be the harbingers of welcome, fresh and charming stars. Bing! Bing!

HOW TO STUDY PICTURES

Bing!—three, six, twenty stars. All the stars in the sky are keeping tryst in this happy pool. Everything darkens, the pool alone sparkles. There is a swarm of stars—all yields to illusion. The sun being gone to bed, the inner sun of the soul, the sun of art, awakes. Bon! there is my picture done!

This expresses the dreaming of a poet, and during the last twenty-five years of his life, when his best work was done, it was in this way that he worked. Years ago his father had given him a little house in Ville d'Avray, near Paris, and thither during the summer the old bachelor repaired with his sister. The time was spent in filling his soul with visions of nature, which, when he returned to Paris, were transferred to canvas. This picture that we are studying was painted in 1851, before Corot had reached his final style. It still shows some traces of classic feeling, particularly in the introduction of figures; but also a taste of what was to follow in the soft blur of foliage that tips the slender stems in the center. Later on he generalized even more freely; his trees become masses of softly blurred leafage, silhouetted tenderly against the delicate vibration of the sky, trembling indistinctly as in a dream-picture, while here and there, like the introduction of the word "Bing" in his letter, are little accents of leaves or bits of tree-trunk, vibrating sharply like the twang of a violin string.

Rousseau's advice, on the contrary, to his pupils was, "Form is the first thing to observe." The point to be noted is that, whereas Corot had begun by observing form and had then escaped as far as possible from it, Rousseau, first and always, based his art upon it. Indeed, at the middle period of his life the scientific instinct asserted itself, and for a while he sank the larger feeling for the whole in too exact a representation of detail. But, during his great periods, he exhibited a mastery in the delineation of the impressiveness of form that has never been surpassed. His favorite tree was the oak, with sturdy arms supporting its weight of leaves and branches, and strong roots, in between the rocks, grasping the firm earth. The strength of nature, her deep embedded force, putting itself forth in stout and lusty growth, continuously vigorous; the mighty force of clouds that replenish the earth; the vastness and grandeur of the sky in the full glory of midday, or the superb pageant of the sunset, as in this picture; in a word, the perennial strength of nature, as contrasted with the little lives of men—such was the theme upon which he spent his life. While Corot drank in nature, nature to Rousseau was entirely outside himself. He was in love with her for her own sake.

This was a grander attitude toward nature than that of Corot. The latter, in modern phraseology, was a temperamental artist; that is to say, he chose from nature what suited his moods and painted her with a certain invariableness of manner, as if there were nothing in nature except what he felt about her. All that he did was lovely, but it was limited in scope; whereas Rousseau, with his broad impersonal vision searching nature for what she had to tell him, painted in every picture a different subject. It was the phases of her inexhaustible story, a story as old as mankind and that will outlive the last of humanity, that he treated; and it is for this reason, because he suggested the continuity of her elemental forces, even while depicting a certain phase, that one may rightly describe him as the epic poet of the Barbizon School.

The truth of this would be more evident if we had the opportunity of seeing a number of Rousseau's pictures alongside of a number of Corot's; but even from the comparison of these two examples I think it may be gathered. The *Dance of the Nymphs* is a morning poem; breathing the freshness of a world that, despite of time, is forever innocent and young. The creatures that enliven it, nymphs and satyrs, are the effervescence of fancy, removed very far from the responsibilities and daily experiences of life. The figures which Corot introduces in his landscapes are always embodiments of the spirit of the scene, like the Dryads, Naiads, and Oreads of the old Greek imagining. But in Rousseau's Sunset Scene another day of labor is finished; rest is brooding down upon the tired earth; creatures nearer to nature than beings in the shape of humanity are taking their fill of water before they too settle down upon the earth, that mighty bosom from which all things draw nourishment and on which all rest. Those same cows—or others like them—will inhabit the same scene to-morrow; those sturdy trees and branches will survive another and another day, as they have weathered many; that boulder will defy the effort of time to remove it. The scene, as Rousseau painted it, is typical and elemental; not alone a spot on the edge of the forest of Fontainebleau, but a poem of universal import, whose theme is the ever-present one of earth's enduring strength, and of recurring toil and rest. Rousseau reached this power of elemental expression by continually concentrating his great faculty of observation upon the fundamental qualities of nature, which as compared with man's moods and changes are the same yesterday, to-day, and forever. Corot, on the contrary, nourishing his moods on nature, ended by interpreting these moods of his own rather than nature herself. He is not the great descriptive, epic poet, alive to the mighty forces that underlie the vastness of his subject, but the sweet, lyric singer of a few choice moments. As he said himself: he is the lark; Rousseau, the eagle.

For Corot recognized Rousseau's superiority not only in wider sweep of vision but in his mastery over form; and form is the foundation of all great painting, whether of the human figure or landscape. It is with the close study of forms of nature that all great landscape-painters have begun, even if, like Corot, they subsequently try to merge the form in the expression of the sentiments which the objects of the landscape arouse. For the painter cannot represent spirit to the mind, except by representing to the eye a real suggestion of the form in which it is embodied. This is the lesson of all the landscape-painting which has followed upon the new movement of the Fontainebleau-Barbizon artists.

Landscape to-day is the most living branch of painting; nowhere more so than in our own country. American painters have continued the nature-study and poetic feeling of the Barbizon men, and often have gone farther than they in the rendering of light and air and of the manifold variety of nature's coloring. But whenever we come upon men of commanding talent, such as

HOW TO STUDY PICTURES

George Inness, Alexander Wyant, and Homer Martin among those who are dead, and such as Tryon, Murphy, Horatio Walker, Winslow Homer, and very many others among the living, we shall find that while often they prefer to subordinate form to poetical impression, it is with the precise and patient study of form that they first began. Upon this firm foundation they have subsequently erected the spiritualized fabrics of their poetic fancies. They have not builded castles in the air, but delicate structures planted firmly upon the facts of earth. Hence the hold they take upon the perceptive faculty; for they reach us first through our experience, and then delight our imagination.

CHAPTER XXII

JULES BRETON
1827- .
French School

JEAN FRANÇOIS MILLET
1814–1875
Fontainebleau-Barbizon
School of France

HERE are two pictures of peasant subjects, and, as it happens, with similar titles: Jules Breton's *The Gleaner,* and *The Gleaners* by Jean François Millet.

With what a proud carriage Breton's girl strides through the field! How painfully Millet's women are stooping! Their figures are clumsy, uncouthly clad, and you cannot see their faces. This girl, however, is dressed in a manner that sets off her strong and supple form; her face is handsome and its expression haughtily independent. As the meek women stoop, each carries one of her hands behind her back. If you imitate for yourself the action of leaning down and extending one hand, you will find that the other has an involuntary tendency to go back in order to maintain the balance. This natural tendency of the human body to secure its balance by opposing direction of its parts is a principle that the best artists rely upon to produce a perfect poise of rest or movement in their figures.

Now study the arms in Breton's picture. The left one—with what a gesture of elegant decision it is placed upon the hip!—while the right has the elbow thrown out with an action of freedom and energy. Evidently the girl is not tired, or the elbow would seek support against the chest. Her hands, too, are finely shaped, and the fingers spread themselves rather daintily. I wonder if so light a grasp as that of the right hand on a few ears of wheat would really hold the sheaf in place upon her shoulder. I wonder, also, how her bare, shapely feet withstood the pricks of the stubble. I notice that Millet's women have prudently kept on their clumsy wooden sabots.

But now turn the inquiry toward your own experience. If you went into a wheat-field where peasants were gleaning, would you expect to see a beautiful, proud girl like Breton's, unfatigued by her toil, or homely women like Millet's? I fancy you would be more likely to meet the latter, and I doubt if anywhere in France you might come across such a type as Breton's, which is rather that of the women of the Roman Campagna, a noble remnant of the classic times. She is unquestionably a beautiful creature.

But beauty does not consist only in what is pleasing to the eye ; there is a beauty also which appeals to the mind. "Truth is beauty, beauty is truth." Perhaps if we study Millet's picture we shall find that it has a beauty of its own in its truth to nature. His women are not posing for their picture. Quite unconscious of anybody's gaze, they are absorbed in their toil, doing what they are supposed to be doing in the simplest and most natural way. They are very poor, these peasants; working early and late, and despite all their labor keeping body and soul together with difficulty; a meek, God-fearing race, roughened and drawn out of shape by toil.

With what an intimate insight into the lives of these people as well as into their occupation Millet represents them! He paints them, not as if he were a city gentleman visiting the country, but as if he belonged to their own class. And, as a fact, he did. He was the son of a small farmer, and had bent his own back under the scorching sun and felt the smell of the earth in his nostrils. But an uncle, who was a priest, had taught him as a boy, so that in his manhood he read Shakspeare and Virgil in the original texts. Therefore, although he was of the peasant life, he was greater than it, and brought to the interpretation of its most intimate facts a largeness of view and depth of sympathy which make his pictures much more than studies of peasants. They are types. He painted a picture of a sower that is now in the Metropolitan Museum, New York; and when we have once grasped the fullness of its sufficiency, it becomes to us the type of *The Sower;* so that we could not look on another picture of similar subject without instinctively comparing it in our mind with Millet's.

Breton, on the other hand, had never toiled in the fields; he pursued the usual routine of study through the art schools, whereas Millet, "wild man of the woods," as the other students called him, tried them only to abandon them. He could not master, or bring himself to care about, the elegancies and refinements of drawing as practised in the schools. In these Breton is proficient; he has also written very creditable poetry, so that, when he went into the fields for subjects, he had the teaching of the schools in mind and the sentiment of a poet in his heart. Accordingly he freely translated the peasant into both.

Note, then, these two ways of reaching a poetical result: Breton had beautiful ideas and used the peasant as a peg on which to hang them; Millet, with no direct thought of being poetical, sought only to portray the truth as he saw and felt it. But he has represented the dull, homely facts with such an insight into the relation which they bear to the lives of the people engaged in them, that he has created—and this is the great accomplishment of the poet—an atmosphere of imagination around the facts.

Which of these two methods of poetic creativeness is, *per se,* the better,—whether the starting-point shall be from the imagination, which uses the facts merely as a string to thread its beads upon, or from the facts themselves as the groundwork or justification of the web of imagination woven over them,—is not to be determined here or, probably, anywhere. It is better worth while to regard these two methods as periodically asserting themselves. Thus in the splendid days of the Italian Renaissance the Breton point of view was the one in vogue. In our own era, however, that of Millet has prevailed both in literature and painting. The present is an age of naturalism, and one of the master-minds which helped to make it so was Millet.

His early life was very close to nature. His father's farm was at Gruchy, in the hilly department of Manche, which juts out like a promontory into the English Channel. In that narrow strip the sea is nowhere far off.

He grew up with the air of the hills and of the sea in his nostrils, both conducive to sturdiness of character and to the development of imagination, if a boy chances to have any. And the young Millet had. He knew nothing of art or artists, but he had the desire to represent what he saw, and in the interims of work upon the poor farm he would copy the engravings in the family Bible, or take a piece of charcoal and draw upon a white wall. By the time he was eighteen, a family council was held, and it was decided that the father should take him into Cherbourg and consult a local painter as to Jean's prospects. The painter advised his studying art, and undertook to teach him. However, he worked in Cherbourg only two months, for then his father died and he had to return home to resume his work as a farm laborer. Five more years he labored, until the municipality of Cherbourg provided a subsidy to enable him to go to Paris to study. He was now twenty-three, a broad-chested Hercules, awkward and shy, his big head covered with long fair hair; with nothing to denote intellectual force except a pair of piercing dark-blue eyes. Delaroche, to whose studio he attached himself, was kind to him, but he himself could not understand the large classical pictures that the master painted. To him they seemed artificial, with no real sentiment. Ringing in his ears, even then, as he used to say in later life, was the " cry of the soil "; memories of his home life, that in some way he wanted to learn to paint. Delaroche's studio was no place for him, and after a little while he left it.

Then followed eight years of beating the air. He married, and had to bestir himself for a living. He tried to paint what the people seemed to like—pretty little figure subjects; but prettiness was not in his line, and the attempt to seek it disgusted him. Suddenly he made the great resolve to paint what he wished to and could paint, and, in 1848, produced *The Winnower*. It represented a clumsy peasant, in uncouth working-clothes, stooping over a sieve as he shakes it to and fro. From the academic standpoint, a shockingly vulgar picture! Yet it sold for five hundred francs ($100)! Millet now had the courage of his convictions.

His friend Jacque, afterward the celebrated painter and etcher of sheep and poultry, told him of a little place with a name ending in "zon," near the forest of Fontainebleau, where they could live cheaply and study from nature. The two painters, with their wives and children, rumbled out of Paris in a cart, which took them to the town of Fontainebleau. Thence they proceeded on foot through the forest. It was very wild in those days. "How beautiful!" was Millet's constant exclamation. Arrived at Barbizon, they were welcomed at Ganne's Inn by Rousseau, Diaz, and the other artists who lived in the village, and invited to the evening meal. When a fresh painter came into the colony, it was the custom to take down from the wall a certain big pipe, that, as the newcomer puffed at it, the company might judge from the rings of smoke whether he was to be reckoned among the "classicists" or "colorists." Jacque was proclaimed a colorist, but, some uncertainty being expressed concerning Millet, the latter exclaimed, " Ah! well, if you are embarrassed, put me in a class of my own." "A good answer," cried Diaz, "and he looks

THE GLEANER   JULES BRETON

THE GLEANERS JEAN FRANÇOIS MILLET
LOUVRE, PARIS

strong and big enough to hold his own in it." The little pleasantry was prophetic.

But its fulfilment was deferred for many years, during which Millet worked on in poverty; pictures that now would bring large sums of money being refused at the exhibitions of the Salon and finding no purchasers. A hint of his condition is contained in a letter to his friend Sensier, acknowledging the receipt of twenty dollars: "I have received the hundred francs. They came just at the right time. Neither my wife nor I had tasted food for twenty-four hours. It is a blessing that the little ones, at any rate, have not been in want."

It was only from about his fortieth year that his pictures began to sell at the rate of from two hundred and fifty to three hundred francs each. Rousseau, who had himself known the extremes of poverty, was the first to give him a large sum, buying the *Wood-cutter* for four thousand francs, under the pretense that it was for an American purchaser. It was resold at the Hartmann sale in 1880 for 133,000 francs. By the beginning of the sixties, however, Millet's reputation was no longer in question. At the World's Exposition of 1867 he was represented by nine pictures and received the grand medal. In the Salon of 1869 he was on the hanging committee! But he still continued what has been happily called his "life of sublime monotony"; his sojourn in Barbizon being interrupted only during the war in 1871, when he retired to Cherbourg, painting there some fine pictures of the sea. He died in 1875, at the age of sixty, and was buried in the little churchyard of Chailly, overlooking the forest. A rock in the latter bears a bronze tablet on which the sculptor has represented side by side the bust-portraits of Rousseau, the father of modern French landscape, and Millet, the artist of the people who work in the fields.

In his own words, Millet tried to depict "the fundamental side of men and things." His subject was the peasant life: not the representation of it such as one sees in opera, nor the pretty, sentimental aspect of it; but the actual drama of labor year in and year out proceeding through the four seasons; the "cry of the soil," echoing in the hearts of the patient, plodding, God-fearing toilers. Everything was typical. We have spoken of his *Sower*. Of another picture the critic, Castagnary, wrote: "Do you remember his *Reaper*? He might have reaped the whole earth!"

The secret of it is twofold. Firstly, Millet conceived of his subject as if it were an Epic of Labor; he himself gave to a series of his drawings the title *The Epic of the Fields;* so that all he did was imbued with a deep seriousness and high sincerity. In one of his letters he explains what was in his mind as he painted *The Water-Carrier*,[1] which is now in the possession of Mr. George W. Vanderbilt and at present on exhibition in the Metropolitan Museum, New York.

In the woman coming from drawing water I have endeavored that she shall be neither a water-carrier nor a servant, but the woman who has just drawn water for the house, the water for her husband's and her children's soup; that she shall seem to be carrying neither more nor less than the weight of the full buckets; that, beneath the sort of grimace which is natural on account of

[1] The original title was *Femme qui vient puiser de l'eau.*

the strain on her arms, and the blinking of her eyes caused by the light, one may see a look of rustic kindliness on her face. I have always shunned with a kind of horror everything approaching the sentimental.[1] I have desired, on the other hand, that this woman should perform simply and good-naturedly, without regarding it as irksome, an act which, like her other household duties, is one she is accustomed to perform every day of her life. Also I wanted to make people imagine the freshness of the fountain, and that its antiquated appearance should make it clear that many before her had come to draw water from it.

Secondly, in the representation of a subject, as may be gathered from his letter, he looked only for the essential, the fundamental thing in the gesture or characterization. In another letter he says: "I have been reproached for not observing the *detail;* I see it, but I prefer to construct the *synthesis,* which as an artistic effort is higher and more robust." This gift of his can be more readily studied in his drawings and etchings, in which with a few lines he gives the whole character of a pose or gesture. He never was a facile painter, so that his greatness as an artist is perhaps more discernible in the black-and-white than in the colored subjects. Certainly in his crayon drawings, lithographs, and etchings he proved himself to be one of that limited number of artists who may be reckoned master-draftsmen. Few have displayed in an equal degree the rare gift of expressing the maximum of character with a minimum of lines. Moreover, the character that he expresses is

[1] The only picture of his that can possibly be suspected of sentimentalism is *The Angelus,* the weakness of which is that the point on which it largely depends for its motive is not to be gathered from the picture, but has to be learned from the title.

of that grand and elemental quality which places him, despite the difference of subject-matter, in the neighborhood of Michelangelo.

Millet's influence produced a host of painters of the peasant, among whom the strongest are the Frenchman Lhermitte, and Israels the Dutchman. These, like him, have represented their subject with sympathy and with understanding also. Breton, with whom we have contrasted Millet, did not.

CHAPTER XXIII

GUSTAVE COURBET
1819-1878
Realistic School of France

ARNOLD BOECKLIN
1827-1901
Modern German School

A GLANCE at these two pictures—Boecklin's *Isle of the Dead* and Courbet's *Funeral at Ornans*—reveals at once a great contrast.

In Boecklin's composition the horizontal line is subordinated to the vertical ones; these spire up or tower in bastion-like masses, lifting our imagination with them. In Courbet's, however, the almost level line of the landscape shuts down like a lid upon the parallel horizontal group of figures; the only vertical line that detaches itself is that of the crucifix; but this is too slight to overcome the impression that the composition holds our thoughts to the ground.

These differences of composition correspond to the differences of the artists' motives. Boecklin sought to produce an effect of solemn grandeur, of tranquil isolation, not unmixed with awe; of contrast between the monumental permanence of the island and the frailty and insignificance of the boat, which carries the mourner and the dead over the shifting water to the dead's long home. On the other hand, in Courbet's picture there is no grandeur either of sentiment or appearance; none of the awe that belongs to isolation nor much of the solemnity that attaches to a funeral, for even the ecclesiastical ceremoniousness is offset by the grave-digger in his shirt-sleeves and by the presence of a dog. As for the crowd, some few are mourners, but the rest, drawn thither only by curiosity, or in some cases, as we may judge from their costumes, in an official capacity; all very ordinary every-day people, going through with the business according to the usual routine. For, while Boecklin's picture is a vision of the imagination, Courbet's is a record of facts, the fact of committing a corpse to the ground, as the artist had seen it in his native town of Ornans; a record, so entirely prosaic, that very likely it repels us at first, though it may end by fascinating us for the very reason of its uncompromising truth to reality.

Courbet, in fact, was a realist; Boecklin, a painter-poet. The two ideas, although wide apart, are not absolutely separated, for we shall see presently that the German's poetry was based upon reality and that the Frenchman's realism could yield a measure of poetry. Yet, for a while, it will be better to study the two separately.

We have noted how the classic motive, under the influence of David, marked the beginning of the nineteenth century, and was carried on by his followers, particularly by Ingres. Also that it was attacked, on the one hand by the Romanticists, under the leadership of Delacroix, and on the other by the group of artists at Barbizon who made the study of nature their motive; and that amid this group of naturalists Millet was the great naturalist painter of the peasants, representing them exactly as they appeared in the pursuit of their daily employments.

COURBET—BOECKLIN

But in 1850, when Courbet painted the *Funeral at Ornans,* Millet was known only to a few beyond the limits of Barbizon; none of those Barbizon men had as yet influenced the world; Paris itself, the center of the arts, was the citadel of Classicism. If it was to be stormed, it must be by a personality more robust and with more love of giving and taking hard blows. Such a one was Courbet.

Ornans, his birthplace, is near the beautiful valley of the Doubs, close to the western boundary of Switzerland, and it was here as a boy, and later as a man, that he absorbed the love of landscape, of streams and waterfalls, overhung with rocks and trees, and of quiet pools where the deer steal down to drink; subjects that often occupied his brush. That they did so, in itself marked his difference from classic painters of his time, who cared nothing for landscape; but his main difference was of a much more positive kind.

He was by nature a revolutionary, a man born to oppose existing order and to assert his independence. Of massive build, with a sprinkling of German blood in his veins, broad-shouldered, thick-necked, with a face framed in black hair, and features that might have been modeled from an Assyrian bas-relief, he had that amount of bluster and brutality which makes the revolutionary count in art as well as in politics. And in both directions his spirit of revolt manifested itself.

He started for Paris with the purpose of studying law; but, being arrived there, began to study art. Yet he did not attach himself to the studio of any of the prominent masters. Already in his country home he

HOW TO STUDY PICTURES

had had a little instruction in painting, and now turned for more to the masterpieces of the Louvre. Even in front of these, however, he did not play the part of a submissive student. He looked them over to see what he could gain from them, and gradually discovered a method of painting that would best serve his purpose to be independent of everybody, to see with his own eyes and to paint just what he saw. At first his pictures were not sufficiently distinctive to arouse any opposition, and were admitted to the Salon. So, too, was *The Stone-Breakers,* in which he first displayed his characteristic self. This picture, representing two laborers in uncouth costumes by the roadside, one kneeling as he breaks the stones, the other planting his figure firmly to sustain the weight of a basketful of stones which he is moving,—a picture in which there is no grace of composition, but the strongly painted rendering of an actual episode in the lives of the poor,—declared itself amid the classical surroundings in the Salon of 1851 as, " a rough, true, honest word, spoken amid elaborate society phrases."

Then followed the *Funeral at Ornans,* which the critics violently assailed: " These burlesque masks with their fuddled red noses, this village priest who seems to be a tippler, and the harlequin of a veteran who is putting on a hat which is too big for him "; " A masquerade funeral, six metres long, in which there is more to laugh at than to weep over "; " The most extravagant fancy could not descend to such a degree of triviality and hideousness "; " He means to sneer at the religious ceremony, since the picture has a defiant and directly brutal vulgarity. He has taken pains to expose the repulsive, ludicrous, and grotesque elements in the members of the funeral party."

It will discount the force of these so-called criticisms, to remember that *The Stone-Breakers,* such a subject as Millet might have chosen, was slighted because it represented mere laborers in ragged and dirty clothes, "an excessively commonplace subject,"—and that Millet's pictures at that time were being rejected by a public accustomed only to the peasants of the comic-opera stage.

Indeed the real offense of Courbet's pictures was that they represented live flesh and blood; men and women as they really are, and as really doing the business in which they are engaged,—not men and women deprived of personality and idealized into a type, posed in positions that will decorate the canvas; frigid, marbleized figures like those of Ingres, or tinted and china-like, such as those of Bouguereau. Among these classical and semi-classical painters, whose art was built on formulas, this huge peasant pushed his way, elbowing them roughly, treading intentionally on their toes. They winced at the realities of life—very well, he would give them the realities as strongly, and, if need be, as disagreeably as possible. He spent his evenings at a restaurant where younger artists and the young writers of the school of Balzac congregated. "I am a democrat," he would tell them; and this too, mind you, in the days of Napoleon III. "By doing away with the ideal we shall arrive at the emancipation of the individual. I admire Velasquez, because he saw things with his own eyes, but these imitators of Raphael and Pheidias—pah! It is the greatest impudence to wish to paint things one has never seen, of the appearance of which one cannot have the slightest conception. Better paint railway stations, the views of places through which one travels, the likenesses of great men, engine houses, mines and manufactories, for these are the saints and miracles of the nineteenth century." He advocated painting things as they are, and proclaimed that *la vérité vraie* must be the aim of the artist. So at the Universal Exposition of 1855 he withdrew his pictures from the exhibition grounds and set them in a wooden booth, just outside the entrance, with a big lettering over the door, " Courbet—Realist."

Like every revolutionary, he was an extremist. He ignored the fact that to every artist the truth of nature appears under a different guise according to his way of seeing and experience; and he chose to assert that art is only a copying of nature and not a matter also of selection and arrangement. But in periods of deadness and insincerity, the mute appeal of a Millet living afar off in the quiet woods is unheeded; it needs a big combative fellow, with self-advertisement and beat of drum and loud-voiced blustering exaggeration, to get a hearing and compel a following. It was this part to which nature had fitted Courbet, and which he played with gusto, to the dismay of the academical painters, but attracting the younger men to a fresh study of nature and compelling older men, like Bouguereau and Gérôme, to infuse some semblance of life into their pictures; giving a death-blow also to the idea that prettiness is beauty.

In his contempt for prettiness he often chose subjects which may fairly be called ugly; but that he had a sense of beauty may be seen in his landscapes; and that mingled with it was a capacity for deep emotion, appears in his marines, these last being his most impressive work. Moreover, in all his works, whether attractive or not to the student of mere subject, he proved himself a powerful painter, painting in broad, free manner, with a fine feeling for color, and with a firmness of pigment that made all his representations very real and stirring. Since his day, and in consequence of his pounding influence, painting has to a considerable extent broken loose from the shackles of conventional formulas, and the sickliness of mere prettiness and sentimentality. The painter, instead of being satisfied to tint his pictures, has learned the lesson of painting, and gone again to nature for his motives and instruction. Modern art thereby is more vigorous and wholesome.

While recognizing this, however, we must not forget that Courbet went too far in condemning the Classicists, just as the latter exceeded reason in their wholesale condemnation of him. We cannot agree with them that to represent life as it really appears, is vulgar and commonplace; nor with him that painting needs no formulas, that it can ignore, for example, rules of composition; that it is impudence to paint what one has never seen, and foolish to learn of the great masters of the past; that "imagination is rubbish and reality the one true muse."

For while art should draw continual nourishment from nature, we must remember that nature is not art. For art displays itself in selecting from nature and arranging what it has borrowed in such a way as to produce a balanced harmonious ensemble. Thus, the wide landscape spread out before us, as we sit on a hilltop, may seem, as is so often the case in nature, a perfectly balanced whole; yet, if the artist selects a portion of it suitable for the size of his canvas, he will have to adjust the parts of this part, add to them, or leave out some details, if he would make his picture balanced and harmonious. There is no doubt that Courbet himself did this in the case of his marines and landscapes, notwithstanding his assertions that he painted only just what he saw. In a word, he had the artist's instinct of selection, however much he may have kicked against the restrictions of rules.

And now that we realize something of the man and of his motives as a painter, let us turn again to his *Funeral at Ornans*. "A masquerade funeral," the critics called it; "a sneer at the religious ceremony,"—but surely the bearers are performing their task with a simple sense of responsibility; the coffin is not sensationally forced into prominence, but, on the contrary, introduced into the picture with much reserve; priest and crucifer may display no emotion, but they are showing ordinary attention to their duties; one of the little acolytes, as a boy will, is showing inattention, but throughout the rest of the group, the persons are exhibiting different varieties of feeling from deep affliction to almost complete indifference, just as one may observe to-day on any occasion of a largely attended funeral.

A sensationalist would have emphasized every point that could extract our sympathies—the coffin, the beauty of the service, the grief of the mourners, the yawning grave. Everything would have been keyed up to a dramatic intensity. But Courbet, with a wider vision, and perhaps a larger sympathy, has viewed the incident in its

FUNERAL AT ORNANS   LOUVRE, PARIS   COURBET

THE ISLE OF THE DEAD BOECKLIN

real relation to life. "Loss," as Tennyson says, "is common to the race"; death plunges a little circle of near and dear ones into grief, and causes a slight stir of respectful interest in a somewhat larger circle of social or business acquaintances; but the world, outside of them, goes on its way of work and pleasure, and nature, as typified in that level line of landscape, is absolutely indifferent. When you come to think of it, this picture, by merging the poignancy of grief in surroundings of mere respect, and by framing the little incident in the vast indifference of the world outside of it, has struck a deeper note of human tragedy than any highly-wrought-up spectacle of mere sorrow could have done. It also proves how much greater than his theories was Courbet himself. The reason is, that he had the faculty of great portrait-painters of seizing the character of his subject; not so much on the few occasions that he really painted portraits, but in a more general way in all his work. Whether it was landscape, marine, or men, women, or animals, that he painted, he represented the physical aspect of the subject with such force and actuality, that every one of his subjects suggests an actual individuality. You may note this in the faces and figures of the people round the grave. They are all real people, who for a few minutes have left their real concerns in a real world to pay their respects to the reality of death.

And now let us turn to Boecklin's *Isle of the Dead*. While Courbet stands firm and steady on the earth, the German painter-poet lifts our imagination into the upper region of the spirit. The little boat with the upright figure, robed in white (not in black, observe), is the focus-point to which the composition is adjusted, and to which our eyes are drawn in preparation for the start of our imagination. Compare this ferry-boat with that of Charon's in Delacroix's picture of *Dante and Virgil,* the agony of writhing forms, Charon's terrific energy, and in the distance the flames of Phlegethon. Here the boat with its quick and dead is isolated; an inexpressible calm broods over it; its littleness approaches noiselessly a greater calm, a vaster isolation. Its frailty upon the shifting water bears the chances and changes of mortality to a resting-place that has the suggestion of immemorial permanence. I find myself thinking of that solitary peak above Vailima, where what is mortal of Robert Louis Stevenson reposes. Far down below upon the island shore is the lapping of ocean that to human eye stretches shoreless; around and above the bed of rest, the sky's infinity; not "earth to earth, dust to dust," but the atom of spirit united to the Universal Spirit. So Boecklin has pictured the entrance of the Dead into the infinite seclusion from all we call the world, into communion with the immensity of the Elements.

It is characteristic of him that he has not attempted to lift our imagination to such heights by representing the island in a purely imaginary way, as a spot that the elements unaided have fashioned out of nature. Men have been here before; living, vigorous men, who have walled off the encroachments of the ocean, set up piers of hewn stone; possibly planted the cypresses, certainly honeycombed the rocks and built up tombs. An island such as this may exist somewhere; it is not geologically impossible, and might have been wrought to its purpose of a burial-place, as this has been. Thus, always, Boecklin's imagination is based upon facts; and from these facts of knowledge we can proceed, step by step, to the point where knowledge ceases and imagination makes a leap into the beyond.

To appreciate this, let us glance at the process of Boecklin's own development as a painter. The son of a Swiss merchant, he was born in Basel, "one of the most prosaic towns in Europe." At nineteen he entered the art school at Düsseldorf, then the center of the school of sentimental and anecdotal pictures, but was advised by his master to proceed to Brussels, where he copied the old Dutch masters. In this way he learned the actual art of painting, which in Germany had been neglected, the subject being held of more importance than the method of representing it. From Brussels he passed to Paris, and studied in the Louvre, whence he made his way to Rome. Though he returned for a time to Germany and after 1886 lived until his death in Zurich, the country which affected his life, where he lived during that period in which his particular genius unfolded itself, was Italy. It was from the Roman Campagna, sad and grand, with its vast stretches, broken by ruins; from the fantastic rocks of Tivoli, where the Anio plunges down in cataracts, overhung with luxuriant growth of trees and shrubs and vines; from the smoothly sloping hills near Florence, dotted with villas and olive orchards, overlooking the valley and the winding of the Arno, that he drew the inspiration for his landscapes.

Like the Frenchmen, Poussin and Claude Lorrain, in the seventeenth century, and many other German artists of his own time, he introduced into his pictures "a harmonious blending of figures with the landscape." But, unlike these other painters, he does not depict some historical, mythical, or Biblical subject and then make his landscape conform to the action and sentiment of the figures. With him the love of landscape was first and foremost; whereupon, having conceived the mood and character which his landscape should express, he put in figures to correspond with them. This, as we have seen, is what Corot did, whose figures are embodiments of the spirit of the scene. But Boecklin went much further than he in this direction.

In the first place, in the range and variety of the moods of nature which he interpreted, so that his figures, the offspring of his landscapes, touch deeper and more varied notes. Here in the narrow solitude of rocks and trees, a hermit is scourging his bare back, before a rude cross, while a raven hovers overhead; elsewhere on a rocky hillside the silence is broken by the cry of Pan, who grins to see how he has startled the goatherd and his goats; or again, robed figures move in a stately single line through a sacred grove, while others bow before a smoking altar. Further, as the Greeks peopled their streams and woods and waves with creatures of their imagination, so Boecklin makes the waterfall take shape as a nymph, or the mists which rise above the water-source wreathe into forms of merry children; or in some wild spot hurls centaurs together in fierce combat, or makes the slippery, moving wave give birth to Nereids and Tritons. Yet even here his imagination works with originality. These sea-creatures, lolling on the rocks or floating lazily on the water, are full of sensuous enjoyment; there is cruelty in their faces as there is beneath the surface of the smiling sea. Nor are his centaurs shapely, with grand heads, like the Greek ones; they are shaggy and shambling with primitive savagery, creatures of a fierce time while the world was still in the making.

Boecklin's imagination went even further; he invented new forms, as in *A Rocky Chasm*, where there issues from a crevice a kind of dragon, web-footed, with long craning neck and a pointed feeble head, a creature as eerie as the dim abyss in which it harbors.

He was, in fact, a Greek in his healthy love of nature and his instinct for giving visible expression to her voices; a modern in his feeling for the moods of nature; and in his union of the two, unique. Moreover, he was a great colorist. "At the very time," writes Muther, "when Richard Wagner lured the colors of sound from music, with a glow of light such as no master had kindled before, Boecklin's symphonies of color streamed forth like a crashing orchestra. Many of his pictures have such an ensnaring brilliancy that the eye is never weary of feasting upon their floating splendor. Indeed, later generations will probably honor him as the greatest color-poet of the century."

Boecklin as well as Courbet was a man of fine physique and wholesome robustness; but, whereas the German's mind was as sane as his body, the Frenchman's lacked this admirable poise. He had always been a revolutionary in art, and lost no opportunity of being one in politics. From the consequences of his share in the Revolution of 1848 he was shielded by some influential friends; but, when the French army had been defeated by the Germans at Sedan in 1871 and the terror of the Commune had been established in Paris, he threw himself into the turmoil, and received from the self-constituted government the position of Minister of Fine Arts. He managed to save the Louvre and the Luxembourg from the fury of the mob, but in order to do so had to let it wreak its madness on the Vendôme column. Nevertheless, when order was restored, he was held accountable for the destruction of the latter, and was fined a large sum which more than swallowed up his fortune, and in addition he was banished. Broken in spirit, he retired to Vevay on the Lake of Geneva, to die.

CHAPTER XXIV

DANTE GABRIEL ROSSETTI
1828-1882
*Pre-Raphaelite Brotherhood,
England*

WILLIAM HOLMAN HUNT
1827-
*Pre-Raphaelite Brotherhood,
England*

IN 1850, the year in which Courbet's *Funeral at Ornans* aroused the anger of the French critics, London was amused by the appearance of Rossetti's *Ecce Ancilla Domini* ("Behold the Handmaid of the Lord") and Holman Hunt's *A Converted British Family Sheltering a Christian Missionary*. It was not only the pictures, but even more the pretensions of their authors that excited ribaldry. A year before, these two young men, Rossetti being then twenty-one and Hunt twenty-two, had joined with another young painter, John Millais, and with three young sculptors, James Collinson, Frederick George Stephens, and Thomas Woolner, and with Rossetti's younger brother, William M. Rossetti, in forming a society. They had taken to themselves the title of the Pre-Raphaelite Brotherhood, and were in the habit of affixing to their signatures the letters, P. R. B.

The object of the Brotherhood was revolt against existing views and conditions of art; in its original intention not unlike the revolt of Courbet, a plea for realism. He was ridiculing the dry formalism of the Classicists, and scoffing at the way in which painters allowed themselves to be bound by the "worn-out" traditions of Raphael; advocating instead a representation of nature as it actually appears to the eye of the painter. In like manner the Brotherhood protested against the cult of Raphael, which, since its introduction into England by Sir Joshua Reynolds, had reduced the teaching of art to arbitrary rules about lines of grace and stately compositions, flowing draperies, and artificial poses, substituting a cast-iron system for the free and truthful rendering of nature. But while the sturdy Courbet flung all traditions aside and found his motives in the present, the Brotherhood, under the dominating influence of Rossetti, who, as we shall see, was already a deep student of Dante and filled with the spirit of the thirteenth and fourteenth centuries, sought the impulse of a new tradition in the painters who preceded Raphael: Fra Angelico, for example, and Botticelli.

These "Primitives" belonged to the springtime of the Renaissance, looking out upon the world with fresh young eyes; even their lack of skill in drawing and their *naïve* sentiment were refreshing in comparison with the stilted, pompous insincerity and soullessness of the modern followers of Raphael. Even the latter himself was attacked by Ruskin, who had stepped forward as the expounder and champion of the Brotherhood's ideals. After citing with what truth to the facts of nature the great masters, and especially Titian, rendered every detail of the foregrounds of their landscapes with most laborious fidelity, he proceeded to contrast the unreality of Raphael's conceptions, taking, as a text, his cartoon of *Christ Walking upon the Water*.

D. G. ROSSETTI — HOLMAN HUNT

Note [he says] the handsomely curled hair and neatly tied sandals of the men who have been out all night in the sea mists and on slimy decks. Note their convenient dresses for going a-fishing, with trains that lie a yard along the ground, and goodly fringes—all made to match, an apostolic fishing costume. Note how Peter especially (whose chief glory was in his wet coat girt about him, and naked limbs) is enveloped in folds and fringes, so as to kneel and hold his keys with grace. No fire of coals at all, nor lonely mountain shore, but a pleasant Italian landscape, full of villas and churches, and a flock of sheep to be pointed at; and the whole group of apostles, not around Christ, as they would have been naturally, but straggling away in a line, that they may all be seen. The simple truth is, that the moment we look at the picture we feel our belief in the whole thing taken away. There is visibly no possibility of that group ever having existed, in any place or on any occasion. It is all a mere mythic absurdity, and faded concoction of fringes and muscular arms, and curly heads of Greek philosophers. Now the evil consequences of the acceptance of this kind of religious idealism for true, were instant and manifold. So far as it was received and trusted in by thoughtful people it only served to chill all the conceptions of sacred history which they might otherwise have obtained. Whatever they could have fancied for themselves about the wild, strange, infinitely stern, infinitely tender, infinitely varied veracities of the life of Christ, was blotted out by the vapid fineries of Raphael. The rough Galilean pilot, the orderly custom-receiver, and all the questioning wonder and fire of uneducated apostleship, were obscured under an antique mask of philosophic faces and long robes.

And having made a stand for truth to nature and the probabilities of fact, Ruskin concludes with the statement of his belief that in modern times, and especially in northern climes where people are so much dressed up in clothes, the representation of physical strength and beauty can no longer be the highest aim of art; and in an age which is before all things intellectual, painting should make spiritual expression, instead of form, the object of its most serious study. The art of the new age must be religious, mystic, and thoughtful, and at the same time true to nature. And it was because the Pre-Raphaelite Brotherhood seemed to recognize this, that he asserted it was going to be epoch-making.

Probably no critic of art ever had such a knowledge and love of nature as Ruskin, and few have equaled him in the intuitive appreciation of what is fine in art. But he was so much bigger a man than a mere art critic,—a moralist, a scientist, instinctively religious, versed in literature, and possessed of rare literary gifts,—that he could not help looking at painting, as it were, through these different-colored glasses and wishing to have it conform to the color of each. He could not, at any rate he did not, recognize the independent status of painting: that it is not primarily a means of inculcating morals, of teaching religion or science, or of playing second fiddle to the more elaborately explanatory possibilities of literature; but that it is first and foremost a visible expression of material things, just as music is of immaterial ideas. The latter is independent of morals, religion, and of descriptive or dramatic story, although it may contribute very forcibly to all of them. So painting may; yet this is not its primary function. It is an independent art, whose chief concern is with external appearances.

Moreover, though Ruskin was as earnest an advocate of truth to nature as Courbet, he did not understand the meaning of artistic truth. While Courbet sought a powerful generalization of the whole subject, expressed by means of a broad and large technic, Ruskin taught that the artist should render every characteristic detail with minute exactness. If he painted rocks, for example, he must show unmistakably to what particular geological species they belonged; and in his foregrounds must render the blades of grass and the flowers with "the most laborious botanical fidelity." The artist, whose proper function is to reveal to eyes less sensitive and trained than his own "a new heaven and a new earth," he would have had pother over nature with a microscope, emulating the patient investigations of the botanist and geologist. In fact, he preached—for he was even more a preacher than an art critic—a sort of religion of truth, that tended to enslave the artist's freedom of vision and imagination still more than the requirements of the church had done in the days of the Early Renaissance. The result was for a long time disastrous to English painting and to English public taste; for it established as a standard of excellence a petty rendering in smooth, precise manner of the little insignificances, at the expense of the larger truth of the whole. Ruskin was fond of quoting from the Bible, but missed the application of one text—"Woe unto you, scribes and Pharisees, hypocrites! for ye pay tithe of mint and anise and cummin, and have omitted the weightier matters of the law. Ye blind guides, which strain at a gnat and swallow a camel."

The Brotherhood, as a compact group, bound together by a common regard for sincerity and high purpose, lasted only a short time. Its members drifted into separate lines of work, yet its influence upon art both in England and on the Continent was far-reaching. However, the direction which it took may better be considered after we have studied the two men, Rossetti and Holman Hunt, who proved to be the most distinctively original members of the disbanded Brotherhood.

Ruskin's contention that modern art must be concerned with spiritual expression was realized in Rossetti; that it must be religious in motive and truthful to the minutest detail, in Holman Hunt. This will be apparent in a study of the two pictures here reproduced. In *The Blessed Damozel* our interest is drawn toward the face of the woman looking down; everything else is contributory to the impression that it arouses; even the title excites our wonder. Who is she, and why that expression of her face? In *The Light of the World,* however, it is the matter-of-factness of the picture that first attracts us. Its title, even if we have not immediately noticed the crown of thorns, makes us aware that the figure is Christ. But there is here no grandeur of drapery, or noble pose, or elevated type of countenance. The last is that of a man of the people; only the splendor of the gold-embroidered cloak and its jeweled clasp suggest that the man is more than ordinary. He knocks at a door, overgrown with vines and weeds, a door, therefore, that has remained long shut. Every spray and leaf and flower is lighted sharply by the lantern. Behind the figure, forming a halo round the head, appears the full moon. We remember the text, " The

THE BLESSED DAMOZEL   DANTE GABRIEL ROSSETTI

OWNED BY THE HON. MRS. O'BRIEN

LIGHT OF THE WORLD   HOLMAN HUNT
KEBLE COLLEGE, OXFORD

foxes have holes, and the birds of the air have nests; but the Son of man hath not where to lay his head."

The appearance of this picture in 1854 had a peculiar timeliness. For many years a great awakening had been going on in the Church of England, corresponding to the political, social, and industrial awakening that was spreading over the country as a result of the extension of the franchise by the first Reform Act, and of the introduction of steam and railroads. As a set-off to what seemed to many minds only a material revival, began a religious one, the nursery and stronghold of which was the University of Oxford, so that it became known as the Oxford Movement. Its aims were threefold: to uphold the direct descent of the Church of England from the days of the Apostles, to promote religious piety, and to bring back to public worship the beauty of ritual that it had had prior to the Reformation. Everywhere throughout the land the clergy and people had been asleep, the cathedrals and churches had fallen into decay, but the new spirit of devotion aroused a longing to revive the outward beauty of the past, and one of the most important phases of the movement became the Gothic Revival. The consequence was that, while the most energetic movement in French art at that time was toward a true representation of the world of to-day, the English one devoted itself to a renewal of the past; and not of the classic traditions, but of those of the Middle Ages.

One can now understand how this picture, *The Light of the World,* appealed to the religious feeling of its day. People saw in the doorway overrun with vines and blocked with weeds, an allegory of what had been the condition of the churches and their congregations before the awakening; until Christ, with the lantern of truth, had stolen in upon the night of spiritual sleep, and aroused the sleepers with his knock. After its exhibition in London it went on a pilgrimage throughout the country, and hundreds of thousands of copies were sold in engravings.

In the first place it represented Christ, not in the conventional classic draperies, but in his capacity of priest, in the revived vestments of the church—the alb and cope; moreover, not with a head like a Greek philosopher's, but with the features of a man of the people and the expression of a visionary. In the second place, the picture was full of highly wrought detail; beautiful plant-forms that recalled the delicate traceries of Gothic decoration: metal-work and jewelry and embroidered needlework, the crafts which were being revived in the service of religion. Furthermore, the very exactness with which all these were rendered gave pleasure to a public, that under Ruskin's instruction had learned to look for two qualities in a picture—a beautiful story, preferably a religious one, and a patiently accurate representation of detail.

The success of the picture determined the future course of Hunt's work; which has remained religious in subject and minutely realistic. He visited the Holy Land, that he might study the type and characteristics of the descendants of the Bible personages, the appearance of the sacred landscape, the customs of the people, their mode of life, and the implements and utensils of daily use. Accumulating the results of his researches, he sought by means of exact rendering of modern conditions to get as near as possible to the probable conditions of the past.

The most remarkable example is *The Shadow of the Cross,* in which he represents Christ in the carpenter's shop in Nazareth. He not only gave him the homely appearance of an ordinary artisan, but carried the truth to facts so far as to paint him naked except for a leather apron; a strong brown-skinned man, with the muscles shown and even the hair upon the breast and legs. In front of him is the bench at which he has been planing, and shavings of wood cover the floor. He has paused for a moment's rest and is stretching his arms, and the evening sun streaming through the window throws the shadow of his body upon the wall in the form of a cross. This suggestion is so solemn, and the intensely religious conviction of the artist so apparent in the picture, that, what might have been merely a dry archæological inventory, is lifted up to unmistakable nobility. And this, notwithstanding the harshness of coloring, the abrupt lines of the composition, the lack of atmosphere, and the baldness and metallic glitter of the textures. In fact, despite the absence of those qualities which one looks for in good painting, Hunt's pictures are strangely impressive.

Indirectly they gave rise to a new motive in religious painting. Touched by the human as well as the spiritual beauty of the Saviour's life, artists, such as Fritz von Uhde in Germany, and Lhermitte in France, have represented him as once more visibly moving among men. The former, for example, has interpreted the subject of *Let the Little Children come unto Me,* by a scene in a village school in the Bavarian Alps. From the sunshine outside the Saviour has stepped in, and the peasant children are gathered round with looks of wonder, drawn to him by the sweetness of his invitation. Lhermitte, on his part, among other kindred subjects, pictured a family of peasants at their lunch, bowing their heads, while Christ himself, seated at the humble board, pronounces a blessing on the food. Religion to these people is the chief solace of their lives of toil, and so unquestioning is their simple faith, that the miraculous appearance of the Christ, treated with utmost reverence, as it is, seems to have a touching and beautiful naturalness.

And now let us turn to Rossetti. His father, an Italian patriot, who had sought refuge in London, where he became professor of Italian at King's College, was a distinguished Dante scholar. His children were all gifted. Maria Francesca, the elder daughter, wrote a critical work, entitled, " The Shadow of Dante "; Christina, the younger, became celebrated as a poet; and their younger brother, William Michael, is a well-known writer and critic. Dante Gabriel, the subject of our present study, was poet as well as painter.

He was extraordinarily precocious, very early acquainted with Scott and Shakspeare, and the author at six years old of a drama in blank verse. But the chief influence of his childhood was the worship of Dante. He knew the poems by heart. " The mystical poet became his guide through life and led him to Fra Angelico, the mystic of painting." He attended Cary's drawing-school and the schools of the Royal Academy; but could not find in their systematic methods the help he wanted; therefore he sought the advice of Ford Madox Brown, and eventually of Holman Hunt. He was impatient to paint the pictures that thronged his brain, and impatient of the dry routine of steady instruction, and in consequence never acquired a complete command of drawing. Perhaps he was encouraged not to try for it, in consequence of his fondness for subjects from Dante and his instinctive feeling that they must be represented with the almost childlike simplicity of feeling, the mystic dreaminess and sweetly embarrassed manner of Fra Angelico and the other "Primitives" who adorned the early garden of the Renaissance. For in his heart he belonged to that time; it was as if the spirit of those children of painting had, after many transmigrations, become reincarnated on the banks of the Thames.

And while he persevered in painting, he was continually experimenting in poetry. The exquisitely beautiful poem, afterward pictured in *The Blessed Damozel,* was written in his nineteenth year. The picture was not painted till 1879, when he was fifty-one. In the interval he had known the woman who became to his life and art what Saskia had been to Rembrandt's. In 1850 he met Miss Elizabeth Siddal, a milliner's assistant, who was introduced to him as a model. According to William M. Rossetti she was " tall, finely formed, with a lofty neck, and regular, yet somewhat uncommon features, greenish blue, unsparkling eyes, large perfect eyelids, brilliant complexion, and a lavish wealth of coppery golden hair." She satisfied at once his conception of a perfectly balanced soul and body, of soul-beauty shining through the beauty of form, which was his ideal of woman. She became also his ideal of Beatrice, and as such he painted her many times. He loved her, but for some reason marriage was postponed for ten years, and then after scarcely two years of married life she died. But the memory of her abided with him, and almost all his subsequent painting was a representation, in one character or another, of his Beloved. And, with the years, her type of beauty expanded, losing its girlishness in richer ampleness, becoming more glorified in his imagination.

By the time that he painted *The Blessed Damozel,* he was broken in health, old before his time, and not far from death. In 1870 the volume of his poems had been published, and attacked violently by Robert Buchanan under the title of, "The Fleshly School of Poetry." Suffering from the loss of his wife, and being the victim of insomnia, he was wounded out of all proportion to the circumstances, fancied that a conspiracy had been formed against him, and became a prey to the most morbid sensibility. In his misery he grew more addicted to the use of chloral, which he had taken to alleviate insomnia. Only at intervals, encouraged by his friends, who clung to him, could he work.

There is, therefore, a great tragedy embodied in this picture. Read the poem, written in the springtime of his life, when yet he was only dreaming of what love might be. Is it not strangely prophetic, that even then, it was not the possession, but the loss of the Beloved, that filled his thoughts?

> The blessed damozel leaned out
>   From the gold bar of heaven;
> Her eyes were deeper than the depth
>   Of waters stilled at even.
>
> . . . . .
>
> Herseemed she scarce had been a day
>   One of God's choristers;
> The wonder was not yet quite gone
>   From that still look of hers;
> Albeit, to them she left, her day
>   Had counted as ten years.
>
> . . . . .
>
> It was the rampart of God's house
>   That she was standing on;
>
> . . . . .
>
> So high, that looking downward thence
>   She scarce could see the sun.
>
> . . . . .
>
> "I wish that he were come to me,
>   For he will come," she said.

Since those lines were written, she had come to him, possessed him, been taken from him, and become his forever.

Devotion to this one woman was the source at once of strength and of weakness to his art. Of strength, because, in the first place, it attracted him to outward appearances and gave form and substance to his dreams, and taught him to express the invisible through the visible, while enabling him to realize the conceptions with which his mind was stored and suggesting others to his imagination. On the other hand, it was a source of weakness, because it narrowed him to one type on which he perpetually harped with variations, so that masses of coppery golden hair, heavy-lidded dreamy eyes, a mouth with curling lips, and a long full throat appear and reappear with various degrees of exaggerated emphasis; while his imagination, absorbed in the contemplation of one idea, gives birth continually to one slightly varying form of highly wrought sentiment. He retreats from the manifold sensations of the open, sun-cleansed world, into a hothouse, whose air is laden with the fragrance of the orchid.

Yet we should remember that this single devotion to one type, while it limited his art, may have been necessary to it, the only thing that could have ripened the fruit of which it was capable. We have seen how Dante, and especially the poet's mystic love for Beatrice, filled his early thoughts. When he met Elizabeth Siddal, he met his own Beatrice; henceforth she was to be to him the incarnation of his own spiritual life, the inspiration of his art as the Florentine damozel had been to Dante's. Nor, while she was the companion and nourishment of his spiritual solitude, is it to be assumed that but for her he would have gone outside himself and nourished his art with the rains and sunshine of the actual world. As we have said, he did not belong to our own age, but to Dante's.

By the latter, and the poets of his time, who followed the " sweet new style " that had been derived from Bologna, love was regarded as the mark of the gentle heart and the service of love as the means of realizing the ideals of the spirit, so that the particular woman was rather a visible embodiment of these ideals than a being to be loved and possessed in a human way. If, as seems well-nigh certain, this was also Rossetti's conception of art and life, it is clear he could have found the best within him only by this exclusive devotion to one type.

He lived in a dream-world, thronged with emotions. These soul-thoughts, too deep, too wide, too vague and infinite to be captured by brush or pen, being inexpressible, he yet tried, as far as possible, to express, sometimes in poems, sometimes in pictures. The latter are brilliant in color, glowing with brightly hued fabrics, precious stones, and flowers; a world of glorious fancy, in which the figures live as in a trance. Never since Perugino had there been figures so wrapped in spiritual solitude as these. But Rossetti's are fuller of expression, suggesting not only mystic ecstasy but a wide range of spiritual expressiveness. Yet, like the Umbrian artist's, they are calm in attitude and slow in gesture, and through this very immobility express the most vivid intensity of inner life.

Though courting seclusion in his London home, at Cheyne Walk, Chelsea,[1] Rossetti nevertheless became the center of a group of men whose influence on art has been wide-spread. Among them were William Morris, Burne-Jones, Walter Crane, George Frederick Watts, Swinburne, the poet, and the novelist and poet, George Meredith. Through Morris and Walter Crane a new impulse was given to decorative art. Sick of the tedious,

[1] The home of artists, also, so wide apart as Holbein and Whistler.

soulless repetition of Renaissance ornament, these men went farther back to a study of Gothic and Celtic ornament, which led them to a study of nature's plant- and flower-forms as motives for decoration. Out of this arose a new spirit of invention, which spread over Europe and to some extent has appeared in America, resulting in the revival of a desire for beauty in objects of art-craftsmanship, and in an increase of original creative skill on the part of the designers, until decorative art has once more become a live one.

That phase of Pre-Raphaelism which is represented by Rossetti, "the painter of the soul," was continued by Burne-Jones and was welcomed in France by some artists who were tired of the long series of pictures dealing with the external life of peasants and social functions. They too began to try and express the subtle emotions of the spirit; and from France the new movement extended to Germany, Switzerland, Belgium, and Austria. The Brotherhood, in its beginning, had started a magazine, called the "Germ." Only four numbers appeared; but the seed, scattered, after long years brought forth flowers, the blue flowers of idealism.

CHAPTER XXV

KARL THEODOR VON PILOTY	MARIANO FORTUNY
1826-1886	1838-1874
Munich School of Germany	Spanish-Parisian School

IN the *Spanish Marriage* there is a profusion of beautiful detail to gladden the eye ; in the canvas by Piloty, a great deal to stimulate our appetite for historical incidents. We already feel a curiosity to become acquainted with this particular one; we reach for a history to discover who these people are and how they happen to find themselves in the circumstances represented; and, having read the story, we shall proceed to search the picture to identify the persons and see how the incident has been portrayed. All of which has, strictly speaking, nothing to do with the appreciation of the painting, as a painting. On the other hand, to appreciate the *Spanish Marriage,* we need no help from the outside; the incident depicted explains itself. We note the moment selected is the signing of the register; and, having done so, we are free to enjoy without any interruption the brilliant groups of figures and the exquisite delicacy of the rococo screen and the other details of the sacristy ; or, if we were facing the original, would step backward, so that the sparkle and luster of its coloring might affect us as a whole.

Further, let us contrast the two pictures from the point

HOW TO STUDY PICTURES

of view of composition. In Fortuny's the figures are sprinkled like gay flowers across the canvas, and surrounded by open spaces; the impression produced being one of spaciousness and dignity, united to elegant sprightliness. In that of Piloty, however, the figures, following the line of a letter S, occupy almost all the composition. Except for the little piece of ground in front and the view beyond the arch, there are no quiet spaces in the picture, and both these, you will observe, are cut into by crossing lines. Moreover, Fortuny has massed his shade beyond the screen, giving a depth and mystery to the distance that lend additional piquancy to the figures in the foreground, while helping to unite them into one composition. Piloty's composition, however, with its scattered light and shade, is arranged to give prime importance to the center group composed of Thusnelda and her child and handmaids, and a somewhat slighter prominence to the emperor, Tiberius, and the bevy of court ladies. Below the latter are the lighted figures of the old bard and the German soldier to whom he is bound, which form, as it were, a prelude to the central mass of light.

Now, while the composition of each picture is regulated with deliberate artifice, Fortuny's is so tactful that the scene appears real and impresses us at once as a single harmonious whole, in comparison with which Piloty's seems artificial and confused and broken up. Perhaps the confusion is intentional, the artist seeking in this way to create a suggestion of stupendous impressiveness, corresponding to the strange, variegated, tumultuous spectacle that the actual incident must have pre-

THUSNELDA AT THE TRIUMPH OF GERMANICUS   KARL THEODOR VON PILOTY
METROPOLITAN MUSEUM, NEW YORK

SPANISH MARRIAGE

MARIANO FORTUNY

sented. If so, in order to attain his object, he has sacrificed the unity of his picture, which, as it now stands, is really a combination of several compositions,—the group with the bear in the front; the group of women; the emperor's group, and that of the senators at the back welcoming Germanicus, the conqueror,—a distribution of separate incidents ingeniously linked together.

And now examine more closely the individual figures. Those in the *Spanish Marriage,* how they brim with life and character! Note the attitude of the priest, as he rises from his chair and leans over the table while the bridegroom signs his name. What an elderly fop the latter is, arrayed in a delicate lilac costume! The bride is in a white gown, trimmed with flowered lace, and has a wreath of orange-blossoms in her luxuriant black hair. She is toying with a fan, enjoying its pretty decorations, while she listens to the talk of a girl friend, who leans forward with a most delightful gesture of dainty grace. How cleverly the artist has suggested in the conduct of all the people present, that this union of age and youth is not an affair of the heart! Observe particularly the indifference which the couple sitting on the right display to what is going on ; while an old man has removed to a far corner, and sits with his hat on his head, as if in contempt of the whole proceeding.

Nor in Piloty's picture is there any lack of characteristic gestures and poses ; every figure enacts some separate part in the drama ; each is drawn with correctness and power. Yet, I suspect, the sum total of the impression that we receive is not so much of life and reality as of an elaborate spectacle, such as one may occasionally see on the stage of a theater. We can scarcely escape the suspicion of artificiality. The tableau has been arranged by an ingenious stage-manager, who has packed it with stirring situations and piled effect upon effect. The scene-painter and costumier having done their share, he has drilled the crowd of supernumeraries until every one of them knows what he is expected to do and does it with all his might, as if the success of the whole depended upon his individual effort. The result is magnificent, but overpowering, unreal, stagy. It is too ambitious and self-important, too suggestive of the high-sounding programme, announced by a German historian of the period. "We stand," he wrote, "with our knowledge, culture, and insight, on a summit from which we overlook the whole past. The Orient, Greece, and Rome, the Middle Ages, the Reformation and Modern times, spread like a universal panorama before us. . . . To bury one's self in the past, to get at the most essential meaning of its life, to awaken what is dead by knowledge, to renew what has vanished by art . . . such is the vivifying work of our time."

But is this picture vivifying? It may succeed in wakening knowledge of the past, but does it renew its life? Certainly it is interesting as an illustration to that page of history which relates how Thusnelda, the wife of Harminius, a German prince, was betrayed by her own father, Segestes, into the hands of the Romans, in order to curry favor with Germanicus. The latter general's success had aroused the jealousy of Tiberius. Roman emperors lived in constant fear of the ascendancy of a victorious general, so Germanicus was recalled and allowed a triumph, which the queen is compelled to adorn. Her humiliation the miserable Segestes is forced to witness, as he stands, a butt for the gibes of the senators on the emperor's right. In the latter's bowed head may well be brooding a dread of Germanicus, and of the menace to Rome, if these magnificent Barbarians should ever discover their own strength and the Romans' growing weakness.

In my last sentence, you will observe, I have obtruded an idea of my own. You will not find it recorded in the brief account by Tacitus of this episode; it can only be guessed at by inference from this picture. But I obtrude it intentionally, to suggest how much more effectively a writer could represent this scene. He would make you realize, not only the outward appearance of the spectacle, but also the inward emotions that are stirring in the individual·actors. He would fathom, not only the thoughts in the brain of Tiberius, but those of the woman who proudly marches past him; those of the Roman ladies; of that bard and the German warrior to whom he is bound; of that woman on the left who darts her arm and imprecations at the captive queen; of the people vociferously applauding the victorious general; and of what lies concealed in the mind of the conqueror, calmly uplifted against the lighted distance.

The fact is that a picture of this sort, by attempting to represent so much, passes beyond the point at which it can be a single unified whole; steps outside of its own special province as a record of what the eye can grasp without assistance from other sources, and challenges rivalry with literature, on the latter's own ground, and, therefore, naturally is worsted. A clever writer could represent this scene to your imagination, and move your emotions, much more vividly than this picture does.

This is true of most so-called "historical" pictures. There have been exceptions, notably the *Surrender of Breda* by Velasquez, to which we have alluded in another chapter. But in that everything is made subordinate to one episode and to one moment in it,—namely, that in which the Vanquished hands the key of the city to the Victor. On the part of the one is exhibited noble resignation; on that of the other, an equally noble magnanimity; in this most trying ordeal each proves himself a hero. For our enjoyment of the picture we do not need to know their names or the circumstances that lead up to the incident. Although the event commemorated occurred in Velasquez's lifetime, he passed beyond the local and temporary and gave his representation a typal significance.

But this is precisely what Piloty has not done. Like most of the "historical" painters, he has selected a subject, that would yield opportunity for striking contrasts and for display of skill in drawing and archæological research; and then, by crowding the canvas with learned details, cleverly represented, seeks to impose upon the spectator an impression of something grander than the ordinary—heroic. For, as a rule, the "historical" painter thinks that the representation of life of his own day is "vulgar"; he has learned to draw the human form and draperies after classic models, idealizing nature; and then rummages amid the dust of antiquity, to find subjects that will demonstrate his skill in representing the draperies and the nude. Turn to Piloty's picture and note the old bard on the right of the foreground. The figure is typical of the whole attitude of mind of these classical, historical, heroical painters. The body is represented partly nude, and the drapery is so arranged that the old man could not possibly walk. What could be more obviously dragged in for effect?

Most of these painters are able draftsmen, although their figures are generally coldly correct and formal, or stilted and bombastic; but few of them are good painters. Piloty, however, was an exception. He received his education at the Munich Academy, under men who were inclined to boast that they were not painters and to look down on the "colorers," just as the Classicists of the French School proclaimed that "form is everything."

But after he had visited Venice, Antwerp, and Paris, he came back a skilful painter, who could render correctly the color appearance of any object he represented. Munich was ripe for something new, and his popularity was immediate. In 1852 he was appointed professor at the Academy, and by the great number of pupils who flocked to him and the influence that he extended throughout Germany, revived in that country the art of painting.

Moreover, his work, though academical, abounds in sentiment and dramatic characterization; qualities that found a ready response in German taste. For the Germans, like the English, are disposed to prefer a picture which tells a story. Piloty's, as we have seen, were historical in theme; but a very large part of modern German painting has been occupied with the little *genre* picture. These are of social or peasant life, in which the personages, generally set in an interior, are enacting some pretty sentimental scene. They are for the most part cleverly painted, so far as representing the color appearance of the objects is concerned, but usually, like Piloty's pictures, without any suggestion of real atmosphere or of the subtleties of light. It is in this respect that Piloty is not a "painter," compared with Fortuny.

The latter, after receiving the usual academical training at the School of Fine Arts in Barcelona, won the Prix de Rome. But while he was studying the old masters in Rome, war broke out between Spain and the Emperor of Morocco.. Fortuny, now twenty-three years old, received a commission from the Town Council of Barcelona to proceed to Africa and paint the exploits of the army. This experience of a few months changed the whole current of his life. The brilliance of Southern sunshine, the glowing colors of the scenery, the richness of the costumes, and the splendor of decorated trappings and weapons, the glittering movement of the life of the people—all these things fascinated him and drew his imagination into the direction of light and color. Other painters before him had been attracted by the charms of the South and the Orient, but none up to that time had so absorbed the inspiration of the color splendors, or the variegated movement of the life.

At first he introduced these qualities into a series of Moroccan subjects; then passed on to pictures, like our present one, with which his memory is particularly identified. They represent interiors decorated profusely in the style of Louis XV, known as Rococo, because the ornamentation included imitation of rockwork, shells, foliage, and intricacies of scrollwork, elaborate and profuse. These countless irregularities of surface, and the gay silk and lace and velvet costumes of the period, offered the fullest scope for color and reflected light.

Painting with an extraordinary dexterity, with a delicate sense of color-harmony, and with an impetuosity of fancy that is truly astounding, he split the light into a thousand particles, till his pictures sparkle like jewels and are as brilliant as a kaleidoscope. When he went to Paris he made a great sensation and became attached to the circle of which Meissonier was the leader. The latter's pictures are like his in the minuteness and elaborateness of their craftsmanship, but do not show the same exquisite color-sense, or skill in representing the diversities of light and atmosphere. In fact, Fortuny himself became the vogue.

He set the fashion for a class of pictures, filled with silks and satins, *bric-à-brac* and elegant trifling, distinguished by deftness of hand, but possessing no higher aim than to make a charming bouquet of color with glancing caprices of sunshine. Because they were cleverly painted they attracted extravagant admiration; but now that clever painting has become more general, their reputation has declined.

CHAPTER XXVI

ÉDOUARD MANET	JOZEF ISRAELS
1833-1883	*1824-*
Impressionistic School of France	*Modern Dutch School*

WHAT a contrast these two pictures present! Their very titles indicate the different point of view in the two artists. *The Old Scribe* has in it the ring of an appeal to our sympathy and interest; *Girl with a Parrot,* on the contrary, is barren of any sympathetic suggestion. Manet, in fact, had no feeling for his subject, except in so far as it contributed to a purely artistic intention; but Israels added to an intention, equally artistic, the further one of entering into the humanness of his subject. He has been through his long career the painter of the Dutch poor, as Millet was of the French peasants; a painter whose work always echoes a clear note of poetry. At the same time he has been the chief influence in the modern revival of Dutch art. On the other hand, while the influence of Manet upon modern art has been even greater, his hold upon the imagination of the layman has been very slight. He was essentially a " painter's painter."

We will consider him first; because an understanding of what he did will help also to a fuller appreciation of Israels, since the latter, like all modern artists who are really painters and not mere tinters, was to some extent influenced by him.

Manet's great work was to carry further and complete the teaching of realism begun by Courbet. The latter's realism consisted mainly in his point of view, in his habit of selecting subjects from nature and treating them as naturally as he could, with the sole purpose of representing the person or thing as it appeared to his eye. But while his subjects were realistic, his rendering of them in many respects was not. He painted realistic subjects with a recipe that he had invented for himself by studying the old masters. For example, he enveloped his pictures in what has been irreverently called "brown sauce"; moreover, his figures, rocks, waves, and trees, were real enough in form, but apt to be of a uniform rigidity of texture. Manet's further contribution was to add to realism of subject a realism of representation; to render the particular texture of each object and to surround all with nature's light and air. He restored to painting a knowledge of the truths which had been discovered by Velasquez.

This great artist had been forgotten during nearly two centuries. At length in 1857, on the occasion of the Manchester Exhibition, he was revealed to the English. The biography of him by Sir William Stirling was translated into French; Paris began to be aware of his pictures in the Louvre, and from them to be directed toward the Prado at Madrid, where the bulk of his work exists. Manet was the first to become a pupil of the Spanish master.

Now we may remember that Velasquez proved himself original, both in the way of looking at a subject and in his way of representing it; each distinguished by extraordinary realism, his motto being, "Truth, not Painting." He represented only what could be embraced by one comprehensive glance, subordinating everything to a vivid impression; and then represented what he saw as he really saw it. And the secret of that reality was that he saw everything through and in the light which surrounded it. Velasquez, like Rembrandt, painted light. But the latter, under his gray Northern sun, painted with light for the purpose of expressing the *inward* meaning of things, whereas the Spaniard retired from the glowing Southern sunshine out of doors into the gray light of his studio, for the purpose of representing realistically the *externals* of his subjects. He discovered that the subject, viewed under these conditions, appeared much flatter than it was usually represented; that form, so viewed, does not stand out with sharp contrasts of light and shade, but that it is really composed of a series of planes, reflecting more or less of light; and that the appearance of color also is the result of various degrees of light reflected. Moreover, he discovered that distance from the eye affects the prevailing or "local" color of objects, the atmosphere which intervenes introducing successive veils of gray; so that the accurate rendering of those variations resulted in a new manner of representing distance,— namely, not by lineal, but by atmospheric perspective.

Manet for some years had been studying the old masters, learning from them their different tricks of painting and producing pictures somewhat after their likeness. But all that he had learned was a knowledge of mannerisms. Until he became acquainted with the work of Velasquez, he had discovered no guiding principle or firm basis. He was modern to the finger-tips; and the Paris of his day, under the influence of Balzac, was vibrating with the realistic spirit. Courbet had demanded that painting also should be realistic in subject and point of view. But what about the method and technic of painting? Was it satisfactory to serve up a modern subject in the old brown sauce of the Bolognese? If not, how could a technic be found that would express in painting the modern spirit of analysis and subtlety that had been developed in modern literature? The answer was found in the art of Velasquez.

He had been dead just two hundred years; yet, strange fact, in his point of view he had anticipated the modern artistic tendencies toward realism, and, what was still more wonderful, had discovered for himself truths in nature that could be applied to painting so as to produce truth of artistic representation. The key-note of his discovery had been light; the study, the analysis, and the painting of light in all its different manifestations upon the surfaces of objects. To Manet, rediscovering the truth through Velasquez, and to the men who were drawn with Manet to this new-old source of inspiration, the watchword became "Fiat Lux," "Let there be Light." The subsequent story of modern progress in painting may be summed up in the one word—light. The rendering of values has become the chief technical aim of the painter; nature is being studied afresh, in order to search out and record the infinite manifestations of light;

HOW TO STUDY PICTURES

in place of a pompous grandiloquent style of meaningless painting, there has grown up one that is distinguished by keen observation, subtle discriminations, and delicate truth of rendering.

The two artists, whom we are considering in this chapter, represent pretty well the two streams into which this new energy of nature-study has flowed. Manet was satisfied with the joy of painting; content to be simply and purely a painter; but Israels has used his knowledge and his skill as a means to body forth the poetic sentiments aroused by his interest in human and physical nature.

At Nadar's gallery, in 1871, Parisians flocked to see the work of Manet and the other men of this new group. The catalogue contained a great deal about "impressions"—for instance, *Impressions of my Pot on the Fire; Impressions of a Cat Walking.* In his criticism Claretie summed up the impressions and spoke of the exhibition as the "Salon des Impressionistes." Thus was started the name " Impressionists," which unfortunately has stuck. For it is misleading, the distinguishing aim of the so-called Impressionist School having been to study light, so that they might fitly be called "Luminarists."

The object of the new group was to teach, that the first requisite of a painter is to be able to paint. This, of course, was an attack once more on the academical and classical school, which says the first requisite is to be able to draw. It tried to enforce its point by saying it did not matter what was painted so long as it was painted well: subject was of little account; the first consideration was the painter's ability to paint. This new creed was summed up in the phrase "Art for Art's sake." The conflict over these catchwords stirred up a great deal of dust, which, however, by this time has cleared away, so that we can better understand the matter at issue.

Remember, in the first place, it was a battle-cry, the rally of this new school of realism, against the insufficiency of Courbet's realism on the one hand, and the dry formalism, on the other, of the Academy. Now, as we have had occasion to remark before, men, when they get to the fighting mood, are not troubled overmuch about logic and reasonableness. It is not the well-weighed statement, recognizing both sides of the question, that will stir their blood; but a catchword, exaggerating their own side of it, to be flung at the adversary with a certainty that, when it reaches him, it will make him dance with fury. Such was this "Art for Art's sake," shouted and reshouted, partly because it involved a great truth, perhaps even more, however, *pour enrager les bourgeois,* or, as we say in English, to make the Philistine squirm; the Philistine being that person, either artist or layman, who is perfectly satisfied with mediocrity, and above all things does not want to have his pet notions disturbed.

Now, over in England, at the period we are considering, Ruskin was contending that the highest aim of art is to teach, to uplift, especially to teach religion; which, stated in an exaggerated way, implied that the subject is the main thing. Across the water from Paris came the retort, *À bas le sujet, l'art pour l'art.* Neither was altogether right, neither altogether wrong.

Will an art, that is based only on a keen eye and nimble fingers, satisfy men and women who have minds and souls?

On the other hand, will painting, based on beautiful ideas, satisfy us if it does not make its chief appeal to us through the eyes? if it does not reach our brain through the medium of enjoyment of the sense of sight?

Has not every art its medium of expression; the poet reaching our capacity for the highest through the medium of words; the musician, through that of sound?

But the painter, who cannot help approaching us through our sense of sight—will he, on the one hand, be wise in paying less attention to what he sees and the rendering of it than the poet does to his words, the musician to his sounds and harmonies? On the other hand, should he be satisfied to appeal *only* to our eyesight and leave our brains and souls untouched?

From the point of view of the layman he should not be; and those artists, who limit their appeal to the eyesight and the enjoyment derived from the sense of seeing, will have a limited following. But let us try to understand that the point of view of the layman and of the artist, however much they may draw together, must always be separate.

For what is the layman? He is the man who does not happen to be a specialist on the subject that is under discussion. If the subject is the buying and selling of silks, then the artist is among the laymen; but if painting, then, the buyer and seller of silks. Now, since the latter, if he is to be a good buyer and seller of silk, must find his occupation very absorbing,—so much so, perhaps, as to make other things seem of secondary importance,— can we not understand how the painter may become absorbed, even exclusively, in the rendering of light and atmosphere, and in the power of discriminating with most delicate assurance between different values? It is the thing he can do better than a great many others; it therefore exercises the keenest activity of his brain, and fills him with that stimulating joy which a man gets in doing what he knows he can do well. He may even not trouble himself about the effect his work will have upon other people; but if so, he differs from the buyer and seller of silk, who has to be concerned with the effect that his commodity will produce, when it is made up into a dress and worn by a lady at some social function. The able merchant is skilled in the values of silk and gives value to his public. It may be the better for the artist and for *his* public, if he can do the same.

Once more, then, I ask you to look at a picture through the eyes of the artist who painted it. In no other way can you be interested in this *Girl with a Parrot* by Manet. I might have selected for illustration that other picture by him in the Metropolitan Museum, *The Boy with a Sword,* one of his best works, in which he came nearest to the power of his master, Velasquez. But, besides being beautifully painted, it has a winsome charm of subject, which is not usual with Manet, so that the selection would have given a wrong impression of his work. The latter, as a rule, is quite uninteresting in subject, not infrequently downright unpleasant; what we must expect to find in it ordinarily is only the technical charm, the refined taste displayed in the color-scheme, and the subtle skill with which light and values, atmosphere and textures, are depicted.

The light in this picture is dull, uniform, and pervasive. The photograph has falsified the effect by making the background appear dark. In the original it is a drabbish gray, a slightly yellower gray than the dove-gray on the wings of the parrot, whose head, on the contrary, is a whitish gray. Again, the glass of water at the top of the stand is gray, but a much lower tone in the darker parts, and a much more sharply whitish tone in the high lights; while, still again, the pan on the floor is of dull pewter, a lighter gray than that of the wall and less light than the parrot's head. So far, you observe, the artist has played upon grays. As a musician might explain it, he has given several modulations of the chord of gray, including the major and minor, the augmented and diminished. In other words, he has made a color-harmony of slightly differing tones of gray; taking pleasure in observing and rendering those slight distinctions, and also in noting how differently the light is reflected from the different surfaces,—in a sort of dull and smothered way from the plaster on the wall; deep and lustrous from the bird's wing; more softly broken up from the feathers on the head; sharp and pellucid from the glass, and with duller luster from the pan. The result is, that by careful discrimination between the various actions of light, he has given us a real appreciation of the textures of the different objects—a refinement of realism in the way of painting that is far beyond the realism of Courbet.

The color of the gown is that of faded rose-leaves; that

GIRL WITH A PARROT   ÉDOUARD MANET
METROPOLITAN MUSEUM, NEW YORK

THE OLD SCRIBE   JOZEF ISRAELS

is to say, very pale rose in the shadows, a pale straw-color where it catches the light. The modeling has been obtained by varying these two tones, according to the amount of light contained in the various parts of the silk; the only approach to shadows being some dove-gray tones, where you see the dark spots round the edge of the right arm, and under the hand and cuff of the left. Notwithstanding that the artist limited himself to these few tones, and chose a gown which hangs from the shoulders with very few folds, he has made us realize the balloon-like roundness of the garment, and, moreover, the existence of a figure underneath it. Again the expression, faded rose-leaves, describes the prevailing hue of the face and hands; the latter are practically of the same color as the gown; yet we shall have no doubt, especially in the original, that the texture of the one is silk, of the others flesh, because of the method of the brushwork. Upon the dress it was laid on in sweeps; upon the flesh-parts, in circular strokes and dabs.

So far, then, as we have examined the color-scheme of the picture, it is a harmony of faded rose-leaves and gray; but to prevent it from being tame, to make it resonant and vibrant, certain notes of positive color were introduced; for example, the black velvet band round the neck, a crimson tail to the bird, and the yellow rind of the orange. I may add that this clear note of yellow receives a dull echo in the drabbish-yellow sand, mingles with the rich brown of the wooden pedestal, and reappears more noticeably in the lighter brown of the girl's hair.

By this time I hope we have entered sufficiently into the point of view of Manet, when he painted this picture, to discover that the problem, as it presented itself to him, was not one of a girl or a parrot, but purely a painter-problem—to render by means of paint the real appearance of objects as revealed by light. By limiting the range of his palette, he increased the difficulty of the problem and thereby his own joy in solving it; and, moreover, produced a very delicate harmony of color, which to a sensitive eye gives somewhat the kind of pleasure that the ear receives from a delicate harmony of sound.

We are now in a position to understand the value of Manet's contribution to modern painting. Guided by the example of Velasquez, he once more introduced real light into pictures; sometimes bright light, sometimes, as in this example, subdued light, but light as it illumines space and is contained on the different surfaces of objects. To reënumerate: he rediscovered the natural truth, that objects in light appear flatter than they do when placed in a dark studio, with light shot down on them from only one direction; that in the light there are scarcely any shadows, and that modeling, therefore, is not to be obtained by lights and shadows, but by careful rendering of the planes of more and less light; and that by means of this careful study of values, the textures also of objects could be best expressed. Lastly, he rediscovered the subtleties of nature's color-harmonies as revealed by light.

These principles and practices were almost simultaneously adopted by other painters, among whom Whistler was one, and are now generally accepted, so that modern art is distinguished by a great number of men who are clever in the technic of the brush. It is not difficult to understand what a fascination it must be to a painter to be able to reach such subtlety of observation and rendering; nor that, in the early days of the movement especially, when few attained to it, those few should be disposed to feel that it was all that a painter need strive for. "Art for Art's sake," however, will never satisfy those who have something to say, something within themselves that they must express; and such a one was Israels.

He was born in Groningen, and at first destined for a rabbi. But, after leaving school, he entered the small banking business of his father, and often went to the big bank of the Mesdags to deposit money. The rich banker's son, H. W. Mesdag, became the famous painter of the sea; the poor banker's son, the greatest all-round painter in Holland, foremost in restoring modern Dutch art to the high position it had occupied in the seventeenth century. For during the subsequent century, and until the middle of the nineteenth, Dutch artists had forsaken the nature-study of their own land and people, and had gone after the Italian grand style, turning out historical pictures or classic landscapes, cold, inanimate, and conventional.

It was in the hard, dry, unatmospheric, academical manner that Israels learned to paint; first at Amsterdam and later at Paris, where he worked under a pupil of David's and then entered the studio of Delaroche, just as Millet was leaving it in despair. For, like the latter, Israels, the "Dutch Millet," as he is often called, was shy and awkward, and he, too, starved in Paris. Then he returned to Amsterdam, took a room, and tried to paint as Delaroche had taught him; such pictures as *Prince Maurice of Nassau Beside the Body of his Father* being the first he sent to exhibitions.

But the circumstance of a severe illness changed the current of his life. To recover his health he went to the little village of Zandvoort, near Haarlem; and there lodged with a ship's carpenter. Buried away among the sand-dunes, far from the pretenses and contentions of the studios, with sea and sky stretching away into the distance and simple fisher-folk around him, he began to see with his own eyes and to feed his imagination upon the realities. As Millet at Barbizon, so he at Zandvoort began to discover artistic material for his brush in the big-framed men and women, uncouth from the daily repetition of hard toil; to enter with sympathy into their lives of patient endurance; and to include in his study of humanity what was so intimately associated with it, the sea and sky and land and the interiors of the homes.

He could not at once shake off the effects of academic training, and his early peasant pictures still betray a design to make the spectator smile or weep by telling a pretty, moving story, assisted by little accidents of gesture or facial expression. Gradually, however, his work became broader and bigger, dealing, as Millet's did, with the essentials; for the expression of sentiment he relied more and more upon the emotional suggestion of color, light, and atmosphere. Living in Amsterdam, he learned from Rembrandt the spiritual significance of light; and, like Manet, he learned to paint with light. While he has painted landscapes and marines, his most characteristic pictures represent dim interiors, with the light entering from a small window, stealing throughout the room, and subtly detaching certain objects into faint relief.

Such a one is *The Old Scribe*. The light is concentrated on the pallid face, the white beard, and the scroll; these being the main features of the subject; the soul, as it were, of the fact. Less prominently it touches the accessory features: a bunch of pens, the ink-pot, a glass water-pitcher, and—a pair of crutches. Lame, therefore shut off from active life; pallid, because cribbed in a little attic—the brightness of the outer world only a means to an end of his close life-work— "Work, while it is yet day," for at night the tired eyes cannot work. High forehead, as of a man of intellect; mobile mouth expressive of deep emotions; intellect and emotions narrowed down to the endless transcribing of texts. The head of a dreamer—the hands big like those of a laborer, yet full of sensitiveness; note how the left is spread upon the parchment, not only keeping it down, but corresponding also in feeling to the delicate and tender expression of the other one. This hand, yes, even the movement of the pen which it guides—how they correspond with the expression of the face! Then the rude, rough-hewn manner of the drawing, joined to the subtle delicacy of the silvery light—this latter more apparent in the original than in the reproduction—what a suggestion they yield of the "simple annals of the poor," the unflinching, patient facing of the necessities and realities; the grayness of the existence and the heroism!

But it is neither the gray, monotonous life nor the tragedy of the poor that Israels always depicts. He has represented also the hardy vigor of the fishermen at work; the coyness of young lovers, as in *The Bashful Suitor* of the Metropolitan Museum; the tenderness of motherhood, and the gladsomeness of little children. It is in this wider range of sympathy that he is bigger than Millet; and, as a painter, using the resources of light and atmosphere, he excels him; so also in his renderings of the ocean and in his freer use of landscape. It was one of the regrets of Millet, at the end of his life, that he had not made as much of landscape as he might have done.

Under the influence of Israels and the Barbizon artists, the Dutch have learned once more to find the inspiration for their painting in their own country and among their own people. Guided by the teaching of Manet and the other "luminarists," they have found a new motive in the study of local nature. Nowhere are such soft and tender effects of atmosphere, such a freshness of moist and vivid coloring as in Holland; and between these two extremes of mistiness and freshness her modern painters have produced a range of art that is characterized by dignified simplicity and by the charm of profound intimacy and heartfelt tenderness.

CHAPTER XXVII

PIERRE PUVIS DE CHAVANNES
1824–1898
French Mural Painter

JEAN LÉON GÉRÔME
1824–1904
Semi-Classical School
of France

PUVIS was a lover of Virgil; Gérôme, very partial to subjects derived from ancient Rome. Yet, despite their classical tendencies, no two men could have been more different in their motives and methods; so that a comparison of the two will help to bring out very sharply the characteristics of each. Let us approach them first of all through the examples here illustrated.

Gérôme's reproduces that moment in the gladiatorial sports of the Colosseum when one of the combatants has been defeated and the victor looks toward the galleries. The vestal virgins turn down their thumbs; if the emperor follows suit, woe to the vanquished! Both the title and the manner of representation record very clearly a precise incident of actual fact. But in Puvis's neither title nor treatment has a definite reference to facts; the painting is concerned with an idea, namely, the relation of the arts to nature. Its subject is an ideal one; its rendering idealized.

Let us examine the two more closely. Gérôme's picture represents only the fragment of a scene. We might not have noticed this, since there is enough included to explain and complete the meaning of the incident, were we not comparing it with the Puvis. But the composition of the latter is complete and sufficing, and it does not occur to us to imagine anything outside the limits of the canvas. The reason is that the parts are so beautifully balanced as to create a feeling of perfect harmoniousness in the whole; every figure is placed with a scientific precision just where it needs must be in order to secure this effect of poise, and with an equal precision the various features of the near and distant landscape have been adjusted to the figures. The whole is an arrangement of full and empty spaces, regulated by the severest logic of cause and effect.

Again we notice that the total result in Puvis's canvas is one of exquisite placidity, while that of the other is assertiveness and turmoil. It is not sufficient explanation of the difference to say that the two subjects are essentially different; or to add that Gérôme had a preference for subjects of dramatic intensity, and that the work of Puvis is always marked by calm. Let us discover the deeper reason of the difference. It lies in the way in which each of the two artists, respectively, has approached his subject.

If we examine the faces of the spectators in the Colosseum, we shall find that each is strongly individualized with its particular character of strong emotion; but the faces in the other picture seem like those of persons moving in a dream. An even stronger note of contrast is represented by the two men, in Puvis's painting, who are moving a large stone. Here is an operation demanding exertion; yet, if we compare the amount of muscular force which they are exerting even with that displayed in the arms of the vestal virgins, not to mention the action of the gladiator, we are inclined to think it will take them a long time to place that stone finally. Their movements are such as the circumstances demand, but so controlled that the operation will be prolonged until the color fades from the canvas. And neither they nor the other figures grouped near them can be thought of as having to go home presently to supper; as the full-fed people in Gérôme's picture, we feel sure, will do as soon as the butchery is despatched. His scene is *momentary, incidental;* that of Puvis's *permanent* and *elemental.* We feel, in fact, that the Puvis figures have not been brought here, but that they belong here; that they belong to the landscape, as the landscape does to them; that while the one endures, the other will. Moreover, just as the winding river, though it is really a scene near Rouen, is typical of all such river scenes, and as the apple-trees, though they differ, all represent a certain type of tree, so the figures are typical. Some are nude, others in classic draperies, still others—the group of the three women on the left, for example, and that opposite one of the architect, sculptor, and painter—in costumes reasonably modern ; yet by this unusual mixture no feeling of incongruity is aroused. They all seem to be of the same race, mingling quite naturally ; a race by itself, not belonging to any particular time or place ; a race resembling our own, yet not to be found anywhere on earth. To repeat: it is the *elemental* and the *perma-*

nent that Puvis sought to express; the *incidental* and the *momentary* that occupied the attention of Gérôme.

By this time it is fitting to mention, what you have probably perceived already, that while the *Pollice Verso* is an easel-picture, intended to be studied in detail, Puvis's is a mural decoration, designed for the embellishment of a certain architectural space in the Rouen Museum. I did not mention this at first, because you might then have assumed that the contrasts we have noted resulted from this difference in the intention of the two paintings. But it is not so. If Gérôme had been commissioned to make a decoration based upon the Puvis subject, he would not have conceived or carried it out in the same way as Puvis has done. In the Panthéon at Paris several great painters have contributed so-called decorations; yet, compared with the decorations of Puvis in the same building, that really decorate it, their paintings are huge illustrations. And so, we may be sure from the character of his work, would a decoration by Gérôme have been. But mural decoration is a thing apart from other painting.

Just what the proper characteristics of mural painting are, and what they are not, may be learned by a visit to the Boston Public Library. The walls of the staircase hall have been decorated by Puvis de Chavannes; the frieze of the delivery-room by Edwin A. Abbey; and four spaces in an upper hall by John S. Sargent. Now it is very likely that one who visits the Library for the first time, if he is not a student of mural decoration, will glance at the Puvis panels with a mild sort of interest, but will not find his attention forcibly arrested or detained. He knows, perhaps, that they represent in allegorical fashion the contributions made to civilization by *Philosophy, Astronomy, History, Chemistry, Physics,* and by *Pastoral, Dramatic,* and *Epic Poetry,* while the large space contains a representation of the *Nine Muses Rising from the Earth to greet Genius.* But the general effect seems unassertive, the symbolism a little vague, the figures unsubstantial, and the coloring thin and tame.

So, passing on, the visitor enters Abbey's room. Ah! knights in armor; beautiful women; strange old interiors of church and castle; a fight of six against one: a weird scene of a sick man upon his couch, and filing past him a procession of men and women carrying curious objects; a boat rocking on the waves; a flower-eyed maiden whom a youth appears to be forsaking—these and much more flash forth from the wall in strong and brilliant colors and prick the visitor's interest. What are they all about? Good fortune! Here is a printed description of the various scenes! It appears they are taken from one of the oldest legends of our race, the Quest of the Holy Grail. Here is fodder a-plenty for the mind! Eagerly the visitor reads the printed matter and identifies the various scenes, and has his views of how they do or do not correspond with his understanding of the story.

As he leaves this room and passes again through the hall, I wonder whether he spares a moment for another glance at the Puvis panels; and, if so, whether he notes how reposeful they seem after the various excitements of the Abbey series. Perhaps not—yet. He mounts the stairs to the Sargent room, so that his eyes are raised and catch sight first of a panel in the center of which kneels a huddled mass of men and women, bowed in prayer or lifting up their hands in supplication. Over them stand in threatening attitudes the figures of an Egyptian and an Assyrian king, and round about the group are flashes of crimson wings, the Egyptian sphinx, the goddess Pasht with black and gold pinions, a bird-headed god, a lion, and other objects.

A second time: "What is it all about?" a question fortunately answered by the printed explanation. The latter is invaluable, especially when the visitor proceeds to examine the bewildering labyrinth of symbolic forms, taken from Egyptian mythology, which fill the ceiling space. How tired his neck becomes, and possibly his brain, by the alternate reference to the book and to the ceiling! He experiences quite a relief when his eyes come down to a lower level and are greeted by a row of stately figures, prophets of the Old Testament, as he sees by the name written under each. How pleasant to be able to enjoy them without laborious study of a printed page! Very likely the visitor is already familiar with them, for their photographs have appeared in great numbers throughout the country. The popular taste, not always right in such matters, has justly singled them out as the best feature of Sargent's earlier decoration. For there is a later one; as the visitor turns, it greets him from the other end of the hall. Here again is a row of figures, this time of archangels; but most noticeable is the treatment of the upper part, where figures, symbolizing the Persons of the Trinity, sit enthroned. Their

INTER ARTES ET NATURAM PUVIS DE CHAVANNES
ROUEN MUSEUM

POLLICE VERSO
IN PRIVATE OWNERSHIP
GÉRÔME

forms are enveloped in ample draperies, flatly painted with little or no modeling, large expanses of rich dusky coloring, against which the heads and hands, some ornamented borders, and forms of doves, make spots of animation. But the general impression is of flatness and simplicity, forming a background of subdued grandeur to the central group of the Crucifixion. Flatness of painting and simple ample masses—these qualities Sargent borrowed from the Byzantine artists who decorated with paintings and mosaics the walls of churches in the Middle Ages. They were poor draftsmen, unskilled also, as we have noticed earlier, in the actual craft of painting; yet their designs were so impressive in their large simplicity, that to this day their work, from the standpoint of decoration, wins the admiration of artists.

Flatness of painting, simple ample masses, large simplicity of design—as the visitor descends the great staircase, will he notice, I wonder, that these are characteristics also of the Puvis panels; that what contributed so much to the grandeur of Sargent's latest work is in a technical sense the fundamental quality of Puvis's? Perhaps it was because of their flatness, their lack of elaborate modeling, the large simplicity, or, if you will, the comparative emptiness—of their design, that he had paid little heed to them before. Now, if he has the curiosity to look into the Abbey room, he will observe in the latter's paintings the very opposite qualities—elaborate modeling, exuberance of parts in the design, a general contradiction of orderly quiet. Then possibly, since he is no longer curious about their subjects, nor dividing his observation between them and the printed key, but looking at them solely as decorations, he may miss something of the suave, stately calm that distinguishes the work of Puvis.

The fact is that Abbey is an illustrator on a grand scale; Puvis, on a grander scale, a decorator. Abbey's work is grand because he has taken one of the noblest themes in literature, and with much archæological knowledge, and upon large canvases, has represented the story with considerable dramatic and poetic feeling. Puvis's, on the other hand, is grander because his work joins hands with what is bigger and grander than itself, —namely, the architecture,—and by union with it has been lifted up.

This is the point to which we have been slowly traveling : Puvis had what neither of the other painters possesses, at least to anything like the same extent,—the true instinct of the decorator. This instinct reasons the matter out in the following way. The part must be less than the whole ; therefore the painted panel cannot compete with the total effect of the architecture, of which it is only a detail ; to try to make it stand out conspicuously is to excite an invidious comparison, whereas to make it blend harmoniously with the architecture is to secure from the latter a reinforcement of the painting. Moreover, the space to be decorated, except in the case of a curved ceiling, is a flat solid mass, which terminates the vision ; therefore, while the decoration is introduced as a pleasing variety to the general effect of masonry, it should not interfere with the intentions of the latter; it should not, as the artists express it, "make a hole in the wall"; give, that is to say, an impression that you are looking through the wall at some scene beyond, but should preserve the essential condition of the wall: its solidity and flatness. Once more, since the painting is to decorate a certain wall space, its composition of lines and masses should be chosen with particular reference to the shape of the space; some of the lines, for example, should repeat, while others should be in contrast to, the contours of the space, and the masses should be arranged so as to present a perfect balance within the space. Moreover, the lines of a building are generally simple, the wall spaces spots of quiet strength; therefore the composition of the painting will do well to imitate this simplicity of line and quietness of masses, so as to give the idea of structural arrangement; to be what artists call " architectonic " in character.

To sum up, the decorator should recognize that his work is subordinate to the architecture; should make it harmonize with the latter in composition and color, preserve the flatness of the wall space, and have a distinctly structural or architectonic character. Let us examine how Puvis, to whom is due the credit of having revived in the nineteenth century the true principles of mural painting, exemplified them in his work. It should be mentioned, in passing, that, unlike the Boston Library, some of the buildings in which his work appears are inferior specimens of architecture, but that did not deter him from sticking to the theory of subordination.

We will consider his work under the two heads of his choice of subject and method of painting. Puvis de Chavannes came of an aristocratic family which had resided for three hundred years in Burgundy, so that, as

HOW TO STUDY PICTURES

a French writer says, he inherited the racial tendency toward poetry and the enjoyment of nature. On the other hand, his father was an engineer of bridges and roads in Lyons, and the son, after receiving a classical and mathematical education in that city, proceeded to the Polytechnic in Paris, with a view to adopting his father's profession. But, his health breaking down, he made a trip to Italy and came back determined to be a painter. He started, then, with an acquired taste both for the classics and for mathematics, with logical as well as poetical tendencies. It was not until he was thirty-five years of age that the accident of some vacant panels in a new house, belonging to his brother, drew his attention to mural decoration. Of one of the drawings he made an enlarged copy and sent it to the Salon. Its acceptance encouraged him to go on in the same vein, and two years later he exhibited the decorative canvases, *War* and *Peace*. One of them was purchased by the government; when Puvis, not willing that the two should be separated, made a present of the other. They are now in the museum at Amiens, and mark the beginning of his public career as a mural painter.

The conception of their subjects is the reverse of realistic. In the *Peace,* for example, many of the figures are nude; they are grouped with the regard for beauty of line that distinguishes the work of the classicists, but, unlike them, Puvis already shows his love of landscape. Yet in three important respects this work differs from his later ones. In the first place, the figures are massed one behind the other; secondly, their forms are ample and roundly modeled; and, thirdly, the eye is detained by the beauty or character of individual figures. As the French say, there are fine *morceaux* in the painting, and it was applauded by the authorities.

But Puvis's logical mind argued, not immediately but by degrees, that anything which distracts attention from the whole must be avoided ; that the massing of figures, necessitating contrasts of light and shade, interfered with the flatness of the design ; that in every way perfection was to be reached through simplification. Accordingly he reconsidered even the character of his subjects. The allegory must be rendered in a manner as abstract as possible, so that the mind of the spectator may be in no wise occupied with " What is it all about? " nor drawn away for a moment from the first and final thought that this is a decoration.

The conception having been reduced to abstract expression, it followed that the method of painting, also, must be as unobtrusive as possible. Therefore Puvis reduced the amount of modeling ; relied more and more upon the contour-lines of his figures and their position in the composition ; distributed them in successive planes, sprinkled over the landscape, and flattened the bulk and distance of the latter into a simple patterning of colored forms ; reducing also the strength of the color, heightening continually the key of it, and relying more and more upon subtle rendering of values. His progress became a constant search for what was essential, and a leaving out of everything that might possibly distract attention from the whole and disturb the absolute simplicity of effect which it was his growing purpose to attain.

HOW TO STUDY PICTURES

It was charged against him that this increasing tendency to leave out rather than to put in resulted in large barren spaces and in carelessness of drawing; and that his color, becoming paler and paler, was anemic. No doubt there is some justification for the criticism; indeed the panels at Boston show instances of imperfect drawing. But there never was a prophet yet crying in the wilderness that did not fall into exaggerations; it is by them that he compels a hearing; and Puvis, by his attack upon the kind of historic fiction that was being made to do duty as decoration, perhaps had need to run into extremes. As to his color, he proved himself a modern of the moderns. Not even Manet himself could juxtapose his flat tones with more precise discrimination of their relative values. Puvis's skill in this respect is manifested particularly in the landscape parts. He selects for the sky a tone of blue that has more light in it than the greens of the earth, and varies the tones of the latter by almost imperceptible gradations of light and less light tones. In this management of values and knowledge of forms and construction, he is the equal of the best professional landscape-painters; and the result is that, while his landscapes give an impression of space and seem filled with air that surrounds the figures, they also give the impression of being flat to the wall.

The truth of this is apparent, I think, even in the reproduction of *Inter Artes et Naturam*, though we miss the effect of the color. But try to imagine the color of the grass to be tender green, such as in early April, sprinkled with pale-yellow flowers, while a bunch of purple iris grows beside the water-basin; that the costumes of the women include pale rose and lilac and silvery white; those of the men, gray and blue ; that the distant landscape is veiled in luminous bluish haze, and the whole scene bathed in a soft glow. In this landscape, whose tranquillity is not marred by a single flutter of disturbance,—an abstract expression of nature's calm,—the figures move and have their being, abstracts of humanity, suggesting by their positions and gestures the abstract ideals of the artist. In the original they are not as prominent as in the black-and-white reproduction, the colors tending to blend them with the landscape, so that the spectator is less inclined to examine them separately. They dwell apart from him, creatures of his own likeness, but purged of materialism ; embodied spirits, in a scene that is of the earth, but not earthly, breathing the spirit of nature as she reveals herself in moments of exalted calm to the contemplation of the painter and the poet.

And poet by instinct, as well as painter, was Puvis himself; moreover, a vigorous, red-blooded man, with healthy enjoyment in the good things of life, and an admiration of what is strong and bounteous in human and physical nature. Yet in his art the instinct of the decorator, as we have seen, led him to avoid these qualities, as being too assertive for the province of mural decoration, until by a process of severely logical experiments he was able to depict not form, but its essence and abstract suggestion. The result is that his decorations do not impress upon us the idea of paint ; they seem rather to have grown upon the wall like a delicate efflorescence.

HOW TO STUDY PICTURES

In the case of Gérôme's pictures, however, one does not lose the recollection of paint. Throughout it is the cleverness of drawing and skill of representation that divide our attention with the subject. He belonged to the family of the classicists, was learned in composition and drawing as they are taught in the schools, and fond of classical and drapery subjects. But he also borrowed of the realists and gave his men and women something of individual character; he borrowed also of the romantic and anecdotic painters, so that his pictures tell exciting stories; moreover, he had traveled in Egypt and brought back a certain feeling for glowing light and color. In consequence, therefore, of his touching so many varieties of popular taste, he was a most popular painter and received every honor that the French nation bestows upon success. But, being so accomplished in many directions, he was really master in none, and the artistic judgment of the world has already turned its thumb down upon his excessive reputation.

CHAPTER XXVIII

JAMES ABBOTT McNEILL WHISTLER   JOHN SINGER SARGENT
1834-1903   1856-
American   American

THESE pictures, like their respective authors, present a strange contrast. The Sargent, so brilliantly assertive, is the work of a reticent personality; while the Whistler, so tenderly reticent, is the creation of an artist who was brilliant and assertive.

There is an antithesis in these two cases between the man and his work that is by no means uncommon in the history of art. Without attempting an explanation of this, we may note, as helping toward it, that an artist puts into his work what there is of best and strongest in himself; also that some artists, holding their art very sacred, erect around it a barricade, and adopt a personal manner that, as it were, shall throw the world off the scent; somewhat as the plover wheels around in the air with noisy cry, in order to distract attention from her nest, which is tucked away remote from disturbance in a different direction.

The work of both these men has an original force, that has influenced countless other painters, and yet its inspiration was borrowed. Both owe much to the lesson of Velasquez; Sargent also to that of Franz Hals and

HOW TO STUDY PICTURES

Raeburn, while Whistler gleaned from Manet and the Japanese. The originality of each consists in adapting what he has derived to the spirit of his own age and surroundings, and in giving his own work an independent vitality, that has become, as I have said, an example to others.

This statement may serve as a useful definition of originality. The latter is rarely, if ever, doing something new, but giving to a thing that has been done before some new force and meaning. Now that we are reaching the end of our survey of painting, we may look back and see that the progress has been for the most part a series of renewals, of men carrying forward and farther what they had received from others. The most notable example of this in the whole story is that of Raphael, who has been called " the Prince of Plagiarists," and yet his work is unique. It is not the search after or discovery of new ideas that makes an original man, so much as his ability to reclothe the old with some newness of appearance or meaning out of his own stock of individuality.

When Sargent entered the school of Carolus-Duran he was much above the average of pupils in attainment. He had been born in Florence, in 1856, the son of cultivated parents; his father, a Massachusetts gentleman, having practised medicine in Philadelphia and retired. The home life was penetrated with refinement, and outside of it were the beautiful influences of Florence, combining the charms of sky and hills with the wonders of art in the galleries and the opportunities of intellectual and artistic society. Accordingly, when Sargent arrived in Paris, he was not only a skilful draftsman and painter, the result of his study of the Italian masters, but also,—which has had perhaps an even greater influence upon his career,—young as he was, he already had a refined and cultivated taste. This at once stood him in good stead, for his new master, though a very skilful painter and excellent teacher, was otherwise a man of rather showy and superficial qualities. He too had studied in Italy, but later in Spain, and it was chiefly upon the lessons learned from Velasquez that he had founded his own brilliant method. This method Sargent, being a youth of remarkable diligence with an unusual faculty for receiving impressions, soon absorbed. He painted a portrait of his master, which proved he had already acquired all that the latter could give him. Then he went to Madrid and saw the work of Velasquez with his own eyes; subsequently visiting Holland, where he was greatly impressed with the portraits by Franz Hals. Let us see how these various influences are reflected in his work.

In the accompanying picture we may trace the influence of Velasquez in the noble simplicity of the lines, in the ample dignity of the masses, in the single impression which the whole composition makes and the quiet sumptuousness obtained by the treatment of the black and white costumes, a treatment at once grand and subtle. Moreover, the whole picture has the highbred feeling and stateliness of manner, the powerful directness and at the same time self-restraint, that Sargent had found in the old Italian portraits. Yet the suggestion of the picture is thoroughly modern; not only do the ladies belong to to-day and vibrate with life, but in the actual technic of the painting there is vitality of brushwork: now a long sweep of a full brush, now a spot of accent, a touch-and-go method, brilliantly suggestive, terse, quick, vivacious, and to the point, qualities that are best summed up in the French word *esprit*. They are peculiarly French; and in his possession of them Sargent shows the influence of his training and life in Paris, and proves himself a modern of the moderns.

Yet in his case this *esprit* is rarely carried to excess; and when it may seem to be, as in some of his portraits of ladies, one may guess that he took refuge in this pyrotechnic display of brushwork because he could find nothing else in the picture to interest him. Usually, he seems to have received an almost instantaneous impression of his subject, vivid and distinct, to the setting down of which are directed all his subsequent efforts; and they are often long and patiently repeated. It is not a deep impression; as a rule, takes little account of the inward man or woman, but represents with amazing reality the visible exterior, illumined by such hints of character as a keen observer may discover in manner or speech and general appearance. Sometimes, however, it would appear that he had been unable to establish a sympathetic accord with his subject; and these are the few occasions when he seems mainly preoccupied with the technic, or the still fewer ones in which there are evidences of tiredness or fumbling in the brushwork.

In the acquirement of the latter a strong influence was

PORTRAIT OF THE ARTIST'S MOTHER   JAMES A. McNEILL WHISTLER
LUXEMBOURG GALLERY, PARIS

PORTRAIT OF THE MISSES HUNTER   JOHN S. SARGENT
BY PERMISSION OF MR. CHARLES E. HUNTER

WHISTLER—SARGENT

Franz Hals. From him Sargent caught the skill of modeling the faces in quiet, even light, of building them up by placing side by side firm, strong patches of color, each of which contains the exact amount of light the part of the face reflected, and of giving to flat masses of color the suggestion of roundness and modeling. While French *esprit* is noticeable in his portraits of ladies, his male ones recall rather the manly gusto of the old Dutch painter. Moreover, in his placing of the figures in the composition, and in the pure, luminous tones of his flesh-tints, he often reminds one of the Scotch artist, Raeburn.

In addition to portraits, he has executed some mural decorations for the Boston Public Library, the theme of which is the *Triumph of Religion*—illustrating certain stages of Jewish and Christian history. One portion presents in an intentionally complicated composition the confusion of gods and goddesses of Egypt; another, also with deliberate intricacy of arrangement, the persecution of the Jews under Egyptian and Assyrian tyrants. Then in the frieze below stand the *Prophets* of the Old Testament, those of *Hope* and those of *Lamentation;* large and simple forms, following one another in beautiful, simple lines of rhythmic gravity. Upon the wall at the opposite end of the room appears a symbolic representation of the *Redemption of Man,* treated in the spirit of Byzantine decoration, but without the Byzantine formalism and unnaturalness in the representation of the figures. This panel, the latest executed, is the best, being a remarkable example of grafting the skill of modern painting upon the old stock of Byzantine mural decoration, which still remains, by reason of its flatness of treatment, its general simplicity of design and occasional elaboration of parts, the most distinctly mural form of color decoration that has ever been applied to a wall. The *Prophets* share this simplicity of design, but the other two panels, partly because of the confusion of their design,—although there is no reason why a pattern should not be elaborate and intricate,—still more because of the immense amount of literary allusion that they contain, and without a knowledge of which they are unintelligible, may be reckoned the least successful.[1]

These decorations exhibit a very beautiful side of Sargent's mind that has been only partially developed; a deeper insight into the significance of the subject than his portraits suggest. The latter are distinguished rather by an audacious vivacity of method, and an extraordinary appreciation of the value of the things which lie upon, or only a little below, the surface. In this respect he offers a great contrast to Whistler.

If you turn to the latter's *Portrait of the Artist's Mother,* you will recognize at once that "audacious" and "vivacity" are terms that cannot be applied to it; also, that the interest it arouses is a much deeper one than you feel in Sargent's picture. For Whistler, not a brilliant brushman, was interested most in what could not be presented to actual sight, but suggested only. Here it is the tenderness and dignity of motherhood and the reverence that one feels for it; not the first blossom-

[1] For the point of this criticism the reader may compare the chapter on Puvis de Chavannes.

ing of motherhood, as in Raphael's Madonnas, but the ripened form of it. What the man himself is conscious of owing to it and feeling for it, what the mother herself may feel, as she looks back with traveling gaze along the path of hopes and fears, of joy and pain, that she has trodden. This miracle of Motherhood, most holy and pure and lovely of all the many miracles of life, continually repeated in millions of experiences, Whistler has represented once for all in such a way that this picture will remain forever a type of it.

By what means did he produce this universal, typal significance? Ultimately, of course, by the way in which he has composed and painted the picture; but, before that, through the attitude of mind with which he approached the task. If we succeed in understanding this attitude, we shall have learned a clue to all this artist's work.

You remember that Leonardo cared less for the appearance of things than for the spirit or essential meaning that was concealed behind the veil of the outward appearance. He was in this respect the opposite of Dürer, just as Whistler was of Sargent. He shunned the obvious, however brilliantly portrayed. Now the least obvious of the arts is music. Music steals into the soul of a man and fills it with impressions; into the soul of another man with impressions, varying according to his experience and feeling; and so on into the souls of countless others, with always varying impressions. Moreover, the impression received by each individual is not a definite one, or limited except by the individual's capacity. The impression grows and grows until it loses itself in a distance that we can seek toward but never reach; it passes into the universal.

Why has not painting the power to affect us so indefinitely? Because it must begin by representing concrete things: figures and objects that we can see and touch, and to which we have given names. Therefore much of our attention is distracted by voluntarily or involuntarily identifying these things which have names, so that the general impression, the essence of the artist's conception, of which these names are unavoidable accidents, is clogged and circumscribed by them. Accordingly, if the painter desires, as Whistler did, to raise his own art toward the abstract and universal appeal of music, it must be by diverting attention as far as possible from the means that he is obliged to employ.

At one period of his career Whistler almost completely discarded form and objects, relying, as far as possible, entirely upon the effects of color to produce the impression; calling these canvases, in which different tones of one or more colors would be blended, "nocturnes," "symphonies," "harmonies": terms borrowed from the art of music, the abstract significance of which he was striving to emulate. The public, being addicted to names and to being interested in concrete things, asked, "What are they all about?" and, receiving no answer, scoffed.

But even to Whistler these canvases were only in the nature of experiments. The pictorial artist cannot get away from the concrete; visible and tangible objects must engage his attention; he must found upon them his abstract appeal. Let us see how Whistler did it, interrupting for a moment our study of his paintings by a glance at his work in etching, for all through his career he was etcher as well as painter. Among his early works with the needle is a series of views of the Thames: the row of picturesque old houses that lined the water at Chelsea, where he lived for many years, the wharves, the shipping, boat-houses, and bridges. In the suggestion they give of constructive reality, of detail, and of the actual character of the objects represented, they are marvelous. Not even a man exclusively in love with the appearances of things could render them more convincingly. Then, having mastered the character of form, he set to work to make the objects in his etchings subordinate to the general impression he wished to convey; giving more and more attention to the evanescent qualities of light and atmosphere. Having learned to put in, he became learned in leaving out; and in his later series of Venetian etchings confined himself to a few lines contrasted with large spaces of white paper. But the lines are used with such comprehension and discretion, that they are sufficient to suggest the character of the objects, while the chief meaning is given to the empty spaces. These cease to be mere paper; they convey the impression of water or sky under the diverse effects of atmosphere and luminousness, and by their vague suggestiveness stimulate the imagination.

Remembering Whistler's preference for suggestion rather than actual statement, one can understand his fondness for etching, since the latter demands an effort of imagination, first of all upon the artist's part to translate the various hues of nature into black and white, and then upon the spectator's to retranslate these into hues of nature. And while this is so in the case of *color*, it is much more so when it comes to the point of creating an illusion of *atmosphere* simply by means of a few lines on a sheet of white paper. And a correspondingly keener imagination is demanded of the spectator, which may be a reason why many people prefer the master's earliest *Thames Series*.

In the *Portrait of the Artist's Mother* black and white again form important ingredients, combined with the gray of the wall and the very dark green of the curtain; the grave harmony being solely relieved by the soft warmth of the face. Is it necessary to say that this prevailing gravity, so choicely reserved, and this accent of tenderness, contribute very largely to the emotion aroused in our imagination? Reserve, if it is deliberate, is a quality of force and may be one of dignity. That it shall be so here is assured by the contrast between the upright line of the curtain and the diagonal curving line of the lady's figure, and by the quiet assertion of these two masses. Observe how the latter are painted so that they shall count as masses, with only enough suggestion of modeling to make us feel in one case the folds of the curtain and in the other the figure beneath the dress. The severity of these masses is assuaged by the two gathering-points of intimate expression, the hands and the head. The former are laid one above the other with a gesture of exquisite composure, their color rendered more delicate and tender by being shown against the white handkerchief.[1] The gray wall behind

---

[1] Compare how Rubens placed the dead body on a white cloth in his *Descent from the Cross*. See page 182.

the head assists in creating an illusion of atmosphere, enveloping the head in tenderness, while the little accents of dainty suggestiveness that appear in the white cap soften the immobility of the face. In this is concentrated the calm and tender dignity to which every other part of the canvas has contributed. I speak of "calm and tender dignity," but who shall capture into exact words the qualities of mind and feeling which lie behind that searching gaze? That face speaks to each and every mother's son with different appeal; it speaks in a universal language, that each can understand but no man can fully comprehend. Yet, once again, let us note that the expression of the face is not an isolated incident, but the center and climax of a corresponding expression that in a more general way pervades the whole canvas; the result of the exquisite balance of the full and empty spaces and of the tender dignity of the color-scheme of black and gray.

Whistler's fondness for gray, which even caused him to keep his studio dimly lighted, just as the Dutch artist Israels does, may be traced to his study of Velasquez, as also his subtle use of black and white, and the preference he shows for sweeping lines and ample imposing masses. Often in the apparently haphazard arrangement of the masses and spaces there is a suggestion of the Japanese influence, as well as in the introduction of a hint of something outside the picture. Note, for example, the apparently accidental spotting of the picture on the wall, and the portion of another frame, peeping in, as it were, from outside. From both Velasquez and the Japanese he learned the power of simplicity and subtlety; the value of leaving out rather than of putting in; the charm of delicate harmonies, the fascination of surprise, and the abiding joy of suggestiveness. They helped him to give expression to the preference, which he shared with Leonardo, for the elusive rather than the obvious.

Whistler and Sargent belong to America, but are claimed by foreigners as, at least, citizens of the world, cosmopolitans. Sargent, with the exception of a few months at distant intervals, has spent his life abroad; Whistler, since about his twentieth year, was a resident of Paris and London, occasionally visiting Holland. The artistic influences which affected both were those of Europe. Yet their Americanism may be detected in their extraordinary facility of absorbing impressions, in the individuality evolved by both, and in the subtlety and reserve of their methods, qualities that are characteristic of the best American art.

CHAPTER XXIX

CLAUDE MONET	HASHIMOTO GAHO
1840-	1834-
Impressionist School of France	Modern School of Japan

WE touched upon Oriental art at the very beginning of our story. Then it was the Byzantine offshoot of it that we were considering, and the efforts of Giotto to liberate painting from the shackles of its traditions. Now, however, it is the art of Japan that claims our attention, and it does so because, as we saw in the previous chapter, it has been a source of some fresh inspiration to Western painting. The latest phase of the latter is represented in Monet, while Gaho is the foremost living artist in Japan. They are both landscape-painters.

We have seen that Manet was the founder of the modern impressionism, yet in the minds of the public Monet stands forth as the most conspicuous impressionist; and, as his later pictures are painted not in masses of color but with an infinity of little dabs of paint, the public is apt to suppose that this method of painting is what is meant by impressionism. Now Monet, like Manet, is an impressionist, in that what he strives to render is the effect vividly produced upon the eye by a scene; and, working always out of doors, he goes further than this, in trying to represent the exact effect of a scene at a certain hour of the day. It is the fleeting, transitory mood of nature that he represents. For this reason he was one of the first to be attracted by the Japanese paintings and colored prints which began about the sixties to be brought over in considerable numbers to Paris. For one of the characteristics of the Japanese work is, that it catches the fugitive gesture or movement in the elasticity of its momentary appearance.

But the method which Monet uses to render his effects is a totally different matter from his way of seeing nature, and of itself has nothing to do with impressionism. Nor was he the originator of the method of painting in dots or dabs. The first to practise it was a French painter but little known, named Seurat, who had studied very closely the experiments in light and color made by certain scientists, among others by Professor Rood of Columbia University, and then applied the theory to the practice of painting. Seurat was followed by Pissarro, and then by Monet, and later by many others, among them our own American painter, Childe Hassam. But, since Monet stands out from all of them as the big original man, this innovation in the handling of pigments will be identified with him.

Let us trace the train of causes which led to this result. Though a Parisian by birth, Monet's early years were spent at Havre, where Boudin, the painter of harbors and shipping, frequently resided. It was he who, attracted by the young Monet's taste for drawing, advised him to go out of doors and study nature. The young man did so, but was interrupted in his studies by being drawn as a conscript and drafted to Algeria. Here he came under the spell of the brilliant Southern sunshine. To his study of nature was added a special enthusiasm for the effects of sunlight. This was increased when he visited England during the disturbed period of the Franco-Prussian War, and became acquainted with the experiments in the painting of light that had been made by Turner. Thus, a second time, an English influence affected the course of French painting. Forty years earlier the appearance at the Salon of pictures by Constable had stimulated " the men of 1830 " to go out to Barbizon and study nature; and now Turner gave the stimulus to Monet to supplement and advance the study which they had achieved. The rendering of light became the problem of his artistic endeavors. Then it was that on his return to France he became acquainted with the principles of Seurat and Pissarro, and found in them a practical means of fulfilling what was to be his particular *rôle* in art as the leader of the " luminarists."

His aim was to render the appearance of nature as seen in out-of-door light,—*plein air*, as the French call it,—and especially the various effects of sunlight. Aided by the experiments of the scientists and by his own keen observation, he discovered certain facts which had escaped the notice of less keen eyes unaided by science; for example, that green, seen under strong sunshine, is not green, but yellow; that the shadows cast by sunlight upon snow or upon brightly lighted surfaces are not black, but blue; and that a white dress, seen under the shade of trees on a bright day, has violet or lilac tones. Science had proved that these are facts, and the keen, cultivated eye of the artist corroborated them. Here was a new insight into realism.

Thus far, however, science had only opened up a new faculty of seeing; could it also suggest a method of reproducing in paint the effects thus seen? Professor Rood had made experiments by covering disks with various colors, and then revolving them and noting the color produced while the disk was in motion. This suggested a new way of applying the pigments to the canvas. Instead of blending them upon the palette, the artist placed them separately side by side upon the canvas, so that the blending might be done by the eye of the spectator, standing at the required distance from the picture. As Pissarro himself said, the idea was " to substitute the optical mingling for the mingling of pigments, the decomposition of all the colors into their constituent elements; because the optical mingling excites much more intense luminosity than the mingling of pigments."

If you stand close to a picture by Monet, you see only a confusion of dabs of different-colored pigments laid on the canvas with separate strokes of the brush-point, in consequence of which this method of painting has been called the *pointilliste* method. But, if you step further back, these dabs begin to mingle, until they no longer appear separate but merged into a single harmonious effect.

Let us refer to the illustration of the *Old Church at Vernon*. It reproduces pretty well the effect of the separate dabs—the points, or stippling, as they are also called; but, unless you are familiar with some of the originals of Monet's pictures, it will hardly suggest to you the blending of these dabs. The searching eye of the camera has reduced the effect of distance and mechanically registered the multiplicity of paint spots, so that the picture looks somewhat as it would if we were standing where we ought not to stand to view it properly—namely, close by. Accordingly we receive an impression of a gritty, confused surface, and of a very wabbly, unsolid-looking church, rising up into a sky that seems veiled in crape. For here again, and in the water of the foreground, the camera has played us false. It did so, you may remember, in the drab-gray background of Manet's *Girl with a Parrot*, making it appear too dark; and here the darkness of sky and water is even more exaggerated, since in the original they are a very delicate dove-gray.

For the hour represented is early on a summer's morning, when the vapors that have been sleeping over meadows and river are touched by the "rosy-fingered dawn" and, palpitating in the growing warmth, begin to float skyward and disperse. All the air is a-tremble with silky opalescent mist, through which trees and buildings glimmer scarcely more substantial than their reflections. You can now appreciate why the outlines of the church are rendered so uncertainly, why its mass presents so little of the solidity of architecture. The church, like everything else in the scene, appears to be trembling in the soft, quivering atmosphere. If you have witnessed such an early sunrise, and could see the original of this picture, you would not need my word to recognize the truth with which the phenomenon is represented.

HOW TO STUDY PICTURES

We may discover here a clue to the kind of motive which interested Monet, as well as to the method he adopted to realize it. It was not the church as a specimen of architecture that for the time being interested him, but its aspect under the influence of a certain evanescent mood of nature. With the same end in view, he painted his famous series of the *West Front of Rouen Cathedral:* under varying light-effects of early morning, of full sunlight, of fog, of the last rays of the sun, of afternoon, and so on. The venerable pile is represented with sufficient hint of shape and construction to make us realize its presence, yet it is not its material reality that affects us, but something quite as real, possibly even more so: namely, the influence upon our spirit of its presence when bathed in the tenderness, or glory, or mystery of light. The pictures will not give you the actual appearance in its whole or detail of the architecture as a photographic print would do. But imagine yourself dispensing with a lens and wooden box and a sensitized plate inside it, and receiving the impression of the lighted cathedral through your eyes on to the sensitized plate of your imagination, and so securing a spiritual impression, a spirit picture. It would be somewhat like what Monet has produced in these cathedral pictures, and in a host of others, including the one we are studying.

It was indeed a higher kind of impressionism that Monet originated, one that reveals a vivid rendering, not of the natural and the concrete facts, but of their influence upon the spirit when they are wrapped in the infinite diversities of that impalpable, immaterial, universal medium which we call light, when the concrete loses itself in the abstract, and what is of time and matter impinges on the eternal and the universal.

This is the secret also of the spiritual impression produced by Corot's pictures of the dawn and evening; everything trembles on the edge of those gray skies of his through which the eye travels forward, until imagination takes its place and the spirit dips into the illimitable. For Corot could make us feel that the bit of sky which he reveals to us is a part of the infinite ocean of light. But Monet's range of expression is much wider than Corot's; partly because his sensitiveness to color is keener and more embracing, partly because he has found a new way of rendering the color impressions by means of paint. For this reason he has gone farther in the representation of light than Rembrandt, Velasquez, or Turner. He does not have to stimulate the appearance of light by surrounding it with shadows as Rembrandt did; nor is he bound to the tangible, visible objects of his subject, as was Velasquez, in representing their values or the amount of light which each contained; nor, again, tempted to escape from the tangible appearances, as Turner grew to be. The secret of his freer, fuller power is that he uses a method of painting which, while it is clumsy and gross compared with the tenuous medium of light that he is representing, yet enables him to suggest a higher key of light and more nearly to suggest the essential characteristic of light, namely, its vibrative quality.

For let us remember that light is a form of energy that travels in waves through space, until it reaches us, when it floods the sky and pours over all the earth, swimming through transparent objects, turned from its direction, as it is refracted in its course through objects of varying transparency, tossed in a shimmer of luminous reflections from the surfaces of opaque objects; an energy that streams, or throbs, and darts in and out, pulsating continually with vibrations.

It is an approximation toward this suggestion of movement that the *pointilliste* method of painting permits. When we try to read from a book whose print is too small for our eyesight, the little dots of black are apt to irritate our brain, until the whole page presents an unsteady, quavering blur, very painfully fatiguing because it oppresses us with a sense of feebleness. But suppose that, instead of dots of black, we are looking at dabs of color, which, when they blend, suggest a mass of foliage quivering with light; then the sensation is pleasant. Instead of the eye being distressed by the sense of feebleness, it has been gladdened by a surprise of new perception; and as our eye has had a share in creating the surprise, our imagination receives so much the pleasanter stimulation. We are not gazing helplessly at a blur, but likely to enjoy a sensation of vibrating color; color, that is to say, with all the stir of light about it.

The artist in another way also has made it possible for us to see more sensitively. For example, to our unaided sight a stretch of sea may appear to have a prevailing hue of blue, or, more definitely, perhaps, a greenish blue. Monet, on the other hand, with an eye that is by nature keener and trained to an exquisite sensitiveness, sees the blue and paints in blue dabs, notes the greenish blue and adds dabs of green. But he sees much more; the presence of yellow it may be, or white in the strong sunshine,

OLD CHURCH AT VERNON   CLAUDE MONET

SUNRISE ON THE HORAI　　　　　　　　HASHIMOTO GAHO

and of pink and rose and violet. All these constituent colors he places side by side in minute patches, and immediately the latter begin to act and react on one another, as a number of bright people will do upon one another, when assembled together in a room. I will mention only one recognized fact: red, yellow, and blue, being regarded as the primary colors, and the combinations of any two of these—namely, red + yellow = orange, yellow + blue = green, blue + red = purple—being regarded as secondary colors, it has been demonstrated that the juxtaposition of any secondary with the remainder primary will heighten the brilliancy of each. Thus, orange and blue are mutually enforcing; so green and red, and yellow and purple. While this law applies everywhere in painting, it applies with more subtlety and vivacity when the color spaces, instead of being big, are split up into an infinite number of tiny fragments; for the result may be likened to an intricate web, scintillating with numberless dewdrops. And there is yet another source of vivacity in this method of painting; namely, that the light is not reflected in broad masses from the canvas, but from each one of these separate patches dart reflections, which melt and mingle like the play of light upon minute threads of gossamer.

In this way Monet and his followers have based their method of painting upon the facts discovered by scientists in their study of light, and have thus made great advances in the rendering of light by means of pigments. It must be remembered, however, that the latter are poor substitutes for the colored light which they try to reproduce. White paint, for example, which represents the lightest or highest note of color in pigments, is infinitely inferior in luminosity to white *light*. So, while it is often said that these artists have raised the key of color, it would be more correct to say that they have raised the key of the shadows. By substituting for black and brown or red shadows delicate blue and violet ones, they have increased the general appearance of lightness, and by the increased vivacity and subtlety due to the *pointilliste* method of laying on the paint, have more nearly approximated to the effect produced upon the eye by the vibrations and the brilliancy of sunlight.

In this necessarily brief account of Monet's work I can add only one more particular—that it is absolutely objective. Corot was a poet at heart, seeking through nature to express his own subjectivity—himself; and this is the attitude of the majority of landscape-painters. Monet, on the contrary, is an eye, analyzing what it sees; the brain behind it is filled with passion, but with a passion aroused and satisfied entirely from without. The result is that, while most painters interpret through nature a mood of their own, Monet interprets those of nature purely; and through the frame of his picture we gaze, as through an open window, at nature herself appealing to us, if we have eyes to see, *directly*.

Yet many people are honestly unable to admire his pictures. The eyes of some are physically incapable of blending into one the separate patches. Others, again, by their temperament have so marked a preference for the solidity and facts of nature, that this spiritualized suggestion of it troubles them. I think one is to be congratulated if one can appreciate both the tremendous reality of Rousseau, the spirituality of Corot, and also the marvelous suggestion to one's spirit and imagination that may be found in Monet.

Now it is the suggestiveness to spirit and imagination that is the key-note of the Japanese motive. Buddhism teaches the impermanency and unreality of matter; that matter is but a limited symbol of the universal soul. The Japanese laugh at our Western art, that tries to represent the human form and the forms of nature exactly. Our artists, they think, in the first place are feeding themselves upon what is not real, but an illusion; and, in the second place, are trying to make the spectator believe that what he sees on the canvas is a real man, or fish, or mountain. He is trying to prop up an illusion with a lie.

Now this is an idea not very dissimilar to the teaching of our own philosophers, from Plato to Herbert Spencer, but so far removed from our ordinary way of regarding this world and our relation to it, that I mention it only to get a starting-point for trying to understand how the Japanese feel toward art. We may state it briefly in the following way.

Matter is impermanent, the forms in which it appears to the eye are temporary. We ourselves were taught at school that the extent and shape of our earth are continually changing; and in Japan these changes are very frequent and remarkable, owing to the volcanic nature of the islands and to the almost daily occurrence of earthquakes. "Rivers shift their courses," writes Lafcadio Hearn, "coasts their outline, plains their level; volcanic peaks heighten or crumble; valleys are blocked by lava floods or landslides; lakes appear or disappear. Even the matchless shape of Fuji, that snowy miracle which has been the inspiration of artists for centuries, is said to have been slightly changed since my advent to the country; and not a few other mountains have in the same short time taken totally new forms. Only the general lines of the land, the general aspects of its nature, the general character of the seasons, remain fixed. Even the very beauty of the landscape is largely illusion,—a beauty of shifting colors and moving mists." This was written in 1895, after the author had been living in Japan for about ten years.

This impermanent matter is the temporary manifestation of the Universal Spirit, which alone is eternal. In every form of nature, great or small, resides for the time being an atom of the Universal Spirit. It is this atom of spirit that is the life of the form in which it resides, determining its character. The Japanese speak of this inward spirit as " kokoro."

The highest aim in art, says Hashimoto Gaho, *is to express this kokoro.* A picture that gives merely the temporary appearance of the objects of nature is not a work of art; it becomes such only if it manifests an expression of the "kokoro," or, in his own word, if it manifests "kokoromochi." At first sight this might seem like Corot's expression of the spirit of dawn and evening; but Corot put into his pictures what was in himself, whereas with Gaho the "kokoro" is entirely outside himself, residing in the object before him, actually there, whether Gaho himself were asleep or awake, alive or dead, having nothing to do with himself. Rousseau, therefore, to whom nature was an objective study, who tried to represent the strength that lies in the rocks themselves, and the sinewy vigor that directs the growth of the oak, comes nearer to Gaho's idea of it; and Monet also, who has been described as only an "eye." On the other hand, we remember that the old Greeks also believed that there was a spirit in the waterfalls, the mountains, the trees; but in their art they represented it in human shape, as nymphs, naiads, oreads, dryads. This aim, however, is the very opposite to that of the Japanese artist, who strives to get away as far as possible from the accidents of impermanent form. In his attempt to do so he simplifies, generalizes, and conventionalizes.

So do Western artists, but not for the same purpose or to the same extent. They want to represent the human form or the landscape as its material form really appears to the eyes; but, not being able to imitate every hair on the head or every leaf and blade of grass, they are forced to give a general appearance of hair, of foliage, or of grass,—they simplify and generalize. Then they make marks on the canvas which are not like leaves, but which we have all agreed to accept as suggesting the appearance of leaves; in fact, they conventionalize: but, observe, mostly with the intention of forcing upon us the material fact of these things being leaves. Some of our artists, however, say: "We do not care about representing leaves, but only the impression produced on our minds by them"; and these men whom we call impressionists, because of their going farther in generalization and conventionalizing, approach nearer to Jap-

HOW TO STUDY PICTURES

anese art, by the example of which, we must remember, however, they have been largely inspired.

Now the Japanese artist, taught by his religion to value spirit more than matter, portrays material form only because he is obliged to make a material habitation for its " kokoro "; but he does not dwell on form. On the contrary, he tries to draw your attention away from the fact of his subject being a woman or a tree; he eliminates as far as possible the aggressiveness of form, and accordingly simplifies, conventionalizes, and generalizes more than the Western artists do.

In the first place, he does not use oil paints, by means of which his Western brother gives solidity and elaboration to his objects. The Japanese artist paints with water-colors upon silk or paper, using thin transparent washes of color, manipulating his brush with a delicacy and decision that are superior to anything in Western painting. With one stroke of his brush, moving freely from the shoulder,—for he kneels on the floor and works above his silk or paper,—he can render, for example, a branch of a plum-tree, using the flat side and bearing more heavily on one end so as to render the shadow at the same time as the light part, and twisting the brush on to its edge to indicate knots or joints or such like. This in itself represents a wonderful skill in generalizing and simplification. It has led also to a wonderful skill and expressiveness in the use of line.

This is the second point to be noted: Gaho himself says that Japanese painting is founded upon line, that by varieties of modulation of its breadth and of dark and light the line itself may be made to manifest " kokoromochi."

Thirdly, the colors are laid on flat; forming a pattern of very subtle harmony.

Fourthly, the composition is not based on set forms of balanced arrangement, but is distinguished rather by irregularity, by its unexpectedness and surprises. Nor is it designed to hold our attention entirely within the frame. Often the spray of a flower, or a branch, belonging to some plant or tree that we cannot see, peeps into the picture, as if to remind us that there are other things beyond this tiny view, and that the latter is only an atom of the universe. We have noted, in the previous chapter, Whistler's borrowing of this device in the *Portrait of the Artist's Mother*.

Fifthly, conventionalization is carried to a point where to Western eyes it seems strange. For example, we may look through a number of prints by different artists, and the women's mouths will all be represented by a similar arrangement of lines, which to us does not convey the idea of a natural mouth. To the Japanese, however, it does; and they would retort that many of our conventions in painting seem to them equally unintelligible and unreasonable. For, remember, that conventions are a sort of shorthand appeal to memory and experience; wherefore, since there is so much in the Japanese memory and experience that must remain unknown to us, we can never fully appreciate the conventions of their painting.

Every one of these characteristics of Japanese art that I have enumerated has influenced modern Western art. Space will not permit me to particularize, but if you will bear them in mind when you examine pictures by Degas and Whistler, the latter's Venetian etchings especially and the work of many American and foreign illustrators, you will be able to discover the traces of the influence unmistakably.

There is one other point among so many that might be alluded to. A Buddhist text declares that *he alone is wise who can see things without their individuality*. And it is this Buddhist way of seeing, as Lafcadio Hearn says, which makes the greatness of true Japanese art. One might explain this by saying that the Japanese artist discards the accident of individuality in favor of the type, but it is even more than this—that in the Particular he tries to express a portion of the Universal, regarding even his composition, for example, not as a complete finite arrangement but as a fragment of what he imagines as a universal geometry.

And now let us turn to Hashimoto Gaho's *Sunrise on the Horai*. The Horaizan is the Japanese Earthly Paradise; the dream-place of peaceful and exalted contemplation. Gaho, contrary to custom, has represented it upon the mountain-tops and pictured it in the purest hour of all, in the freshness of early sunrise. The sun itself is veiled in the vapor that rises up from the steep valley, at the bottom of which are the rice-fields, whither the laborers are already wending for their day's toil. Down there are the lives of men, their joys and sorrows, the multiple units of the human hive. All below is clouded in uncertain mists, but up here it is clear and serene; the foreground, a miniature panorama of mountain scenery, with pines, the symbol of eternity, and pagoda pleasure-houses of the soul; further back, a cone-like peak of spiritual desire and mountain ramparts, barring the approach as yet to the ultimate Beyond.

Study, first, the linear arrangement: the broken level lines of the foreground, the soaring lines of the peak, the lines as of longing piled upon longing of the mountain mass, and then that diagonal line that fades into invisibility. Then from its gradual lifting up into height, and from its flight into the immensity of distance, the imagination settles back to the assured certainty of the foreground and the intimacy of the pine-trees, those familar objects of the Japanese landscape.

Study, secondly, the exquisite gradations of tone, and the way the darks and lights are distributed in the composition, the occasional accents of dark, and the value of the empty spaces. There is perhaps nothing in painting which may give so pure and rarefied a joy as the way in which the Japanese artists give you the effect of definition melting into indefiniteness, and this picture of Gaho's is a fine example of the effect. It states just enough to render the imagination active, and then leaves it to its own wandering.

It is this suggestiveness to the imagination, moreover the decorative beauty and expressiveness of the lines and masses of the composition, and the choiceness and originality of the color-harmonies, rich or delicate, as the case may be, but always subtle, that are among the conspicuous charms of Japanese painting. These may be enjoyed, even when the subject refers to experiences that we do not share or is represented by means of conventions unfamiliar to us. In the accompanying example these limitations are scarcely to be felt.

HOW TO STUDY PICTURES

Japanese painting has already taught our Western artists a good deal ; it has a further lesson for all of us, if only in the matter of simplification. How little there is in this picture, and yet how choice and meaningful the details that are introduced! The same is characteristic of the Japanese home life. The home is simple, adorned by a few choice treasures, stored in the little closet or *tokonama*, and taken out for the occasional enjoyment of the family or to greet the visit of a guest. The life, too, is outwardly simple. Though Japan has adopted Western notions, and undertaken the *rôle* of a first-class nation, with all the intricacies of trade relations, the appearance of the cities and of the outward life of the people is almost as simple as ever. In fact, there has never been a nation, at any rate since the great days of Athens, whose art so closely reflected its outward life and the soul which it embodies.

CONCLUDING NOTE

WE have come to the end of the study that we set out to make. Step by step, we have marked the evolution of modern painting, from the Byzantine traditions which prevailed before Cimabue down to the latest possibilities introduced by the *pointilliste* method of Monet.

We have made the acquaintance of a majority of the greatest artists ; of those who, being themselves men of originality, exercised a wide influence on others. In studying their points of view, and their methods of rendering what they saw in the way they felt it, we have gained a general insight into pictorial methods and motives, that will enable us to appreciate the infinite varieties of the same as they appear in other artists.

Turn by turn, we have visited different countries, according as the art of painting flourished in them simultaneously, or as it declined in one and reappeared with vigor in another. And, doing so, we have found that the manifestations of art have varied in response to the racial and temporary conditions of each country; and, while we have not attempted to explain genius as the result of these, we have examined how they influenced it.

We have seen how one impulse of movement followed another ; all of them involving truth, but none monopolizing the whole truth ; in fact, that the manifestations and possibilities of painting are wide and various as human nature. From this study, also, we should have discovered that the enjoyment to be derived from pictures is not only the satisfaction of our own predilections, of what most appeals to ourselves individually, but the interest to be gained from studying pictures as the record of the feeling and experience of other minds.

We have gained a fairly comprehensive bird's-eye view of the whole field of painting ; sufficient, if our study must stop here, to enable us to recognize the landmarks of the subject ; but offering, if we are able to step down and pursue the study in detail, a convenient groundwork for investigation.

It is not by the much, unavoidably omitted, that I beg the usefulness of this book may be judged, but by the value of what is included.

ORIENTA POINT,
   MAMARONECK, N. Y.

A BRIEF BIBLIOGRAPHY OF BOOKS ON ART READILY PROCURABLE

Italian Schools.—Berenson, Bernard: The Florentine Painters of the Renaissance; The Venetian Painters of the Renaissance; The Central Italian Painters of the Renaissance (New York, 1897). Blashfield, E. H. and E. W.: Italian Cities (New York, 1900). Brinton, S.: Renaissance in Italian Art (London, 1898). Crowe, J. A., and Cavalcaselle, G. B.: History of Painting in Italy (London, 1866). Morelli, G.: Italian Painters. Translated by C. J. Ffoulkes (London, 1892–1893). Ruskin, John: Mornings in Florence (Orpington, 1875); Modern Painters (London, 1846, 1860). Symonds, J. A.: Renaissance in Italy (London, 1875); Sketches and Studies in Italy and Greece (London, 1874). Vasari, G.: Lives of the Painters. Edited by E. H. and E. W. Blashfield and A. A. Hopkins (New York, 1897). Modern Painters. Muther, R. (See General Reference.) Willard, A. R.: History of Modern Italian Art (New York, 1900).

Flemish School.—Fromentin, E.: Les Maîtres d'Autrefois (Paris, 1876). Kugler, F. T.: Handbook of Painting: The German, Flemish, and Dutch Schools. Remodeled by Dr. Waagen, revised and in part rewritten by J. A. Crowe (London, 1874). Van Dyke, J. C.: Old Dutch and Flemish Masters. Engravings by Timothy Cole (New York, 1895). Modern Painters. Muther, R. (See General Reference.)

German School.—Alexandre, A.: Histoire populaire de la peinture: École Allemande (Paris, 1895). Colvin, A.: Dürer (Encyclopædia Britannica, Edinburgh, 1883). Kugler, F. T.: Handbook of Painting: The German, Flemish, and Dutch Schools. Revised by J. A. Crowe (London, 1874). Woltman, A.: Holbein

BIBLIOGRAPHY

and his Time. Translated by F. E. Bunnett (London, 1872). Modern Painters. Muther, R.

Dutch School.—Bode, W.: Studien zur Geschichte der holländischen Malerei (Brunswick, 1883); Rembrandt (Paris, 1898); Franz Hals und seine Schule (Leipsic, 1871). Fromentin, E.: Les Maîtres d'Autrefois (Paris, 1876). Gower, R.: Guide to Public and Private Galleries of Holland and Belgium (London, 1875). Kugler, F. T.: Handbook of Painting: The German, Flemish, and Dutch Schools. Revised by J. A. Crowe (London, 1874). Van Dyke, J. C.: Old Dutch and Flemish Masters. Engravings by Timothy Cole (New York, 1895). Modern Painters. Muther, R.

Spanish School.—Ford, R.: Handbook for Spain (London, 1855). Justi, C.: Velasquez and his Times. Translated by A. H. Keane (London and Philadelphia, 1889). Stevenson, R. A. M.: The Art of Velasquez (London, 1895). Stirling-Maxwell, Sir W.: Annals of the Artists of Spain (London, 1848); Velasquez and his Works (London, 1855). Muther, R. (See General Reference.)

French School.—Alexandre, A.: Histoire populaire de la peinture: École Française (Paris, 1893). Berger, G.: L'École française de peinture (Paris, 1879). Blanc, C.: Les artistes de mon temps (Paris, 1879). Brownell, W. C. (New York, 1901). Dilke, Lady: French Painters of the Eighteenth Century (London, 1899). Duret, Théodore: Les peintres impressionistes (Paris, 1879); Histoire d'Édouard Monet (Paris, 1902). Gautier, T.: L'Art moderne; Romanticism. Goncourt, E. and J. de: L'Art du XVIIIme siècle (Paris, 1881–1882). Guibal: Eloge de Poussin (Paris, 1783). Moore, G.: Modern Painting (New York, 1893). Pater, Walter: Imaginary Portraits; A Prince of Court Painters (Watteau) (London, 1887). Sensier, Théodore: Rousseau (Paris, 1872); Life and Works of J. F. Millet (Paris, 1881). Stranahan, C. H.: History of French Painting (New York, 1895).

English School.—Armstrong, Sir W.: Gainsborough and his Place in English Art (New York, 1898). Bate, P. H.: English Pre-

BIBLIOGRAPHY

Raphaelite Painters (London, 1899). Chesneau, E.: The English School of Painting (London, 1885). Maccoll, D. S.: Nineteenth Century Art (Glasgow, 1902). Phillips, C.: Sir Joshua Reynolds (London, 1894). Redgrave, S.: A Century of Painters of the English School (London, 1890). Rossetti, W. M.: Ruskin, Rossetti; Pre-Raphaelitism (London, 1899). Wedmore, F.: Studies in English Art (London, 1876); Masters of Genre Painting (London, 1880). Muther, R. (See General Reference.)

Japanese Art.—Amsden, Dora: Impressions of Ukiyo-ye (San Francisco, 1905). Fenollosa, F. E.: Review of the Chapter on Painting in " L'Art Japonais," 1885. Gouse, Louis: L'Art Japonais (Paris, 1883). Hearn, Lafcadio: Kokoro (Boston, 1896). Okakura-Kakuzo: Ideals of the East (New York, 1904). Muther, R. (See General Reference.)

General Reference.—Bryan's Dictionary of Painters (New York, 1902). Champlin, T. D., Jr., and Perkins, Charles C.: Cyclopedia of Painters and Paintings (New York, 1887). Cox, Kenyon: Old Masters and New. La Farge, John: Great Masters of Painting. Lubke's History of Art. Translated by Clarence Cook. Masters in Art (Boston). Muther, R.: History of Modern Painting (New York, 1896). Van Dyke, J. C.: History of Painting; Art for Art's Sake; How to Judge of a Picture. Woltmann and Woermann: History of Painting.

American Painting.—American Art Review. Caffin, C. H.: American Masters of Painting. Hartmann, S.: History of American Art (Boston, 1902). Isham, Samuel: History of American Painting. (In press.) Mason: Life and Works of Gilbert Stuart. Tuckerman: Book of the Artists.

GLOSSARY OF TERMS

Abstract: opposed to *Concrete* (q.v.); viewed apart from concrete form; e.g., *the abstract beauty of a line*, where the line not only serves to inclose a form but has an independent beauty of its own (66). So also, *abstract beauty of color*, where color is independently a source of esthetic enjoyment, apart from the object to which it may belong. So, also, *music is the most abstract of the arts*, because it is entirely withdrawn from the concrete and appeals directly to the esthetic sense, and thence to the imagination (451, 452). For further remarks on abstract, see *Concrete*.

Academic: having the qualities that characterize the official standards of excellence maintained by the Academy of Painting and Sculpture, founded in France by Louis XIV. These have varied from time to time in details, but are based upon a preference for form over color; and upon an idealization of form, in imitation of the purity of antique sculpture. Hence the synonym *Classic*. Perfection of line and form is aimed at in preference to individuality and character.

Action: the gesture or attitude of a figure, expressive of character or sentiment. See *Expression, Movement*.

Æsthetic. See *Esthetic*.

Analysis: opposed to *Synthesis* (q.v.); the process of distinguishing between and studying separately the ingredients of an object. Thus the analysis of an elm involves an examination of its stem, the spread of its branches, the way in which the smaller are attached to the larger and the latter to the stem, the character of the foliage both in masses and in individual leaves, the effect upon the color and form of the foliage under the action of sunlight or of wind, and so on. Most of the great artists have trained themselves at first by severe analysis, after which they render their subject by means of synthesis. Having learned to put in, they become learned in leaving out.

Architectonic: literally, of or pertaining to construction; having the qualities of form and structure deliberately built up to produce a desired effect upon the imagination: e.g., *the architectonics of poetry* — that is to say, the form and structure of versification. *The architectonics of a picture*, in allusion to the formal arrangement of its lines and masses, its *full and empty spaces* (q.v.); more particularly of a composition planned to occupy and conform to a given space in connection with architecture — *a mural painting* (q.v.).

Arrangement: a principle of composition whereby the artist, having selected from a variety of details the ones best adapted to his conception of the subject, arranges them, with deliberate intent, to produce a certain impression on the spectator (99 et seq.). See *Selection*.

Art: by its derivation from a Greek word, "to fit," means primarily the fitting of form to an idea.

Art for art's sake: a catchword adopted in the last quarter of the nineteenth century by the followers of Manet, who asserted that the first requisite of a painter was to be able to paint. They began by saying that the subject of a picture was of little importance, the main thing for the artist being an opportunity of artistic expression; and, in their disgust of the, so-called, story-telling picture, in which considerations of painting as painting are sacrificed to mere attractiveness of subject, ended by asserting that subject was of no importance at all. Now that the dust of argument is settled, it has established the truth that, as Professor John C. Van Dyke says, "the art of a picture is not in the subject but in the manner of presenting it."

Articulation: the art of joining together; for example, of correctly joining the branches

GLOSSARY OF TERMS

of a tree to its trunk, the leaves to the branches, the flower and leaves to the stalk, and the latter to the stem; the accurate rendering of the joints or articulations of the human body. Both the actor and the painter recognize the fact that the joints are the seats of expression.

Atmosphere. The world, out of doors and indoors, is filled with air, more or less illumined with light. It surrounds every object, affecting both their shape and color. The outlines even of objects near to us are seldom sharp, and become more blurred and indistinct as the objects lie further from the eye. The colors, too, as they recede, become grayer in appearance — seen, as it were, through intervening veils of atmosphere. Many painters represent the figures and objects with uniform sharpness and distinctness; there is no suggestion of atmosphere in their pictures. Others, however, by rendering the effect of lighted atmosphere upon the outlines and colors of the objects (see *Values*), make them appear to be surrounded, as in nature, by an *envelope* of lighted air, and to occupy their proper plane in the depth of atmosphere. Moreover, it is to be noted that, as atmosphere varies according to time of day, locality, and season, it becomes to our imagination a source of expression in nature.

Breadth and simplicity: the results of a painter's ability to see the large significance of things; to view his subject, as it were from afar off, so that it is seen apart from its littlenesses of detail in its essential character. When a painter can so stand back from his subject and see it in this broad, general way, and then by simple, effective brushwork suggest to us a similarly broad comprehension of its essential character, we speak of the breadth and simplicity of his work. See Hals, 195 et seq.

Chiaroscuro: derived from Italian *chiaro* = clear, + *oscuro* = obscure; French equivalent, *clair-obscur*; English, light and shade. The distribution in a picture of light and shade, introduced for one or more purposes: (1) the functional use, to suggest the modeling of form, the raised parts catching various quantities of light and the depressed being in various degrees of shadow; (2) the decorative use, to produce an agreeable pattern by a contrast of lights and darks; (3) the expressional use, to arouse by such variety an appeal to our emotions. As a method of modeling it is less true to nature than modeling by means of a rendering of the values (*q.v.*); as a method of emotional expression, when used, for example, by Rembrandt, who made his lights emerge from a bath of darkness, or by Rubens in his *Descent from the Cross*, its mingling of clearness and mystery has a wonderful effect upon the imagination.

Classic. See *Academic*.

Colorist: one who uses color not merely to increase the reality of appearances in his picture, but as a means of emotional expression. He thinks and feels in color, conceives his subject as an arrangement not so much of form as of color, and moves us by his color-harmonies, as a musician by his harmonies of sound.

Colors, cold and warm: yellow suggests the color of sunlight and flames, and red the glow of a fire and of sunlight seen through moist atmosphere; we associate with these colors and with their union, orange, the idea of warmth. On the other hand, blue suggests the color of the ocean, of the sky after rain, and of the evening sky in the upper part removed from the sunset glow, and when blended with yellow, it is the cooling ingredient in the resultant green. We associate with blue the idea of coolness. Moreover, science, as well as the observation of artists, has proved that in bright sunlight the tint of shadows contains blue. See Reynolds's doctrine about cold and warm colors, 274.

Composition: literally, the placing together of parts to produce a whole; in art, the parts must be harmoniously related to one another and to the whole, and the latter must be distinguished by balance and unity. It involves a twofold process of selection and arrangement: the selection of parts best suited to one another and to the whole, and the arrangement of them so as to produce by the actual direction and character of the lines and by the disposition of the masses and spaces an impression upon the esthetic sense, and, in higher works of arts, upon the imagination. It cannot be too thoroughly understood that composition is the structural basis of painting, as it is of poetry and of music; and that its appeal to sense or imagination is an abstract one — that is to say, primarily independent of the subject-matter. See 98 et seq.

GLOSSARY OF TERMS

Concrete: opposed to *Abstract*; viewed as existing in connection with objects and substances. Thus the picture of a landscape conveys a concrete impression of trees, water, sky, ground, etc., and may do no more. On the other hand, it may stimulate an abstract impression, for example, of exquisite restfulness, so that in the enjoyment of this the actual shapes and appearances of objects and substances, perhaps even their very existence in the picture, may be forgotten. Again, a composition so harmoniously balanced and unified, such as that of Raphael's *Disputà*, may so captivate the imagination that it is only upon a second visit one becomes conscious of the concrete facts of the figures and what they represent. Remember, the abstract is as much a fact to the spirit and the imagination as the concrete is to the senses of sight and touch. See *Abstract*.

Construction: the act or result of building up a structure — for example, the construction of the human figure, so that we are made to realize beneath the flesh its framework of bones and joints and muscles. In this sense we speak of the figure being good or faulty in construction. Similarly we examine the construction of a landscape: has the painter made us realize the firm earth or rocky foundation beneath the grass of a meadow; the special character of stoutness or suppleness in trees and plant forms; the actual quality of construction in waves and clouds, and so on? In a picture, as in a building, it is not the outside appearance which first meets the eye that is of chief importance, but the underlying, embedded, construction.

Contour: inclosing forms; e.g., *contour lines of the figure.*

Convention, Conventionalisation. If we grant, for example, that a painter cannot represent absolutely all the leaves on a tree or all the hairs in a man's beard, it follows he must adopt some method of suggesting to us the appearance of the mass of leaves or hairs. He adopts some convention of representing it, some arrangement which our memory and experience will immediately interpret to mean a mass of leaves or hairs. It is to be noted that the artist takes advantage of memories and experiences, which in a general way we share with him, so that by association of ideas his convention is intelligible to us. But if the convention — as, for example, the one employed by the Japanese to suggest the human mouth — is founded upon memories and experiences foreign to our own, we shall probably find it not immediately intelligible.

Distemper: a medium of painting used before the development of oil-paints. The color ingredient was ground in water, and in order to give it substance, — or, as the artists say, "body," — so that it would not sink too much into an absorbent material like canvas, and to fix it so that it would not, when dry, rub off a hard one like wood, white of egg or some other glutinous ingredient was stirred in. As a medium of picture-painting it was superseded by oil-painting, but, with glue as a medium, is still used by scene-painters and, under the name of calcimine, by house-decorators.

Drawing: the manner of representing objects on a flat surface; (1) specifically, as contrasted with painting, by means of pencil, pen, or crayon; (2) in a general sense, including painting, referring to the quality of the representation: e.g., *the drawing of that figure is good; the other is weak in drawing.*

Elemental: of or pertaining to first principles; hence based upon what is fundamental and essential, unimpaired by the details of individual differences. Such, for example, was the character of Millet's drawing, 251.

Elusive, Elusiveness: the suggestion, in a work of art, of what eludes the grasp of the eye; e.g., *the elusive quality of Velasquez's contour line*, partly definite, partly melting into indefiniteness, because he rendered the blurring effect of light creeping round their edges (192). Also the suggestion of what even eludes the grasp of the imagination; thus Leonardo (121, 122) and Hashimoto Gaho (477) essayed to suggest the mystery of humanity and nature.

Engraving: (1) the process of cutting a picture *into* steel or copper, or *out* of wood; (2) the result so obtained. It is to be observed that in the case of steel or copper the picture is below the surface of the material, and the ink is forced by a roller into the grooves, out of which, in the process of printing, it is sucked up by the damp paper driven down into the grooves under great pressure. On the other hand, in wood-engraving the picture stands up above the rest of the block, just as type is raised; the ink adheres to the raised parts, and the paper, as in printing

GLOSSARY OF TERMS

from type, receives the impression. The depressed kind of printing is sometimes called *intaglio*; the raised, *relievo* or *cameo*.

Esthetic: literally, able to be apprehended by the senses; hence, with special meaning, of or belonging to an appreciation of the beautiful: e.g., *the esthetic taste*.

Etching. This, like steel- and copper-engraving, is (1) a process; (2) the result of an intaglio printing, only that the lines of the picture instead of being graved with a "burin" are *bitten* into the copper by acid. The copper plate having been covered with a thin layer of melted wax and asphaltum and blackened with lamp-smoke, the artist draws his picture on it with a needle or similar instrument. This easily furrows its way through the soft wax, and discloses, wherever there is a line, the bright copper. The plate is then plunged into a bath of nitric acid, which bites into the exposed lines, leaving the wax-covered portions intact. Then, the wax having been removed, ink is rolled into the grooves and a print taken, as in steel- or copper-engraving. This is the bare statement of a process which involves many modifications, and which is distinguished from that of engraving on steel or copper by the greater freedom of drawing which it permits and by the qualities of the line and tone obtained; for the action of the acid being somewhat uneven, the line in etching is more sensitive, and the "blacks" can be made richer in tone than is possible in line-engraving.

Expression: the revelation of character and sentiment in a work of art. Thus we speak of *the expression of a figure*, meaning that its pose and gesture are significant of character and that there is a suggestion in the figure of the life-spirit which animates it. Similarly we may speak of *the expression of a landscape*, referring to the way in which the artist has expressed the character of rocks and trees, water, and so forth, or to the way in which he has made the landscape interpret a mood of feeling, either his own or one that he conceives as existing in nature itself.

Expressional: of or pertaining to expression; e.g., the expressional use of line and color — that is to say, their use not only for the purpose of representing the appearances of objects, but also as an independent source of appeal to the emotions. See *Abstract*.

Feeling: (1) a sympathetic comprehension; e.g., *a feeling for form*, implying both a correct observation of form and also an appreciation of its characteristic qualities. Similarly, *a feeling for light and atmosphere*. (2) The evidence of sympathetic comprehension; e.g., *the figure is excellent in feeling*. (3) As an equivalent for *Sentiment* (q.v.).

Flat painting: where the color is laid on with little or no indication of modeling by means of *Chiaroscuro* (q.v.).

Fore-shortening: the art of representing on a plane surface in true perspective objects as they appear to the eye, especially those objects or parts of objects which extend toward the spectator on a line between his eyes and the center of the object.

Fresco: literally, "fresh"; painting in water-color upon the still damp plaster of a wall, so that the plaster and the painting dry together and become inseparable. The process is more fully described, p. 147.

Full and empty spaces: used of composition, as a convenient term to distinguish those forms in the design which are of primary importance to the delineation of the subject, from those forms or open spaces which are of subsidiary importance to the subject and are introduced chiefly to complete the harmony and balance of the composition. (See p. 100.) That the empty spaces may also be of importance to the subject, see "space-composition," p. 80.

Generalization: the process of discovering and rendering the essentials of a subject, so as to represent a summary of its salient characteristics.

Genre: a kind of picture representing ordinary in-door and out-door life; especially the Dutch pictures of the seventeenth century, which depicted domestic scenes and the pastimes of the peasants. It is to be noted that while these were the subject of the picture the design of the Dutch artists was not to *illustrate* them, but to make them the basis of a *pictorial* treatment (q.v.).

Gesture: literally, the mode of carrying; the carriage of a figure or of a part of it, as the head, the arm, or hand, expressive of character or sentiment. Practically the equivalent of *Action* (q.v.). See *Movement*.

GLOSSARY OF TERMS

Glazes: thin layers of transparent color brushed over the whole or parts of a picture in its final stages to produce a desired *tone* (*q.v.*).

Grand style: an imposing method of composition, embodying elevated feeling, brought to perfection by the great Italians of the Renaissance (102). Long after the death of Tintoretto, the last of the great Italians, its influence continued to lead smaller men in all countries to imitate its manner without being able to reproduce its spirit. Hence innumerable affectations and mannerisms.

Greek: the English equivalent of Græci, the name by which the Romans designated the people who called themselves *Hellenes*, after a mythic ancestor, Hellen. Their territory, which comprised a portion of the mainland (Thessaly and Epirus), the Isthmus of Corinth, and the peninsula of the Peloponnesus and adjacent islands, was known to themselves as *Hellas*, to the Romans as Græcia, hence Greece.

Half-tone: a method of photographic reproduction by which it is possible to render mechanically not only the extreme darks and lights of a picture, but also the intermediate tones; hence the name. A picture or a photograph of it is set up before the camera and photographed through an intervening glass screen, upon which a series of parallel lines, vertical and horizontal, very close together, have been graved. The effect of this is to split up the impression upon the negative into innumerable pin-point dots. The negative is then laid over a copper plate which has been covered with a sensitized film, and is exposed to light in the usual way of making a print. Where the negative is black (that is to say, in the lightest parts of the original or final picture), the light does not penetrate through, and therefore the film remains intact, but in the successively less dark parts of the negative (which in the positive are represented by the successively less light parts of the picture), the light in varying degrees disintegrates the film. Consequently, when the plate is plunged into a bath of acid, only these portions are bitten into in their varying intensity. The result is a plate bristling with minute pin-points biggest in the darkest parts, smaller in those less dark, and according to their size is the amount of ink which they receive from the ink-roller as it passes over the plate. Similarly, when the paper passes over the plate it receives its darkest impressions from the biggest points and varying degrees of less dark from the smaller points. This is the process used in the illustrations of this book, and the pin-points, if not visible to the eye, may readily be detected through a magnifying-glass.

Harmony: an arrangement of diversities into a unity of effect, so as to produce an impression of completeness and perfection; e.g., *a harmony of lines, a color-harmony*. It is to be noted that the impression is complete. Where a painter uses color, as many do, only to increase the resemblance to real objects, the tints could, as it were, be shuffled like a pack of cards, without impairing the completeness of the whole. But if the painter is a colorist (*q.v.*) and plays with color as a musician does with notes, then the least alteration, such as the subsequent fading out of parts of the picture, disturbs the balance and unity of the color-composition as much as if notes in a musical composition should be dropped out or transposed.

Hellas, Hellenic. See *Greek*.

Heroic: relating to something larger than life; e.g., *a statue of heroic size*. Hence something presumed to be nobler than ordinary experience; e.g., *Poussin's heroic treatment of the human figure, Claude's heroic landscapes*. Accordingly, it is used as a synonym for *Classic* (*q.v.*).

Hole in the wall: a term used in connection with *mural painting* (*q.v.*). It implies that the painting, instead of preserving the impression of being upon a flat, solid surface, makes one feel as if one were looking through an opening to some scene beyond; we say of such that *it makes a hole in the wall*.

Ideal: (1) that quality in a picture which represents a mental or spiritual idea embodied in the external form: cf. Titian's *Man with the Glove* (127); (2) the assembling into one single representation of the qualities of perfection which appear separately in many individuals: e.g., *an ideal treatment of the human figure, an ideal landscape*.

Imagination: the faculty of picturing the universal in terms of the particular. Boecklin, for example, in his *Isle of the Dead* (365 et seq.), while adhering to the facts of an island and a boat approaching it, makes one realize the vastness of the infinite soul into which the atom of soul is received.

GLOSSARY OF TERMS

Impressionism: the faculty possessed by some painters, notably Velasquez, of receiving an immediate and vivid impression of a subject in all its salient features, and of retaining the same keenly in his mind, while he painted, so that the rendering of it produces upon ourselves a similarly immediate and irresistibly vivid impression. Such is the immediate vividness of Velasquez's *Maids of Honor*, that Gautier summed up his admiration of its realism of appearance by exclaiming, "Where is the picture?" (179)

Infinite: our world with countless others swims in an ocean of ether, the limits of which extend beyond our powers of comprehension. Human life is like children paddling in the shallow water of an ocean that stretches away and loses itself upon an unattainable horizon. Some artists—Corot, for example, in his skies—suggest that what he shows us is a part of this infinity. It is this suggestion of the infinite or universal, which appears in the works of all artists who make a powerful appeal to the imagination, and is a quality that painting may share with poetry and music.

Kokoro: a Japanese term to express the life-movement of the universal spirit, temporarily manifested in *impermanent matter* (472).

Kokoromochi: the expression of *kokoro*, without which a picture is not a work of art.

Legion of Honor: a French military and civil order of merit, instituted in 1802 by Napoleon I. It consists of several ranks: grand officers, grand crosses, commanders, and knights.

Light and shade. See *Chiaroscuro*.

Local color: the prevailing color which belongs to an object, irrespective of the variations produced in it by light and shade, and by the reflections of neighboring colors (191, 406).

Luminarists: a term first used in this country by Professor John C. Van Dyke as a substitute for the name impressionists, to designate Manet and his followers, since their chief motive was the study and rendering of light.

Medium: (1) the particular method of representation employed by the artist; e. g., painting, engraving, etching, etc.; (2) the material or tool so employed: e. g., oil-paints, water-colors, the burin, needle, etc.; (3) the liquid in which the color ingredient is dissolved: e. g., oil, water, or water mixed with a glutinous substance.

Monumental: having qualities suggestive of structural grandeur and permanence, so as to be conspicuously impressive, as a monument is; e.g., *a monumental statue, a monumental composition*.

Mural painting or decoration: a painting on a *wall*; one, however, that is not merely applied to the wall or to some other surface space of a building, but is so planned as to become an integral element of the architectural design (426 et seq.).

Naïve (ni-eve'), French: artless, unaffectedly simple.

Naïveté (ni-eve-tay'), French: the quality of artlessness and of unaffected simplicity, as of the child-mind.

Naturalistic: pertaining to or concerned with the study of nature's appearances.

Nature: from the artist's standpoint, comprises the external appearances of all things.

Neutral: neither black, which is the equivalent of darkness, nor white, the equivalent of light, but the intermediate gray. Thus a neutral tint is one with a strong infusion of gray; e.g., *neutral green* = a grayish green. So red may be *neutralized* into a warm gray, blue into a cool gray, and yellow into drab. Similarly, a neutral *tone* (*q.v.* (1)) is applied to a color the luminosity of which is neither low nor bright, but intermediate like the gray of dawn. In this respect we may speak of a picture as being of warm or of cool neutral tones.

New Learning, the: (1) the knowledge of Greek literature, diffused by the Greek scholars, who became scattered over Europe after Constantinople had been taken by the Turks in 1453; (2) the commencement of the scientific spirit of inquiry, resulting from the teaching of Copernicus (1473-1543) that the sun was a fixed body and that the earth as well as the other planets moved round it.

Objective: of or belonging to the object studied; opposed to *Subjective* — of or belonging to the mind of the subject who studies: e.g., *the objective point of view*, directed toward the study of what the artist perceives in the object, unbiased by any feelings of his own (130, 289). Cf. *Subjective*.

Pagan: Latin *paganus*; literally, a dweller in a pagus (village), a rustic. These were

GLOSSARY OF TERMS

the last to be reached by the spread of Christianity, so that the early Christians of the Roman Empire used pagan as a general term for heathen, or idol-worshipers. In our own time we rather use it, free of any religious significance, to describe that tendency in the Italian Renaissance which resulted from the study of the antique marbles and of Greek literature. Once more, though without any belief in them, the artists and poets revived the ancient myths, and joyed in imagining a young world, in which the forces of nature were visibly embodied; wherein Pan sported with fauns and satyrs, and the countryside was thronged with nymphs: Oreads traversing the mountain slopes, Dryads and Hamadryads threading the groves, and Naiads hovering in the mist of streams and fountains, while Tritons and Nereids frolicked in the ocean (143).

Painter's painter: a studio-term used to signify that such and such a painter, because he cares little for the subject of his picture as compared with the technical problems of painting, and in solving the latter displays unusual skill and facility of brushwork, is likely not to interest the general public and can be properly appreciated only by his fellow-painters (404).

Paintiness, painty: qualities in a picture that obtrude on us a consciousness of paint; so that the painter seems to have been interested in the paint for its own sake, rather than as a means only of representing truth of appearances.

Particular, opposed to *Universal* (q.v.): of or belonging to the individual, the temporary, and the local.

Personal equation: an error common to all the observations made by some one person; especially in noting the exact moment of transit of a star across the thread of his telescope. Hence, in a general sense, the particular, personal impression produced upon the eyes and mind of each individual, as a result of his peculiar qualities of eyesight, and of mind, temperament, and experience.

Perspective: the act or result of representing on a plane surface the third dimension of depth or distance; so that the objects in the picture may be made to appear at varying distances from the eye and to occupy varying planes in the distance. This may be accomplished: (1) by decreasing the size of objects in proportion to their distance from the *fixed point of sight* of the artist, and by making all lines which go back from it converge toward an imaginary *vanishing-point*, determined upon by the artist either inside or outside of the limits of his canvas. Such, in brief, is lineal perspective. Atmospheric perspective, on the other hand, is obtained by the artist noting and rendering accurately the diversities in the amount of light contained, respectively, in all the colors of the objects, and the variations effected in the *local colors* (q.v.) by the intervening planes of *atmosphere* (q.v.) (190, 191).

Pictorial: having qualities that properly and exclusively belong to a picture. It cannot be too often stated that a picture in the true sense of the term is much more than a mere representation of facts and objects. It is a completely independent method of arousing the esthetic sensations. While in poetry the total impression reaches us by degrees, a picture flashes it upon our consciousness at once; while the sculptor is confined to form and to such color as light and shade may suggest, the painter has at his disposal the whole gamut of color: moreover, he can represent his figures in all the charm and added force of their surroundings; can choose his own manner of lighting, and invest his subject with the magic of atmosphere. When he recognizes in line and form and color, tone, light, and atmosphere, a wealth of opportunity that belongs only to his particular art, and relies mainly upon these to impress us, we speak of the pictorial quality of his work.

Pigment, or paint: the coloring ingredient mixed in a medium of oil or water.

Placing: the act of making every object in a picture duly occupy its proper place in the perspective, and of giving it a just amount of distinctness or indistinctness according to its distance from the front.

Pointilliste: a method of laying the paint on the canvas, originated by Seurat and developed by Monet. Instead of the colors being blended on the palette, they are laid on the canvas pure, in minute points, or dots, or stipples, the eye of the spectator being relied upon to blend them (460, 461, 464).

Polder: Dutch word for pasture-lands.

Quality: that which gives a thing distinction or characteristic charm. E.g., *observe the quality in that wave*; it has been painted in such a way as to show that the painter

GLOSSARY OF TERMS

comprehended its structure and movement and has appreciated the subtleties of its color and of the effects of direct, reflected, and refracted light.

Realist: in painting, one whose attitude of mind, being purely objective, leads him to be satisfied to depict objects as they appear to exist, independently of personal bias or of any attempt to idealize.

Rhythm: in a composition, the harmonious repetition of parts which are related mutually to one another as well as to the whole. Thus in Sargent's *Frieze of the Prophets* there is a rhythm of form or rhythmic flow of lines and forms, following one another with that general resemblance and individual difference which characterize the flow of ocean waves.

Romantic: painters or writers; those whose motive is to idealize facts so that they may be a means of expressing and arousing emotions.

Scheme of color, or color-scheme: a systematic arrangement of the colors in a picture with the intention of producing a harmonious completeness of effect. It corresponds to the arrangement of notes in a harmony of sound, and, like it, would be disturbed by the displacement or loss of any of the individual notes.

Selection: a principle of composition and drawing whereby the artist selects from the mass of possible details such as are essential to the expression of his purpose (99 et seq.). See *Arrangement*.

Sentiment: in a work of art, the expression of the feeling which the artist conceives toward his subject.

Simplification: a principle of composition and drawing whereby the artist reduces the representation of his subject to its simplest essential expression: (1) either, as in Millet's drawings, to enforce the essentials of the figure and the gesture and action of it; or (2), as in Puvis's mural paintings, that they may not be too obtrusive and so distract attention from the architecture.

Subjective, opposed to *Objective* (q.v.): of or belonging to the mind of the subject who studies and represents an object; e.g., *the subjective point of view*, which leads the artist to care less about representing the appearance of the object than about making his representation express some mood or feeling of his own (130, 289).

Subtle: literally, fine-woven, like a spider's web; hence involving fine discriminations: e.g., *a subtle rendering of values*, in which the delicate differences in the quantities of light have been very sensitively noted; *a subtle color-scheme*, in which there is an absence of strong contrasts and instead a play upon colors only slightly different in *tone* (q.v.); *a subtle conception*, one distinguished by intricacy of motive and delicate shades of thought.

Suggestion, suggestive: opposed to *Obvious* (1) in method, (2) in motive. Sargent's portraits, for example, represent the obvious appearances of his subjects, but with a manner of brushwork entirely the reverse of obvious, conveying an impression of reality not by detailed imitation but by a summary of masterly suggestions. Leonardo's method, on the other hand, was much more obvious, yet his *Monna Lisa* eludes our clear comprehension, and subtly stimulates the imagination. In the third place, Whistler's *Portrait of the Artist's Mother* is an example of suggestiveness to the imagination as regards both method and motive.

Symphony: literally, a harmonious blending of vocal or instrumental sounds; hence a blending of colors that appeals to the sensuous imagination: e.g., *a symphony in gray, a symphony in silver and blue*.

Synthesis, opposed to *Analysis* (q. v.): literally, the arrangement of different parts into a whole; hence the process by which an artist, having analyzed his subject and discovered its essential characteristics, makes a summary of these in such a way as to suggest the fundamental characteristics. "I have been reproached," said Millet, "for not observing the *detail*; I see it, but I prefer to construct the *synthesis*, which, as an artistic effort, is higher and more robust" (251).

Tactile imagination: "the imagined sensation of touch"; a term originated by Mr. Bernard Berenson. "Psychology," he writes, "has ascertained that sight alone gives us no accurate sense of the third dimension. In our infancy, long before we are conscious of the process, the sense of touch, helped on by muscular sensation of movement, teaches us to appreciate depth, the third dimension, both in objects and in space. . . . The essential in the art of painting is somehow to stimulate

GLOSSARY OF TERMS

our consciousness of *tactile* values, so that the picture shall have at least as much power as the object represented to appeal to our *tactile imagination*."

Technic, or technique: the principles and practice of artistic craftsmanship.

Temperament: the individual temper, mental constitution, and disposition of a person; hence, in a general way, a person's particular bias of feeling or peculiar make-up of nervous sensibility. When an artist, as most modern ones of poetic or imaginative tendency do, betrays this peculiar bias of feeling in his work, he is spoken of as *a temperamental artist*, and his work, as being largely *influenced by temperament*.

Texture: the surface of an object, represented in such a way that the substance of which it is composed is made to appear real to the eye, and that through our *tactile imagination* (q.v.) we may have an imagined sensation of the pleasure of its feel to the touch.

Tone: (1) the degree of luminosity in color; e.g., *a low-toned picture*, in which there is a prevailing absence of luminosity; (2) the intensity or depth of a tint: e.g., *a deep tone of red, a delicate tone of gray*; (3) the existence in a picture of a prevailing color: e.g., *a tonal arrangement*, signifying that, although many colors are introduced, we are made to feel that they are subsidiary to one prevailing color.

Type: literally, one of a group of objects that embodies the characteristics of the whole group to which it belongs. Hence we speak of *The Sower* by Millet as having the significance of a type or as being typical in character, because it summarizes the actions and gestures which more or less characterize the operations of all sowers, who sprinkle the seed as they stride over the soil.

Universal, opposed to *Particular* (q.v.): the quality in a picture which makes us look beyond the personal, local, or temporary significance to a significance limited only by the extent of our experience and imagination.

Value: the quantity of light contained in the color of an object and of parts of the same. Thus a gown, the *local color* (q.v.) of which is pink, will show diversified *tones* (q.v.) of pink, according to the amount of light on the exposed parts and the amount of less light in the channels of the folds; and by representing these values accurately the painter without the use of shadow will obtain an effect of modeling. Cf. Manet's *Girl with a Parrot*, 412, 417. Again, a field, the local color of which is green, will show grayer and grayer green as it recedes from the eye, owing to the neutralizing (see *Neutral*) effect of the successive planes of intervening atmosphere. By rendering accurately the values of these greens a painter may suggest distance and *atmospheric perspective* (q.v.).

INDEX

INDEX

A

Abbey, Edwin A., mural decorations of, in Boston Public Library, 426, 427; his work compared with Puvis de Chavannes's, 433; an illustrator on a grand scale, 434

Abstract-concrete, qualities of painting, 66, 452. See *Glossary*

Academic (or classic) in French painting, the, Poussin the father of, 239; suited to genius of French, inherited from the Romans, 240; characteristics and effects of, 241; in figure and landscape seeks as near as possible to perfection, 253; Delacroix's criticism of, 315; precise about form, neglects color, 316; a translation of sculpture into painting, 317; benefit of, as a standard, 321. See *Glossary*

Academy in Rome, French, founding of, 240

Academy of Painting and Sculpture, French, origin of, 240; principles and advantage of, 241

Accessories in a picture, significance of, exhibited in Van Eyck's *Virgin and Donor*, 119; in Holbein's portrait of Georg Gyze, 126, 131

Adam [Michelangelo], 155

Adoration of the Lamb [the Van Eycks], 45

Adoration of the Magi [Botticelli], 55

Adoration of the Magi [Dürer], 109 et seq.

Adoration of the Shepherds [Correggio], marvel of light and shade, 157

"Afflatus," 146

Allegorical subjects, 61, 62

Allegory of Spring [Botticelli], 61

Amsterdam, Rembrandt studies in, 224; settles in, 225; Ruisdael moves from Haarlem to, 229; claims to be Hobbema's birthplace, 242; Hobbema dies in, 250; Israels settled in, 420

Anatomy Lesson, The [Rembrandt], 212

Angelico, Fra (frah ahn-jay'lee-ko), 37 et seq.; *The Annunciation* compared with Van Eyck's *Virgin and Donor*, 37; most remarkable example of a religious painter, 38; the minute finish and yet breadth and simplicity of his style, 38; his early life, 46; admitted to the Dominican monastery, 46; example of two personalities—painter and devout monk, 47; influenced by the illuminators and by Ghiberti, Donatello, Brunelleschi, 47; at San Marco while Michelozzo enlarged it, 48; the arcaded loggia appears in *The Annunciation*, 48; this example of his maturity examined, as to composition and subject, 49; as to color, 50; the impression received of his work in San Marco, 50; complete union of the artist and the devotee, 51; his influence on Rossetti, 372, 385

Angelus, The [Millet], title of, criticized, 351, note

Annunciation [Fra Angelico], 37 et seq.

Antonello da Messina (an-tone-ayl'lo dah mays-see'nah) discovers the Van Eycks' secret of oil-painting, 45

Antwerp, 195

Apollo Belvedere, 320

Architectonic quality in composition, explanation of, 102; characterizes academic style, 241; important in mural decoration, 435. See *Glossary*

Architecture, influence of, on painting, 47, 48, 53; value of, when introduced into a picture, 81 et seq.; Northern and Southern kinds compared, 94

Arena (ah-ray'nah) chapel, Padua, 18

Art, primary meaning of the word, 5

"Art for art's sake," it is said, should be the painter's aim, 171; its value as a principle considered, 409 et seq. See *Glossary*

Art is not nature, 99

Art of portraiture, Dutch art an, 197

Artist, composition of an, 4, 5

Assisi (ahs-see'see), Upper and Lower Churches of, 18

Atmosphere in a picture, (?) arbitrary and conventional kind of, 123; Correggio's use of, 144; suited to the dreamy luxuriance of his imagination, 148; (?) atmosphere of nature, rendered by Masaccio, 29; by Leonardo. 122, 123; atmosphere with color and light and texture the qualities of Venetian painting, 161; Velasquez suggests perspective by rendering it, 191, 192; varying luminosity of, studied by Constable, 301; suggested in Whistler's etchings, 454. See *Glossary*

Augsburg, free imperial city, 93; birthplace of Holbein, 137

Avenue, Middelharnis, The [Hobbema], 242 et seq.; compared with *The Valley Farm*, 289

B

Baglioni (bal-ye-owe'ni) family at Perugia (pay-ruzh'yah), 81

Balance and unity in composition obtained by selection and arrangement, 99; organic unity in nature, 100; equilibrium of full and empty spaces, 100;

INDEX

repetition and contrast of lines and masses, 100, 101; everything focused to a point, 101; geometric design, 102; architechtonic or structural unity, 102; beauty primarily dependent on balance and unity, 102

Barberini (bar-bay-ree'nee) family, *bon mot* about, 251

Bar'bizon, 249, 322 et seq.

Barcelona, birthplace and patron of Fortuny, 402

Bardi (bah'dee) Chapel, S. Croce (san'tah crow'chay), Florence, 18

Bargello (bah-jel'loh) Chapel, Florence, 18

Bartolommeo Colleoni (bah-tol-ome-may'oh col-lay-oh'nee) statue, 71, 84

Bartolommeo, (bah-tol-ome-may'oh) Fra, 50, 104

Basel, Holbein, Erasmus, and Froben at, 138; in clutch of the Reformers, 139; birthplace of Boecklin, 367

Bashful Suitor, The [Israels], 422

Bath, Gainsborough settles in, 284; Beau Nash leads the fashion in, 284

Beautiful Gate of the Temple [Raphael], 164

Beauty, what is it? as expressed by the Greeks, Correggio, Michelangelo, 155; views of Winckelmann, Lessing, Keats, Delacroix, 319; may exist in character of subject and individuality of artist, 320; in truth, 340

Beauty in a picture, what produces, 6

Belle Jardinière, La (lah bel jah-dee'nee-air) [Raphael], 104

Bellini, Gentile (jayn-tee'lay bayl-lee'nee), 31, 71, 132

Bellini, Giovanni (jo-vahn'nee), 68 et seq.; his debt to Mantegna, Verrocchio, and Squarcione, 71; the sculptural calm of his figures, 72; Dürer's judgment of him, 72; his work compared with Titian's and that of Phidias, 77; in it Byzantinism reached its highest truth to local facts, 77; the influence of Greek culture is seen in it at its highest point, 78; his introduction of architectural forms, 81-84; Titian worked with him, 132

Bellini, Jacopo (yah-ko'poh), 31, 71

Bentivogli (bayn-tee-vohl'ye) family at Bologna (bo-lone'yah), 31

Bentivoglio (bayn-tee-vohl'yoh), Cardinal, patron of Claude, 251

Berenson, Bernard, quoted: Florentines masters of several crafts, 18; space-composition, 80; on "tactile" sense, 120

Blashfield, Edwin H., quoted *re* Veronese, 164

Blessed Damozel, The [Rossetti], 376 et seq.

Blue Boy, The [Gainsborough], a challenge to Reynolds (?), 274

Boccaccio (bok-kahch'yo), his stories the evangel of the modern world, 54; portrait in Raphael's *Parnassus*, 106

Boecklin, Arnold, 353 et seq.; his *Isle of the Dead* a composition in which the horizontal is subordinated to the vertical, a work of imagination, 353; compare the boat with Charon's in Delacroix's *Dante and Virgil*, 366; a sense of infinite seclusion, yet the isle has been modified by man, 366, 367; he introduces a harmonious blending of figures and landscape like Poussin, Claude, and Corot, and has a Greek faculty of interpreting landscape by creatures of like nature, 368; but invents new forms, 369; greatest color-poet of the century, 369; born at Basel, enters Düsseldorf, but advised to go to Brussels; thence to Paris and Rome; the latter the great influence upon his career, 367

Bologna (bo-lone'yah), 31

Boston Public Library, decorations in, 426 et seq., 449, 450

Bottegha (bot-tay'gah), the studio-workshop of early Italian artists, 12, 96

Botticelli, Alessandro (ah-lays-sahn'dro bot-ti-chel'lee), 52 et seq.; inspired by the new study of Greek, 52, 53; pupil of the goldsmith Botticelli, 55; at the court of the Medici, 55; pupil of Fra Lippo, a realist, but himself a poet and dreamer, 56; fond of allegorical subjects, 61, 62; his *Venus* and *Madonnas*, 62; his compositions, decorative patterns, 64, 65; poor anatomist, but a great draftsman, 65; abstract beauty of his line, 66; his yearning fulfilled in Giovanni Bellini and Raphael, 67

Boucher, François (frahn'swah bou'shay), successor to Watteau, 304; voluptuous insipidities of, 313

Boudin (bou-dan), Eugene Louis, influence on Monet, 458

Bouguereau (bou-gair-roh), W. Adolphe, affected by Courbet, 358

Boy with a Sword [Manet] nearest of his works to Velasquez, 411

Brabant, Flemish school of, 66

Bramante (brah-mahn'tay), design of, for St. Peter's, 156

Brancacci (bran-karch chee), Chapel of the, Church of the Carmine (kah'mee-nay), Florence, 29

Breadth and simplicity, illustrated in Giotto, 17; in Hals, 205, 206; result of mental power, 207. See *Glossary*

Breton, Jules (zhool bray'ton), 339 et seq.; his *Gleaner* examined, 339, 340; she is type of woman of Roman Campagna, 340; uses peasant as a peg to hang his own poetry upon, 342; represents his subject without sympathy or understanding, 352

Brinton, Selwyn, quoted *re* princely houses of Italy, 32

" Brown sauce " of Courbet, 405, 407

" Brown tree " in a picture, 290

Bruges, Flemish school of, 37-67

Brunelleschi (broo-nayl-lays'key), 47

Burger-Thoré, quoted *re* early life of Rousseau, 325

Burial of Wilkie at Sea, The [Turner], 299

Burne-Jones, Sir Edward, intimate with Rossetti, 389; a "painter of the soul," 390

Burney, Fanny, her first impressions of Mrs. Siddons, 273

Byron, Lord, influence on Delacroix, 307; one of the leaders of romanticism, 318

[496]

INDEX

Byzantine influence: Byzantium gateway of East and West, 9; meeting-place of Oriental and Greek art, 10; Byzantine art of illuminators and decorators, character of, as encouraged by the church, 10; reaches its highest point as expression of religion in Perugino, 70, 71; as expression of truth to facts in Giovanni Bellini, 77; St. Mark's a triumph of Byzantine art, 160, 161; Sargent influenced by Byzantine art, 433, 449

C

Campanile (kam-pah-neel'ay), Florence, 81
Caravaggio (kah-rah-vuj'jyo), 232
Carlo Dolci (kah'lo dohl'chee), 232
Carolus-Duran, Charles Auguste, teacher of Sargent, 442
Carpaccio (kar-parch'chyo'), 163
"Cavalier Painter, the," Van Dyck, 207
Cellini, Benvenuto (bane-vay-noo'to chellee'nee), 322
Cesena (chay-zay'nah), 31
Charles I of England bought Mantegna's *Triumph*, 35
Chelsea, Holbein welcomed in, 139; Rossetti lived there, 389; scene of much of Whistler's sojourn and work, 453
Chiaroscuro (kee-ah"rohs-koo'roh) (see *Light and shade*), Giotto's elementary use of, for modeling, 17; Leonardo, by subtlety of, secures poetic and emotional effect, 122; one of the prevailing qualities of Venetian painting, 161; Tintoretto's use of, 175; emotional expression of, in Rubens's *Descent from the Cross*, 182, 183, 190; Velasquez substitutes for, study of values, 190, 191; unifying effect of, in Rembrandt's *Sortie of Banning Cock Company*, 213; Rembrandt's use of, 214, 215, 216; Fortuny's treatment of, compared with Piloty's, 392; Manet revives Velasquez's study of values, 407; appearance of light and shade in open-air light, 459. See *Glossary*
Children of the Shell [Murillo], 209 et seq.
Christ Walking on the Water [Raphael], Ruskin's criticism of, 372, 373
Chrysoloras, Manuel, Greek scholar, 55
Church, influence of the, on painting: insists on types to express dogmas, 10; Masaccio and Mantegna break away from the flat formalism encouraged by the church, 21; conventional ideas still determine character of compositions, 56; Murillo, a painter for the church, 210
Cimabue (chee-mah-boo'ny), 8 et seq.; *Madonna Enthroned*, reason of similarity to Giotto's, 9; his picture carried in procession, 11; adopts Giotto as pupil, 12; his treatment of form and drapery, 12, 17
Classicists versus Romanticists, 318, 319, 320; versus Rousseau and Millet, 326, 349; versus realists, 355-358; versus impressionists, 408, 409
Classic in French Painting. See *Academic*
Classic or heroic landscape, Poussin the father of, 238; suggested by Italian landscape, 238; principles of, 241; illustrated in Claude's *Landing of Cleopatra*, 242, 243; Claude advances it beyond Poussin, 252; the cause of its popularity, 253; Constable's revolt from it, 288 et seq.; Turner's rivalry of Claude, 291, 292; Corot's early preference for, 327, 328
Claude Gellée, called Lorrain, 242 et seq.; his classic compared with Hobbema's natural treatment, 242-249; his early life and journey to Rome, 250; first cook, then assistant to the painter Agostino Tassi, 250; revisits France for two years, 251; returns to Rome in company of Charles Errard, 251; attracts notice of Cardinal Bentivoglio and wins European fame, 251; left forty-four etchings, also two hundred sketches now owned by the Duke of Westminster, and called "Liber Veritatis," 251, 252; his conception of the ideal or heroic landscape, 252; his study of sunshine, 252; helped to found the academic or classic in French art, 253; his work suited the taste of the time and remained popular all through the eighteenth century, 253
Clothes, influence of, on painting, 118
Color and music compared: Delacroix felt in color as a musician does in sounds, 307; Boecklin and Wagner likened, 369; Manet's modulation of a chord of gray, 412; Whistler's effort to reach the abstract appeal of music, 451, 452
Colored forms, nature seen as an arrangement of, 316
Colorists and color: Van Eyck's brilliant, rich color, 40, 45; Memling's rich and life-like, 64; Bellini anticipates the other great Venetian colorists, Giorgione, Titian, and Veronese, 84; Rubens's splendor of color, 184; local color, 191, 406; color weak point of Poussin and classic school, 241; Watteau studies the coloring of Rubens and the Venetians, 258; splendor of Turner's color-schemes, 299; Delacroix felt in color, and made it a means of emotional appeal, 307, 317; academic school disregard color, 316; Charles Blanc's extraordinary statement, 319; Boecklin greatest color-poet of the century, 369; Manet's delicate color-schemes, 412, 417, 418; Whistler's color-harmonies, 452, 454, 456; Professor Rood's experiments in light and color studied by Seurat, Pissarro, and Monet, 458; effect of strong sunshine on colors, 459; decomposition of colors and optical mingling instead of mingling of pigments, 460; Monet's range of color wider than Corot's, advantages of the *pointilliste* method of laying on color, 463; vibrating color, 464; primary and secondary colors, and heightened effect by combination, 469; colored pigments inferior in luminosity to colored light, 469; raising the key of color, 470; flat coloring and subtle harmonies of the Japanese, 475, 477. See *Glossary*
Comedies, French and Italian, 258
Communes, or Republics, of Italy, 31
Composition: Van Eyck's combines large

INDEX

spotting and minute elaboration, 39; the balancing of full and empty spaces, 79; effect of suggesting the third dimension, "space-composition," Perugino's mastery of it, 80; strengthening of composition by introducing architectural forms, 81; monumental quality of Bellini's, 81; character of the latter's figures in keeping with the architectural settings, 83; Raphael's mastery of composition, 98; nature seen through a window will lack composition, 99; composition analyzed, 98–102; selection and arrangement, 99; balance and unity, 99; natural or conventional arrangement, 99; full and empty spaces, 100; the equilibrium of them in Raphael's *Madonna degli Ansidei* yields suggestion of wonderful composure, 100; vertical, horizontal, and curved lines contrasted and repeated, 100, 101; a focus point of whole, 101; basis of design geometric, 101, 102; architectonics of composition, and affect of on the imagination, 102; in *Madonna degli Ansidei* the expression of faces is only a refinement of the qualities already expressed in the composition, 103; this picture contrasted with Wolgemuth's *Death of the Virgin*, 103; German preference for detail over structural dignity, 103; Raphael's, built up to affect the imagination, 104; noble spotting of light and dark in Titian's *Man with the Glove*, 132; composition of line and of light and shade in Rubens's *Descent from the Cross*, 181, 182, 183; Poussin's composition of figures and landscape in *Et Ego in Arcadia*, 237; seductive charm of the same in Claude's *Landing of Cleopatra*, 242; Hobbema's harsher arrangement, 243; exquisite pattern of forms and sky space in Watteau's *Emburkation*, 257; composition of Boecklin's *Isle of the Dead* and Courbet's *Funeral at Ornans* compared, 353 et seq.; study of arrangement of masses in Whistler's *Portrait of the Artist's Mother*, 454; Japanese arrangement of line and tone, 474, 475; illustrated in Hashimoto Gaho's *Sunrise on the Horai*, 476, 477. See *Glossary*

Composition of light and less light, 193
Composition of light and shade, 182
Conception of subject, 6
Concrete-abstract, how far painting expresses, 452. See *Glossary*
Constable, John, Hobbema set the path for, 255; Gainsborough born near his birthplace, East Bergholt, Sussex, 283; 287 et seq.; a miller's son brought up near *The Valley Farm*, or *Willy Lott's House*, 287; studied at Royal Academy schools and from works of Hobbema and Ruisdael, love of nature led him back to the river Stow, 288; *The Valley Farm* compared with Claude's *Landing of Cleopatra* and Hobbema's *Avenue*, 288, 289; "Painting is with me another name for feeling" 288, 289; "Where are you going to place your brown tree?" 290; his fidelity to nature and interpretation of his own mood make him the father of modern landscape, 290; his simple life in Sussex and at Hampstead, 300, 301; studied the varying luminosity of the atmosphere, 301; his landscapes exhibited in Salon, 1822–1827, attracted Delacroix and influenced Rousseau, 323

Constantinople taken by the Turks, 162
Contrast and repetition in composition, 100 et seq.
Conventionalization of Western and Oriental artists compared, 473 et seq. See *Glossary*
"Conversation Pieces," Hogarth's, 270
Coronation of Napoleon I at Notre Dame [David], 315
Corot, Jean Baptiste Camille (zhahn bahteest' cah-mee'yel coh'roh), one of the painters of the *paysage intime*, 249; 322 et seq.; the lyric poet of the Fontainebleau-Barbizon School, 323; suggestion of music and songfulness in his *Dance of the Nymphs*, 323, 324; his escape from form to render the effect of form upon the senses, 324; his parents, 324; father makes him allowance, 327; his first visit to Italy, 328; masters the skill in drawing moving objects and learns to generalize, 328; after third visit to Italy comes under influence of Rousseau, 328; describes the sensations produced upon him by early morning and evening, 328, 333, 334; his final style, 334; his attitude toward nature compared with Rousseau's 335, 336, 337; the figures in his landscapes compared with Boecklin's, 368; his rendering of skies, 463; his attitude toward nature compared with Monet's, 470; his expression of nature's spirit compared with the Japanese idea of "kokoro," 472
"Corporation picture," 211
Correggio (cor-rage'jyo, Antonio Allegri (ahl-lay'gree), 142 et seq.; represents the pagan element of the Renaissance, 142, 143; his *Marriage of St. Catherine*, without religious fervor, a poet's golden dream, 143, 144, 145; his use of glazes, 148; his *Marriage* compared with Michelangelo's *Jeremiah*, 153; his type, physical loveliness joined to loveliness of sentiment, 155; sketch of his life, 157; his trouble over the "fry of frogs" and his wife's death, 157; his triumph of light and shade in the *Adoration of the Shepherds*, 157; retires from Parma to Correggio, 157, 158; his influence upon Reynolds, 276
Côtés de Grandville, Rousseau's first masterpiece, 326
Courbet, Gustave (goo'stahve coo'ur-bay), 353 et seq.; his *Funeral at Ornans* compared with Boecklin's *Isle of the Dead*, 353, 354; realist and revolutionary, 355; avoids the studios and studies in the Louvre, 355, 356; his first work, *The Stone-Breakers*, 356; *Funeral at Ornans* criticized, 356; advocates "la vérité vraie," 358; his broad, firm manner of painting, 359; the *Funeral* seriously judged, 360, 365; his share in the Revolution of 1848, 369; in the Commune, his banishment and death, 370; his truth to nature com-

[498]

INDEX

pared with Ruskin's teaching, 374, 375; his "brown sauce," 405; his teaching of realism carried further by Manet, 406, 407
Cranach, Lucas, 141
Crane, Walter, influence of, on decorative art, 389, 390
"Cry of the soil" (*Le cri de la terre*) heard by Millet, 343
Curved lines contrasted with vertical and horizontal, 100 et seq.
Cuyp (kipe), Aelbert, 252

D

Dance of Death [Holbein], 138
Dance of the Nymphs [Corot], 323 et seq.
Dante (daan'tay), Giotto's portrait of, 18; swan-song of the Middle Ages, 54; his portrait in Raphael's *Parnassus*, 106; Taine's estimate of, 146; Rossetti a student of, 384; the ideals of his spirit realized through Beatrice and the service of love, 388, 389
Dante and Virgil [Delacroix], 304 et seq.; compared with Boecklin's *Isle of the Dead*, 366
Daubigny, Charles François (sharl frahn'-swah dow-been'ye , 322
David, Jacques Louis (zhack loo'ee dah'-veed), 304 et seq.; his art a protest against that of Watteau's successors, 304; his *Oath of the Horatii* cold, calculated, and self-conscious, 304; its subject considered, 304; a suspicion of staginess, 305; David a part of the Revolution, 308; his *Horatii*, founded upon Roman models, incites to Roman Republicanism, 308, 313; David, appointed Minister of Fine Arts, imposed his Roman taste on public and private life; it suited the spirit of the time, 313; the naturalism of his portraits of Marat and Napoleon, 314; and of his *Coronation*, 315; his banishment to and death in Brussels, 315; his legacy of classicism, 315; his *Horatii* compared with Delacroix's *Dante and Virgil*, 316, 317
Death of the Virgin [Wolgemuth], 103, 104
Decline of Italian art, 177, 232
Decomposition of colors into their constituent elements, 460 et seq.
Definition melting into indefiniteness, 192, 477
Degas (day'gas), Edgard, 475
Delacroix, Ferdinand Victor Eugène (ewe'-zhane day-lah-crwah'), 304 et seq.; his art a protest against David's, his *Dante and Virgil* examined, its subject, 306; its color-scheme, 307; product of the Romantic movement, 307, 308; he represents the fervor of individualism, 308; ridicules the Academy's search for ideal beauty, 315; his *Dante and Virgil* compared with David's *Horatii*, 316, 317; a great colorist, 317; influenced by the Romantic writers, 318; Blanc's "criticism" of him, 319; his assertion that beauty is not the only end of art, 319; the Academy's opposition to him, 320

Delaroche (day-lah-roh'she), Hippolyte, teacher of Millet, 343; of Israels, 419
Descent from the Cross [Campana], 224
Descent from the Cross [Rubens], 175, 178 et seq.
Despots, Italian, brilliant and terrible life of, 32
Detail, Flemish skill in, illustrated by Van Eyck, 39, 40; by Memling, 64; German taste for, 103; Dürer's skill in rendering detail and in giving it significance, 119, 120; Holbein's elaboration of, to suggest character of his subject, 131; Meissonier's untruthful truth of, 189; Van Dyck's rhetorical treatment of, 205, 206; Hogarth's anecdotal, 260, 261; Corot escapes from, 324; freely generalizes, 334; Rousseau for a period too exact in representing, 335; Western and Japanese generalization and conventionalization of, compared, 473 et seq.
Diaz (dee'ahz) de la Peña, Narciso Virgilio, 322, 326, 344
Dido building Carthage, Turner emulates Claude in, 291
Dimensions, the three, 17
Disputà (dees-poo-tah') [Raphael], its design based upon one of Perugino's, 105
Distance, effect of, upon the imagination, 80
Distemper, the medium of, 8. See *Glossary*
Distinction, quality of, 282
Dobson, Austin, quoted on *Marriage à la Mode*, 265
Doge Leonardo Loredano (doje lay-o-nah'-do lo-ray-dah'no), portrait of [Giovanni Bellini], 77
Doge's Palace, Venice, embodiment of the temporal life of Venice, 160; its decorations, 163
Domenichino (do-may-nee-kee'no), Poussin studies with, 232
Dominici, Giovanni (jo-vahn'nee do-mee-nee'chee), founder of the order of Dominicans, 46
Donatello (doh-nah tayl'loh), influence on Masaccio, 24; on Fra Angelico, 47
Dosso-Dossi (dos'so dos'see), 32
Dramatic and scenic contrasted, 170, 174
Drapery, treatment of: Giotto's rudimentary but functional use of, 17, 17; superior character and fluency of Masaccio's, 23; Mantegna's liny and stiff, 24; origin and explanation of this treatment, 33, 34; sculptural and monumental character of Giovanni Bellini's, 84; Reynolds's treatment in the *Mrs. Siddons*, 281
Drawing, the child's way of, 64
Ducal Palace, Venice. See *Doge's Palace*
Dupré, Jules (zhool doo-pray'), 249, 322, 326
Dürer (doorer-rer'), Albrecht, his opinion of Giovanni Bellini, 72; Wolgemuth his master, 85; 109 et seq.; most representative of the German race, 109; his skill of draftsmanship, qualities of his work, 110; Dürer's genius characterized by the genius of the Germans, 111; his admiration of Luther and work in engravings for the publisher Koburger, 117, 118; did

INDEX

not possess the gift of ideal beauty, due to influence of German Renaissance being moral and intellectual rather than artistic, 118; his skill in suggesting textures and the significance of appearances, 119, 120; difference between his work and Leonardo's summarized, 124; his art must be joined with Holbein's to represent completely the genius of the German race, 141
Dutch art an art of portraiture, 197
Dutch School, 195-254, 404-422
Dutch war of independence, 195 et seq.

E

East Bergholt, birthplace of Constable, 283, 287
Eastern and Western ideals, difference between, 9, 471, 476
Ecce Ancilla Domini [Rossetti], 371
École des Beaux Arts (ay'cole day bohs ahr), 241
"Eighth Discourse," Reynolds's, on warm and cold colors, 274
Elemental and permanent compared with incidental and momentary, 425
Elemental quality in painting, the: elemental geometric figures, 102; the elemental quality the secret of the elevation of Michelangelo, 155; Rousseau's suggestion of it, 336, 337; Millet's, 352; Puvis de Chavannes's, 425; Whistler's search for it, 451, 452; Japanese idea of "kokoro," 472, 473. See *Glossary*
Elusiveness in painting, Leonardo's love of, 121, 124; Velasquez's appearing and disappearing lines, 192; Whistler's preference for, 456; Japanese skill in, 477. See *Glossary*
Embarkation for Cythera [Watteau], 256, 257, 258, 259
English School, Early, 255-303
English Pre-Raphaelite School, 371-390
Engraving and painting compared, 117
Engraving on copper, 110, 260. See *Glossary*
Engraving on wood, 110. See *Glossary*
Entombment, The [Giotto], 22
Entombment of Christ [Mantegna], 35
Erasmus, friend of Holbein, 130; driven from Basel by the Reformation, 139
Errard, Charles, one of the founders of the French Academy in Rome, 251
Esprit (ays'pree) in brushwork, 444
Etching, process of, 221. See *Glossary*
Etchings, Whistler's, constructive reality and detail of Thames series; economy of line in Venetian series, 453; characteristic of the artist's love of suggestiveness, 453, 454; betray the Japanese influence, 475
Et Ego in Arcadia [Poussin], 228, 238
Everdingen, Allart van, 229
Exaggeration of Michelangelo, 156; of Tintoretto, 175
Experience and feeling, influence of, on the artist, 4 et seq.
Externals, joy of the painter in, 21, 22

F

False realism, 189
Family of Darius, The [Veronese], 169
Father of modern landscape, the, Constable, 287
Feeling and experience, influence of, on the artist, 4 et seq.
Ferrara (fer-rah'rah), 31, 32
"Fiat Lux" (fee at loox), "Let there be Light," 407
Fighting Téméraire, The [Turner], 299
Figure, rigidity of the academic, 316
Figures, placing of: heads above heads in Byzantine painting, 8; Giotto begins to suggest a third dimension, 17; Masaccio to place his figures in air, 29; figures treated as a pattern of forms by Botticelli, 64; figures stretched across in one or two planes, as in low-relief sculpture, by Mantegna, 34; by Wolgemuth, 95; by Poussin, 232; by David, 308; seen as through a veil, as in the case of Leonardo, 121; placed in melting atmosphere by Correggio, 148; enveloped in light by Velasquez, 190; an arrangement of colored forms in harmonious relation, 316; distributed by Puvis in separate planes, to avoid contrasts of light and shade, 437
Filippino (fee-leep-pee'no) Lippi, 29
First of the moderns, the, Velasquez, 194
Flat painting, Byzantine, 17, 20; Hals's, flat tones, 205; Puvis's, 433, 437. See *Glossary*
Flemish art, one of choice perfection of detail, 38
Flemish School, 37 et seq., 52 et seq., 177 et seq., 195 et seq.
Florentine artists masters of several crafts, 18
Fontainebleau, 322
Fontainebleau-Barbizon School, 322-352
Form, idealization of: Botticelli's abstract beauty of line, 65, 66; Perugino's forms expressive of "soul-solitude," 69, 70; Giovanni Bellini's grand type of physical and mental perfection, 72; Leonardo's forms expressive of the mystery of inward beauty, 121, 122, 123; Michelangelo's, of mental emotions, 154; Murillo's, of religious sentiment, 210; Rembrandt's expressive of the soul, 216; Poussin's poetic treatment, 239; Watteau's idealism, 257; academic idealization, 253, 315, 316; Boecklin's idealization founded upon facts, 366, 367; Rossetti's, upon devotion to one woman, 387-389; Puvis de Chavannes's, upon simplification, 437
Form, the rendering of: Giotto's advance in, 12, 17, 18; Masaccio's further advance in, 22, 23; the impulse given to, by sculptors, 24, 29; Flemish love of, 39, 64; influence of architecture on, 48, 81-84, 434-437; Dürer's mastery in, 119, 120; Velasquez's skill in, by means of values, 191; flat modeling of, in clear light by Hals, 205; Millet aimed at a synthesis of form, 351; force of character in Courbet's rendering of form, 365; Whistler

[500]

INDEX

shunned the obviousness of form, 451 et seq.; Japanese belief in the impermanence of matter and temporariness of form, 471

Form the first thing to observe, Rousseau's advice, 334

Fortuny, Mariano, 391 et seq.; his *Spanish Marriage* compared with Piloty's *Thusnelda*, 391; its composition, 392; the life and character of the figures, 397; his birth and training in Barcelona, 402; won the Prix de Rome, then visited Morocco and became fascinated by the light, color, and movement of the South, 402; his Rococo subjects characteristic, 403; skill in painting, and vogue in Paris, 403; set the fashion for *bric-à-brac* pictures, 403

Fragonard, Jean Honoré, 304

Francis I, 322

Frari, Church of the, Titian buried in, 137

French, the, inheritors of Roman tradition, 239, 240

French schools, 228–271, 304–370; 404–440

Fresco, 18, 147. See *Glossary*

Froben, printer and publisher, 138, 139

Fromentin (fro'mon-tan), French painter and critic, quoted on Flemish art, 46; on the Dutch School, 197; on Rembrandt, 214

"Fry of frogs," 157

Fugitive gesture or movement, 458, 461

Full and empty spaces: balance of, in composition, and its effect upon the imagination, 79; explanation of, 100 (see *Glossary*); Puvis's treatment of, 424; special value of empty spaces in Whistler's Venetian etchings, 453; Whistler's, in the portrait of his mother, 454, 455; and in Gaho's *Sunrise on the Horai*, 477

Fundamental side of men and things, the, Millet tried to depict, 350

Funeral at Ornans [Courbet], 353 et seq.

G

Gainsborough, Thomas, 272 et seq.; his *Portrait of Mrs. Siddons* compared with Reynolds's, 273; refutes Reynolds's doctrine concerning cold and warm colors, 274; not dramatic, but simple and of delicate refinement, 282; his "distinction" as an artist, love of music and simple things, 282, 283; sketch of his career, 283, 284; eulogy on him pronounced by Reynolds, 285; his art spontaneous and poetic, 285

Gallic genius compared with German and Anglo-Saxon, 266

Ganne's Inn, Barbizon, 344

Generalization, to a certain extent inevitable, 4; Corot learns the value of, 328; Western and Oriental methods compared, 473, 474. See *Glossary*

Genius shaped by environment, 111 et seq.

Genre, Dutch, compared with Hogarth's, 270. See *Glossary*

Geometric forms in composition, 102

George, Saint [Donatello], influence on painting of, 24, 47

Georg Gyze, Portrait of [Holbein the Younger], 125 et seq., 184

Germ, The, 390

German and Italian Renaissance compared: the Italian primarily an artistic movement, the German an intellectual one, 112; German movement closely identified with the arts of printing and engraving, 117; owing to climate, Italians study human form, Germans render the character of clothes, 118

German art, character of: profusion of detail, 103; stern, tender, enigmatic, as in Dürer, 111; decorative feeling, eager curiosity, elaboration, as in Holbein, 141; abounding in sentiment and dramatic characterization, in Piloty and genre works, 401

German history, summary of, 86–94

German School, 85–141, 353–370, 391–403

Gérôme, Jean Léon (zhahn lay'on zhayrome'), Rousseau slighted in favor of, 327; Courbet's influence on, 358; 423 et seq.; his *Pollice Verso* compared with Puvis's *Inter Artes et Naturam*, 423, 424, 425; unlikely to have painted true decoration, 426; great popularity, and causes of it, 440

Ghiberti's (ghee-bare'tee) doors, influence on painting of, 24, 47

Gilles (zhee-yeel') [Watteau], 258, 259

Giorgione (jor-jo'nay), 84, 137

Giotteschi (jot-tays'key), followers of Giotto, 18

Giotto (jot'toh), 8 et seq.; pupil of Cimabue, 11; his advance toward natural truth, 12; suggests the third dimension and uses light and shade in a functional way, 17; sculptor and architect as well as painter, 18

Girl and Pigs [Gainsborough], 282

Girl with a Parrot [Manet], 404 et seq., 461

Giulio Romano (jool'yoh roh-mah'noh), 232

Gleaner, The [Jules Breton], 339 et seq.

Gleaners, The [Millet], 339 et seq.

Glory of Venice [Veronese], 164 et seq.

Golden age, a, 143 et seq.

Golden Calf, The [Tintoretto], 173

Goldsmith, Oliver, friend of Reynolds, 285

Gonzaga (gon-zah'gah) *Welcoming his Sons* [Mantegna], 22 et seq.

Gothic feeling, characteristics of, 66, 67; expressed its desire of beauty first in architecture, 94; descended from the religion, savage and cruel, of Asgard, 95

Gothic revival in England, product of the Oxford Movement, 381; Holman Hunt's *Light of the World* imbued with the spirit of, 381, 382; effect of, on modern revival of decoration, 390

Greek art and Greek religion connected, 9

Greek culture and study, recovery of, by the Western world, 54, 55; Botticelli inspired by, 52, 62; influence of, seen in highest form in Giovanni Bellini, 77, 78; united to Christianity by Raphael, 88; he retells the Greek myths and interprets Bible story in Hellenic guise, 106; important consequences of this, 107; Ruskin's criticism of it, 373

[501]

INDEX

Greek sculpture, Giovanni Bellini's work compared to it, 72, 77; Michelangelo's contrasted with, 154
Greuze, Jean Baptiste (zhahn bah-teest' grooerz), 267
Gruchy (groo'shee), Millet's birthplace, 342
Guido Reni (ghee'do ray'nee), 232

H

Haarlem, scene of Hals's life, 198 and note; and death, 207; birthplace and early home and finally deathplace of Ruisdael, 229, 230; one of the towns claiming to be the birthplace of Hobbema, 242
Hals, Frans, 195 et seq.; first of the great Dutchmen, 198; his meeting with Van Dyck, as told by Houbraken, 198; comparison of the two men, 198, 199; his *Portrait of a Woman* contrasted with Van Dyck's *Marie Louise*, 199, 200; his mastery of hands, 199, 200; his portraits typical of Dutch School, 205; his method of painting, 205; broadly surveyed externals of his subject, 206; his work indicative of fine qualities of mind, 206, 207; for over a hundred years overlooked, now esteemed highly, 208
Hampstead, Constable's later home, 301
Hands, expression of, 199, 200
Hanse towns: their trade with Venice and Genoa, 93; their privileges and importance, 140
Hashimoto Gaho (harsh-moh'toh gah-hoh'), 457 et seq.; foremost living artist in Japan, 457; suggestiveness keynote of Japanese motive, 471; based upon Buddhist beliefs, 471-472; Gaho's doctrine of "kokoromochi," 472; of Japanese painting being founded on line, 474; his *Sunrise on the Horai* examined, 476; its linear arrangement, 477; its tonal composition and value of empty spaces, 477
Hassam, Childe, 458
Hayman, Frank, 283
Hearn, Lafcadio, quoted as to changing character of Japanese landscape, 471, 472; and as to the source of true greatness in Japanese art, 476
Hedge, Dr. F. H., his definition of Romantic, 292
Hell, in the Campo Santo at Pisa, 53
Hellas, Hellenic, 53, 105. See *Glossary*
Hellenic guise, Bible stories clothed in, by Raphael, 106, 107
Helst, Bartholomeus van der, 211
Heroic landscape. See *Classic or heroic landscape*, also *Glossary*
High Renaissance, 21
Historical painting and painters, 400
Hobbema (hob'bay-mah), Meindert, 242 et seq.; three towns claim to be his birthplace, 242· his *Avenue of Middelharnis* compared with Claude's *Landing of Cleopatra*, 242; the composition of the *Avenue*, 243; its subject studied, 244; his landscapes represent the *paysage intime*, 249; little known of his life, 250; his truth to nature less than Constable's, 253, 254

Hogarth, William, 255 et seq.; the first English painter, 255; his, a new kind of pictures, 256; linked to Watteau's by the influence of the drama, 259; personal characteristics, 260; subject of the *Marriage à la Mode*, 260, 265; Austin Dobson's praise of it, 265; indorsement of his qualities as a painter, 266; difference between him and Watteau partly racial, 266-268; he reflected four influences: Puritan morality, power of the middle class, the drama, and rise of English prose, 268, 269; his line of beauty, 269, 270; his "Conversation Pieces," how they differ from Dutch genre, 270; summary of difference from Watteau, 270, 271
Holbein the Elder, 138
Holbein the Younger, and Dürer, grand figures in German art, 85; 125 et seq.; his *Portrait of Georg Gyze* compared with Titian's *Man with the Glove*, 125-127; his enjoyment in the truth of facts, 127; his art, objective, particular, realistic, 128; his attitude of mind made him a realist, 129, 130; his elaborate detail compared with Titian's simplification, 131; minuteness of his modeling, 131; sketch of his career, 137-140; its contrast to Titian's, 140, 141; his place in German art, 141
"Hole in the wall," 434. See *Glossary*
Homer, Winslow, 337, 338
Hooped skirts, effect of, on Velasquez's style, 193
Hoppner, John, 286
Horizontal lines, expression of, illustrated in architecture of Southern Europe, 94; contrasted with vertical, 100; effect of excess of, 353, 365
Houbraken quoted concerning Hals and Van Dyck, 198
Hugo, Victor, the leader of French Romanticism, 307; production of his "Hernani," 318
Hunt, William Holman, 371 et seq.; member of Pre-Raphaelite Brotherhood, 371; its motive and ideals, 371, 372; Ruskin to the rescue, 373, 374; the latter's contention that modern art should be religious in motive and truthful to minutest detail realized in Hunt, 376; the *Light of the World* examined as to subject, 376; it fitted in with the Oxford Movement and Gothic Revival, 381, 382; he visits the Holy Land, 382; the *Shadow of the Cross* described, 382; his influence on foreign artists, 383, 384

I

Idealist and realist, Rembrandt a union of, 214
Idealization, examples of: Botticelli's Virgin and Venus, 62; Perugino's sexless, soul-saturated figures, 69, 70; Bellini's elevation of local facts into noble types, 77; Raphael combined the intensity of the religious feeling with the impersonal serenity and happiness of the pagan, 88; Leonardo's types elusive, less

INDEX

visible to eye-sight than to soul-sight, 121, 123; Titian's idealization of a mood, 127; Van Dyck's idealization of elegance and manners, 199; Claude's improvement upon nature, 242, 243; the academic improvement on the human figure, 253; Watteau's rainbow-hued visions of grace, 256, 257; Boecklin's idealization based on facts, 366, 367; Puvis seeks for the permanent and elemental, 425, 437, 439. See *Glossary*

Ideals of the West and East different, 9

Illustrators influenced by Japanese art, 476

Imagination, the, effect of distance and space upon, 78; stimulated by experience of physical sensations, 79, 80; Michelangelo's appeal to, 154, 155; Rembrandt's power of moving, 214, 216; how the sky appeals to, 231; Boecklin bases on facts his appeal to, 366, 367; music's abstract appeal to, 451; the concrete appeal of painting to, 452; Whistler's appeal to, through suggestiveness, 452-456; effect upon, of Corot's skies, 463; suggestiveness to spirit and imagination the keynote of Japanese painting, 471, 477

Imitation of Italian art, Flemish art loses its identity in, 67; German art also, in seventeenth and eighteenth centuries, 141; caused Velasquez to be forgotten, 194; also Hals, 208; Rembrandt to be despised, 226, 227; Reynolds founded his style on, 276; Constable broke away from, 288

Immortals, the, 240

Impermanence of matter, Japanese belief of, 471, 472

Impressionism, modern: Manet revives Velasquez's study of light, 407; origin of name, which is a misnomer, 408; the impressionists should be called luminarists, 408; their cry of "Art for art's sake," 404 et seq. See *Glossary*

Impressionism of Monet, popular misapprehension of, 457; goes further than Manet and Velasquez, and learns from Japanese to seek the fleeting mood of nature, 457, 458; his method of painting, of itself, has nothing to do with impressionism, 458

Impressionism of Velasquez, instant and complete, and vividly retained, 190; a realism of vision, rendered with true appearance of light, 190, 191, 192

Impression on the eye and on the mind contrasted, 129

Incidental and momentary compared with elemental and permanent, 425

Individuality, Winckelmann says that the highest beauty is devoid of, 319; Delacroix says that style depends upon individuality of artist, 319, 320; Millet's peasants not individual, but typal, 341, 350; Puvis's avoidance of, 437; Buddhist text, "He alone is wise who can see things without their individuality," 476

Ingres (an'gur), Jean Auguste Dominique, follower of David, 354; his frigid, marbleized figures, 357

Inness, George, 337, 338

Institute of France, 240, 241

Intense feeling, Rembrandt and Ruisdael the only notes of, in Dutch art, 230

Inter Artes et Naturam [Puvis], 423 et seq. See *Glossary*

Ipswich, Gainsborough resided at, 283

Isaiah [Michelangelo], 276

Isle of the Dead [Boecklin], 353 et seq.

Israels, Jozef, 404 et seq.; painter of the Dutch poor, 404; destined for a rabbi, then helped in his father's bank, 419; schooled first in the academical manner, under Delaroche, 419; settled in Amsterdam and tried to paint historical subjects, 420; ill-health took him to Zandvoort, where he began to study nature and the fisher-folk, 420; back in Amsterdam, he at first painted rather anecdotal and sentimental pictures, but gradually learned to make light the main source of expression of sentiment, 420; illustrated in *The Old Scribe*, 421; its broad yet delicately sensitive treatment, 421; more range of motive than Millet, better painter of light and atmosphere, and makes more of landscape, 422; his influence on Dutch art, 422

Italian history, summary of, 86 et seq.

Italian influence. See *Imitation of Italian art*

Italian School, 8-176

J

Jacque, Charles (sharl zhack), 322, 344

Japan, art of, 471 et seq.; Japanese art compared with Occidental, 471

Japanese art, influence of, on Whistler, 455; on Monet, 458

Japanese art, related to life, 478

Jeremiah [Michelangelo], 142 et seq.; compared with Reynolds's *Mrs. Siddons*, 276

Johnson, Samuel, friend of Reynolds, 285

Judgment, The, in the Campo Santo at Pisa, 53

Judith with the Head of Holofernes [Mantegna], 35

Julius II, Pope, summons Raphael to Rome, 105; commissions Michelangelo, 153

K

Keats quoted, 319

Kemble, family of actors, 272

Keppel, Commodore, afterward Lord, 275

Kneller, Sir Godfrey, 255

Koburger, Antonius, printer, 93, 117

Koeverden claims to be birthplace of Hobbema, 242

Ko'koro, the Japanese idea of, 472, 473. See *Glossary*

Kokoromochi (ko'ko-ro-mo"chee) the expression of "kokoro," 472. See *Glossary*

L

Landing of Cleopatra at Tarsus [Claude], 242 et seq., 288

INDEX

Landscape, a background to figures in Italian art, Perugino's beautiful example, 78; its expressional value, 79; the Dutch painted it for its own sake, 237, 244; "classic" or "heroic," 237, 238; equal balance of landscape and figures in Poussin's pictures, 237; love of, particularly characteristic of Northern nations, 237; influence of, upon the Italian grand style, 238; Claude's rearrangement of nature, addition of architecture, and reduced importance of figures, 242, 243, 252, 253; Constable revives the natural landscape, 287 et seq.; Rousseau founds the modern French school of *paysage intime*, 325 et seq.; American landscape, 337, 338

Las Meñinas (lahs mane-yeen'as). See *Maids of Honor*

Last Judgment [Michelangelo], 156

Last Judgment [Tintoretto], 173

Lastman, Pieter, 224

Lawrence, Sir Thomas, 286

Layman? What is a, 410

Layman's point of view differs from artist's, 410

Leaving out and putting in, 131, 200, 453

Lebrun, Charles, 240, 255

Lely, Sir Peter, 255

Le Nôtre lays out the gardens at Versailles, 253

Leonardo da Vinci (lay-o-nah'do dah veen'chee) fellow-pupil of Perugino, 84; influence on Raphael, 104; 109 et seq.; his *Virgin of the Rocks* compared with Dürer's *Adoration of the Magi*, 109, 120, 121; early life in Florence, maturity in Milan, last three years in France, 110; pupil of Verrocchio, 110; scientist, musician, and painter, 110, 121; peered into the secrets of nature and life, 121, 122; the first to make chiaroscuro yield poetic and emotional expression, 122; the subtlety and delicacy of his method illustrated in the *Virgin of the Rocks* and the *Monna Lisa*, 123; his type of woman's beauty, 123; his work full of mystery, sensitive, strangely alluring, but baffling and elusive, 124; recapitulation of his qualities, 142; anticipated the perspective of light, 191; one of the Fontainebleau School, 322; traits in him shared by Whistler, 451

Lessing quoted: truth to nature first condition of beauty, 319

Lethière, Guillaume (gheel'yome lay'ti-air), 323

Let the Little Children come unto Me [Von Uhde], 384

"Let there be Light," "Fiat Lux," the motto of modern painting, 407

Leyden, birthplace of Rembrandt, 224

Lhermitte, Léon Augustin (lay'on ohgoos'tan lair'meet), 352, 383, 384

"Liber Studiorum," Turner's, 252, 298

"Liber Veritatis," Claude's, 252, 298

Life and movement, 65, 169, 328

Light, modelling by: Velasquez, 190, 191; Hals, 205; Manet, 417

Light, Monet's rendering of, 463 et seq.

Light a form of energy, 463

Light and shade. See *Chiaroscuro*

Light of the World [Holman Hunt], 376 et seq.

Line, functional use of, 17; decorative use of, 65, 66; compositional use of, 100, 101, 102; at the same time expressional use of, 102; for another union of compositional and expressional lines compare, 181, 182; Correggio's lines of grace, Michelangelo's of power, 155, 156; elusiveness of Velasquez's contour lines, 192; Hogarth's line of beauty, 269; academic ideal line, 315, 316; Millet's synthetic line, 351; economy of line in Whistler's etchings, 453; Japanese painting founded on line: its subtlety of expression, 474; Japanese line melting into indefiniteness, 477

Lippo Lippi, Fra (frah leep'po leep'pee), 56

Local color, 191, 406. See *Glossary*

Local truth idealised by Giovanni Bellini, 77

London in 1526, 139

Lord Leighton's *Procession of Cimabue's Madonna*, 11

Lorenzetti (low-raynt-say'tee) brothers, 20, 53

Louis XIV, 240, 255, 256

Louis XV, 256

"Luminarists," 408, 422. See *Glossary*

Luther's influence on Dürer, 112, 117

M

Madonna and Child with St. Jerome and the Magdalene [Correggio], 157

Madonna degli Ansidei (dail'ye ahn-seeday'ee) [Raphael], 97 et seq.

Madonna Enthroned [Cimabue], 8 et seq.

Madonna Enthroned [Giotto], 8 et seq.

Madonna Gran Duca (grahn doo'ca) [Raphael], 104

Madrid, 223

Maids of Honor, The, "Las Meñinas" [Velasquez], 178 et seq., 269

Malatesta (mal-ah-taste'ah) family at Rimini, 31

Manet (mah'nay), Edouard, 404 et seq.; his *Girl with a Parrot* compared with *The Old Scribe* by Israels, 404; carried further and completed the realism of Courbet by realism of representation, 405; first studied and borrowed from the old Italian masters, then learned anew the truths concerning light discovered by Velasquez, 406, 407; "Let there be Light" became new watchword, 407; the "Salon des Impressionistes" in 1871, 408; the position of the Impressionists considered, 408-411; in *Boy with Sword* approaches nearest to Velasquez, 411; his *Girl with a Parrot* examined: its color-scheme, 412, 417, 418; enumeration of his qualities, 418; his influence on others, 418, 419

Mantegna, Andrea (ahn-dray'ah mahn-tane'yah), 20 et seq.; at Padua what Masaccio had been at Florence, 21; established the status of painting inde-

[504]

INDEX

pendent of the church, 21; his *Gonzaga Family* examined: character and individuality of the heads, 23; attitudes stiff, drapery limp, 24; learned of sculpture, 24; of Giotto's frescoes in Padua, 30; and of his teacher Squarcione's casts of antique sculpture, 30; assisted his master in the Church of Eremitani, 30; friendship with the Bellinis, 31; summoned to Verona by Gonzaga, 31; companion of scholars, 33; the influence of sculpture in his picture of the Gonzaga family, 33, 34; his skill in perspective, 34; his *Triumph of Cæsar*, 34, 35; his engravings *The Entombment* and *Judith* described, 35, 36

Man with the Glove [Titian], 125 et seq.

Marat, portrait of [David], 315

Marco, San (san mar'ko), monastery of, 48 et seq.

Mark's, St., embodiment of the spiritual life of Venice, 160, 161

Marie Louise von Tassis, portrait of, [Van Dyck], 198 et seq.

Marriage à la Mode [Hogarth], 260 et seq.

Marriage at Cana, The [Veronese], 169

Marriage Contract, The [Hogarth], 260, 265

Marriage of Bacchus and Ariadne [Tintoretto], 173

Martin, Homer, 337, 338

Martyrdom of St. Agnes [Tintoretto], 174

Masaccio, Tommaso (tome-mah'so mahsahch'chyo), 20 et seq.; to the fifteenth century what Giotto had been to the fourteenth, 20; finally reclaimed painting from Byzantinism, 21; his *St. Peter Baptizing* examined: advance in use of nude and in character and correctness of form, 22, 23; influenced by Donatello and Ghiberti, 24; but discovered for himself the placing of figures in atmosphere, 29; where his chief works are, 29; like Leonardo, he anticipated the study of light by Velasquez, 123

Massys, Quentin, 67

Medici (may'dee-chee) family at Florence, 31, 55, 87

Mediums not confused by the French, 266, 267

Mediums used by artists: distemper, 8; fresco, 18, 147; oil, 45, 147; engraving on wood, 110; engraving on copper, 110; etching, 221. See *Glossary*

Meissonier (mice-own'yen), 189, 403

Memling, Hans, 52 et seq.; his naïveté tinctured with gentle sentiment, 53; his *Virgin Enthroned* mingling of realism and conventionalism with touches of symbolism, 56; a preoccupation with the natural appearances, 61; a record of facts treated with pleasing fancifulness, 63; he presents the facts obvious to touch and sight, 63; in the distant detail he paints not as he sees, but as he knows, the child's way of drawing, 64; his figures, compared with Botticelli's, heavy and stockstill and posed for effect, 65; little known of his life, 66

Meredith, George, 389

Mesdag, H. W., 419

Meyer (mi'er), Jacob, patron of Holbein, 138, 139

Meyer Madonna [Holbein], 138

Michelangelo Buonarroti (meek-el-ahn'-jel-o bwone-ar-ro'tee), 142 et seq.; influenced by Masaccio, 20; the tumult of the Renaissance represented in him, he is an embodiment of its soul, 143; his *Jeremiah* filled with the profundity of his own thoughts, 145; ranked by Taine with Dante, Shakspeare, and Beethoven, 146; continually at war with the world, 146, 147; the *Jeremiah* painted in fresco, a medium just suited to the artist, 148; a sculptor's feeling in the picture, 153; the wonder of the Sistine Chapel, 153; with him the human form made to express mental emotions, 154; his soul-communion with Vittoria Colonna, 155; the elevation of soul in his work, lines of power, tremendous energy, even torment, 155; dares to ignore anatomy and exaggerate, 156; architect, sculptor, painter, poet, his connection with the design of St. Peter's, his death and will, 156

Michelozzo (mee-kel-obt'so), architect of San Marco, 48

Middle class, influence of, 268

Millet, Jean François (zhahn frahn'swah mee'lay), erects a tombstone to Rousseau, 327; 339 et seq.; his *The Gleaners* compared with Breton's *The Gleaner*, 339; the truth to nature in Millet's, 340, 341; a peasant himself, but educated, 341; his pictures are types: e.g., *The Sower*, 341; "Wild Man of the Woods," 341; Millet's poetry compared with Breton's, 342; his early life at Gruchy, 342, 343; becomes a pupil of Delaroche, 343; *The Winnower* is sold and fixes his career, 344; sets out with Jacque for Barbizon, 344; years of poverty, final recognition, 349; tried to depict the fundamental; his epic of labor, 350; he himself describes his aim, 350, 351; a great draftsman, 351

Miniature painters of manuscripts, influence of, 38, 47

Miracle of St. Mark [Tintoretto], 170 et seq.

Mirror, nature a, 303

Momentary and incidental compared with permanent and elemental, 425

Momentary appearance, 458

Monet (mo'nay), Claude, 457 et seq.; in the eyes of the public the most conspicuous impressionist, 457; his impressionism, in advance of Manet's and Velasquez's, influenced by the Japanese, 457, 458; his method of painting, 458; his early life at Havre, induced by Boudin to study nature, 458; as a soldier in Algiers, came under the spell of sunshine, visited London during the Franco-Prussian War and studied Turner, light became his study, 459; he learned the effects of color under open-air light, 459; Professor Rood's investigations suggest the application of paint in separate dabs, 460; the eye mingles them, 460; his *Old Church at Vernon* examined, 460, 461; his *Rouen Cathedral* pictures, 462; his higher kind of impres-

[505]

INDEX

sionism, 462; compared with Corot, Rembrandt, Velasquez, Turner, 463; his *pointilliste* method of painting, 464, 469; raising the key of shadow, 470; he is an eye, 470; people honestly unable to admire his pictures, 470
Monna Lisa (mon'na lee'zah) [Leonardo da Vinci], 123
Montefeltri (mone-tay-fayl'tree) family at Urbino, 31
Monumental, explanation of, 81, 82, 83. See *Glossary*
Mood of the painter expressed, in Titian's *Man with the Glove*, 126; in Corot, 335
More, Sir Thomas, patron of Holbein, 139, 140
Morris, William, 389
Motives, various, of Italian art, 159
Motley quoted regarding Antwerp, 195
Movement and life, 65, 169, 328
Mrs. Siddons as the Tragic Muse [Reynolds], 272 et seq.
Mrs. Siddons, Portrait of [Gainsborough], 272 et seq.
Mural decorations, qualities of, considered, 434 et seq. See *Glossary*
Mural decorations, by Puvis, Abbey, and Sargent, in Boston Public Library, 426 et seq., 449, 450
Murillo, Bartolomé Estéban (bah-tol-o-may' a-stay'bahn moo-reel'yoh), 209 et seq.; his *Children of the Shell* examined: its subject and the models of the figures, 209, 210; very popular in his day and since, 210, 211; his early life in Seville, 222; visits Velasquez in Madrid, 223; his success, and death from a fall, 224
Murphy, J. Francis, 337, 338
Music and color compared. See *Color and music*
Muther, Richard, quoted, on David, 314, note; on Boecklin, 369
Mystery in a picture, 292, 293
Mystic Marriage of St. Catherine [Correggio], 142 et seq.

N

Napoleon I, 314
Naturalism, the present an age of, 342
Nature a mirror, 303
Nature and nature study, 302, 303
Nature must be corrected, academic principle, 315
Netherlands, the, 195
New Learning, the, 54 et seq., 107. See *Glossary*
Night Watch, The. See *Sortie of the Banning Cock Company*
Northcote, James, quoted regarding Reynolds, 276
Nude figure, 22, 118, 154
Nuremberg, free imperial city, 93; Dürer's birthplace, 110

O

Oath of the Horatii [David], 304 et seq.
Objective point of view, 127, 130. See *Glossary*

Official standard, advantage and disadvantage of, 241
Oil-painting perfected by the Van Eycks, 45, 69
Old Church at Vernon (vair'none) [Monet], 460 et seq.
Old Scribe, The [Israels], 404 et seq.
Open-air (*plein air*), 300, 301, 459
Optical mingling of color, 460
Orcagna (or-cahn'yah), 53
Originality, 105, 276, 442
Oriess quoted regarding Rembrandt, 224
Ornans (or'non), birthplace of Courbet, 354, 355
Outlines of objects in nature not sharp, 316
Ovetari (o-vay-tar'ee) family, 30
Oxford Movement, the, 381

P

Pagan feeling of the Renaissance, 88, 143. See *Glossary*
Pageant pictures, 163
Painting, independence of, 21, 374
"Painting another name for feeling" (Constable), 288
"Painting is nothing more than drawing" (academic theory), 319
Paradise [Tintoretto], 175
Pater, Walter, definition of Romantic, 292
Pavia (par-vee'ah) altarpiece [Perugino], 69 et seq.
Paysage intime (pay-ee-sahzh' an-teem'), 249, 254, 289, 322, 325
Peace and War [Puvis], 436
Permanent and elemental compared with momentary and incidental, 425
Perspective, lineal, 17, 34, 191; atmospheric, 29, 191
Perugia (pay-ruge'yah), 31, 70, 97
Perugino. See *Pietro Vannucci*
Perusing pictures with a printed key, 427, 428
Peruzzi (pay-root'see) Chapel, S. Croce (san'tah crow'chay), Florence, 18
Peter Baptizing the Heathen [Masaccio], 20 et seq.
Petrarch (pay'trark), 54, 106
Phidias (fi'dee-ahs), sculpture of, 72, 77, 357
Picture, proper way of seeing a, 3
Pietà (pee-ay-tah') [Michelangelo], 155
Pietro Vannucci (pee-ay'tro vahn-nooch'-chee), called Perugino (pay-roo-gee'no), 68 et seq.; his painter-like point of view tempered with sentiment, 68; among the first in Italy to perfect the use of oils, 68, 69; the painter of soul-solitude and spiritual ecstasy, 69; his figures personification of soul-rapture, 70; he represents the highest development of Byzantinism as an expression of religion, 70, 71; his type different from Bellini's, 77, 78; his use of landscape and its effect on the imagination, 78, 79, 80; his skill in "space-composition," 80; a pupil of Verrocchio, 84; by repetition, his type became affected and sentimental, 84
Piloty (pee-loh'tee), Karl Theodor von, 391 et seq.; composition of his *Thusnelda*

[506]

INDEX

compared with Fortuny's *Spanish Marriage*, 392, 397; its stage-like elaboration, 397, 398; a too ambitious programme, 398; the story of the picture, 398, 399; it encroaches upon literature, 399, 400; compared with *Surrender of Breda*, 400; his practice the same as that of other historical painters, 400, 401; unlike the majority, a good painter, 401; his career in brief, 401; his work abounds in sentiment and characterization, so related to German domestic genre, 401, 402; his limitations as a painter, 402

Pisa (pee'zar), the Campo Santo in, 53
Pisano, Andrea (ahn-dray'ah pee-zah'-noh), 24
Pissarro, Lucien (loo'see-an pees-sah'ro), 458, 459
Pizzolo, Niccolo (neek'ko-loh peets'so-loh), 30
Plagiarism, 105, 276
Plein (plain) *air* (open-air), 300, 459
Pleydenwurff, Hans (pli'den-vurf), 96
Poetic creativeness, methods of, 342
Poetic tendency of the Barbizon artists, 323; that of Millet and Breton compared, 342
Pointilliste (pwine'teel-yeest) method of brushwork, 460, 464. See *Glossary*
Point of view, the artist's, 4; differs from the layman's, 410
Pollice Verso (pol'lee-kay vair'so) [Gérôme], 423 et seq. See *Glossary*
Portrait of the Artist's Mother [Whistler], 450 et seq., 475
Poussin (poos'san), Nicolas, 228 et seq.; his *Et Ego in Arcadia* compared with Ruisdael's *The Waterfall*, 228; born in Normandy, 231; learns drawing from casts and from prints after Raphael, 232; goes to Italy and attaches himself to Domenichino, 232; influence of sculpture apparent in *Et Ego*, 232; and of Raphael, 237; he becomes influenced by the Italian landscape, 237, 238; the subject of the *Et Ego*, 239; his work was the origin of the "classic," or "academic," in French art, 239, 240; his weakness in color, 241
Prado, 194
"Praise of Folly," Erasmus's, illustrated by Holbein, 138
Pre-Raphaelite Brotherhood, 371, 372 et seq.
Primitives, the, 372
Princely families, rise of. 31
"Prince of Plagiarists," Raphael, 105, 442
Prose, rise and influence of English, 269
Puritan influence, 268
Putting in and leaving out, 131, 200, 453
Puvis de Chavannes, Pierre (pee'air peu'veez der sha-vahn'), 423 et seq.; his *Inter Artes et Naturam* compared with Gérôme's *Pollice Verso*, 423; its unity and completeness and placidity, 424; its calmness due to the expression of what is permanent and elemental, 425; a mural decoration, 426; his conception of mural decoration to be gained by comparing his work at Boston with Abbey's and Sargent's, 426-433; the qualities of his work — flatness of painting, simple ample masses, large simplicity of design, 433, 434; his theory of logical subordination to the architecture, 434, 435; his origin and education involved a union of logical and poetic tendencies, 436; his *War* and *Peace*, 436; gradual simplification of theme and technic, 437; excessive simplification, 438; his skill in the landscape parts, illustrated in *Inter Artes*, 438, 439; the abstract qualities of his art, 439; his decorations seem to have grown upon the wall like a delicate efflorescence, 439

R

Racine, 253
Raeburn, Sir Henry, 286; influence on Sargent, 442, 449
Raphael Sanzio (rah'fay-el sahnt'ayoh), influence of Masaccio on, 20; Botticelli's yearning after the antique fulfilled in, 67; 85 et seq.; contrast between his art and Wolgemuth's, 85; it combines the religious and the pagan feeling, 88; his influence over his assistants, 96; representative of the Umbrian, Florentine, and Roman schools, 97; his early life in Urbino, and with Perugino in Perugia, 97; his *Madonna degli Ansidei* betrays the influence of the master, but already surpasses his work, 18; its composition studied, 100, 101; its beauty primarily dependent upon its "architectonics," 102, 103; the composition of the *Death of the Virgin* contrasted, 103; Raphael's idealization, 104; the sources from which he drew his composite type, 104; the "Prince of Plagiarists," 105; his work in Rome, 105, 106; retold the legends of Hellas and clothed the Bible story in Hellenic guise, 106; his influence upon the thought of his own day and of posterity, 106, 107, 108; his influence upon Poussin, 232, 237; on Reynolds, 276; the revolt from it of Courbet, 357; of the Pre-Raphaelites, 372; of Ruskin, 373
Realism: Lippo Lippi satisfied with the study of external form, 56, 61; Wolgemuth's prosaic imitation, 110; an attitude of mind, as shown in Holbein, 125-130; Velasquez's realism of unity and realism of impression, 189; Meissonier's false kind of realism: compare Memling's, 64, 189, 190; Velasquez's realism of rendering light, 190, 191; and of representing form, surrounded by lighted atmosphere, 192; realism of Dutch genre and of Hogarth compared, 270; Courbet's *la vérité vraie*, 358; his *Funeral at Ornans* a fine example of realism, 360, 361; Ruskin's doctrine of exact realism, 374, 375; the same illustrated in Holman Hunt, 382, 383; to Courbet's realistic point of view and choice of subject Manet adds a realistic truth of rendering, borrowed from Velasquez, 407, 412; Monet's further insight into realism of appearance, 459, 460. See *Glossary*
Realist and idealist, Rembrandt a union of, 214
Reaper, The [Millet], 350

INDEX

Reformation in Germany, 112
Rembrandt, Van Rijn (rin), 209 et seq.; one of the few great original artists, 209; a realist and idealist in one, 209, 214; his *Sortie of the Banning Cock Company* did not satisfy his clients, 211; had proved himself a realist in the *Anatomy Lesson*, 212; the *Sortie* examined, 212; originally called the *Night Watch*, 213; really a study of light, 214; Fromentin considers the subject of the picture did not warrant this treatment, 214; his estimate of Rembrandt summarized, 214, 215; Rembrandtesque treatment of light and and shade, 215; a source of emotional gesture, 215; finally tried to paint with light alone, which involved sacrifices, 215, 216; the example of his *Syndics of the Cloth-workers' Guild*, 216; "Prince of Etchers," 216, 221; his aim and achievement as compared with Murillo's, 222; sketch of his career, 224; early life in Leyden, 224; settles in Amsterdam, 225; success and marriage to Saskia, ten years' happiness, 225; dispute over the *Sortie* and death of Saskia, 225; his friendship with Jan Six, 226; his financial troubles, 226; his last portrait of himself, 226; after his death soon forgotten, and in the eighteenth century his work despised, 226, 227; his restoration to honor in the nineteenth century, 227; influences Israels, 420; his stimulation of the effects of light by means of shadow compared with Monet's *pointilliste* method, 463
Renaissance in Italy and Germany compared, 111 et seq., 118
Repetition and contrast in composition, 100 et seq.
Reserve, a quality of force, 454
Resurrection [Correggio], 157
Revolution, French, 256, 308
Reynolds, Sir Joshua, 272 et seq.; his *Mrs. Siddons* compared with Gainsborough's, 272, 273, 274; his "Eighth Discourse" on warm and cold colors, 274; regulated his art and life on safe principles, a man of the world, 274, 275; birth and boyhood, 275; visit to Italy with Commodore Keppel, 275; his deafness, 275; studied Raphael, Michelangelo, Rubens, Correggio, and the Venetians, 275, 276; his success in combining for himself something of the style of each, 276; the pose of the *Mrs Siddons* recalls Michelangelo's *Isaiah*, the attendant figures those in the *Jeremiah*, 276; intimate with Garrick and Burke, Samuel Johnson, Oliver Goldsmith, and other celebrities of his day, 281, 285; strong inclination toward the dramatic, 281
Ribera (ree-bair'rah), Roman, 223
Rimini (ree'mee-nee), 31
Robbia, Luca della (loo'kah dayl'lah robe'-byah), 47
Rocky Chasm, A [Boecklin], 369
Rococo, style of Louis XV, 402. See *Glossary*
Roman Empire, break up of, 86 et seq.
Romans, characteristics of, inherited by the French, 239, 240

Romantic, romanticism, 292, 307, 318, 323. See *Glossary*
Rome, sack of, 145
Romney, George, 286
Rood, Professor, his scientific investigations into light and color help Monet and others, 458, 460
Rossetti (ros-set'tee), Dante Gabriel, 371 et seq.; his *Ecce Ancilla Domini* appears in 1850, 371; a member of the Pre-Raphaelite Brotherhood, 371; a student of Dante, he leads the other members back to the "Primitives," 372; realizes Ruskin's theory that modern art should be concerned with spiritual expression, 376; *The Blessed Damozel*, 376; his father, an Italian patriot in refuge in London, student of Dante, 384; extraordinarily precocious, 384; Dante, his guide, leads him to Fra Angelico, the mystic of painting, 384, 385; impatient of the routine of art study, 385; poem of "The Blessed Damozel" written in 1846, met Miss Siddal in 1850, painted the picture in 1879, 385; her personal appearance described, 385; satisfied his conception of perfectly balanced soul and body, 386; after ten years of waiting married her, lost her two years later, 386; suffered from this and from Buchanan's attack on his poetry and became victim to insomnia and chloral, 386; the tragedy of *The Blessed Damozel*, 386, 387; his single devotion to his wife's memory source of strength and weakness to his art, 387, 388; his conception of woman like Dante's, 388, 389; his life at Chelsea and intimates, 389; as a painter of the soul succeeded by Burne-Jones, 390; his influence led to the revival of idealism in foreign painting, 390
Rossetti, William M., member of the Pre-Raphaelite Brotherhood, 371; his description of Miss Siddal's appearance, 385
Rousseau, Théodore (tay'o-dore roo'sob), Hobbema the forerunner of, 249; 322 et seq.; leader of the Fontainebleau-Barbizon School, 322, 326; epic poet of the group, 323; the eagle, 324; influenced by the work of Constable and by the Dutch landscapes in the Louvre, he leaves the studio of Lethière and sketches about the plain of Montmartre, 323, 326; his *Edge of the Forest of Fontainebleau* compared with Corot's *Dance of the Nymphs*, 323, 324; its solidity of form and clear decision of line, 324; his early poverty, 325; boyhood dreams, 325; first a student at the Polytechnic, 325; *Côtes de Grandville*, his first masterpiece, awarded a medal, 326; then officialdom slighted him, Diaz's protest, 326; sad domestic life, 327; a final insult of the authorities probably hastened his death, 327; the oak, his favorite tree, characteristic of himself and work, 335; based his art on form, and during a period with too exact detail, 335; broad impersonal vision that sought after the elemental in nature, 335, 336, 337; his mastery of

INDEX

form—and form is the foundation of great painting, 337
Royal Academy established, 286
Rubens, Peter Paul, compared with Veronese, 170; 177 et seq.; ranks with Rembrandt and Velasquez as among the greatest, 178; his *Descent from the Cross* compared with Velasquez's *Maids of Honor*, 178; examined as to subject, 179, 180; its appeal to the "tactile imagination," 180, 181; its arrangement of line, 181, 182; of light and shade, 182, 183; he visits Madrid and meets Velasquez, 183; his *Marie de Medici* series in the Louvre, 184; his treatment of light compared with Velasquez's, 190; his mastery of the human form and splendor of color, 193; ambassador from court to court, 193, 194; teacher of Van Dyck, 197; his coloring studied by Watteau, 258; by Reynolds, 276; his drawing and color by Delacroix, 317
Ruisdael (rise'dale), Jacob van, 228 et seq., *The Waterfall* compared with Poussin's *Et Ego in Arcadia*, 228; its character of subject borrowed from Everdingen, 229; his early work in Haarlem his best, 229; non-success drove him to Amsterdam, where the popularity of Everdingen's Norway scenes induced him to emulate them, 229; their sternness akin to his own sad life, 229; returned in poverty to Haarlem and died in an almshouse, 230; in respect of sadness akin to Rembrandt, 230; the beauty of the skies in his pictures, 230, 231; his works studied by Constable, 288
Ruskin, John, his excessive praise of Turner has harmed the latter's reputation, 302; champions the Pre-Raphaelite Brotherhood, 372; his criticism of Raphael's *Christ Walking upon the Water*, 373; his doctrine that modern painting should make religious or spiritual expression rather than form its object of study, 374; could not or would not recognize independent status of painting, 374; overlooked the meaning of artistic truth, 374, 375

S

Sacrifices made by Rembrandt, 215
Sargent, John Singer, 441 et seq.; the antithesis in work and personality of Whistler, 441; his style borrowed from Velasquez, Hals, and Raeburn, yet has original force, 441, 442; early life in Florence, 442; already a skilful draftsman and painter, nurtured on the Italian masters, entered the studio of Carolus-Duran, 442, 443; a refined and cultivated taste, 443; visited Madrid and then Holland, 443; in the *Portrait of the Misses Hunter* Velasquez's influence seen in line and mass and unity of impression, 443; also the influence of the stately directness of the old Italian portraits, 443; yet thoroughly modern, 443; the *esprit* of his brushwork French, 444; especially notable in his female portraits, the influence of Hals and Raeburn more in the male ones, 445; his impression confined to what is on or near the surface, 444; his mural decorations in the Boston Public Library described, 428, 449; intentional complexity in the ceiling and lunette, need of printed clues, 428; the frieze of the *Prophets* immediately intelligible and finer as a decoration, 428; the latest panel, the *Redemption of Man*, full of the Byzantine influence, the grandest; flatness of painting, simple ample spaces, and large simplicity of design, 433, 449; a background of subdued splendor to the raised central group, 433; remarkable example of unison of ancient and modern technic, 450
Sarto, Andrea del (ahn-dray'ah dail sar'to), 322
Saskia van Uylenborch, Rembrandt's love for, 225; like Rossetti's for *his* wife, 385
Savonarola (sah-\one-ah-ro'lah), 50
Scenic and dramatic contrasted, 170, 174
Scholarship, Greek and Roman, revival of, at Gonzaga's court, influencing Mantegna, 32, 33; Petrarch and Boccaccio's zeal for, 54; Botticelli mingles with scholars at the court of Lorenzo de' Medici, 55; influence of, upon Giovanni Bellini, 78; upon Raphael, 88
Science anticipated by Leonardo da Vinci, 120
Scott, Sir Walter, one of the leaders of the Romantic movement which inspired Delacroix, 307; one of the latter's favorite authors, 318; also Rossetti's, as a boy, 384
Sculpture, influence of, on painting: Masaccio learns of Ghiberti and Donatello, 24; Mantegna from Squarcione's collection of antique casts, 30; so did Giovanni Bellini, 71; Verrocchio, sculptor more than painter, influenced Giovanni Bellini, taught Perugino and Leonardo da Vinci, 71, 84; early German painters imitated the Gothic sculpture, 95; the feeling of sculpture in Michelangelo's *Jeremiah*, 153; Poussin's study of casts and low-reliefs reflected in his *Et Ego in Arcadia*, 232; David went back to Roman sculpture, as seen in the *Oath of the Horatii*, 304, 308, 316, 317; "the marble manner only requires a little animating," Winckelmann, 319
Scuola di San Rocco (squo'lah dee sahn roke'ko), 173
Seeing things without their individuality, Buddhist text, 476
Selection and arrangement in composition, 99 et seq. See *Glossary*
Sentiment expressed by color, light, and atmosphere, in Israel's case, 420. See *Glossary*
Seurat (seu'rah), George, originator of the *pointilliste* method of painting, 458, 459
Seville, birthplace of Murillo, 222
Sforza (sfort'sah) family at Florence, 31
Shadow of the Cross, The [Holman Hunt], 383
Shakspeare ranked by Taine with Dante, Beethoven, and Michelangelo as the four

INDEX

most exalted in art and literature, 146; source of inspiration to Delacroix, 318; read in English by Millet, 341; a favorite author of Rossetti's boyhood, 384
Siddal, Miss Elizabeth, lover, wife, and inspiration of Rossetti, 385–389
Siena (see-ay'nah), the brothers Lorenzetti in, 20
Simplicity, simplification: everything but essentials left out in Titian's *Man with the Glove*, 131; Puvis's large simplicity of design, 433; he reduced his theme to abstract expression, then simplified his technic to insure no distraction from the unity of effect and its relation to the architecture, 437; the "leaving out" in Whistler's etchings, 453; tender dignity in the simple massing in the portrait of his mother, 454; simplification of Western and Japanese artists compared, 473, 474; the value of the empty space in Gaho's *Sunrise on the Horai*, 477. See *Glossary*
Sistine (sees'teen) Chapel, 153 et seq.
Six Gallery, Amsterdam, 226
Six, Jan, 226
Sky: Perugino's distance and space-composition, 78; enlargement and interpretation of the sentiment of his figures, 79; skies of Holland proverbially grand, 230; Ruisdael's fine skies, 231; painters of powerful imagination and feeling revel in the rendering of, 231; Turner's skies of vast grandeur, 299; the cloud effects of Northern countries make them the home of natural landscape painting, 300, 301; Corot's love of the, 333, 334, 463
Sortie of the Banning Cock Company (The Night Watch) [Rembrandt], 211 et seq.
Soul-solitude, Perugino the painter of, 69
Sower, The [Millet], 341
Space-composition, Perugino's mastery of, 80; Raphael's supreme distinction, 98
Spanish Marriage, The [Fortuny], 391 et seq.
Spanish School, 177–194, 209–227, 391–403
Squarcione (squar-chee-owe'nay), his collection of casts helps to educate Mantegna, 30; also Giovanni Bellini, 71
Stage, influence of, exhibited by Watteau and Hogarth, 256, 258, 259, 260, 261, 269
Stanze (stahn'zer) of the Vatican, 105
Steelyard, merchant of the, 140
St. Mark's embodiment of the spiritual life of Venice, 160; its beauty akin to the qualities of Venetian painting, 161
Stone-Breakers, The [Courbet], 356, 357
Story in a picture: Hogarth's anecdotal with a moral, 260, 268; due partly to the influence of the new literature of novelists, 269; difference of Dutch genre, which is mainly concerned with the pictorial aspect, 270; German fondness for historical and story-telling genre, 401, 402; the literary element in Abbey and Sargent's decorations in the Boston Public Library, 427, 428, 450
St. Paul's Cathedral, 208, 285
St. Peter's, design of, 156

Subjective point of view, 127, 130. See *Glossary*
Sudbury, birthplace of Constable, 283
Suggestiveness to one's imagination, 450 et seq., 471, 477. See *Glossary*
Sunrise on the Horai [Hashimoto Gaho], 457 et seq.
Surrender of Breda [Velasquez], 183, 400
Swanenburch, Jacob van, a teacher of Rembrandt, 224
Swinburne, Algernon, friend of Rossetti's, 389
Symonds, John Addington, quoted regarding Tintoretto, 173
Syndics of the Cloth-workers' Guild [Rembrandt], 216

T

Tactile imagination, the stimulation of, 80, 120, 180. See *Glossary*
Taine quoted: of Giovanni Bellini, 77; of Michelangelo, 146
Talma, French actor, first to act the Horatii in Roman costume, 305
Tassi, Agostino (ah-jose-tee'no tahs'see), 250
Technic, what it is, 5, 63. See *Glossary*
Temperamental attitude, the, 126, 127, 290, 335. See *Glossary*
Temporary appearance of objects will not constitute a work of art, 472
Terribilità of Michelangelo, 156
Terrible side of Italian Renaissance, 32, 53, 54, 70, 143
Textures, effect on the imagination of, 79, 80; Dürer's skill in rendering, 119; Manet renders them by rendering the varying quantities of light, 412, 417; and by manner of brushwork, 417. See *Glossary*
Thinker, The [Michelangelo], 155
Thrale, Mrs., quoted, of Mrs. Siddons, 273
Tiepolo [tee-ay'po-lo], 232
Tintoretto, 159 et seq.: he and Veronese the most characteristic of Venetian art, 159; the motive of the latter partly religious, classical, and realistic, but chiefly the joy and pageantry of life and pride of Venice, 159; bringing of the body of St. Mark to Venice, 160; St. Mark's and the Doge's Palace the symbols of her spiritual and temporal life, 160, 161; the decoration of St. Mark's; its beauty of color, light, and atmosphere also characteristic qualities of Venetian painting, 161; an art of display and some exaggeration, 162; Tintoretto's paintings in the Hall of the Great Council, 163; his frieze of portraits of seventy-six doges, 163; his work has a strain of dramatic poetry, 169; his *Miracle of St. Mark* compared with Veronese's *Glory of Venice*, 170; his is dramatic, the other scenic, 170; the value of the story in his *Miracle*, 171, 172; the dramatic movement, beauty of color, and emotional use of light and shade in the treatment, 174, 175; sought to combine the drawing of Michelangelo and the coloring of Titian, 172; son of a dyer,

[510]

INDEX

hence his name, 172; copies the work of Titian and the casts of Michelangelo's Medicean figures, 172; his study of suspended figures, 172; first important work, *The Last Judgment* and *The Golden Calf*, 173; his work in the Scuola di San Rocco, 173; his *Marriage of Bacchus and Ariadne* and *Martyrdom of St. Agnes* prove his mastery of tender, tranquil subjects, 174; his usual impetuous force, "Il Furioso," 174; "while Tintoretto was the equal of Titian, he was often inferior to Tintoretto," 174; makes his figures emerge from darkness into light, 175; a mind teeming with ideas, lightning-bursts of inspiration, rapid realization on the canvas, 175; his colossal *Paradise* confused and exaggerated, 175; buried in Santa Maria del Orto, where his first work was done, 176

Titian (tish'yan). See *Tiziano Vecelli*

Tiziano Vecelli (tit-zee-ah'no vay-chel'lee), called Titian, 125 et seq.; his *Man with the Glove* compared with Holbein's *Portrait of Georg Gyze*, 125; the mood of a man, 126; abstract, exalted, idealized, 127; reflection of the artist's self, a mood of his own subjectivity, 130; composition large, simple, grand, a triumph of simplification, 131; wonderful composition of dark and light, 132; born at Pieve, of an old family, in the Cadore district of the Alps, 132; at eleven years of age a pupil of Gentile Bellini, later of Giovanni, 132; worked with Giorgione, 137; his distinguished patrons, 137; great in portraits, landscape, religious and mythical subjects, 137; luxurious home at Biri, 137; died at the age of ninety-nine of the plague, 137; the world was to him a pageant and he represented it with the brush of a supreme colorist, 141; the culmination of the art of Venice, 159; Watteau learned color from him; 258; Delacroix also, 317

Triumph of Cæsar [Mantegna], 34, 35

Triumph of Death, in the Campo Santo at Pisa, 53

Troyon, Constant (troh'yon), 322, 326

Truth, not painting (*Verdad no pintura*), said of Velasquez's work, 179

Truth to nature the first condition of beauty (Lessing), 319

Tryon, Dwight W., 337, 338

Turner, Joseph Mallord William, 287 et seq.; contrast between his *Ulysses Deriding Polyphemus* and Constable's *Valley Farm*, 287, 290; most imaginative landscape-painter, 290; subject of the *Ulysses* studied, 291; in his *Dido building Carthage* he imitated Claude, 291; then he would be himself — Turner, 292; after a visit to Italy began his finest period of twelve years, ending with *The Fighting Téméraire* and *The Burial of Wilkie at Sea*, 292, 299; his work romantic in so far that it involved mystery, 292, 297; and strangeness, 297; the contradiction of his life and art, 297, 298; sketch of his life: a barber's son, precocious, pupil of the Royal Academy, exhibited at fifteen, 298; unrivaled in water-color, his "Liber Studiorum" an emulation of Claude, an unfair rivalry, 298, 299; experimented in the rendering of light and atmosphere, trying to raise the key of color, 299, 300; his squalid life and generous will, 300; Ruskin's excessive admiration, 302

Typal expression in painting: Michelangelo's *Jeremiah*, 155; Millet's *The Sower*, 341; Whistler's *Portrait of the Artist's Mother*, 451. See *Glossary*

Types of picture repeated by the Italians, 105

U

Uhde (oo'der), Fritz von, 383

Ulysses Deriding Polyphemus [Turner], 290 et seq.

Unity and balance in composition, 99 et seq.

Unity of impression, 189

Universal spirit manifested in matter, 472, 476. See *Glossary*

Urban VIII, a patron of Claude, 251

Urbino (ur-bee'no), Raphael's birthplace, 97

V

Valenciennes, birthplace of Watteau, 256, 258

Valley Farm, The [Constable], 287 et seq.

Values: the varying quantities of light contained upon varying planes of objects, 191; Velasquez's skill in rendering, 191; Hals's rendering of, in broad, flat tones, 205; Manet rediscovers from Velasquez the study of light and, 406, 407; his *Girl with a Parrot* analyzed, 412, 417; Puvis's skill in, 438. See *Glossary*

Van Dyck, Sir Anthony, 195 et seq.; Houbraken's anecdote of, and of Hals, 198; his method of work, 199; comparison of his portrait of Marie Louise, with Hals's portrait of a woman, 199, 200, 205, 206; sketch of his career, 207, 208; the quality of his idealization, 249; the quality of the distinction in his work, 282

Van Dyke, John C., quoted upon Hogarth, 266. See *Glossary*, under "Luminarists"

Van Eyck, Hubert, 39, 40, 45

Van Eyck, Jan (zhan van eyck), 37 et seq.; his *Virgin and Donor* compared with *The Annunciation* by Fra Angelico, 37; the art of each has a minute perfection of finish, inherited from the miniature-painters, 38; the *Virgin and Donor* described, 38, 39; its composition one of large and handsome spots, wrought over with elaborate ornamentation, 39; characteristic of Flemish spirit and the national skill in craftsmanship, 39; but with Jan and Hubert van Eyck details do not detract from a general grand significance, 39; the elaboration of the picture studied, 40; its rendering of textures and fine, brilliant coloring, 40; the brothers were the first to use oil-colors successfully, 45; their secret discovered

INDEX

by Antonello da Messina, 45; their joint work, *The Adoration of the Lamb*, 45; in the two brothers Flemish art, born out of handicrafts, reached full growth, 45, 46; Jan in the service of Philip the Good, as "varlet and painter," 45; his work grave in sentiment, resplendent in character, 46
Van Loo, Jean Baptiste, 304
Van Marcke, Emil, 322
Varlet and painter, Jan van Eyck engaged as, 45
Vasari (va-sah'ree) quoted, 55
Velasquez (vay-lahs'keth), Diego Rodriguez de Silva, 177 et seq.; his *Maids of Honor* compared with Rubens's *Descent from the Cross*, 178; the work of his maturity, 178; the actual incident depicted, 179; "illusion so complete, where is the picture?" 179; an illustration of his motto, "Truth, not painting," 179; Rubens visits the Spanish court for nine months, 183; Velasquez visits Italy; his decorative painting, *The Surrender of Breda*, 183, 184; the difference between its conception and treatment and Rubens's series of *Marie de Médicis*, 184; the *Maids of Honor* a new kind of picture, product of a new kind of eyesight, of a new conception of realism, 184; its realism of unity a realism of impression, 189; Meissonier's *1807—Friedland* contrasted, 189; an instant and complete impression, 190; its lighting compared with that of the *Descent from the Cross*, 190; a study of natural light, direct light, half-light, and reflections, 190, 191; of the degrees of grayness of the atmosphere as it recedes from the eye, 191; a new kind of perspective, that of atmosphere, anticipated by Leonardo, 191; local color and values, 191; Velasquez's study of light leads him to avoid sharp outlines, 191, 192; the elusiveness of his lines, 192; saw his subject at a single glance, received a vivid impression of it, and then rendered it as a single impression, 192; the picture is a composition of light and less light, 192, 193; the curious costumes may have influenced him in avoiding the Italian grand manner, and compelled to something new, 193; the constrained life of Velasquez, the exuberant freedom of Rubens's, 193; for two centuries forgotten, now honored as "the First of the Moderns," 194; his influence upon Manet and modern painting, 405-406; on Whistler and Sargent, 441, 443, 455
Venetian art, motive of, combined something of religious, classic, and realistic motives, but chiefly is concerned with the joy and pageantry of life and the pride of Venice, 159; qualities of, 161
Venice, sketch of the history of, 160 et seq.
Venus, cult of, 62
Vérité vraie, la (lah vay'ree-tay vhray), Courbet's motto, 358
Veronese, Paolo Caliari (pah'o-lo cal-ee ah'ree vay-ro-nay'zay), ranks with Giorgione and Titian as the greatest Venetian colorists, 84; 159 et seq.; he and Tintoretto most characteristic of Venetian art, 159; the motive of that art concerned chiefly with the joy and pageantry of life and pride of Venice, 159; St. Mark's and Doge's Palace symbols of her spiritual and temporal power, 160, 161, 163; the beauty of color, light, and shade, and atmosphere in St. Mark's, characteristic of the qualities of Venetian painting, 161; his *Glory of Venice* described, 164; magnificent in balance as in motive, 164; only rivaled by his *Marriage at Cana* and *Family of Darius*, 169; its characteristics: facility of execution, life and movement, unity of effect, luminous rich color and transparent shadows, 169; his point of view simply that of a painter rejoicing in the splendor of external appearances, the very incarnation of the Italian Renaissance, 169; exuberant fancy and facility, calm strength and restraint, 170; the *Glory of Venice* compared with Tintoretto's *Miracle of St. Mark*, 170; the former scenic and the latter dramatic, 170, 174; how he resembled Rubens, 170, 175
Verrocchio (vay-roh'kyo), goldsmith, painter, and sculptor, 55; influenced Bellini, teacher of Perugino and Leonardo, 84
Versailles, 253
Vertical lines, expression of, characteristic of the eager, soaring spirit of Gothic architecture, 94; contrasted with horizontal and curved in Raphael's composition, 100, 101; lifting up the imagination, as in Boecklin's *Isle of the Dead*, 353
Vibration of light and color, the *pointilliste* method of Monet suggests the, 463, 464
Vinci, Leonardo da. See *Leonardo*
Virgil, study of, by Millet, 341; by Puvis, 423
Virgin, cult of the, 62
Virgin and Donor [Jan van Eyck], 37 et seq.
Virgin Enthroned [Botticelli], 56 et seq.
Virgin Enthroned [Memling], 56 et seq.
Virgin of the Rocks [Leonardo da Vinci], 109 et seq.
Visconti (vees-kone'tee) family at Milan, 31
Vite, Timoteo (tee-mo-tay'-o vee'tay), 97
Vittorino da Feltre (vee-tore-een'oh dah fayl'tray), scholar, 32
Vivarini, Alvise (al-vee'zay vee-vah-ree'-nee), 163
Votive pictures, 95
Vouet, Simon (see'mohn vou'ay), 255

W

Walker, Horatio, 337, 338
War and Peace [Puvis], 436
Water-Carrier, The [Millet], 350
Waterfall, The [Ruisdael], 228 et seq.
Watteau (in French, vaht-toh; English, wot-toh), Jean Antoine, 255 et seq.; the first of French painters, 255; his work distinctively French and original, 255;

[512]

INDEX

a native of Valenciennes, 256; his work, like Hogarth's, a new kind of picture, 256; influenced by the drama, 256; the *Embarkation for Cythera* a rainbow-hued vision of beauty and grace, 256; represents the charm of the court life during the Regency with no hint of storm impending, 256; a mingling of reality and unreality, 257; its dreamy distance, exquisite pattern of composition, delicate chiaroscuro, and brilliant harmony of colors, 257; his idealism, as with all great artists, founded on nature, 258; as a lad, drew the antics and gestures of the actors and mountebanks in the market-place, 258; when he reached Paris, added to skill of drawing a study of the coloring of Rubens, Titian, and Veronese, 258; Italian comedies in the salons and gardens of the Luxembourg, 258; his *Gilles*, 258; almost all his work influenced by the study of the comedians, 258, 259; figures and landscape adjusted to make a *mise-en-scène*, 259; this and the dramatic vivacity made his pictures new, 259; the seriousness of his art, his frail health, and sad, retiring disposition, 259, 260; difference between him and Hogarth, 270, 271; the voluptuous insipidities of his followers, Van Loo, Boucher, Fragonard, produced the reaction of David's art, 304, 313

Watts, George Frederick, 389

Western and Eastern ideals, difference between, 9

West Front of Rouen Cathedral [Monet], 462

Weyden (val'den), Roger van der, 66

"What is it all about?" 427, 428, 437

Whistler, James A. McNeill, nearest to Rembrandt as an etcher, 222; one of the first to accept Manet's lessons from Velasquez, 418; 441 et seq.; his work and personality contrasted with Sargent's, 441; borrowed of Velasquez and the Japanese, yet had original force, 442; interested most in what could not be actually presented, but suggested, 450; his portrait of his mother is a type of motherhood, 451; tried to emulate the abstract, universal appeal of music, 451, 452; "nocturnes," "symphonies," "harmonies," 452; his love of suggestion made him etcher as well as painter, 453; the significance of detail in his earlier prints, in the later the significance of economy, 453; the illusion of atmosphere in the Venetian series, 453, 454; *Portrait of the Artist's Mother* examined: the reserve and dignity and tenderness of its composition and color-scheme, 454, 455; traces in it of the influence of Velasquez and the Japanese, 455; his eminent qualities: simplicity and subtlety, economy of means, delicate harmonies, the fascination of surprise, and the joy of suggestiveness, 456

Willy Lott's House. See *Valley Farm*

Wilson, Richard, 301

Winckelmann, German critic, his dictum on the aim of art and on the highest beauty, 319

Winnower, The [Millet], 344

Wolgemuth (vohl'ge-moot), 85 et seq.; the master of Dürer, 85; the difference between his art and that of Raphael as wide as that between the contemporary German and Italian civilizations, 85, 86; art in Germany the faithful handmaid of religion, 88; began with cathedral building, 94; characteristics of the Gothic architecture, 94; stained glass, metal-work, carved wood, and stone, 94; the terrible and grotesque an inheritance from the religion of Asgard, 95; German painters began by imitating the carved work, gradually they learned from the Flemish how to paint, 119; Nuremberg on the main road between Italy and the North: its wealth and importance, 93, 94; Wolgemuth a native of the city, and from his workshop issued the principal pictures of the day, 96; in partnership with Hans Pleydenwurff, 96; after the latter's death married his widow and carried on the business, 96; a business it really was, and the workshop a factory, 96; compare the work in Perugino's *bottegha* and in Raphael's, 96; Wolgemuth's *Death of the Virgin* has no composition in the strict sense, 103; it has the German characteristic of crowded detail rather than structural dignity, 103; attempt to represent the scene naturally, with the actual types of people of the day, 104; the impression it makes is little more than recognition of certain facts, 104

Woman, to Leonardo the symbol of beauty and of the search for beauty, 123

Wood-cutter, The [Millet], 349

Words, be distrustful of, 128

Wren, Sir Christopher, 285

Wyant, Alexander, 337, 338

Z

Zandvoort, Israels first learned to study nature at, 420

[513]

www.ingramcontent.com/pod-product-compliance
Lightning Source LLC
Chambersburg PA
CBHW081213170426
43198CB00017B/2600